SO-BAB-775

How to Be a Successful Internet Consultant

Jessica Keyes

McGraw-Hill

New York San Francisco Washington, D.C. Auckland Bogotá
Caracas Lisbon London Madrid Mexico City Milan
Montreal New Delhi San Juan Singapore
Sydney Tokyo Toronto

Library of Congress Cataloging-in-Publication Data

Keyes, Jessica, (date).
    How to be a successful Internet consultant / Jessica Keyes.
        p.   cm.
    Includes index.
    ISBN 0-07-034531-7 (pbk.)
    1. Business consultants.   2. Internet consultants.   I. Title.
    HD69.C64K49   1996
    004.6'7—dc20   96-18013
                                                                  CIP

McGraw-Hill

A Division of The McGraw-Hill Companies

1 2 3 4 5 6 7 8 9 0   DOC/DOC   9 0 1 0 9 8 7 6

ISBN 0-07-034531-7 (PBK)

The sponsoring editor for this book was Brad Schepp, the editing supervisor was Lori Flaherty, and the production supervisor was Pamela Pelton. It was set in Garamond Light by Jana Fisher through the services of Barry E. Brown (Broker—Editing, Design and Production).

Printed and bound by R.R. Donnelley & Sons Company.

This book is printed on recycled, acid-free paper containing a minimum of 50% recycled, de-inked fiber.

McGraw-Hill books are available at special quantity discounts to use as premiums and sales promotions, or for use in corporate training programs. For more information, please write to the Director of Special Sales, McGraw-Hill, 11 West 19th Street, New York, NY 10011. Or contact your local bookstore.

To my husband and parents

Contents

Introduction

The times, they are a-changing.

Agriculture. Steel. Publishing. Transportation. They're not exactly industries of the past, but they're no longer the wielders of economic miracles, no longer the employer of millions of fresh-faced young people with just diplomas in their hands, or eager immigrants who smile as they gaze at the lady in the harbor. Today's times pivot around one industry, and one industry only: technology.

Technology certainly seems to be the answer. It's certainly the solution for the millions of organizations that use the various forms of it in their businesses, from knitting machines that use software to weave beautiful, complex patterns, to your local Burger King, where pushbutton accuracy does everything from record sales to re-order stock. From distance learning via satellite, to a rural doctor videoconferencing with a medical institution in a large city, technology has become the center of our very way of life.

Now there's a new kid on the block: thousands of computers and millions of people, all connected, all talking to one other. It's the Internet. Once the private communication network of academics and the military, the Internet has opened its arms to welcome the rest of the world.

In particular it's welcoming you. For in this brave, new, interconnected world there's a whole new breed of professional, the Internet consultant.

Tip

Visit the New Art web site at:
www.business-america.com

Equal parts writer, programmer, and graphics expert, the Internet consultant is, in the vernacular of the Web, a "cool" job. And it's a potentially lucrative one. There are thousands of businesses already doing business on the Web. There are more waiting in the wings.

Tip

When you first start out you'll probably be solo, so you're going to need all these skills. As your business grows, your best bet is to hire specialists in the areas of programming, graphic design (. . . and marketing, advertising, etc.).

They're waiting for you—but what do you do if you're not exactly sure what the Internet is? If you don't know a GIF from a JPEG, or maybe think that Java is a new flavor at your local coffee bar? Or are certain that you'll never understand how to run your own business? What do you do to get up to speed fast, get online, and start making money? Read this book.

How to Be a Successful Internet Consultant is for programmers, graphic designers, writers, copywriters, sailors, truck drivers, and anybody else with an inclination to get in on the ground floor of this brave new world. In other words, it's for you. This guide is unique. In this one, not even very fat, volume you'll find everything you need to know to get online and in-the-money.

Tip

You say you're experienced at HTML? Well, this book is still for you. Just skip Part I and proceed directly to Part II. Here you'll get expert advice on starting and staying in business. No matter how good your HTML is or how good a programmer you are, if you can't sell yourself you're out of business.

In the first half of the book you'll find five chapters rich in the techniques of Web development. You'll learn what the Internet is. By the end of Chapter 2 you'll be writing your very own HTML-based home pages. I promise. And by Chapter 3 you'll be conversant in the likes of Java (no, it's not coffee), forms, frames, e-mail, ftp, CGI scripts, and a host of other Web techniques. You'll even learn about sexy things like "shocked" Web pages using Macromedia's Shockwave, VRML, 3D, and animation.

In Chapter 4 you'll go from having two left thumbs to drawing two left thumbs—or at least finding out where on the Web to get free art that shows two left thumbs. Learn about transparency, interlacing, and (ugh!) palette conflict. While artistic talent is nice, in the age of technology you can skim by without it. What you can't skim by is understanding all about Web servers.

Tip

Every chapter is filled with Tips boxes. Here you'll find locations of hot and cool places on the web. Where to get free stuff and other great tips to get you started right away.

Chapter 5 does that. You'll find some interesting case histories here about how other folks handle serving up the Web. You'll also learn how to choose an Internet Service Provider, when you should set up your own site, and when you shouldn't. You'll understand how to pick Web server software, where to find it, and where to install it. RealAudio, databases, secured servers, and chat are topics you won't want to miss.

By the time Chapter 6 rolls around, you'll wonder what's left to cover. But knowing how to code HTML, write a Java script, design a cool graphic and set up a server are only part of being an Internet consultant. The most important part of being an Internet consultant is the business part.

Wow! An Internet book that discusses business? Yes. There are too many folks out there who think that "doing a little work on the side" is being a consultant. From Chapter 6 on out, the In-The-Money section of the book, you'll see how to pay your mortgage with your newfound skills. Heck, it's going to show you how to pay off your mortgage.

Even if you didn't want to start an Internet business, this book would be an excellent reference on what it takes to start and stay in business. It's filled with tried-and-true methods, the ones being used by successful people today. That's what makes it different from all those other marketing and business books out there. They're written by marketing, public relations, and advertising types who "advise" people on business. This book provides advice from someone who's been *doing* the business of technology—your business—successfully for a decade. There's no advice from a marketing guru, just advice from someone in the same boat as you. A boat, by the way, that's still sailing after ten years.

There's no philosophy here, no painful discussions about every nuance of marketing. It's just short, to the point, tried-and-true advice. Much of it is in easy-to-read list form. Rip out those pages, tape them to your PC, and follow the instructions.

Tip

Visit the author's Web sit to locate all of the *hyperlinks* listed in this book, as well as a bunch of other goodies such as shareware—both business and Internet.

http://www.business-america.com

In Chapter 6 you'll learn how to assess the playing field and find out what your competitors are up to. You need this competitive intelligence to figure out what fees to charge and even what to put in your literature. You'll also learn how to create a marketing plan, how to steer your own mission and goals towards success, and the value of building your own Web site.

In Chapter 7 you're going to learn a thing or two about auto-marketing your business, from the Web to telemarketing, from faxmail to getting data to fill your prospect database. You'll even learn a trick or two about making an interactive demo CD to lure business to your front door.

In Chapters 8 and 9 you're going to get a crash course on the traditional techniques of paper-based direct mail, newsletters, sales letters, public relations, and advertising. You're going to find out everything from how to get written about to getting your own articles published. These chapters will answer the questions: When and where do I advertise? How much does it cost? How can I get it cheaper? How do I write a press release? What kind of publicity stunts can I pull to get noticed? What should go into my literature package? My press package? And on and on and on . . .

While Chapter 10 discusses setting fees and taking the plunge into expansion through finding funding, in Appendix A I've provided a slew of prewritten templates that can help you get that money. You can use these samples to write your own proposals, sales letters, and press releases. Use them with my blessing. Finally, there's a glossary, HTML quick reference guide, and a lengthy Internet product and services guide.

There it is, everything you need. A veritable bible of being in the Internet business. Happy Internetting!

1

The business of the Internet

Unless you've been hiding under a rock, the Internet probably is the hottest topic in town. You can't open a newspaper, or turn on the TV or the radio, without WebSpeak coming right at you. We're the Wired Generation. We're tuned in and turned on. We use it for school, to shop, and to conduct our financial transactions. And the more prurient among us use it as a low-res *Playboy* substitute.

There are anywhere from 27 million to 50 million hardy souls (depending on the flavor of statistics you're quoting) web crawling on any given day. Although the initial mix of crawlers was decidedly academic and government, the advent of graphical browsers such as Mosaic and Netscape opened the doors for the rest of us to crawl right in and log on.

The new webcrawler can be anyone, from the business person who needs to look something up, to his son who uses it for homework. A doctor in a remote area might use the Internet to get assistance from a teaching hospital in the city. And her patients might use it to purchase that special something that just can't be found in town. What all these webcrawlers have in common is opportunity. An opportunity to expand one's horizons beyond the geographic and physical borders under which we now operate.

It's a vast opportunity for business as well. Yahoo, one of the original Web indexes, lists over 10,000 corporate sites in their directory. But that's only the tip of the iceberg:

- ActivMedia measured the 1995 growth rate of Web business marketers at an astounding 1800 percent.
- Hambrecht & Quist forecasts Internet-related sales soaring to $14.5 billion in the year 2000—just around the corner.

- A Nielsen Media study finds an astonishing 63 percent of Net surfers are business-related.
- The Internet Society announced that the number of hosts on the Internet has passed the 3.8 million mark.
- Lycos has indexed over 1.53 million Web pages, with possibly thousands being added daily.
- Bluestone reports that the number of business home pages has risen from a mere 30 in early 1993 to more than 50,000 by the end of 1995.
- Hambrecht & Quist forecasts that Internet equipment sales will grow from $500 million in 1995 to $2.5 billion in 2000; network services will escalate from $300 million to $5 billion; software from $250 million to $4 billion; and consulting/integration services will increase from $250 million to close to $3 billion.
- The Internet Engineering Task Force has indicated that it is fast reaching the capacity of *.com* registrations, with over 200,000 commercial names registered (80 percent of which are legal entities).
- Nielsen Media's CommerceNet funded study of Internet usage found that 37 percent of Net surfers were professional, 12 percent technical, and 14 percent administrative/managerial. They also found that 66 percent of the 4200 respondents accessed the Internet through work and spent an average of 5 hours and 28 minutes online.

Businesses see "gold in them thar hills." Indeed, Open Market, an Internet service corporation in Cambridge, Mass., says that between 50 and 100 fully functional business sites are added every day.

For the most part, these sites are marketing-oriented—a virtual advertisement, catalog, or customer service. A smaller percentage of bleeding-edgers actually sell on the Web, but to a certain extent success seems to be limited to those selling computer hardware and software and books; products like flowers and travel are quickly catching on, however.

What does this all mean to you? Simply that you can be on the leading edge of a jobs boom that has the potential of dramatically inverting today's down tick to an exciting up tick.

Someone has to design those home pages, build those databases, and write that copy. And that brings us to the point of this book. *How to Become a Successful Internet Consultant* is unique. It will provide you with all the inside information you need to get started on the road to a lucrative living—thanks to the Internet.

Profile of an Internet consultant

What does it take to become an Internet consultant? Although you found this book in the computer (or maybe Internet) section of the bookstore, an Internet consultant is equal parts graphic designer, copywriter, and programmer. That's what makes this field so exciting—and so unusual.

Most Internet consultants come into the field from the programming side. Given the technical bent of the Internet, this is a natural evolution and one that many programmers have made rather easily. But as the Internet matures, so does its look and field. Gone are the days when a home page could consist of some rather bland text and some silly clip art. Today's home pages must be every bit as graphically appealing as those in your favorite full-color, glossy magazines.

As a result, a new breed of home page designer has jumped into the mix. Graphic designers have added a whole new dimension to the Internet. Colorful graphics, unusual fonts, interesting color schemes, and great designs are a welcome departure from yesterday's gray-on-gray look.

The Internet is anything but static. Not a week goes by without some new bell or whistle being announced, something that will add pizzazz to anyone's page. Today's Internet is very much multimedia-enabled. Audio, video, text, and graphics are the foundation of all of the most successful home pages.

So what does it take to be a successful Internet consultant? All of the above—and a good sense of business to boot. What kind of person will be a successful Internet consultant? Someone who possesses all (or at least some) of these talents, is resourceful, and is willing to work hard at learning and maintaining a level of skills consistent with what I'll refer to as the "cool level" of the Web. And above all, this person needs to possess a level of creativity that can neatly combine the skills of a programmer, the art of a graphic designer, and the savvy of a business person.

Alex Gadea (*alexgadea@virtualscape.com*) of Virtualscape, Inc., located in New York, has been in business for about a year. With a decidedly technical background in computer network consulting, Alex advises folks entering this business to be careful. "Don't think that all you have to do is put up a server and a Web site and you'll be rolling in dough before you know it. The business operates like any other business and without a sound business strategy, you're not going to make it."

Gadea is of the opinion that anyone who goes into business "better have a business plan." Although we'll cover all these issues in depth in the second half of this book, Gadea's points are well worth mulling over. Ask yourself these questions:

- Who is your target market?
- What resources are you going to devote to advertising and other marketing activities?
- How will you plan your expansion(s) and when do you expect them to occur?
- How are you going to maintain your clients and keep them happy?

On the opposite coast, Kent Joshi is grabbing his own piece of the Internet pie. Joshi, all of 28 when this book was written, may be short on years, but he is certainly long on experience. With a résumé that includes both IBM and Microsoft, Joshi feels comfortable in searching out and then securing the Fortune 100 executive as a client.

Joshi is a good example of what it takes to be a successful Internet consultant. When he started his business in 1994, he decided to model it on the successful large consulting firms such as Andersen Consulting and The Gardner Group. Based in Woodland Hills, Calif., The Joshi Group (*www.joshigroup.com*) has a prestigious client list that includes The Disney Company, Nestlé, and Toyota. The company has become successful not only because of their technical skills, but because of their business skills as well.

Joshi recognizes that there are several components to Internet consulting and that one can't be expert in all facets. His advice is "to focus on your strengths. I focus on the areas I am good at and I build strategic relationships for the rest. Not everyone can do all the pieces."

To build these strategic relationships requires good networking. "I tend to attract experts in the field as consultants," says Joshi of his cadre of technical consultants who form his inner circle.

For an Internet consultant, strategic relationships can be external consultants, past clients, referrals from clients, and vendors. This last category may indeed bring the greatest returns. Joshi recommends the various vendor Solution Provider programs, with Microsoft and Netscape high on the list. Both will forward consultant leads. Their take? They get to sell their software.

Understanding the Internet business

The Internet has spawned its own vocabulary. Web. Surf. Infonaut. Net. But the vocabulary of doing business is very much the same as in any business. You must understand the medium of the Internet and the diversity of consulting assignments that you may be able to wrest from it, possess a set of superior skills, and, finally, you must understand how to get into business and stay in business. Those tracking the rise and fall of small business—and make no mistake about it, Internet consulting (at least in the beginning) is very much a small business—know that 95 percent of all small business start-ups fail within the first five years.

Tip

Go to your local bookstore and get a copy of the magazine *BoardWatch*. It lists all of the major BBSs and discusses software to boot.

The medium of the Internet

I'm often amused when I watch television. That's because most television talk shows that cover the Internet phenomenon get it all fouled up. Let's spend just a few words in straightening things out. When Al Gore talks about the Information Superhighway, he is actually talking about *all* of the exits on those millions of miles of cable, fiber optic, and just plain twisted pair that run around the world. The Internet is just one part of the equation. The other part of the equation is made up of services such as CompuServe, Prodigy, America Online, Microsoft Network, and the tens of thousands of smaller BBS's (Bulletin Board Systems) that are so pervasive—and so popular. There are BBS's for virtually every hobby, profession and every interest.

CompuServe, AOL, and the other proprietary online services collectively have over 11 million paying subscribers. Although every one of these services has built a gateway to the Internet (i.e., a facility for easy access the Internet directly through the front door of the proprietary service), the majority of subscribers are fairly dedicated and seem content to spend an equal amount of time between the Internet and behind the closed doors of the proprietary service. Indeed, a good Internet consultant will take the time to explore the opportunities that development on these venues could bring to the client.

Let's say your florist client wants to broaden its exposure. Aside from the Internet itself, the proprietary services do provide ample opportunity. CompuServe, for example, not only provides advertising facilities (for a fee, of course), but also the possibility of hosting a *forum*. Forums are like clubs. Like-minded people gather together electronically for information-mining, and just plain company, surrounding a particular theme. There are potentially millions of people interested in gardening, horticulture, hiking, etc., so it makes sense that a this area would attract a large following.

Tip

There is a wide variety of books that list the addresses for the many thousands of mailing lists. Find one or more appropriate mailing lists at

http://www.tile.net/tile/listserv/index.html

This is the official home of the latest Inet-Access FAQ. It also contains archives of the Inet-Access mailing list.

Hosting the forum gives the client a certain degree of authority that might just translate into increased business. The point is that the excitement over the Internet should not blindside the consultant into missing potential lucrative opportunities on other Information Superhighway off-ramps.

In spite of the fact that it's been noticed by the press only in the past couple of years, the Internet is really several decades old. Built as a Department of Defense (DARPA) project to link computer resources scattered worldwide, it became a mainstay for the research, governmental, and academic communities. In point of fact, quite a few of the 27 million folks on the Internet right now are still of that persuasion. This mix is changing fast, however.

The Internet is really an amalgamation of several different technologies, e-mail being the foremost amongst them. Interestingly, e-mail often is overlooked as a service that can be provided to potential clients. Of course, one e-mail address does not a happy client make— but a mailing list, on the other hand, is invaluable.

Part of any Internet consulting task is to publicize the client's site or just plain publicize the client. What better way to do it than via direct e-mail? But be forewarned, there's a certain "netiquette" involved when dealing with mailing lists. Advertising and blatant self-promotion are just not acceptable. One famous case in point involved two attorneys who basically littered every mailing list with a promotion for their legal services. Since most people subscribe to multiple mailing lists, this "spamming" had the effect of stuffing user mail boxes with tons of duplicate unsolicited mail. It was like getting fifty car wash circulars—all on the same day.

The opposition turned nasty, and a lot of technical know-how was used to get back at these Net perpetrators. The confrontation made the papers and the attorneys made hay by writing a book. To this day, however, the law firm name is synonymous with bad manners on the Internet—something you can't afford if you want to grow a client base and keep your customers happy.

Like the CompuServe forum discussed above, marketing to a mailing list works better if done subtly. This means hosting a new list, or joining an existing list, and making a valuable contribution to the discussion. Our florist company, for example, can make it a point to join as many mailing lists as possible. By offering succinct advice and answers to questions, the person gains a reputation as someone who's knowledgeable in the business—and someone worthy of your business. Of course, each message ends with what is known as a *signature*. This is one or more lines appended to the bottom of every message sent. It contains name, address, and other pertinent information. Many also put in a descriptive line about their business or themselves. Our florist might use a signature as follows:

```
            Joseph Petunia --- Flowers R Us
 123 Main Street     Anytown USA     (800) 555-1212
            "Flowers to the Trade"
```

Tip

Create a signature that really identifies who you are. If your firm name is J. Associates, then add a tagline to it such as "Purveyors of Antiques."

Those in the service-oriented businesses often add a tagline that tries to describe their talents. Marty Winston, a well-known figure in the high-tech PR business, appends the description "SageOp" to his missives in the Public Relations forum on CompuServe. This is a rather creative play on the term *sysop* (system operator) that will be familiar to anyone who has ever used a forum, electronic mailing list, or BBS.

Usenet newsgroups are the flip side of mailing lists and have, in some quarters, something of a dubious reputation. In spite of the fact that Usenet was created to provide a timely, "newsy" information feed to Internet users, many hopped aboard the bandwagon bearing many different agendas. Now there is a proliferation of Usenet newsgroups with such intriguing names as *rec.arts.drwho*, which is a group of folks hooked on the fictional British television character Dr. Who. Other names, particularly in the so-called *alt* hierarchy where new groups are easier to create, are unprintable here.

> ### Tip
> Hop over to *http://www.dejanews.com* to do a quick keyword search on newsgroups that interest you.

The mix of messages in many of these newsgroups sometimes seems to be equal parts on-topic discussions and threads that read like multilevel marketing scams. Make-money chain letters also abound. There has been some press lately on boiler room operations that are preying on unsuspecting Netters by offering business and/or investment opportunities just too good to pass up. A hint here: If it sounds too good to be true, it is. Pass it up. In spite of all these problems, active participation in relevant Usenet newsgroups is a feature that you should add to your list of Internet consulting services.

Most people freely substitute the word *Web* for the word *Internet*. It really does mean two different things. The Web, like e-mail and Usenet, is one part of the Internet, which is itself a part of the Information Superhighway.

The Web (short for World Wide Web or WWW) is really the most exciting part of the Internet and the part that has spawned more new Internet consultancies than any other. The Web is anything but new. It's been around in text-only form for quite some time. Anyone with a Unix shell account from an Internet Service Provider (ISP) has probably toyed with the text-based Web, frequently with a Unix tool named *Lynx*. For the most part, it was used (and still is) to access library or other information content located at various and sundry universities.

The Web in its current form grew in popularity only after the Mosaic "browser," with its graphical user interface (GUI), was born just a few short years ago. Marc Andressen, now of Netscape fame, developed Mosaic when he was still an undergraduate. Mosaic's ability to handle both graphics and text (and now audio, video, animation, and even telephony) opened the Pandora's box that refuses to be closed. For the most part, the bulk of your business will be Web-based. You will design and implement Web-based solutions that are not only a combination of the requisite graphical and textual components, but database programming as well.

> ### Tip
> See the glossary at the back of this book for an explanation of terms you'll need to know.

The Web itself integrates several older Internet technologies in which the consultant needs to be conversant. Many of your clients will ask you to find a way to enable their customers to download a text file or graphics file from the company's Web site. The technology most often used for this purpose is the File Transfer Protocol, usually used as the noun or verb *ftp*. It is a protocol that describes the way files can be transferred over a network. Most networking software already has ftp built into it. But there's a wrinkle. If you want to let customers download and maybe even upload to the site, then the flavor of ftp needed is *anonymous ftp*. For this a bit more technical savvy is required.

Gopher is essentially a simple, text-based menu interface to information on the Internet. It is really a precursor to the Web, but it can used effectively as part of a solution for a client who requires the ability to search and download information. Many companies have implemented gopher servers and sometimes you'll see it used interchangeably with ftp for download purposes. Archie and Veronica are programs that let you search gopher servers for various keywords. A combination of gopher and Veronica, therefore, might just be an inexpensive way to provide "search and download" facilities for a client. It's certainly a solution that should be investigated.

Consulting diversity

There are many ways to put all this knowledge to good use:
- Building sites for clients
- Advertisements
- Catalogs
- Ordering online
- Marketing
- Customer service
- Building "intranets" (internal Internet-like networks not accessible to the outside)
- Hosting client Web sites on your server
- Becoming an Internet Service Provider
- Creating an Internet marketing specialty company

A successful consultant must be able to operate in all of these spheres. While it is possible to make a quick kill designing home pages with sparse graphics and some text, be forewarned that nearly anyone can perform this function. Many do. I've had more than one potential client tell me that her 14-year-old son can build a Web page for less money than I would charge.

CompuServe, Prodigy, and AOL all give their subscribers the opportunity to build home pages. They even provide software to help do it, as shown in Fig. 1-1.

1-1 *Making it easy to develop on the Web.*

To overcome the "Junior can do it" opposition, you'll either have to counter with some serious arguments about what you can do better than "the competition," or simply not compete for the small end of the business at all. I've chosen the latter. For one thing, the margins (the amount of money you actually make vs. the expenses of time, materials, and overhead) are dreadful. Every Tom, Dick, Harry, Mary, Junior, and Granddad who knows a little HTML seems to be in on the act—some charging as low as $100 per job.

Table 1-1 provides a guideline for the median prices you can charge for what I refer to as Level One Internet consulting. Level One is text, graphics, audio, video, tables, imagemaps, and some forms, on from 1 to *n* pages. Level Two consulting is everything on Level One with the addition of programming and databases (i.e., search engines, order taking, etc.).

For the most part, to be successful and build a company you will be required to go after the larger businesses. Getting your feet wet by tackling small business is fine, but move on up the ladder as soon as you can. Small businesses are extremely cost-conscious and want to pay

Table 1-1 Making a Livable Wage Doing Level One Internet Consulting

	Starter	Basic	Plus	Standard	Special	Deluxe
Total Cost	$340	$575	$795	$1,245	$1,875	$2,440
Total Pages	1	2	3	6	12	20
Links	3	6	8	15	30	45
Scanned pictures (in addition to mast and top-of-page graphic)	2	4	5	8	16	24
Words of text (approximate)	200	400	600	1,200	2,400	4,000
Masthead graphic (client-supplied or simple custom graphic incorporation company logo)	yes	yes	yes	yes	yes	yes
Colored lines and bullets	Netscape	Netscape	Netscape	Netscape	Netscape	Netscape
Colored and textured background	Netscape	Netscape	Netscape	Netscape	Netscape	Netscape
Site publicity using SubmitIt	yes	yes	yes	yes	yes	yes
Image Map					x	x
E-mail response link to your e-mail address	x	x	x	x	x	x

very little for what amounts to a lot of hard work. If you stay on this side of the business, you'll find out very quickly that you're working long hours and still not making the mortgage at the end of the month.

Moving on up the ladder to Level Two means you'll also be able to tackle the more interesting projects. It's here where you'll be able to combine imagery, audio, video, animation, databases, programming, e-mail, ftp, and more.

Tip

Keep up to date by subscribing to the free e-mail newsletter Edupage. Send an e-mail to:

listproc@educom.unc.edu

with the message "subscribe Edupage your_name" (without the quotes).

Figure 1-2 shows what a typical Level One page might look like. Salons USA is a chain of beauty salons and spas located throughout the Midwest. You probably can't see the colors, but it is highly colorful. It's about four pages (screens) long, contains information tables, and has provision for automatically e-mailing the company directly

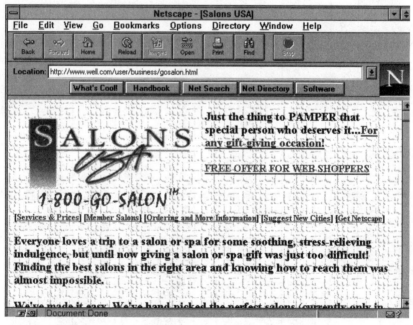

1-2 *A simply constructed home page.*

from the web page. The corporate logo is a graphic image because, at this time, you can't really duplicate unusual fonts on the Web—although that's probably coming, too.

Tip

Unisys has many domain names. Their prime site is called *www.unisys.com*. A launch of a new, exciting computer in Spring, 1996, saw the company enhance this site and several others. The name of the site that describes the new computer is:

www.clearpath.com

The more unique the name, the greater the chance that folks will find your client on the Web.

Unisys is an extremely large hardware and software company. Their Web site is many thousands of pages long. It contains product information, which is available to read online or via ftp download. The site is highly interactive, too. Figure 1-3 demonstrates a part of the reason why the Unisys site is a Level Two site. The ability to request information from the user and then transmit it to a database on the Unisys side required bona fide programming. The Unisys site, by the way, even permits you to request that faxes be sent to your fax machine.

Tip

Not a programmer? Hire one. Your local paper probably has tons of ads for computer and/or Internet consultants. The online services (e.g., CompuServe) have forums where job postings are commonplace. Ultimately you might want to go through programmer associations.

For Internet-related work, try the New York New Media Association:

http://www.nynma.org/

For computer consulting, try the Independent Computer Consultant's Association:

http://www.icca.org/

1-3 *The use of forms.*

Honing your Internet skills

An Internet consultant is only as successful as his or her skill set. The fact that the Internet keeps growing in capability is a double-edged sword, however. On the one hand, it's downright fun to be continually honing your skills, but on the other hand, it's hard work to stay on the high end of the learning curve.

There are several ways to approach the process of keeping your skills up to date. While there are some courses one can take, most notably at the university level, the Internet itself provides you with the best instruction at the lowest cost.

Tip

Most browsers permit you to save the HTML (HyperText Markup Language) of the Web page you are viewing. If you see a page that has something you'd like to learn, save it. Using Netscape, you can see the HTML by clicking on View and then Document Source. Use File, Save As to get it on your hard disk.

An easy way to approach learning is as follows:

1 Read every book and magazine on the subject you can get your hands on.

2 As often as you can, spend an hour or two perusing the Web. Most magazines cover the latest and hottest (or, to use the Web vernacular, coolest) sites. Jot down the URLs (Uniform Resource Locator, or address) and use your browser to take a look-see. If the site has some feature you'd like to add to your bag of tricks, then save the HTML (using the View Source or similar option in your browser). Offline, study the HTML and then copy the part you liked into your code. This works particularly well when you see an interesting Java applet you'd like to use on one of your client sites. The Web really is a self-teaching medium.

3 Use one of the Web search engines to search for topics of interest. There's plenty of free information out there on such interesting topics as HTML, Java, multimedia, CGI scripting, etc. Download and read.

Tip

I started to put together a list of books on the Internet, but I know that I never read bibliographies. Instead, I'd like to direct you to a great Internet source on books. Do a keyword search for "Internet" at:

    http://www.amazon.com

---

4 Subscribe to one or more newsgroups or mailing lists. There's lots of experience out there that you can tap. A list of relevant newsgroups is presented in Table 1-2.

5 If you're going to be chief cook and bottle washer (i.e., artwork, programming, marketing) and you're not quite a Picasso, then invest some time at the local college. For example, in New York City, both the Parsons School of Design and the School of Visual Arts offer courses in digital graphics.

The Internet biz

You can be the most talented of Web designers and the most prolific of programmers, but if you don't *sell* yourself and your business, you'll soon be out of business.

Table 1-2 Mailing Lists of Interest

alt.bbs.internet
>   BBSs that are hooked up to the Internet.

alt.best.of.internet
>   It was a time of sorrow, it was a time of joy.

alt.culture.internet
>   The culture(s) of the Internet.

alt.folklore.internet
>   Internet Myths and Legends.

alt.internet.access.wanted
>   "Oh. OK, how about just an MX record for now?"

alt.internet.commerce
>   Doing business on the Internet.

alt.internet.guru
>   Recognition of people responsible for inet success

alt.internet.media-coverage
>   The coverage of the internet by the media.

alt.internet.talk-radio
>   Carl Malamud's Internet Talk Radio program.

alt.irc
>   Internet Relay Chat material.

alt.irc.announce
>   Announcements about Internet Relay Chat (IRC). (Moderated)

alt.online-service
>   Large commercial online services, and the Internet.

at.network.ping
>   PING - Personal InterNet Gate : Betrieb und Diskussion.

bit.listserv.help-net
>   Help on BitNet and the Internet.

comp.infosystems.announce
>   Announcements of internet information services. (Moderated)

comp.infosystems.interpedia
>   The Internet Encyclopedia.

comp.internet.library
>   Discussing electronic libraries. (Moderated)

comp.internet.net-happenings
>   Announcements of network happenings. (Moderated)

comp.mail.headers
>   Gatewayed from the Internet header-people list.

comp.mail.mime
>   Multipurpose Internet Mail Extensions of RFC 1341.

comp.org.isoc.interest
>   Discussion about the Internet Society.

comp.protocols.ppp
>   Discussion of the Internet Point to Point Protocol.

cu.courses.envd4352
>   internet and related issues

demon.announce

Demon Internet announcements (Moderated)

demon.ip.winsock.dics

DICS PD software to access Demon Internet

*Issues facing a huge Internet (big-internet@munnari.oz.au). (Moderated)info.ietf

*Internet Engineering Task Force (IETF) discussions (ietf@venera.isi.edu). (Moderated)

info.ietf.isoc

*Internet Society discussions (isoc-interest@relay.sgi.com). (Moderated)

misc.news.internet.announce

News bulletins from the Internet. (Moderated)

misc.news.internet.discuss

Discussion of news bulletins from the Net.

tnn.internet.address

Discussions about Internet addresses.

tnn.internet.firewall

Discussions about Internet firewalls.

tnn.internet.www

World Wide Web topics and programs.

tw.bbs.comp.irc

BBS Board of Internet Relay Chat

This really is the ugly part of a consultant's job, the one that most people like the least. It's truly difficult to sell yourself, but someone has got to do it. And if you're a one-person firm, that person has got to be you.

The second half of this book will discuss a consultant's approach to publicizing, marketing, and sales; at this point, however, I just want to set the stage. Here are rules to live by:

1 Marketing and sales skills are every bit as important as your technical and creative skills.

2 You should perform marketing/sales activities at least 20 percent of each week. You should constantly be on the lookout for new business. In other words, you should always be selling. Going to a wedding? The folks at your table are in business, aren't they? Sell them. Are you a member of clubs and associations? If not, join some. If yes, then go to the meetings. Offer to be a guest speaker. Work the room.

3 The second person your company hires should be a salesperson. This leaves you time to do the creative part of the business while your salesperson can get down and dirty into sales.

Now that you're a bit more familiar with the Internet business, let's get into the thick of things. Chapter 2 is a mini-tutorial on how to create Web pages using the latest in Web technology.

Tip

Good search engines:
    http://www.infoseek.com
    http://altavista.digital.com
    http://www.excite.com
    http://www.yahoo.com
    http://wizard.inso.com/
Or use *http://www.search.com* to access 250 search engines all at one time.

2

The code's the thing

The heart of an Internet consultant's business is creating Web sites. No matter how much art and text you have, it'll never look good on the Web if you don't have a thorough understanding of the tagging language that gets you there.

Fortunately, HyperText Markup Language, or *HTML*, is rather easy to learn—especially if you follow the advice I gave you in the last chapter and study the pages of good-looking sites you've seen on the Web.

This chapter will take you through the steps of understanding and applying HTML to your own pages. Along the way we'll get progressively more in-depth as we cover more state-of-the-art features. We'll also take a look at extensions like Java, tools like Adobe's PDF, and even RealAudio. Interspersed through the chapter will be descriptions (and directions on how to download) tools that can help you develop and test your own HTML.

Tip

While there's a ton of information contained in the next few chapters on all things HTML, get yourself an HTML reference book to keep on your desk. Go to *http://www.amazon.com* and do a keyword search on "html." There are descriptions, reviews—and you can even buy the book online.

P.S. I'd recommend one to you, but I have a slew in my bookcase. Buying Web books is addictive!

Getting access to the Internet

Although the majority of the readers of this book are probably technical and already have access in some way to the Internet, there are no doubt some readers who've yet to log on for the first time. There are many ways to get access to the Internet. For example, I gain access through CompuServe, Microsoft Network (MSN comes with Windows 95), and two Internet Service Providers (The WELL in San Francisco and Panix in New York).

I'll recommend to these readers what I recommend to clients who don't have access: Use an established company like CompuServe, America Online, or Microsoft Network. Of the three, MSN probably has the best and quickest customer support, but all are experienced with first-time users—something I can't say for some of the Internet Service Providers (ISPs).

Tip

First-timers should get on the Internet the easy way:

CompuServe
800-487-0453

AOL
800-827-3338

Microsoft Network
800-386-5550

Prodigy
800-221-9318

The proprietary online services realized they had stiff competition and, in the spirit of "if you can't beat 'em, join 'em," they've all quickly provided a gateway to the Internet. (In fact, CompuServe is reported to be planning a phase-out of the private side of their service over the next several years.) Because the competition is fast and furious between all these players, we all reap the benefits of cheaper prices and better features. The least expensive of the lot (at least for now) appears to be the Microsoft Network, which costs about $5 per month plus additional charges for excess time.

You don't even have to wait for any of these services to send you the free software. All you need do is go to any large bookstore that sells magazines and track down one of the many computer magazines. Chances are that bundled inside the shrink wrap is a free copy of software to get you up and running. Because I subscribe to a number of these publications, over time I've collected quite a lot of these free diskettes, which I give to new clients.

Tip

Save those free copies of AOL or CompuServe software that come shrinkwrapped with your computer magazines. They make great freebies to give to clients who've never been online before.

Those hardy souls who don't want to travel down this particular path may choose to do business directly with an Internet Service Provider. An Internet Service Provider (ISP) is a company that sells access to the Internet. It can be distinguished from a proprietary information service like CompuServe or America Online by its emphasis on Internet tools such as Usenet news, Gopher, and the World Wide Web (although CompuServe and company are fast catching up). Put another way, the information services are in the business of being self-contained entities, but have added doorways to the Internet; ISPs are in the business of *being* the doorways.

Typically the basic service the ISP offers you is what's referred to as a *shell account*. Panix, in New York City, offers this service for about $100 a year. Shell is really a euphemistic, computerese expression for a command-line Unix session. (Unix is an operating system that has been around for many years, and it hasn't changed much. For the most part, its difficulty level exceeds the ability level of most non-computer-oriented users.)

Similar to the DOS prompt in many ways, a shell connection provides users with basic services like e-mail, ftp (File Transfer Protocol), gopher, telnet (where you can log into someone else's computer), plus various and sundry other tools. Think of a shell account this way: Your computer pretends to be a dumb, remote terminal that can operate your provider's computer.

The next type of connection, a step up, puts your computer itself on the Internet. Access to the Web in graphical mode (i.e., through Mosaic and Netscape) requires either a SLIP (Serial Line Internet Protocol) or PPP (Point to Point Protocol) connection. These permit one to use a dial-up telephone line to gain access to the very graphical and very full-screen Web.

Tip

To get a list of national and local providers, send mail to:

dlist@ora.com

Yahoo is a good source, too:

*http://www.yahoo.com/Business/Corporations
/Internet_Access_Providers/*

For a combination provider list and survey form that will tell you who the best (and worst) regarded providers are in your area, go to:

http://www.thelist.com/

C¦Net's subscribers ratings:

http://www.cnet.com/Content/Reviews/Compare/ISP/

My Panix PPP connection costs an additional $200 or so per year. But for that amount of money I get unlimited access to the Internet. Therein lies the reason why ISPs are so popular. Where CompuServe and the other well-known service providers charge a monthly base rate and then an hourly fee, many ISPs (not all, mind you) charge merely a one-time fee.

The problem here is level of difficulty. While some of the larger ISPs have tailored their own SLIP or PPP installation diskettes, which are loaded with a Web browser, many other ISPs leave it up to you to obtain and install the tools you need to actually use the connection.

My own experience bears this out. When Mosaic first became popular, I decided to download a free copy of it from a university site. Although it came with extensive written documentation, I still had to spend many hours coding such esoteric things as "IP address" and "subnet mask" to get it to work.

Currently there are three contenders for the "most popular" title in the Web browsing category: Netscape, Microsoft Internet Explorer, and Mosaic in its many flavors. From the end user's perspective they all work similarly—they get you access to the Web. From a developer's standpoint, however, the three flavors act differently and, as a result, make it important to test your pages on all three platforms.

The difference is in the way the browser supports the various versions of HTML. The original Mosiac browser supported HTML 1.0. There are literally thousands of these browsers still in use. Unfortunately, they don't support the newer standard-HTML capabilities, nor the Netscape extensions that have become quasi-standards because of that browser's popularity. Tables, colors, and graphic backgrounds are features that fall into this category.

Netscape, more modern versions of Mosaic (like CompuServe's), and Microsoft's Internet Explorer all support HTML 2.0, with HTML 3.0 fast coming 'round the bend. This chapter will discuss coding using this particular convention, and also address the HTML 3.0 feature set.

Tip

Download a copy of Netscape from:

http://home.netscape.com

Internet Explorer can be found here:

http://www.microsoft.com

Crash course in HTML markup

The HyperText Markup Language (HTML) is composed of a set of elements that define a document and guide its display. It derives from SGML (Standard Generalized Markup Language), which is a markup language oriented toward publishing. For the most part, HTML coding is not programming—unless, of course, you want to get into database queries or start using extensions like CGI and Java (more on that later)—so it's fairly easy to learn. Appendix B presents a complete reference to HTML tags in alphabetical order. What I'd like to do in this section is help you understand the concept and power behind this versatile tagging language.

In writing this chapter I had to make a decision about how to present the material. Most books on the subject present it in tag order. I don't think that's logical. Instead, I'd like to offer this mini-tutorial in the way you'd actually follow links around—sort of a hypertext approach. First, I'll present some simple examples and explain how the code was created. Then I'll elaborate by providing examples of existing home pages and discuss the one or two HMTL techniques that make that page unique. In this way, we'll get to discuss tables, background colors, scrolling text, Java, audio, etc., in a much more logical, intuitive way. Chapter 3 will enlighten you even more by providing advanced HTML topics.

Be aware that HTML is an evolving language and, as I already mentioned, different World Wide Web browsers may recognize slightly different sets of HTML elements. For example, as I put pen to paper, Microsoft's Internet Explorer does not recognize Java applets—but this probably will have changed by the time you read this book.

> ### Tip
>
> For general information about HTML, including plans for new versions, see:
>
> *http://www.w3.org/hypertext/WWW/MarkUp/MarkUp.html*

The basics

Look at the Web page shown in Fig. 2-1. It shows a very simple-looking design. A little text, a few graphics, and some buttons. Now let's see the HTML code for this page. If you were using a browser, you'd locate the page by typing its address or URL (Uniform Resource Locator). When this screen shot was snapped, it was *http://www.well.com/user/ business.*

But first, here's a note on the address. URL stands for Uniform Resource Locator, and *http* stands for HyperText Transport Protocol. Perhaps one day we'll get sophisticated enough to get rid of all the techie buzzwords and just say "get me address = . . . " to find what we want. But for now, just remember the convention.

If you're a Windows person, then you'll notice that the slashes are going in the "wrong" direction (/ instead of the usual DOS-oriented \ ). Just remember that the slash you need is under the question mark,

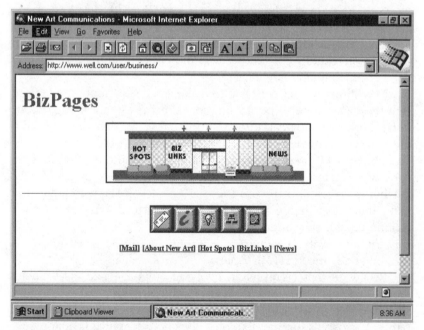

2-1 *The old New Art home page example. Our new one is located at http://www.business-america.com*

as in "Why did they do it this way?" You should soon get used to this reverse (or is it perverse?) convention.

The next part is the actual address. The *www* (which stands for World Wide Web) also is a convention. It's the most common name for the computer on a system that handles Web-related tasks. Most home pages do use it as part of their address. Also notice that I'm typing in lowercase here. Unix sees upper- and lowercase characters as different—not consistently, just when you don't want it to—so it's important to copy the address exactly as you see it, even if the address contains mixed-case expressions.

The string *www.well.com* is what is referred to as the *domain name*. It's the name of the site. Most of the larger companies, whether they use an ISP or connect their own company directly to the Internet, create their own name. Nowadays this is a must activity if the company is to "brand" its Web site. For example, the Unisys site has many domain names. The name *www.unisys.com* came first; then (with the April, 1996, launch of a new computer named ClearPath) came the name *www.clearpath.com*. Since a shareware site was also considered, Unisys created the domain name *www.sharestuff.com*.

Tip

Want to add something interesting to the Web sites you build? The PointCast Network is a free service that broadcasts news and information directly to a viewer's computer screen. Viewers can download the software at the company's Web site:

http://www.pointcast.com

All of the slashes and names after the *www.well.com* specify what directory to look in. In this case, the company is going to the site named *www.well.com* and looking in a directory named */user/business.*

The home page we are examining is named *index.html*. This, too, is a convention. It is the name of the very first file (the index file) the computer loads. Many servers have this default built into the software, although some use the convention *welcome.html* or *home.html*. Since *index.html* is the default, it saves me a couple of keystrokes in getting to the business site. The alternative would be:

http://www.well.com/user/business/index.html

By clicking on the View Menu and selecting Document Source (in Netscape and Microsoft Internet Explorer) or File–Document Source (in Mosaic), you'll be able to see the HTML for this page.

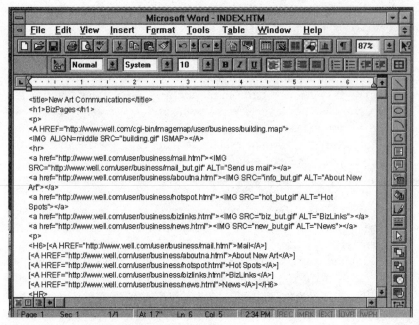

2-2 *The New Art home page HTML.*

> ## Tip
>
> While most commands have complementary beginning and
> ending tags, there are quite a few that will let you get by with-
> out the ending tag. The <BODY> tag is one of them. Although I'm
> not particularly a neat coder, I'd still recommend that your HTML
> be by-the-book, and contain both beginning and ending tags.

All HTML documents are composed of a single element:

```
<HTML>...</HTML>
```

which is, in turn, composed of head and body elements:

```
<HEAD>...</HEAD>
```

and

```
<BODY>...</BODY>
```

To allow older HTML documents to remain readable, the tags
<HTML>, <HEAD>, <BODY> are actually optional within HTML docu-
ments. This is how the page in Fig. 2-2 was created. Let's look at the
HTML in detail and see what makes the document tick.

```
1. <TITLE>New Art Communications</TITLE>
```

The < less-than symbol and > greater-than symbols identify the name of the HMTL tag to the interpreter. All but a few tags really consist of two parts: an open and a close tag. Together they form a *container.* For example, <TITLE> is the open tag and </TITLE> is the close tag. Notice that they are the same except for the addition of the slash (/) in the closing tag. The slash (/) is consistently used in HTML to designate a closing tag or "off" switch. Note that the HTML tag names themselves are not case-sensitive; lower-, upper-, and mixed-case formats work equally well, and are used interchangeably in the examples that follow. Note also, however, that any filenames invoked *within* an HTML tag (more on this later) will have to conform to the casing conventions of the server.

The title tag tells the interpreter the name of the document. It is also used by many Web search engine robots as the descriptor of your site. Search engines, discussed in Chapter 5, are Internet programs whose job is to locate and index all of the millions of pages on the Internet. Many of the robots that perform the explore function of the search engine often make use of the title. (A *robot,* sometimes called a *worm,* is a program that goes out into the Internet to search for information.) So be careful what you call each page. Make the title descriptive. If you have more than one page, do not use the same title on each page.

```
2.  <H1>BizPages</H1>
```

"BizPages" is the visible title of this particular home page (as opposed to the name or <TITLE> of the page that can't be seen by the end user). The <H1>*text*</H1> pair is the most prominent header, which is why the majority of home pages use this in the title. There are five other titles, each of which decrease in size:

```
<H1>...</H1>   Most prominent header
<H2>...</H2>
<H3>...</H3>
<H4>...</H4>
<H5>...</H5>
<H6>...</H6>   Least prominent header
```

These predefined headings can be used to good visual effect, and also make your HTML code a little easier to read.

Tip

Imagemaps are a method of setting more than one anchor in a single image. The publisher of the map specifies areas of the image that can be clicked to follow various hyperlinks. This allows a Web page to have a more user-friendly, GUI-like method of traversing the Web.

3. `<P>`

This is a paragraph header. Most Web page designers use it to force the browser to skip a line. Because HTML interpreters ignore anything other than the first space, to provide for the white space that good graphic design calls for, the `<P>` tag often is used to force a skipped line. The `<BR>` line break HTML tag has basically the same effect. (There's also another way, the `<PRE>`...`</PRE>` or "preformatted" tag pair, which maintains the exact formatting utilized.)

4. `<A HREF="http://www.well.com/cgi-bin/imagemap/user/`
`business/building.map">`
`<IMG ALIGN=middle SRC="building.gif" ISMAP></A>`

This rather lengthy statement not only displays the main graphic on the page, but also points to a "map" that is used to hyperlink the end user to as many pages as there are links on the map.

The `<A>`...`</A>` pair is a link tag. What follows it is usually the HREF parameter, which is short for *hypertext reference*. Here we're telling the browser to look for an image called *building.gif* located at *http://www.well.com/user/business*. The map file called *building.map* also is located here. (Here also is the case-sensitivity situation mentioned earlier. Any information within quotation marks inside a tag, such as a URL, path, or filename, should respect the casing conventions of the server.)

Tip

You can download a free imagemap editor directly from the Internet:

http://www.boutell.com/mapedit/

The GIF-plus-map combination is called an *imagemap*. The map specifies to the browser where to hyperlink when a section (i.e., a set of coordinate pairs) of the associated image is clicked. Although it is possible to create the map manually, there are shareware tools for doing so that make it much easier.

Imagemaps can either be *client-side* or *server-side*. Most imagemaps on the Web today, such as the one above, are server-side imagemaps. This means that there needs to be some sort of CGI (Common Gateway Interface) facility on the server. In the statement:

`<A HREF="http://www.well.com/cgi-bin/imagemap/user/business/`
`building.map">`

notice that */cgi-bin/imagemap/* is added to the actual location of the file stored at *http://www.well.com/user/business*. This is a convention of The WELL, the Internet Service Provider where this server is located.

Chances are good that your server, be it your own or one owned by an ISP, will have a different convention. In all cases, you must contact the system administrator for instructions, or find an example of HTML that already works at your site and copy the code. (Be aware that some ISPs levy a small extra fee for using server-side processes.)

The last part of the statement:

```
<IMG ALIGN=MIDDLE SRC="building.gif" ISMAP>
```

tells the browser that the image *building.gif* (IMG) is a clickable or mapped image (ISMAP), and that the text should be aligned in the middle of the image (ALIGN=MIDDLE). Other possible ALIGN values are TOP and BOTTOM.

MAPEDIT is a *shareware* tool, meaning that you can evaluate it free for 30 days, but then have to forward some small sum of money to the developer to keep it working. MAPEDIT provides a drawing tool that enables you to trace objects within the image. The example shown here has clearly defined shapes, so it was easy to use the MAPEDIT tool to trace around the parts of the building that I wanted to define for a particular hyperlink. MAPEDIT allows you to trace in various shapes, such as a rectangle or a circle. Creating a workable map is as easy as tracing a shape. Associated with each shape is a hyperlink, as shown in Fig. 2-3.

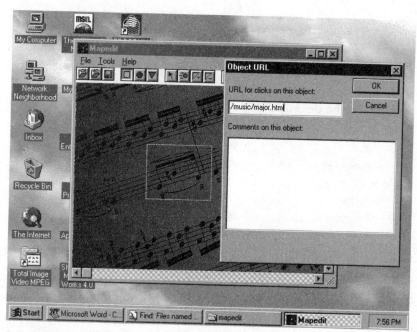

2-3 *Using an imagemap creation program.*

The resulting map file is actually a text file that contains the co-ordinates of each shape (i.e., hyperlink) as shown below:

```
default http://www.well.com/user/business
rect http://www.well.com/user/business/hotspot.html 35,23 70,63
rect http://www.well.com/user/business/bizlinks.html 92,25 133,73
rect http://www.well.com/user/business/news.html 254,24 289,62
```

MAPEDIT, and other utilities like it, assist you in defining the x,y pixel coordinates (e.g., 35,23 and 70,63), which would be difficult to figure out on your own. In the above example, three "hot spots" were defined, that is, areas in the image on which the user can click. If you compare the map above to Fig. 2-1, you'll see that there are three storefronts: Hot Spots, BizLinks, and News.

Because each storefront is rectangular in shape, MAPEDIT's rectangular drawing tool was used. The "rect" in the map definition above tells the browser the coordinates that follow form a rectangle.

The URLs, or addresses, link each clickable area to a specific HTML file. Again, note that it is not necessary to hard-code the specific server each and every time. If this convention had been followed, and all files were located in a single directory, the map could have been coded much more simply:

```
default /
rect hotspot.html 35,23 70,63
rect bizlinks.html 92,25 133,73
rect news.html 254,24 289,62
```

The "default" statement tells the browser that if the user clicks anywhere other than these three predefined quadrants, it should re-display the *index.html* file. If the statement had said "default *error.html*" the browser would have hyperlinked to that file. Since *index.html* is the default HMTL file for most servers, the / indicates that this file should be redisplayed.

5. <HR>

Sometimes you want to create a divider between sections. The <HR> tag does just that. It creates a horizontal rule line.

```
6. <A HREF="http://www.well.com/user/business/mail.html">
<IMG SRC="http://www.well.com/user/business/mail_but.gif"
ALT="Send us mail"></A>
```

This statement is fairly similar to the preceding link statement. It is clickable, but it is not an imagemap. It is an image that, when clicked, will jump or hyperlink the user to another page, or to another location on the same page. In this example, we will hyperlink to a file named *mail.html* if the image (named *mail_but.gif*) is clicked.

Notice the ALT="Send us mail" parameter. If the image is missing or the user turns off the downloading of images (an option in most browsers), the associated text will be displayed.

```
7.<A HREF="http://www.well.com/user/business/aboutna.html">
<IMG SRC="info_but.gif" ALT="About New Art"></A>
<A HREF="http://www.well.com/user/business/hotspot.html">
<IMG SRC="hot_but.gif" ALT="Hot Spots"></A>
<A HREF="http://www.well.com/user/business/bizlinks.html">
<IMG SRC="biz_but.gif" ALT="BizLinks"><A>
<A HREF="http://www.well.com/user/business/news.html">
<IMG SRC="new_but.gif" ALT="News"></A>
```

The next four link statements are exactly the same as shown previously, but display a different image and hyperlink to a different document. Note that each begins with <A HREF=... and ends with the closure </A>.

Also notice that in this example all of the locations *http://www.well.com/user/business/*... are fully specified in the code. This is not necessary, and not even desirable if the server, or the directory on that server, should change. It's best to use relative directory notation. For example, the *business* home page is all stored in one directory—the main one. There was really no need, therefore, to continually encode the full URL *http://www.well.com/user/business.* All files could have been more simply encoded as <A HREF="*filename.html*"> or <IMG SRC="*filename.gif*">. Files located in subdirectories could be encoded like <A HREF="HOTSPOTS/HOTSPOT.HTML">, where *hotspots* is a subdirectory one level below the current directory. This technique permits portability.

```
8. <P>
```

It was necessary to put some white space between the buttons and what appears below it. The handy paragraph <P> tag does the trick.

```
9. <H6>
<A HREF="http://www.well.com/user/business/mail.html">Mail</A>]
<A HREF="http://www.well.com/user/business/aboutna.html">
About New Art</A>]
[<A HREF="http://www.well.com/user/business/hotspot.html">
Hot Spots</A>]
[<A HREF="http://www.well.com/user/business/bizlinks.html">
BizLinks</A>]
[<A HREF="http://www.well.com/user/business/news.html">
News</A>]
</H6>
```

The next set of statements basically reiterate the preceding link statements, but in a different format. Why? Different people use different wsers to search the Internet. A good page design takes this into account. This particular page, while not the most visually exciting, provides three different ways to access the same data. The first, and the most visually stimulating, is the imagemap. The second method is to supply a graphical button for each separate activity.

The last method is purely text-based. Even the fastest conventional (i.e., non-ISDN) modem, 28.8 kbps as of this writing, barely chugs along when overly large images are downloaded. Therefore, a well-designed page will also have an option for text-based retrieval.

Tip

Transfer rates for a 10MB file:

9.6 kbps	2.3 hours
14.4 kbps	1.5 hours
28.8 kbps	46 minutes
56 kbps	24 minutes
128 ISDN	10 minutes
1.54 mbps T-1	52 seconds
4 mbps cable*	20 seconds
10 Mbps cable	8 seconds

* cable is a cable modem

HTML tips from the experts

Probably the best way to learn HTML is to see what other people have done. The Web is a wonderful learning experience—not only for the content that it holds, but also for the way in which it is presented. Newcomers to the profession should make it a point to spend lots of time wandering around.

Tip

Download a trial version of WebWhacker from:

http://www.ffg.com

or Milktruck at:

http://www.milktruck.com

If you see something that's intriguing, make a copy of it for your records. There are several ways to do this. As I mentioned above, most browsers provide a way for you to view and then save the HTML. If the site has multiple pages that you find interesting, you might want to invest in some of the new "page grabbing" software being sold t day. WebWhacker, by the Forefront Group, permits you to download—literally—an entire site's graphics and HTML for your perusal. In Fig. 2-4 I've grabbed part of Microsoft's home page so that I can peruse it at my convenience—when I'm not being charged for it!

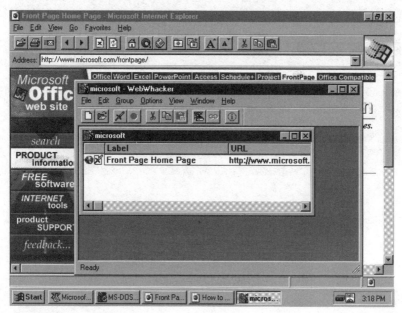

2-4 *Using WebWhacker to "grab" pages.*

Alias/Wavefront is a manufacturer of computer generated-imaging and animation software, so it's logical that they would take some pains to make sure that their home page hit the hot buttons.

Because much HTML is the same across pages, I've isolated only the most interesting of statements. In this way you can build your HMTL knowledge base in a logical, progressive fashion. Just make sure to read carefully the beginning of this chapter, which gives you a primer on HTML, before you wade into the deeper waters of more complex HTML.

One note: Most, if not all, of these advanced HTML techniques require at least HTML 2.0. If your browser is not the most recent, take some time to download the current version from your vendor.

> ## Tip
>
> Download Netscape:
>
> *http://home.netscape.com/comprod/mirror/index.html*
>
> Internet Explorer:
>
> *http://www.microsoft.com/ie/*

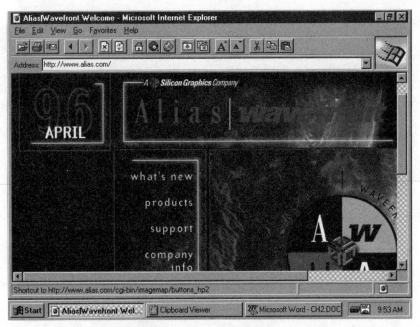

2-5 *The Alias/Wavefront cool page.*

The comment

Professional programmers know the value of a good comment. Because HTML is hard to read, and because you never know who will be maintaining the HTML you start to write, it's a good idea to document your HMTL by inserting frequent and descriptive comments:

```
<!-- HTML Source for Alias/Wavefront  Web Server  -->
<!-- Copyright 1995 Alias/Wavefront - a division  -->
<!-- of Silicon Graphics Canada Limited.           -->
<!-- All rights reserved.                          -->
```

Background colors and text

Ever wonder how to get rid of those unsightly default background and text colors? The <BODY> tag is one of the few statements that does not have an corresponding ending tag (i.e., one containing an "off" slash). Here the developer opted to change the background color (BGCOLOR) to black and the text (TEXT) to white:

```
<BODY BGCOLOR=#000000 TEXT="#ffffff">
```

Colors are specified as RGB (red-green-blue), and each can have a value between 0 and 255. To make matters even more confusing, these numbers must first be translated to hexadecimal.

> **Tip**
> See the colors and get the hex value at:
>   *http://www.snowcrest.net/dougbnt/colrtab.html*
> Or if you want to translate your own RGB value to hex, try the calculator at:
>   *http://www.lne.com/Web/rgb.html*

Controlling font size

Controlling the size of the font gives the developer more control over the look and feel of the final product. The SIZE parameter of the <FONT> tag controls the size of the font (default is 3). In absolute terms, its value can be anywhere from 1 to 7:

```
<FONT SIZE=1>....</FONT>
```

You can also use relative notation. The expression <FONT SIZE=+2> means font size 5, the current size (3) plus 2. The tag <FONT SIZE=−1> means font size 2, the current size (3) minus 1.

> **Tip**
> The <FONT SIZE> tag doesn't work with all browsers. If the size is an important element, use the heading tags <H1> through <H6> instead.

Using graphics

An important part of any Web page is its graphics. The <IMG> statement inserts an inline image into a document. As shown in the tag below, it has its own attributes. For this image the developer decided that no border was preferred. If a border is desired, then its width can be set to a value in pixels (BORDER=n).

```
<IMG NO BORDER ALIGN=LEFT WIDTH=457 HEIGHT=117 HSPACE=0 VSPACE=0
  SRC="/icons/banner1.jpeg"
  ALT="[Alias|Wavefront Top banner image]">
```

> **Tip**
> Another way of saying NO BORDER is BORDER=0.

Again we see the use of the ALIGN attribute, here to align the image to the left of the screen. Essentially what is aligned is the image versus the text on the page. Here the image is aligned to the left of the text. The developer could have also chosen LEFT, TOP, TEXTTOP, MIDDLE, ABSMIDDLE, BASELINE, BOTTOM, or ABSBOTTOM.

While most page designers spend many hours with various and sundry imaging programs such as PhotoShop to create a perfect image, you can also let the browser scale the image to suit your tastes. In this example, the developer decided to scale the height to 117 pixels and the width to 457 pixels; whether this is a scale up or down depends on the original image size. If the image is fine as it comes out of the imaging program, then by all means leave these two attributes out of your HTML statement.

Graphic designers know that a good design is a combination of text, graphics, and the white space that surrounds them. While the page developer basically nullifies the HSPACE and VSPACE parameters by setting them to 0, these parameters can be used effectively to provide space around the image. VSPACE is the space between the image and the text above it and below it. HSPACE is the space between the image and the text to its left and right.

The image is a JPEG, which we will discuss more at length in Chapter 4. At this point all you need to know that it is a form of graphic image that is compressed and can be created easily in any one of a number of imaging programs.

Tip

The best of all places to get information on Java and even applets is Sun's Java home page:

http://www.javasoft.com

or try Symantec's Java hot list:

http://cafe.symantec.com/javacentral/javarelated.html

Using Java and Javascript

Probably one of the more exciting things to come along in the fast-paced world of Web development is Java, from Sun Microsystems. Alias/Wavefront uses it on their page as shown below:

```
<APPLET CODEBASE="../Feature" CODE="scroll_bar.class" HEIGHT=100
WIDTH=600></APPLET>
```

Make no mistake about it. Java is a real programming tool and is not for the Sunday HTML coder—or for the faint of heart. It looks and works like the C++ programming language and requires real programming skills. The upside of Java is that it provides a development environment that can turn what are now essentially text-based pages into a more living document. While it is not the purpose of this book to teach an entire programming language, I would at least like to familiarize you with Java.

Java provides the ability to play sounds, display graphics, run animations, and even distort text in new and unusual ways. Additionally, since it is a bona fide programming language, it can be compiled. Unless you are a programmer, however, Java just might be beyond your patience or capabilities. The best advice I can give, therefore, is to use the Internet itself to find Java applets that you like and then copy them to the home page you are designing.

Java applets follow standard HTML conventions. There is a starting tag and an ending tag <APPLET>...</APPLET>. In the single line of Java above, the developer is telling the browser that the URL (CODEBASE=) where the code is located is in the subdirectory called */Feature*. The code itself is to be called up from a file (CODE=) called *scroll_bar.class*. Height and width, as before, identify the dimensions of the applet in pixels.

You can use Javascript to encode an entire applet directly within the HTML, rather than telling the browser to fetch it from a server.

Tip

An internet newsgroup of interest to Java developers can be accessed directly from your web browser by typing:

news:comp.lang.java

Look at Fig. 2-6 below. You won't be able to see it in a static image, but there is a line of text that scrolls at the very bottom of the

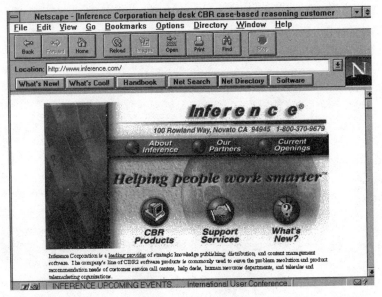

2-6 *Inference's Java scroll.*

> ## Tip
>
> Java and Javascript are two different things. Java is an object-oriented programming language that requires a development tool set to "compile" the Java sourcebook into classes, etc.
>
> Javascript, developed by the joint efforts of Netscape and Sun, is a Java-oriented scripting language that is embedded right in your HTML.

I've included the entire Java script in Listing 2-1. You may copy the code yourself. It is located at *http://www.inference.com*. Notice the scrolling message on the figure. The text for this message is located in the code in the VAR MSG= parameter.

Listing 2-1

```
<HTML>

<!-- *********************************************
    COMPUTER GRAPHICS CREATED BY CARASSO DESIGN
    FOR INFORMATION ON PRICING AND SERVICES,
    CONTACT info@carasso.com
    ********************************************* -->
<HEAD>
<TITLE>Inference Corporation help desk CBR case-based
reasoning customer service CIS help desk customer care
sales automation problem resolution problem
management</TITLE>
</HEAD>

<SCRIPT LANGUAGE="JavaScript">
<!-- Beginning of JavaScript Applet ------------------

/* Copyright (C)1996 Web Integration Systems, Inc. DBA Websys, Inc.
    All Rights Reserved.

    This applet can be re-used or modified, if credit is
    given in the source code.

    We will not be held responsible for any unwanted
    effects due to the usage of this applet or any
    derivative.  No warrantees for usability for any
    specific application are given or implied.

    Chris Skinner, January 30th, 1996.
        Hacked for CNNfn by RD, Jan. 31, 1996
*/
```

```
function scrollit_r21(seed)
{
var msg  = "INFERENCE UPCOMING EVENTS........
International User Conference..... March/April Knowledge
Solutions Seminar Series.....UK Seminar
Schedule........................ INFERENCE
ANNOUNCEMENTS.......... Inference's CBR Express Named
Product of the Year by Call Center Magazine.....
Inference Corporation Expands North American
Distribution.....Six Leading Help Desk Solution Providers
Join Inference OEM Program and Commit to Embed
CBR2.....ICL Sorbus Sign European Wide Deal for Inference
Product..... New CasePoint WebServer Product..... Record
Fourth Quarter Financial Results..... Intergraph
Corporation Customer Success Story..... and New Knowledge
Publishing Division.......... "

   var out = " ";
   var c   = 1;

   if (seed > 100) {
           seed--;
           var cmd="scrollit_r21(3 + seed + ")";
           timerTwo=window.setTimeout(cmd,100);
   }
   else if (seed <= 100 && seed > 0) {
           for (c=0 ; c < seed ; c++) {
                   out+=" ";
           }
           out+=msg;
           seed--;
           seed--;
           var cmd="scrollit_r21(" + seed + ")";
               window.status=out;
           timerTwo=window.setTimeout(cmd,100);
   }
   else if (seed <= 0) {
           if (-seed < msg.length) {
                   out+=msg.substring(-seed,msg.length);
                   seed--;
           seed--;
           seed--;

                   var cmd="scrollit_r21(3 + seed + ")";
                   window.status=out;
                   timerTwo=window.setTimeout(cmd,100);
           }
           else {
                   window.status=" ";
                   timerTwo=window.setTimeout("scrol-
                   lit_r21(100)",75);
           }
       }
   }
}

// - End of JavaScript code ------------- -->
</SCRIPT>
```

Tip

There are lots of Javascript resources on the Web:

The Javascript Resource Center:

http://www.intercom.net/user/mecha/java.html

The Javascript Archive:

http://acwww.bloomu.edu/~mpscho/jsarchive/

Matt's Script Archive:

http://www.worldwidemart.com/scripts/

Tip

Do a search on the word "applet" on *http://digital.altavista.com.* You'll find 10,000 references. That's a lot of applets you can copy. More specific places for applets are:

www.gamelan.com
www.javasoft.com/applets
www.dimensionx.com

Tip

A slew of Java development tools have been announced that makes Java programming a breeze:

AimTech's Jamba:

http://www.aimtech.com/prodjahome.html

Symantec Café:

http://cafe.symantec.com/cafe/index.html

Power Production WebBurst:

http://www.powerproduction.com/products.html

FutureTense Texture:

http://www.futuretense.com/

Sun's Java Workshop:

http://www.sun.com/developer-products/

WinGen:

http://www.pro-c.com

If this full-blown Java looks 'way too complicated for your programming skills, fear not. A slew of visually based Java development tools is on the horizon (see Tip box) that makes Java programming as easy as "drag and drop."

The site map

Many Web sites are fairly large. They consist of dozens, even hundreds of pages. Unisys came up with a good way to help users navigate through their rather extensive site, providing information in their new heterogeneous multiprocessing computer, the ClearPath HMP (Fig. 2-7).

2-7 *Unisys's Clearpath site map.*

The Unisys site map is something that, having reached this point, you could code yourself. It's actually just a series of clickable images that take you to the particular HMTL page of interest.

One of those pages is ShareStuff (*www.sharestuff.com*), a virtual shareware repository. Several hundred thousand hyperlinks are provided to shareware and freeware files.

The HTML files were generated automatically by a series of approximately a dozen programs. Because the number of shareware links was excessive (although a search engine was provided), a browse directory is provided for each operating system such as Unix and Windows 95. Here users can click on a particular subdirectory that lists the shareware programs.

Using tables

Tables are a good way to present rows and rows of data—or merely to lay out elements on a page (use BORDER=0 here). Although it is possible to have variable column lengths, this example shows a rather straightforward way of putting tables together.

Tables are a nuisance to code. Later in this chapter we'll review at least one HTML editor that helps you to put together tables easily, without the fuss and muss of manually coding them.

Tables, like everything else in HTML, come with a start and an ending tag, <TABLE>...</TABLE>. The <TABLE> tag has several attributes. COLSPEC tells the browser the number and width of each of the columns in the table. The ShareStuff table contains 6 columns, each of them 25 pixels in width and left-justified. In this example a border, whose width is 6 pixels, is used to make the table much more prominent.

The ShareStuff Unix directory is rather lengthy; the table contains multiple rows. Since all rows look alike, we'll look at one that is rep-

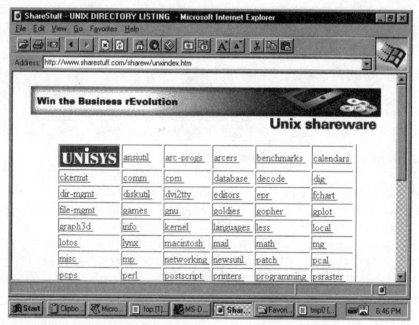

2-8 *Using hyperlinks inside of tables.*

resentative of the entire table. Each row is bounded by
<TR>...<TR> tags. Each row can contain multiple columns and n
have a heading as well as data. Each ShareStuff row has 6 colum
all of them containing data. Each of the columns is called a *cell* and
is defined by the <TD>...</TD>. Data can be in the form of text, image references, or even hyperlinks, as shown in the fragment below.
The user need only click on the text in a cell to hyperlink to another
HMTL file. For example, if the user clicks on the word *artificial,* the
HTML document named *dosx009.htm* is shown.

```
<TABLE COLSPEC="L25 L25 L25 L25 L25 L25" BORDER=6>
<TR><TD><A HREF="dosx0007.htm">archiver </A> </TD>
<TD><A HREF="dosx0008.htm">arcutil          </A></TD>
<TD><A HREF="dosx0009.htm">artificial       </A></TD>
<TD><A HREF="dosx0010.htm">asm_mag          </A></TD>
<TD><A HREF="dosx0011.htm">asmutil          </A></TD>
<TD><A HREF="dosx0012.htm">assembler        </A></TD>
</TR></TABLE>
```

The </TABLE> ending tag is required to complete the table. There
are several other table attributes that can make your tables quite creative:

- CELLSPACING defines the amount of space between cells.
- CELLPADDING defines the amount of space between the edges
  of the cells and what's inside.
- <CAPTION>...</CAPTION> provides a caption for the table.
- <TH>...</TH> defines a cell that contains a boldface heading.
- ROWSPAN is used with the <TH> or <TD> tag and defines the
  number of cells that this one cell will span.
- COLSPAN is used with the <TH> or <TD> tag and defines the
  number of cells to the right of this cell will span.
- NOWRAP is used with a <TH> or <TD> tag to prevent the
  browser from wrapping the contents of a cell.

Tip
A complete ISO-Latin-1 character list can be found at:
www.well.com/user/business/latin.htm

Tip

To create your own background library, use an imaging program like Photoshop to "cut" a small piece of background out of an image you already have on hand, either scanned or taken from the Internet. The dimensions should be no bigger than 765 pixels by 765 pixels. Save this in a directory you call */bkground.*

Using special characters

At times the text must contain a special character such as the © copyright symbol. Most sites copyright their HTML code as shown below:

`<P>&copy;1996 UNISYS.`

Using special symbols requires the ISO Latin-1 character set. The © symbol can be displayed in HTML by using the code "&copy."

Adding imagery and sound

The final stop on our tour is Richard C. Hoagland's site. Hoagland is well known for his theory that there are monuments, actually vestiges of extraterrestrial civilizations, on Mars and the Moon.

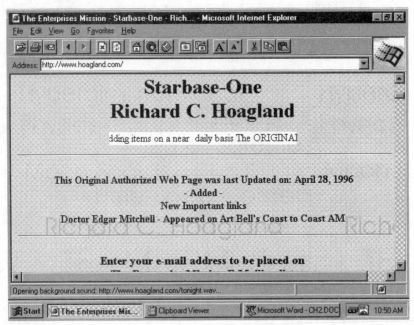

2-9 *An out-of-this-world site.*

His site has some interesting features. First, notice the background. You might not be able to see it from this black and white reproduction, but the background contains ghosted (i.e., very light, hence ghostly) text. You may just be able to make out his name and the words "physics" and "comet" among others.

As you can see from the code below, one can specify a background image in the body tag. Here the file *hoagdrop.gif* (stored in the main directory) is loaded using the BACKGROUND attribute. Again, it is possible to specify the width and the height of the image.

```
<BODY background="hoagdrop.gif" WIDTH="475" HEIGHT="341">
```

Page authors concerned that the overuse of graphics means a slow download can take advantage of the fact that, if the image dimensions are smaller than the area of the full window, the browser will "tile" the image to fill up the width and height of the screen. You therefore can define a very small image file that takes no time to download, and let the user's browser create a pleasing pattern over the whole screen.

The Hoagland site differs from most in that it takes advantage of the browser's ability to handle many forms of data. Data can be in the form of text and graphics, as we have seen, but it can also be in the form of audio and animation. When you load the site for the first time, it might well be disconcerting to hear a male voice saying, "...you're going to see tonight, you will not be disappointed."

```
<BGSOUND SRC="tonight.wav">
```

This statement is part of the <BODY>...</BODY> grouping. As you can see, it loads a file called *tonight.wav*. Those familiar with multimedia will be intimately familiar with audio WAV files.

Using browser helper applications

Browsers come preconfigured with the type of data files they understand without some work on the part of the user. Figure 2-10 shows

2-10 *How a browser understands file types.*

a list of file types that Microsoft's Internet Explorer understands. (Access this through View, Options, File Types.)

These file formats are called MIMEs (Multipurpose Internet Mail Extensions). When a Web server responds to a request for a document from a Web browser (e.g., Netscape or Mosaic), the server announces to the browser the type of data it is sending using MIME.

Your Web browser, whether it be Mosaic, Netscape, Lynx, or some other, understands the MIME mechanism, too. When you click on a hyperlink, the Web server sends a stream of data that includes the MIME type of the data. Your browser reads this MIME type information and decides what to do with the incoming data.

Thus, your Web browser knows what to do with data of the MIME type *text/html* (regular Web pages), or *image/gif* (a GIF image). Built into your browser is the ability to handle properly these and other common types of data. This is how you're able to read most documents you find on the Web, and see most images.

Web browsers can't possibly handle all kinds of data. This is where Web *helper applications* (also called *external viewers*) come in. Web browsers use the MIME information to pass off the data to helper applications. This is how you play Web movies or sound files, and so on.

Given a MIME type to associate with a given kind of data, you can define any program on your computer as a helper application. As a user, all you need do is access the MIME table and add a definition as shown in Fig. 2-11.

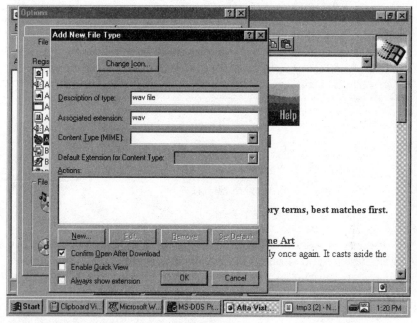

2-11 *Adding a new file type to a browser.*

Tip

Get your artwork, icons, and backgrounds free right on the Web. Start here:

http://www.yahoo.com/Computers/Multimedia/Pictures

Myriad MIME types are provided with most browsers. These include *gif, wav, txt, rtf, jpeg, tif, snd, au, mpeg, avi, mov, zip, tar, exe,* etc. Visit Netscape's site to find a complete list for their browser:

http://home.netscape.com/assist/helper_apps/mimedefault.html

This capability opens the floodgates towards greater creativity on the Web. But be forewarned that different browsers work differently (at least they do now). What works on one might not work on another. The best advice I can give you is to test on all three major platforms: Mosaic, Netscape, and Internet Explorer.

Another difference between browsers, at this time, is the ability to handle the <MARQUEE> tag. The Hoagland site uses it to display a scrolling message. Check the white-with-black text box in the center of the page. (Netscape shows it as static text.)

Tip

There's good news and bad news. If a browser doesn't understand your tag it ignores it. The good thing is that you don't get an error message. The bad thing is that your carefully crafted Web site is not visible to everyone.

```
<MARQUEE BGCOLOR=WHITE WIDTH=50% SCROLLDELAY=2>
```

```
Keep checking here by "RELOADING" periodically, we are
adding items on a near daily basis The ORIGINAL AUTHORIZED
Enterprise Mission - Starbase-One   Richard C. Hoagland on
March 10, 1996 by the Mars Mission Group.
```

```
</MARQUEE>
```

By now you should all be experts in interpreting and using HTML statements, so you should have no trouble reading this one. White is specified as the background color, along with a box width of 50 percent and a scroll delay (the interval between the end of the message and the restart of the same message) of 2.

Using HTML development tools

There's absolutely no reason you can't use your text editor, or even Windows Notepad, to code HTML. After all, it's only a bunch of text and some tags. There's a plethora of tools, however, that do make it easier going for you.

Some Microsoft tools

Users of Microsoft Word 6 for Windows can download free Internet Assistant for Word directly from Microsoft's home page at *http://www. microsoft.com/IntDev/author/.* You can also download an Internet Assistant for Excel, PowerPoint, Access, or Schedule, all of which are parts of Microsoft's Office Suite.

In Fig. 2-12, a document is going to be created from scratch. But that's not always necessary. For example, let's say you have a Word or text document already completed. Wouldn't it be nice to turn it from a word processor version to an HTML version, bullet points and all? That's exactly what Internet Assistant does.

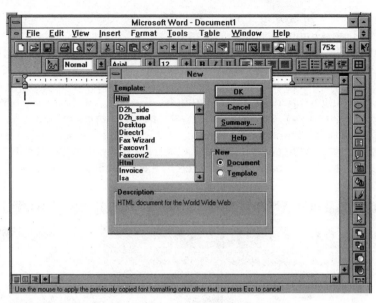

2-12 *Using Word to generate an HTML document.*

Import a document and the Internet Assistant will translate bullets, alignment, etc., to HTML, while allowing you to embed graphics and hyperlinks (Fig. 2-13).

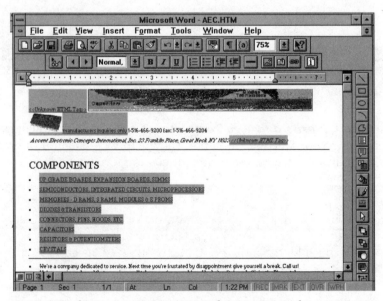

2-13 *Word Internet Assistant translates existing documents to HTML.*

Another Microsoft entry into Web page development tools is FrontPage. Originally slated to cost over $600, it's now sold at the bargain basement price of $149 (or $109 if you're a Microsoft Office user). You can also download a sample version of the product from the Microsoft FrontPage Web site (*www.microsoft.com/frontpage*). We're going to spend a few paragraphs discussing its features so you know what to look for in a good Web site development tool.

Microsoft's FrontPage authoring and management tool is an easy and fast way to create and manage a Web site through HTML, as shown in Fig. 2-14. Its features are described in the following paragraphs.

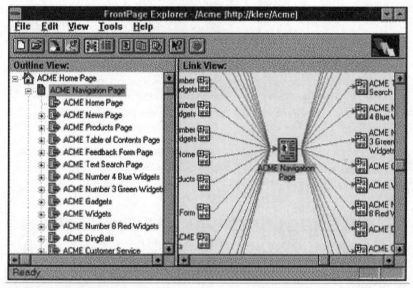

2-14 *FrontPage, Microsoft's professional HTML development tool.*

Web Wizards and Web Templates These are for automatically generating your Web site contents. They help with creation of entire webs, individual pages, interactive discussion forums, and more.

Tip

Keep in mind that there's bound to be a shakeout in the Internet wars. Will Netscape win? Or Microsoft? The tool that you use should be able to handle both. Microsoft's tool, as good as it is, ties you into its own proprietary technology. You might be better off using a third-party development tool. It's interesting to note that many MIS managers are looking at Lotus Notes's new entry into the Web wars as a more neutral third party.

WebBot components WebBot components offer drop-in interactive functionality, greatly streamlining the development process. WebBot components also eliminate the need to write your own scripts or add complicated HTML commands. More than a dozen built-in WebBot components let you easily add such advanced interactive capabilities as navigation bars, discussion groups, full-text search, and registration forms to your site.

WYSIWYG HTML editor With the WYSIWYG Microsoft Front-Page Editor, you can edit and refine previously created Web pages, create brand-new Web pages, and create a custom look by adding text and images to a blank page. Acting as a "mini-browser," the Microsoft FrontPage Editor allows you to view your site during its creation, as others would view your end product across your local network or over the Internet. The Microsoft FrontPage Editor automatically generates the HTML code behind the scenes for you.

HTML tables Create HTML tables on the fly, or use any of number of table templates. Insert rows and columns, and split and merge cells. Create auto-resize or fixed-width tables and cells. Manipulate cell padding and spacing. Create table borders, captions, and header cells. Use any HTML feature within tables, including images. Align tables within text.

HTML frames Create HTML frames using the Frames Wizard or the Discussion Web Wizard. Users can choose from several existing frames templates, or can create a custom frames grid. The frame set is stored into the Web like any other document, with pointers to the documents that are displayed within the frame set.

Autoconvert documents and graphics To include pre-existing information such as press releases, logos, or reports into your site, simply position your cursor at the desired location and insert. The Microsoft FrontPage Editor recognizes and automatically converts Rich Text Format (RTF) or ASCII text into HTML. In addition, a wide range of graphic formats are automatically converted into GIF or JPEG image files.

Tip

Get a free Web PDF maker from Adobe at:

http://www.adobe.com/events/netexpect/webpresenter/main.html

Create links Microsoft FrontPage Explorer's drag-and-drop interface lets you create a link by simply dragging a page or image icon to a specific place on a page in the Microsoft FrontPage Editor. With the Microsoft FrontPage Editor, you can create links to other pages, bookmarks, or Web sites with a few clicks of the mouse. Because all standard file formats and protocols are supported, you can link to any file, such as multimedia or PDF, as well as link to any ftp site, gopher site, or newsgroup. If you add a link to a nonexistent page, the task of completing that page is automatically added to your To Do List.

Hotspots Insert images and add graphical hyperlinks by using the FrontPage hotspot editing capabilities. It's easy—just select an area within an image and FrontPage will guide you the rest of the way.

Tip

Not into Microsoft? Then check out Yahoo for other Web authoring tools:

> *http://www.yahoo.com/Computers_and_Internet/Internet/World_Wide_Web/Authoring/*

> *http://www.yahoo.com/Computers_and_Internet/Software/Data_Formats/HTML/Guides_and_Tutorials*

Search through many more at:

> *http://www.cnet.com/Content/Reviews/Hands/*

Check out Adobe's entry, PageMill:

> *http://www.adobe.com*

Hotspot editing functions Images can be inserted and turned into clickable image maps using the Microsoft FrontPage hotspot-editing functions which include:

- *Image Editing Tools* allow for scalable JPEG compression and transparent GIF image creation.
- *Break Below Images* options include clearing either left or right or both margins, so that text is below any floating image, left or right.

Create and customize forms The Microsoft FrontPage Editor also includes an easy-to-use forms editing function to create and customize virtually any form. Within minutes you can create text fields, radio buttons, scrolling lists, and other form elements. Text fields can be quickly resized by dragging the mouse. You can easily edit any HTML form previously created with or without the Microsoft FrontPage Editor. Output form fields to files or other formats.

Advanced page and character formatting capabilities Create pages without knowing HTML. All of the styles available in HTML are available to you, such as character and paragraph styles (including bulleted or numbered lists), horizontal lines and background images, and colors. But instead of using HTML tags, you format your paragraphs as you would with a standard WYSIWYG word processor, and Microsoft FrontPage automatically generates the HTML code behind the scenes. The Microsoft FrontPage Editor displays the page in the same manner as your Web browser. The Microsoft FrontPage Editor also allows you to display hidden formatting and authoring commands, so that you can have complete control over each page's design and format.

Other advanced editing features New toolbar buttons include multilevel undo and redo, increase and decrease text size, and page forward and back in Editor. Now you can create custom pages and backgrounds and save as page templates. There's a built-in, Office-like spell checker. Microsoft FrontPage generates standard 2.0 HTML and supports the creation of various 3.0 HTML features. It thus creates content that can be viewed by virtually any browser.

Developing hot Web sites with HotDog

Another downloadable Web development tool, this one shareware, is HotDog from Sausage (Fig. 2-15). Its features include:

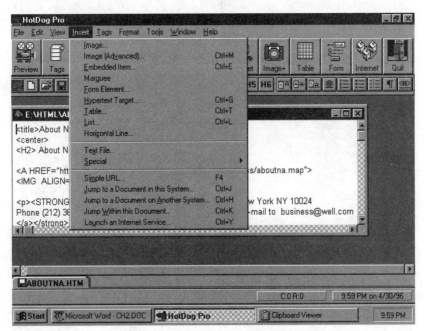

2-15 *HotDog, one of the many shareware HTML tools.*

- Supports both Netscape extensions to HTML, and proposed HTML 3 elements.
- Puts Windows 95-style interface on Windows 3.1 and Windows NT 3.5.

- Supports forms and tables.
- Finds duplicate tags.
- Converts DOS files for use on Unix systems.
- Remembers hypertext links, to minimize retyping long URLs.
- Allows inserting links, images, and text files by drag-and-drop.
- Edits CGI scripts as well as HTML files.
- Allows automatic text replacement when document is ready for preview.

Tip

Download HotDog, one of the more popular shareware Web tools, from:

www.sausage.com

One of the nicest things about HotDog is the ease of creating tables, as shown in Fig. 2-16. All one needs to do is define it; the HTML code is automatically generated. Forms also are easy (Fig. 2-17). You're provided a wealth of choices such as creating radio buttons, text buttons, submit buttons, drop-down list boxes, and more.

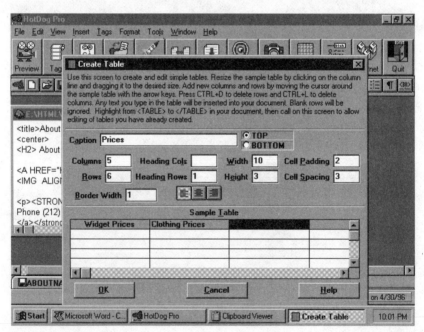

2-16 *Creating an intricate table using a tool.*

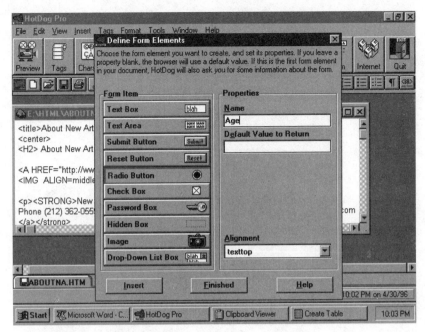

2-17 *Defining a form using a tool.*

Tip

To compete with Microsoft, Netscape has made it a practice to release a new version of Navigator every 6 months. With each new release, a new set of tags is created. Appendix B provides a summary of all the HTML you'll ever need (when this book was written, at least). To get the most current HTML standard tags, surf to the World Wide Web Consortium at:

http://www.w3.org/pub/WWW/

Chapter 3 features more advanced coding techniques.

3

Advanced coding techniques

In this chapter we'll concentrate on some additional techniques for your bag of Web tricks. The goal here is to provide a working tool set of techniques that you can use over and over again to build a wide variety of home pages for, one hopes, an even wider variety of industries.

One of the best things about doing business on the Web, from your customer's perspective, is that they can directly interact with their own customers. What could be better than to market a product on the Web and receive an immediate e-mail requesting more information—or, even better, an order?

Getting mail

This mail feature is available and remarkably easy to design into your pages. Figure 3-1 is the now-familiar New Art home page with its imagemap and buttons. Notice that the leftmost button is one with an envelope. This is the e-mail button. A different designer might have a different design, of course, but an envelope on a button is easy to understand.

When the user clicks on the mail button, a hyperlink goes to a different HMTL file with a different image, as shown in Fig. 3-2.

The page is a rather straightforward request for information such as e-mail address, subject and message. The HTML to code and process the e-mail is shown below:

```
<html>
<TITLE>email</TITLE>
<H1><img alt="" align=middle src=mail.gif> Send email</H1>
<FORM ACTION="http://www.well.com/cgi-bin/mailgate/business"
METHOD="POST">
```

```
<B>Your email address and name:</B><BR>
<dd> <TEXTAREA NAME="from" COLS=68 ROWS=1></TEXTAREA></dd><P>
<B>Subject:</B><BR>
<dd><TEXTAREA NAME="subject" COLS=68 ROWS=1></TEXTAREA></dd><P>
<B>Your Comments:</B><BR>
<dd><TEXTAREA NAME="body" COLS=68 ROWS=5></TEXTAREA></dd><P>
<INPUT TYPE="submit" VALUE="send mail">
<INPUT TYPE="reset" VALUE="cancel">
</P>
</FORM>
</html>
```

3-1 *The old New Art home page.*

Tip

Keep current on development tool sets. Read the Daily Spectrum:

    http://www.spring.com/~ds

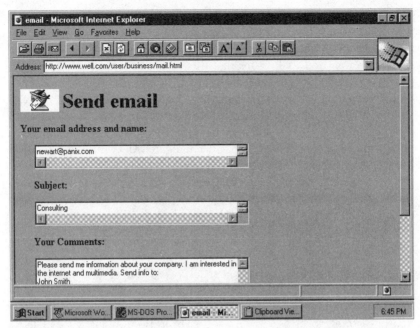

3-2 *Sending e-mail.*

The HTML provides a good working example not only of e-mail, but of forms. The e-mail presented in this example is in the guise of a form that must be processed by the server. In essence, the form takes information from the user and then forwards it to the server. Once it gets to the server, something has to be on hand (i.e., some kind of program or script) to process it. Otherwise it's just so much data.

Tip

Want to add a counter to your site but your ISP won't let you? The folks at *http://www.digits.com* let you use their database, and even show you how to write the simple HTML to place on your page.

For larger clients that require Nielsen-level auditing:

http://www.ipro.com

(This one's not free.)

```
<FORM ACTION="http://www.well.com/cgi-bin/mailgate/business"
METHOD="POST">
```

The HTML code above is what tells the server what to do to it. The requested action is to post the contents of the form to an e-mail.

The program that does this is called *mailgate,* and you can tell from the HMTL that it is a CGI (Common Gateway Interface) script.

Those of you who are using ISP accounts rather than your very own server should make sure that this facility is available. Many ISPs do not permit their clients (i.e., you) to launch their programs from your own directory. To make sure that the system is not overrun with strange and resource-hogging jobs, they prefer that you work through them. In most cases you will find that your ISP has the facilities for such common activities as imagemaps and mailgate. All you need do is read the ISP documentation or speak directly to human tech support.

Salons USA has products and services it wants to sell. After describing its product line, what better way to get orders than through e-mail, as shown in Figs. 3-3 and 3-4?

Tip

Not going through an ISP because you're setting up your own server? Check out Chapter 5. Essentially you'll have to run your own computer, install an operating system (and be familiar with all its nuances), install a Web server (and be familiar with all *its* nuances). Get the picture?

Doing this for a client? Part of your team should be a programmer familiar with installing Web server software.

Not ready to take credit card numbers over the Internet, this company made the decision to request a fax number so that an order

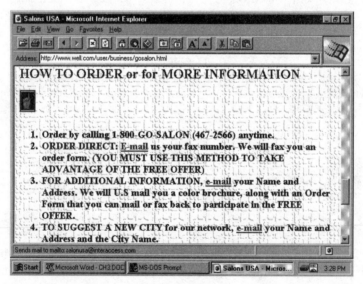

3-3 *Getting to e-mail via hyperlinks.*

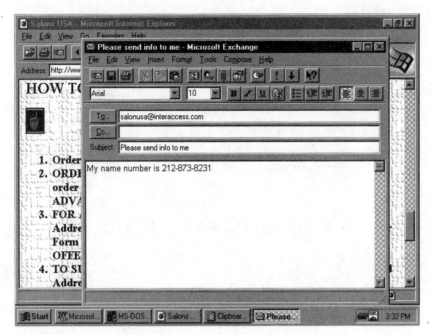

3-4 *The results of the "mailto" CGI script.*

form could be sent to the customer. The customer merely uses the hyperlink provided on the word *e-mail* and off the message goes.

```
<ol>
<li>Order by calling 1-800-GO-SALON (467-2566) anytime.
<li>ORDER DIRECT: <a href="mailto:salonusa@interaccess
.com">E-mail</a> us your fax number.  We will fax you an
order form.  (YOU MUST USE THIS METHOD TO TAKE ADVANTAGE
OF THE FREE OFFER)
<li>FOR ADDITIONAL INFORMATION, <a href="mailto:
salonusa@interaccess.com">e-mail</a>  your Name and
Address.  We will U.S. mail you a color brochure, along
with an Order Form that you can mail or fax back to
participate in the FREE OFFER.
<li>TO SUGGEST A NEW CITY for our network, <a
href="mailto:salonusa@interaccess.com">e-mail</a> your
Name and Address and the City Name.
<li>OR CALL/WRITE  US at 1001 Green Bay Rd, Winnetka, IL,
60093 (847) 441-7225/</ol>
```

The HTML above is the way it was done, a variation on the preceding approach and one that uses the automatic e-mail capabilities of most browsers.

Notice that it is an ordered list <OL> . . . </OL>. Each numbered item is tagged with an <LI> tag. Number 2, Order Direct, contains a hyperlink to the standard "mailto:URL" structure, an easy way to achieve e-mail without using forms. Note, however, that some older browsers do not support this feature and will produce an error message.

Tip

Getting good at writing HTML? You might want to join the Internet Developers Association (IDA).

http://www.association.org

The form's the thing

The form is the basis of most information systems. Data are collected on forms and displayed on forms. Forms are fast becoming the manner in which information is collected on the Internet as well. Forms are used in a wide variety of environments, including e-mail, catalog shopping, and search engine criterion entry.

Tip

Jetform, maker of electronic form-creation and -filling products, has created Web-based versions of its products. A trial version of JetForm Filler is available from:

http://www.jetform.com

Be forewarned, however, that not all browsers support forms at this time. Since it is becoming quite the standard, my guess is that by the time you read this section, only a small percentage of folks won't have forms-enabled browsers. In addition, for a form to work properly, the server where your HTML resides must be able to process those forms. If you don't know, ask. If you can't get your administrator or the ISP on the phone, then try it out for yourself and see what happens.

The e-mail form is an excellent example of how this HTML coding technique works.

```
<FORM ACTION="http://www.well.com/cgi-bin/mailgate/business"
METHOD="POST">
```

A form must start with the <form> tag. Next it must indicate the action that is to be taken when the form is sent to the server. In our example the form is sent to a script called *mailgate*.

The Form tag has many options, or attributes. As usual, there is always someplace on the Web itself to look for a great example of how to do it.

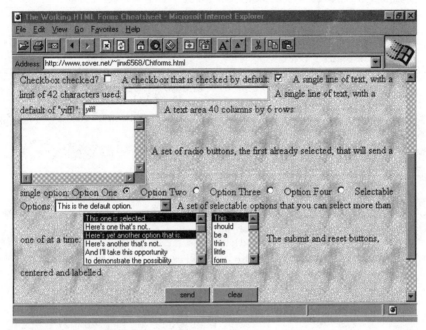

3-5 *How to do forms.*

Jinx-tigr's form cheat sheet is not meant to be used as an example of great style; it is meant to be used as an example of how to code HMTL forms. (It also illustrates powerfully that placement of carriage returns in HTML is almost entirely arbitrary, and is done primarily for the human reading the source code. The last option in the long skinny list has been word-wrapped for this book; in the source, it is all on one line that stretches off to infinity. Either way, the browser displays it just the same.)

```
<form method="post"
action="mailto:jinx6568@sover.net">

Checkbox checked?
<input name="checkbox checked" type=checkbox
value="yes">

A checkbox that is checked by default:
<input name="default checked" type=checkbox checked
value="yes">
```

A single line of text, with a limit of 42 characters used:
```
<input name="single line of text" size="42">
```

A single line of text, with a default of "yiff!":
```
<input name="default text is yiff" value="yiff!">
```

A text area 40 columns by 6 rows:
```
<textarea name="textarea" rows=6 cols=40></textarea>
```

A set of radio buttons, the first already selected,
that will send a single option:
```
Option One <input name="radio button" type=radio
value="one" checked>
Option Two <input name="radio button" type=radio
value="two">
Option Three <input name="radio button" type=radio
value="three">
Option Four <input name="radio button" type=radio
value="four">
```

```
Selectable Options:
 <select name="Selectable Options">
      <option selected>This is the default option.
      <option>Here's another option.
      <option>Here's yet another option :)
      <option>You can keep going indefinitely.
      </select>
```

A set of selectable options that you can select more than
one of at a time:
```
 <select name="Multiple Options" multiple size=7>
      <option selected>This one is selected.
      <option>Here's one that's not..
      <option selected>Here's yet another option that is.
      <option>Here's another that's not..
      <option>And I'll take this opportunity
      <option>to demonstrate the possibility
      <option>of making the window scroll
      <option>and look cool! There are ways to
      <option>select multiple options on this
      <option>input field- for Mac it is
      <option>command-click, for instance.
      <option>However, simply clicking will
      <option>turn off the other options, and
      <option>the form can be used in that way.
      <option>Just remember that a user can
      <option>turn on more than one option if
      <option>they know how.
      <option>This form field is set to
      <option>seven lines displayed in the
      <option>window at one time, with the
      <option>"size" attribute.
      </select>
```

```
<select name="Thin Form" multiple size=7>
        <option>This
        <option>should
        <option>be a
        <option>thin
        <option>little
        <option>form
        <option>cause
        <option>the
        <option>form
        <option>fits
        <option>its
        <option>width
        <option>to
        <option>the
        <option>widest
        <option>line
        <option>in
        <option>the
        <option>form
        <option>you
        <option>know.

<option>In<option>fact<option>you<option>could<option>do
<option>it<option>like<option>this<option>and<option
>perhaps<option>even<option>omit<option>the<option>send
<option>buttons<option>getting<option>a<option>frame
<option>effect<option>without<option>frames!<option>Just
<option>a<option>prank<option>that<option>was<option>
brought<option>to<option>you<option>by<option>the
<option>magic<option>of<option>cut<option>and<option>
paste.<option>*grin*
        </select>

<input type=hidden name="Finally, here is how you can get
rid of obtrusive input fields when stealing forms and
filing off the serial numbers ;) Here you type the name
of whatever the field is that you want to get rid of"
value="And here you type the default that you want to not
be bothered with">

The submit and reset buttons, centered and labeled.
<p align=center><input type=submit value="send">
<input type=reset value="clear">
</form>
```

Jinx did a good job and little elaboration is needed. You can create text fields of variable length and even set the initial value. You can create radio buttons and even drop-down selection lists.

AT&T's form (Fig. 3-6) is instructive as well. AT&T uses this form to collect information from its 800 customers who want a listing on their free AT&T toll-free online directory. In AT&T's case, however, the contents of the form are not being passed to an e-mail script but to one called *clientfeedback.cgi*. More than likely, the information is being passed to an in-house database for further processing to ensure that the request is from a valid 800 customer, etc.

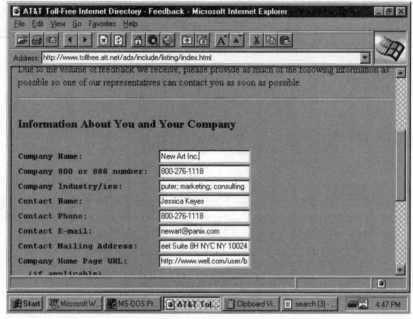

3-6 *Using forms to collect information.*

The <!---> tag indicates that a comment follows. Here the HTML programmer noted the fact that a hidden field named CATCODE with an initial value of "listing" will be sent to the script along with the data the user submits. Another hidden field is included as well. Hidden fields are a great way to send default information to the program that runs on the server. The program needs some information about what to do with what it is being passed; sending a hidden field serves such a purpose.

```
<form action="/cgi-bin/clientfeedback.cgi" method="POST">
<!--- Must include the following hidden fields for the
.cgi --->
<INPUT TYPE="hidden" NAME="CATCODE" VALUE="listing"
SIZE="1">
<INPUT TYPE="hidden" NAME="TOLLFREENUM" VALUE="include"
SIZE="1">
```

Notice that you can intersperse other HTML commands within your form. Here a header is being displayed to make the form more readable. The <pre> preformatted tag is used to ensure that the form is spaced as the HTML coder formatted it.

```
<h3>Information About You and Your Company</h3>
<pre>
```

Our first field "company" is labeled Company Name, takes text as input, and is provided a text box with an initial length (SIZE) of 25. If the user must use more space, he or she can type up to 90 characters before the text box runs out of space. The other pertinent information (800 number, industry, name, etc.) is all entered in the same manner. Note that each field has a field name (NAME) that only the program can see, a label that the user can see, an input type, and a size.

```
<b>Company Name:</b>
   <input type=text name="company" size=25 maxlength=90>
<b>Company 800 or 888 number:</b>
   <input type=text name="comp_num" size=25 maxlength=90>
<b>Company Industry/ies:</b>
   <input type=text name="comp_indus" size=25 maxlength=90>
<b>Contact Name:</b>
   <input type=text name="contactname" size=25 maxlength=90>
<b>Contact Phone:</b>
   <input type=text name="contactphone" size=25 maxlength=90>
<b>Contact E-mail:</b>
   <input type=text name="email" size=25 maxlength=90>
<b>Contact Mailing Address:</b>
   <input type=text name="contactaddress" size=25 maxlength=90>
<b>Company Home Page URL:</b>
   <input type=text name="comp_hpurl" size=25
maxlength=90>
<b>(if applicable)</b>
</pre>
<hr>
```

Tip

A great place to go to find scripts for imagemaps, guestbooks, web indexing, counters, searching, animation and more is:

http://www.iserver.com/cgi/library.html

Because a customer might well not have an 800 number, the words (if applicable) are bolded using the `<B>`...`</B>` tag. The preformatted `</PRE>` ending tag is coded, as well as a horizontal line `<HR>` to set off the form from the information directly below it.

```
<h3>Message Body</h3>
  <input type="submit" value="Submit">
<input type="reset" value="Clear">
<br>
  <textarea name="msg" rows=10 cols=51></textarea>
</form>
```

AT&T has provided the means for a user to enter up to 10 rows of text (each with 51 characters) in a field named "msg." Finally, buttons are provided to Submit and Clear.

Tip

For detailed technical information about the Web in general and CGI in particular, try these:

The World-Wide Web FAQ

http://sunsite.unc.edu/boutell/faq/index.html

Unofficial CGI FAQ

http://www.best.com/~hedlund/cgi-faq/

Yahoo's CGI directory list

http://www.yahoo.com/Computers/World_Wide_Web/CGI_ _Common_Gateway_Interface/

The Web Developer's Virtual Library

http://www.stars.com/

The Usenet newsgroup is:

comp.infosystems.www.authoring.cgi

CGI scripts for processing forms

Unless you're a bona fide programmer, you probably won't want to get involved in coding scripts. You should be familiar with how they work, however, so that you can implement properly the various and sundry freebie CGI scripts that are stored on the Web. The following introduction is adapted from the very fine discussion of scripts written by the NCSA HTTPd Development Team, which is part of the Software Development Group of the National Center for Supercomputing Applications at the University of Illinois at Urbana-Champaign (*http://hoohoo.ncsa.uiuc.edu/cgi/*).

The Common Gateway Interface (CGI) is a Unix-based standard for interfacing external applications with information servers, such as HTTP or Web servers. A CGI program is executed in real time, so that it can output dynamic information.

For example, let's say that you wanted to "hook up" your database to the World Wide Web, to allow people from all over the world to query it. You need to create a CGI program that will transmit information to the database engine, and receive the results back again and display them to the client. This is an example of a gateway, and this is where CGI got its origins.

The database example is a simple idea, but most of the time rather difficult to implement. There really is no limit to what you can hook up to the Web. The only thing you need to remember is that whatever your CGI program does, it should not take too long to process. Otherwise the user will just be staring at the browser, waiting for something to happen. Since a CGI program is executable, it is basically the equivalent of letting the world run a program on your computer system, which isn't the safest thing to do. Therefore, there are some security precautions that need to be implemented when it comes to using CGI programs.

Probably the one that will affect the typical Web user the most is the fact that CGI programs need to reside in a special directory, so that the Web server knows to execute the program rather than just display it to the browser. This directory is usually under direct control of the Webmaster (i.e., the person at the site whose job it is to run all things related to the Web). This effectively prohibits the average user from creating CGI programs. There are other ways to allow access to CGI scripts, but it is up to your Webmaster to set these up for you.

If you have a version of the NCSA HTTPd Web server distribution, you will see a directory called */cgi-bin*. This is the special directory mentioned above where all of your CGI programs currently reside. A CGI program can be written in any language that allows it to be executed on the system, such as:

- Fortran
- perl
- TCL
- any Unix shell
- Visual Basic
- AppleScript

> ## Tip
>
> A good place to find sound files is:
>
> *ftp://ftp.sunet.se/pub/pc/mirror/SimTel/win3/sound*

If you use a programming language like C or Fortran, you know that you must compile the program before it will run. If you look in the */cgi-src* directory that came with the server distribution, you will find the source code for some of the CGI programs in the */cgi-bin* directory. If, however, you use one of the scripting languages (such as perl, TCL, or a Unix shell), only the script itself needs to reside in the directory, since there is no associated source code. Many people prefer to write CGI scripts instead of programs, since they are easier to debug, modify, and maintain than a typical compiled program.

Each time a client requests the URL corresponding to your CGI program, the server will execute it in real time. The output of your program will go to the client.

> ## Tip
>
> You'll need permission to use any copyrighted musical piece:
>
> BZ Rights and Permissions
> (212) 580-0615
>
> BMI
> (212) 586-2000

CGI programs can return myriad document types. They can send back an image to the client, an HTML document, a plain text document, or perhaps even an audio clip. They can also return references to other documents. The client must know what kind of document you're sending it, so it can present it accordingly. In order for the client to know this, your CGI program must tell the server what type of document it is returning.

In order to tell the server what kind of document you are sending back, whether it be a full document or a reference to one, CGI requires you to place a short header on your output. This header is ASCII text, consisting of lines separated by either line feeds or carriage returns (or both), followed by a single blank line. The output body then follows in whatever native format.

Tip

Find your music at:

Associated Production Music
(800) 543-4276

Firstcom
(800) 858-8880

TRF
(800) 899-6874

You can tell the server what kind of document you will be outputting via a MIME type. Common MIME types are things such as *text/html* for HTML, and *text/plain* for straight ASCII text. For example, to send back HTML to the client, your output should read:

```
Content-type: text/html

<HTML>
<HEAD><TITLE>output of HTML from CGI script</TITLE></HEAD>
<BODY>
<H1>Sample output</H1>
What do you think of <STRONG>this?</STRONG>
</BODY></HTML>
```

Instead of outputting the document, you can just tell the browser where to get the new one, or have the server automatically output the new one for you.

For example, suppose you want to reference a file on your gopher server. In this case you should know the full URL of what you want to reference, and output something like:

```
Content-type: text/html
Location: gopher://httprules.foobar.org/0

<HTML><HEAD>
<TITLE>Sorry...it moved</TITLE>
</HEAD><BODY>
<H1>Go to gopher instead</H1>
Now available at
<A HREF="gopher://httprules.foobar.org/0">a new
location</A>
on our gopher server.
</BODY></HTML>
```

Today's browsers are smart enough, however, to throw you automatically to the new document, without ever seeing the above.

If you want to reference another file (not protected by access authentication) on your own server, you don't have to do nearly as much work. Just output a partial (virtual) URL, such as the following:

```
Location: /dir1/dir2/myfile.html
```

The server will act as if the client had not requested your script, but instead requested *http://yourserver/dir1/dir2/myfile.html*. It will take care of almost everything, such as looking up the file type and sending the appropriate headers. Just be sure that you output the second blank line.

Tip

Some sources for CGI scripting tools:

The Bourne shell contains calls to *sed* and *awk*, which convert a GET form data string into separate environment variables:

> *ftp://ftp.ncsa.uiuc.edu/Web/httpd/Unix/ncsa_httpd/cgi/AA-1.2.tar.Z*

This package contains a group of useful PERL routines to decode forms.

> *ftp://ftp.ncsa.uiuc.edu/Web/httpd/Unix/ncsa_httpd/cgi/cgi-lib.pl.Z*

PERL5 is a perl5 library for handling forms in CGI scripts. With just a handful of calls, you can parse CGI queries, create forms, and maintain the state of the buttons on the form from invocation to invocation.

> *ftp://ftp.ncsa.uiuc.edu/Web/httpd/Unix/ncsa_httpd/cgi/CGI.pm-1.53.tar.Z*

If you do want to reference a document that is protected by access authentication, you will need to have a full URL in the Location: specification, since the client and the server need to re-transact to establish that you have access to the referenced document.

There are two methods that can be used to access your forms. These methods are GET and POST. Depending on which method you used, you will receive the encoded results of the form in a different way.

If your form has METHOD="GET" in its <FORM> tag, your CGI program will receive the encoded form input in the environment variable QUERY_STRING. If your form has METHOD="POST" in its <FORM> tag, your CGI program will receive the encoded form input on *stdin*. The server will not send you an EOF on the end of the data; instead you should use the environment variable CONTENT_LENGTH to determine how much data you should read from *stdin*.

When you write a form, each of your input items has a *name* tag. When the user places data in these items in the form, that information is encoded into the form data. The value given by the user for each of the input items is called the *value*.

Form data is a stream of *name=value* pairs separated by the & character. Each *name=value* pair is URL encoded, i.e., spaces are changed into plus signs and some characters are encoded into hexadecimal.

Tip

A good use of frames can be seen at the Business-America site:
http://www.business-america.com

CGI coding is really beyond the scope of this book. I don't want to leave you empty-handed, however, so refer to the Tips to find locations on the Internet where there are CGI scripts already written to do virtually anything you'll ever need to do. Now all you have to do is convince your ISP's Webmaster to let you run them.

Make the picture pretty with frames

When I log into shareware.com (*http://www.shareware.com*) using Netscape or Microsoft Explorer 3.0, I get a choice.

I can choose a frames-based display or not. Frames is an HTML 3.0 feature that most professional programmers know about. It permits you to segment the window into different viewing areas, each with its own color scheme, scroll bars, etc. It's almost as if there were multiple displays instead of one. Frames are generated by three things: <FRAMESET> tags, <FRAME> tags, and frame documents. A frame document has a basic structure very much like your normal HTML document, except the <BODY> container is replaced by a <FRAMESET> container that describes the sub-HTML documents, or frames, that will make up the page.

```
<HTML>
<HEAD>
</HEAD>
<FRAMESET>
</FRAMESET>
</HTML>
```

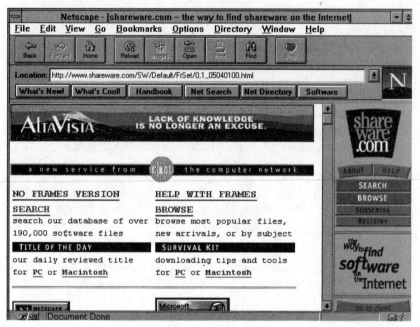

3-7 *What frames look like. This site has since eliminated frames.*

Frame syntax is similar in scope and complexity to that used by tables, and has been designed to be processed quickly by Internet client layout engines.

The <FRAMESET> tag marks the beginning of the main container for a frame. It has two attributes, ROWS and COLS. A frame document has no <BODY>, and no tags that would normally be placed in the body can appear before the <FRAMESET> tag, or the container will be ignored. The <FRAMESET> tag has a matching end tag, and within the container you can have only other nested <FRAMESET> tags, <FRAME> tags, or the <NOFRAMES> tag.

The ROWS attribute takes as its value a comma-separated list of values. These values can be absolute pixel values, percentage values between 1 and 100, or relative scaling values. The number of rows is implicit in the number of elements in the list. Since the total height of all the rows must equal the height of the window, row heights might be normalized to achieve this. A missing ROWS attribute is interpreted as a single row arbitrarily sized to fit.

A simple numeric value is assumed to be a fixed size in pixels. This is the most dangerous type of value to use, since the size of the viewer's window can and does vary substantially. If fixed pixel values are used, it will almost certainly be necessary to mix them with one or more of the relative size values described below. Otherwise the client engine is likely to override your specified pixel value, ensuring that the total proportions of the frame are 100 percent of the width and height of the user's window.

The attribute *value%* is a simple percentage value between 1 and 100. If the total is greater than 100, all percentages are scaled down. If the total is less than 100, and relative-sized frames exist, extra space will be given to them. If there are no relative-sized frames, all percentages will be scaled up to match a total of 100 percent.

The *value** field is optional. A single asterisk character is a relative-sized frame and is interpreted as a request to give the frame all remaining space. If there exist multiple relative-sized frames, the remaining space is divided evenly among them. A numeric value in front of the asterisk gives the frame that much more relative space. The expression *2*,** would give ⅔ of the space to the first frame, and ⅓ to the second.

For example, for three rows, the first and the last being smaller than the center row, the HTML code would be:

```
<FRAMESET ROWS="20%,60%,20%">
```

The following example is for three rows, the first and the last being fixed height, with the remaining space assigned to the middle row:

```
<FRAMESET ROWS="100,*,100">
```

The COLS attribute takes as its value a comma-separated list of values that uses the exact same syntax as the list described above for the ROWS attribute. The <FRAMESET> tag can be nested inside other <FRAMESET> tags. In this case, the complete subframe is placed in the space that would be used for the corresponding frame if this had been a <FRAME> tag instead of a nested <FRAMESET>.

The <FRAME> tag defines a single frame in a frameset. It has six possible attributes: SRC, NAME, MARGINWIDTH, MARGINHEIGHT, SCROLLING, and NORESIZE. The <FRAME> tag is not a container so it has no matching end tag.

The SRC attribute takes as its value the URL of the document to be displayed in this particular frame. Frames without SRC attributes are displayed as a blank space the size the frame would have been.

The NAME attribute is used to assign a name to a frame so it can be targeted by links in other documents. (These usually are from other frames in the same document.) The NAME attribute is optional; by default, all windows are unnamed.

Names must begin with an alphanumeric character. Named frames can have their window contents targeted with the new TARGET attribute.

The MARGINWIDTH attribute is used when the document author wants some control of the margins for this frame. If specified, the value is in pixels. Margins cannot be less than one—so that frame objects will not touch frame edges—and cannot be specified so that there is no space for the document contents. The MARGINWIDTH attribute is optional; by default, all frames default to letting the browser decide on an appropriate margin width.

The MARGINHEIGHT attribute is just like MARGINWIDTH above, except it controls the upper and lower margins instead of the left and right margins.

The SCROLLING attribute can have the values YES, NO, and AUTO, and is used to describe if the frame should have a scroll bar or not. YES results in scroll bars always being visible on that frame. NO results in scroll bars never being visible. AUTO instructs the browser to decide whether scroll bars are needed, and place them where necessary. The SCROLLING attribute is optional; the default value is AUTO.

The NORESIZE attribute has no value. It is a flag that indicates that the frame is not resizable by the user. Users typically resize frames by dragging a frame edge to a new position. Note that if any frame adjacent to an edge is not resizable, that entire edge will be restricted from moving. This will affect the resizability of other frames. The NORESIZE attribute is optional; by default, all frames are resizable.

The <NOFRAMES> tag is for content providers who want to create alternative content that is viewable by frame-incapable clients. A frame-capable Internet client ignores all tags and data between starting <NOFRAMES> and ending </NOFRAMES> tags.

Coding a frames-based document is shown below. The full window is divided into two section or frames. The first frame is them divided into two sub-frames and the second frame is divided into three sub-frames. The HTML files *one.html*, *two.html*, and so on, are coded as any other HTML-based document.

Tip

Download Netscape Navigator from:

http://home.netscape.com/comprod/mirror/index.html

```
<FRAMESET COLS="50%,50%">
 <FRAMESET ROWS="50%,50%">
  <FRAME SRC="one.html">
  <FRAME SRC="two.html">
 </FRAMESET>
 <FRAMESET ROWS="33%,33%,33%">
  <FRAME SRC="three.html">
```

```
  <FRAME SRC="four.html">
  <FRAME SRC="five.html">
 </FRAMESET>
</FRAMESET>
```

The following example uses the <NOFRAMES>...</NOFRAMES> package. Since about 20 percent of browsers in use today are non-Netscape, you should always include this tag in frames-based HTML design.

```
<FRAMESET COLS="50%,50%">
<NOFRAMES>
<h1 align=center><blink>Frame ALERT!</blink></h1>
<p>
This document is designed to be viewed using <b>Netscape
2.0</b>'s Frame features. If you are seeing this message,
you are using a frame <i>challenged</i> browser.
</p>
<p>
A <b>Frame-capable</b> browser can be gotten from
<a href="http://home.netscape.com">Netscape Communica-
tions</a>.
</p>
</NOFRAMES>

<FRAMESET ROWS="50%,50%">
 <FRAME SRC="one.html">
 <FRAME SRC="two.html">
</FRAMESET>
<FRAMESET ROWS="33%,33%,33%">
 <FRAME SRC="three.html">
 <FRAME SRC="four.html">
 <FRAME SRC="five.html">
</FRAMESET>
```

The effect for a frames-incapable browser is shown in Fig. 3-8. Notice the hyperlink to Netscape, which lets the user download the Netscape browser.

As you can see, frames are far less complicated that they look. They add an interesting element to an otherwise very straightforward page. Beware, however: Netscape 2.0 does have some bugs. On occasion, a user clicking on the minimize button will minimize a frame and then wind up getting lost in a maze. The flaw is slated for correction in Netscape 3.0.

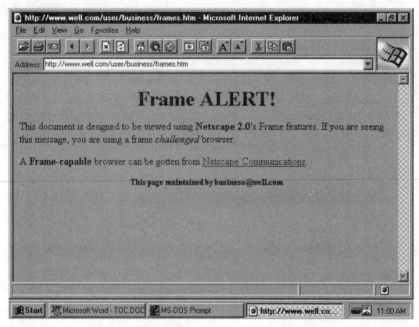

3-8 *HTML knows if the browser is frames-enabled.*

The Shockwave plug-in

Most Internet browsers already come with the ability to display images, audio, and video. One of the hottest products to come on the market is Macromedia's Shockwave, which gives you full multimedia capabilities on the Internet. This comes as no surprise; Macromedia is perhaps the leading vendor of multimedia tool sets. Director, Authorware, and FreeHand are used widely within the professional multimedia developer community.

Tip

Download Shockwave plug-ins from:

http://www-1.macromedia.com/Tools/Shockwave/Plugin/ plugin.cgi

---

Shockwave is basically a set of plug-ins for each of these multimedia tool sets. So if you're a multimedia developer with a large Director portfolio of video, you can use them right in the middle of your Internet home page.

> ## Tip
>
> Developers may develop, and sometimes port, existing code fairly easily to the Netscape Plug-In API. Just a bit of code modification may do the trick. To take advantage of such applications within Navigator, users must obtain and install the plug-in version of the applications. These plug-ins can be thought of as subroutines that operate within the browser itself—without launching a helper application.
>
> Rule of Thumb: Use plug-ins only as a last resort. The odds of getting a user to download the plug-in are low.

There is a catch, of course: To use it. you'll have to keep track of which browsers are compatible with it. Right now it's only Netscape, and even then the plug-in has to be downloaded by those who view your home page. Until the Shockwave plug-ins are automatically provided as an extension to all browsers, as a developer you'll have to weigh the pros and cons of forcing your viewers to spend a not insignificant amount of time in downloading.

Like all software developers, Internet developers sometimes make use of technology when there really is no need to do so. It's technology for technology's sake. A rule of thumb here is to use extensions or plug-ins only if there is absolutely no other way to do it.

Creative sites, like those of ad agencies, publishing houses, and art- or graphic-centric sites, are for the most part the natural venue of multimedia extensions. There seems to be a race, unfortunately, to create the "coolest site." Yahoo, Netscape, and other popular sites perpetuate the problem by publishing "cool site" lists. Since cool is usually defined as an overabundance of multimedia elements, cool sites are pretty much those with lots of graphics and gimmickry. What these guys don't really understand is that a truly cool site is one that is content-rich. If this means text-only, so be it.

But don't be scared off by my philosophical tirade. Make your own decision. If you feel that the site under construction needs a bit of jazz, then by all means use a multimedia plug-in.

A site using multimedia plug-ins but can't be demonstrated easily in the flat representation of a 2D book. The best advice I can offer is to download the Shockwave plug-in yourself; then go to one of the many sites on Internet that already use it to see its capabilities. Finding these sites is easy. Go to *http://altavista.digital.com* and enter a keyword of *shockwave*. About 10,000 sites will appear on the search list. Click on a couple of these to get a feel for the medium.

Of the three Shockwave plug-ins, the one with the most pizzazz is the Director add-in, perhaps because there's something just so intriguing about video on the Web.

In creating a Director movie for playback on the Web, you can use almost all existing Director features—and all of the supporting tools you currently use to produce media for importing into Director—to create high-impact multimedia for the World Wide Web.

In order to turn a Director movie into a Web-enabled movie, the developer must use the Macromedia Afterburner application. Once done, the Director movie is said to be "shocked." Afterburner creates a type of projector designed specifically for the Web. When you convert a movie with Afterburner, it looks and works exactly the same as it did before you converted it. Afterburner simply compresses the movie to reduce download time and converts it to .DCR format. Here's how to turn a standard Director movie into a shocked Director movie.

1 Create the Director movie.

2 Try out the Lingo commands on it.

3 Remove Web-incompatible Director features.

4 Run the Afterburner conversion.

5 Post the movie to an appropriately configured server.

First, create the Director movie, keeping the following caveats in mind. Multimedia delivered over the Internet is limited in size primarily because the majority of users dial in at relatively slow speeds, 14,400 or 28,800 bits per second. At these rates, the user can receive only 1K of information a second. At that rate, it takes a full minute to transfer a 60K file. There is, however, a big difference between theory and practical reality in these numbers. If there is heavy traffic on the Internet host, or there's network congestion, the rate drops even lower.

Within the next few years new technologies such as cable modems will dramatically boost the speed of the network. The size limits imposed by the current technology no longer will be an issue. Authors will be able to deliver Director titles of CD-ROM size—and larger—in real time across the Internet.

For now, keep in mind the download time for your movies and ask yourself:

- Will the user be willing to wait the length of time necessary for the movie to download?
- Is there any way to reduce the size of the movie and shorten the time the user has to wait?

The speeds 14.4 and 28.8 kbps are common modem speeds; 1.5 mbps is the throughput of a shared cable modem line. Make sure you keep in mind data transmission rates, as shown in Fig. 3-9.

Download Times at Common Modem Speeds

Content	Size	Download time at			
		14.4 kbs	28.8 kbs	64 kbs	1.5 mbps
small graphics & animation	30 K	30 secs	10 secs	6 secs	1 sec.
small complete movie	100-200 K	180-300 secs.	90-180 secs.	20-40 secs.	1 sec.
short video clip	500 K	N.A.	120-240 secs.	90 secs.	3 secs.
full size movie	1 M	N.A.	N.A.	180 secs.	6 secs.
MPEG video stream	--	N.A.	N.A.	N.A.	continuous

3-9 *How long it takes to download a file.*

Second, explore what you can do with the new Lingo commands designed for the Web. Several new Lingo commands are available to provide a shocked Director movie with access to the network. The network is essentially an asynchronous place. That is, it takes time to get things from the Net. During downloading, a user can continue interacting with a shocked movie.

Most of the network commands involve starting an operation, then checking to see if it has been completed, and finally getting the results. The Lingo network extensions are different from most Lingo commands, which immediately return the result. These New Lingo extensions can be found at the Macromedia site, located at *http://www.macromedia.com/Tools/Shockwave/Director/create.html#lingo.*

Tip

You can download the latest version of QuickTime from:

http://quicktime.apple.com/qt/sw/sw.html

You shouldn't use any of the standard Director features that are unavailable in movies designed for the Web. The major restrictions in creating Director movies for the World Wide Web have to do with data transmission across a network. For example, the first release of Shockwave doesn't allow linked media. Linked media is a problem in a networked environment because, after successfully downloading a movie, network traffic or other considerations could prevent retrieval of the linked media. At this time Shockwave also doesn't support QuickTime—a direct result of not supporting linked media. However, it should be noted that Netscape 2.0 can play a QuickTime movie through the QuickTime plug-in.

Shocked Director movies can't use movie-in-a-window. Movie-in-a-window is difficult to do properly in a Windows environment and isn't supported by browsers other than Netscape that embed the Shockwave plug-in.

When the movie is finished, convert the movie with the Afterburner application. On Macintosh computers, drag the movie to the Afterburner icon. On Windows computers, double-click the Afterburner icon. In the Open dialog box, select the movie and then save it.

Finally, put a copy of the converted movie on an HTTP server configured for shocked Director movies.

For now, to view a shocked Director movie, users need to have Netscape 2.0 with the Shockwave plug-in. To add a shocked Director movie to an HTML page, use the HTML tag <EMBED>. The <EMBED> tag for a shocked Director movie looks like this:

```
<EMBED SRC="path/filename.ext" WIDTH=n HEIGHT=n
PALETTE=background>
```

Use the WIDTH and HEIGHT arguments to specify the width and height of the image in pixels. Netscape crops the image to the size you specify. The PALETTE argument gives you control over which palette Netscape uses when it plays a shocked Director movie.

Here's an example that shows how to set up the <EMBED> tag for a shocked Director movie named *banner.dcr*, which is 335 by 255 pixels and uses the Director movie's palette for the page.

```
<EMBED SRC="http://www.yourserver.com/movies/banner.dcr"
WIDTH=335
HEIGHT=255 PALETTE=foreground>
```

If the user's browser doesn't support the Shockwave plug-in, the <NOEMBED> tag allows you to substitute a JPEG or GIF image in place of the movie. The <NOEMBED> tag looks like this:

```
<NOEMBED> <IMG SRC="path/filename.ext"> </NOEMBED>
```

You can substitute any HTML source for a shocked Director movie in the syntax of the <NOEMBED> tag. In older versions of Netscape— and on other browsers—the user will see a broken image icon in addition to the substitute image. HTML documents can include more than one movie per page. The user can scroll through the rest of the page while the movie is playing. The user can interact with the movie and enter text from the keyboard into text fields programmed into the movie. The movie itself, using new Lingo commands, can retrieve information from the network and open additional URLs.

Although technically there's no limit to how many movies you can incorporate into a Web page, it's best to include no more than three. When a user leaves a page containing shocked Director movies, the Shockwave plug-in frees the RAM it was using to play the movies.

Because most users will not have the Shockwave plug-in (and might not want to spend the time to download it), your page should have some sort of alternative. Let's assume that for those people who do have Navigator 2.0, you want the page to load a shocked Director movie named *mymovie.dcr* (whose stage dimensions are 160×120). For people who don't have Navigator 2.0, you want to display a JPEG image called *mystill.jpg* (whose dimensions are 60×90 pixels) in place of the movie.

To have an image or text in place of the shocked Director movie on browsers other than Netscape 2.0, you can use a pair of HTML tags understood only by Navigator 2.0: <NOEMBED> . . . </NOEMBED>. When Navigator 2.0 encounters a <NOEMBED> tag, it ignores everything from that point until it reaches the </NOEMBED> tag. Other browsers will ignore both the <NOEMBED> and </NOEMBED> and execute the HTML between the two tags. Here is a sample Java script:

```
<SCRIPT LANGUAGE="JavaScript">
<!-- Hide this script from non-Navigator 2.0 browsers.
<EMBED WIDTH=175 HEIGHT=135 SRC="mymovie.dcr">
<!-- Done hiding from non-Navigator 2.0 browsers. -->
</SCRIPT>
<NOEMBED>
<IMG WIDTH=60 HEIGHT=90 SRC="mystill.jpg">
</NOEMBED>
```

If you view the above sample script with Netscape Navigator 2.0:
   1 The browser will encounter the JavaScript routine and execute it.
   2 If the Shockwave plug-in is installed, *mymovie.dcr* will play.
   3 If the plug-in is absent, the browser will display a broken icon. When Navigator 2.0 encounters <NOEMBED>, it ignores everything between it and </NOEMBED>, and the image *mystill.jpg* will not appear.

If you view the script with any other browser:
   1 The browser ignores the JavaScript routine, thinking that it's just a comment.
   2 When it encounters <NOEMBED> it ignores that as well.
   3 Finally, it displays the image *mystill.jpg* because it doesn't know to skip over anything between <NOEMBED> and </NOEMBED>.

Tip

Java is a bona fide object-oriented programming language. There are some application development tool sets out there to make the development of Java systems easier:

> *http://www.yahoo.com/Business_and_Economy/Companies/ Computers/Software/Programming_Tools/Languages/Java/*

Here's a starter list:

> *http://www.javasoft.com*
> *http://cafe.symantec.com/*
> *http://java.sun.com/java.sun.com/products/JDK/index.html*
> *http://www.roguewave.com*
> *http://www.futuretense.com*

and read the Java programming guide at:

> *http://java.sun.com/progGuide/index.html*

Tip

Check out *JavaWorld* magazine at:

> *http://www.javaworld.com*

Tip

Can't figure Java out? Then grab some applets off the Web and use them on your home page. Be warned though, that Java seems to crash Netscape frequently. Use with care. For best results, surf over to the Java Applet Rating Service:

> *http://www.jars.com*
> *http://java.sun.com/applets/#demos*
> *http://www.science.wayne.edu/~joey/java.html*

Right now only Navigator 2.0 can interpret this JavaScript routine, because it's coded inside a pair of comment tags, <!-- . . . -->. (By the time you read this book most browsers should be able to handle it).

Don't remove the comments. They are necessary for the functioning of this script. Browsers other than Navigator 2.0 ignore anything in an HTML document between a pair of comment tags. Navigator 2.0 supports JavaScript and executes its commands. Notice that the first line after the <SCRIPT> tag begins with an open comment tag <!-- but

doesn't contain a close comment --> tag. Instead, the close comment tag is included on the last line before the </SCRIPT> tag. If you close the comment on the first line, the routine will fail.

Using VRML

Perhaps the most exciting thing to come along is VRML: Virtual Reality Modeling Language. Like Shockwave, it's a plug-in; your home page visitors will have to download a viewer and then go through the laborious process of adding it to their browser before they can see your home page. As mentioned, this process involves going to the home page of the vendor of the plug-in, downloading it, and then installing it.

Tip

Superscape claims that its VRML browser is 10 times faster than first-generation viewers. Download for free at:

http://www.superscape.com

The installation process is quite similar to installing any piece of software, except that the last step entails adding the appropriate MIME (or, as Netscape calls them, "Helpers") to the Browser—unless the setup program does it for you automatically. This is so the browser will recognize the file extension when it comes across one. For example, the plug-in/helper for Macromedia's Director is *x-director.* Other extensions that can be added are DIR (a standard Director movie) or DXR (protected movies that can be played but not opened in Director).

Tip

Protect your PC. It's the heart of your business.

Insure it with Safeware:
(800) 848-3469

Recover your hard disk at Drivesavers:
(415) 883-4232

What makes this pain worthwhile is that VRML lets you create vivid three-dimensional graphics using vectors rather than graphic bitmaps. Download time is minimized. The problem with graphics, as you will discover when you read the next chapter, is that complex, colorful ones simply hog up a lot of room. The original convention, or standard, was that a good page would not have a graphic on it that took up more than 50,000 bytes (just under 50K). Since the average PC modem downloads at a rate of 14,400 bits per second, a simple bit of arithmetic lets us guesstimate that it will take about 28 seconds to download a graphic of this size. While one 50K graphic does not a problem make, a multipage site with many graphics this size does tend to make the viewer see red (the red STOP button, that is).

Even though newer PCs are being configured with 28.8 kbps modems (28,800 bits per second), today's state of the modem art still is too slow. Many home page designers simply ignore this problem, especially those in graphics or advertising who know a lot about good art—but know very little about good technology and the users who are using that technology. Let me fill you in.

Tip

Get into VRML: at WebSpace

http://www.sgi.com/Products/WebFORCE/WebSpace

WebView

http://www.sdsc.edu/EnablingTech/Visualization/vrml/webview.html

WorldView

http://www.webmaster.com/vrml/

WebFX

http://www.paperinc.com/webfx.html

Virtus

http://www.virtus.com/player.html

Users are impatient. They want their information, and they want it now. Even though VRML graphics take us less space than ordinary graphics, they still take up space. Use them only when it is totally relevant to the information you are presenting.

Konstantin Guericke is an executive vice president of Los Altos-based Caligari Corp., one of the leaders in the VRML revolution. He is also one of the more than 70 contributors to the predecessor to this book, *The Ultimate Sourcebook on Multimedia.* His chapter, entitled "The Web in 3D," is an excellent introduction to the subject and will be excerpted briefly here.

Tip

Construct is an Internet design firm that uses VRML heavily. Visit their site to get good ideas:

http://vrml.arc.org/

VRML (pronounced "vermal") stands for Virtual Reality Modeling Language and is to 3D what HTML is to 2D. While HTML specifies how two-dimensional documents are represented, VRML describes how three-dimensional environments can be explored and created on the World Wide Web. Since 2D is really just a subset of 3D, any two-dimensional object can be easily represented in a three-dimensional environment. Tim Berners-Lee, the "father" of the Web, reasons in Mark Pesce's book *VRML: Browsing and Building in Cyberspace* that VRML is the future of the Web—because it is more natural for us to be immersed in a three-dimensional space than to click our way through hyperlinked 2D pages.

Using VRML not only adds sizzle to your Web site, but leverages the fact that each of your visitors has spent his or her entire life navigating in three dimensions. We make sense of the world by quickly analyzing factors such as the speed of approaching objects (e.g., a car), the location of light sources, and the texture of surfaces. Since many of these processes happen subconsciously, a clever designer can guide visitors through spaces and focus their attention without forcing them to make explicit choices. Similar to the real world, the visitor maintains a first-person perspective and completely controls how close to move towards an object and from what angle to view it.

Tip

A great Web 'zine for advanced coders:

http://www.virtualschool.edu/mon/Perl/WebTechniques. html

VRML is simply a scene description language that standardizes how three-dimensional environments are represented on the Web. Unlike programming languages such as C++, VRML does not have to be compiled and run. Rather, VRML files get grammatically analyzed (parsed) and then displayed. Since this is a much faster process, the creation of VRML files is much simpler than programming. It also allows for more interactivity and facilitates incremental improvements.

Here is how VRML works from the user's perspective. First, you have to obtain a tool that "speaks" VRML. There are freely downloadable versions of products such as Caligari Fountain, Intervista WorldView, Paper Software's WebFX, and TGS WebSpace. Some allow just for browsing in 3D, while others allow for various levels of 3D creation and VRML authoring.

> ### Tip
>
> Learn how to: finger, ph query, imagemap, form mail, web us-age analysis, full text searching, HTML analyzer to look for bro-ken links:
>
> *http://www.uic.edu/depts/adn/www_publish/advanced_tool s.html*

A VRML file is loaded the same way an HTML file is accessed, either by clicking on a link or typing a URL and hitting Enter. Based on the speed of your connection and the size of the file, the loading time can be as little as a few seconds or as much as a couple of minutes. Well-structured VRML files will allow your VRML browser to load the file in pieces, which lets you explore right away while the browser fetches more detailed objects and those that are not currently in your view.

As you navigate through the scene, you will notice that some ob-jects are linked. If you click on them, you will jump either to another VRML world or to another media type such as HTML. While this gets you to other places quickly, it leads to the same problem as "jump-ing" from link to link in HTML: You jump from a document on one topic on a server in one place to another document on a different topic in a completely different place. This is what Mark Pesce, co-cre-ator of VRML, calls (by way of Gertrude Stein) "there being no there, there." Contrast this with navigating through a 3D environment. Since you see everything that is in between your origin and your destina-tion, you will experience a sense of continuity, which not only helps us find our way back, but also reassures us viscerally that we know how we got to our destination.

> ### Tip
>
> Links to techie magazines, Net resources, and, of course, the Webmaster's reference guide:
>
> *http://www.aloha.com/~muneoka/therack2.htm*
> *http://www.he.net/~glo-boxx/resource.htm*
> *http://webreference.com*

For example, when we walk through a town, we look around and build a mental map of the place. If someone tells us that we have to turn right at the next intersection, we can visualize this and get to where we want to go. There is a sense of continuity, and we can see how quickly we progress towards our goal. Sometimes we get lost, but this is part of our experience—and often that is how we discover new places or meet new people. Typing a URL and watching the byte counter as the destination loads onto our screen just isn't the same.

While this is not intimidating to experts, the majority of people will only get online if it works like the real world. Abstract URLs are difficult to remember, and jumping from one text fragment to another is not something that people encounter on a daily basis. However, once the Web allows us to use our spatial perception and conforms to the way we work (rather than forcing us to adopt the way computers work), the Web will become just another place we go to accomplish our chores, chat with friends, or learn new skills.

VRML allows for much richer interaction than HTML. When viewing two-dimensional home pages, your options are basically limited to jumping from page to page and looking at images from a fixed, predetermined perspective. When visiting VRML worlds, however, you can choose freely the perspective from which to view the world. In addition, you can navigate unencumbered through 3D environments, the contents of which are limited only by the imagination of their creator.

VRML spaces are inexpensive to build, can be bigger than the earth, and the objects in it can (and often do) defy the laws of gravity. As you walk or fly through such worlds, you can pick up objects and inspect them from all sides; if your VRML application includes authoring capabilities, you can even create and modify 3D objects. Don't like the color of your house? Just repaint it with a few clicks of the mouse! Thus, VRML allows 2D home pages to expand into 3D home worlds. Traditional commercial Web sites can draw in new users by adding three-dimensional environments that are fun to explore, and by providing a natural way to navigate through the information available on the site. Ultimately you will be able to collaborate with other users in context-rich and visually descriptive 3D environments, rather than typing away at the command prompt in a text-based chat room.

The caveat about using VRML is that you need to create a lot of content from scratch and that you may need to hire expertise that you don't have in-house. Not every Photoshop wizard makes a good 3D modeler. Designing a space requires visualization skills that even experienced page layout artists may lack. Many accomplished architects may not make the transition either, since the virtual medium offers opportunities and challenges quite different from those of the physical world.

Most tools today fall in one of the following categories: VRML browsers, VRML authoring packages, or 3D creation tools. Since the whole market is still very young, the tools vary by features, but also by navigation paradigms and object manipulation methods. In addition, the tools differ considerably in terms of ease of learning, ease of use, reliability, price, and system requirements. While VRML is new, 3D creation tools have been around for a long time.

While many CAD packages allow for 3D design, the preferred tools for game designers and multimedia producers have been modeling and animation packages such as Softimage, 3D Studio, Strata Studio, and Caligari trueSpace. While VRML currently does not support animation, it is very likely that it will do so in the future, so it's wise to purchase a 3D creation tool from a vendor who will be able to add functionality as VRML evolves into a language for describing interactive multi-participant environments.

Tip

A great source of VRML info:

http://rsd.gsfc.nasa.gov/users/delabeau/SystemP/VRML.html

The VRML repository is located at:

http://www.sdsc.edu/vrml/

Some VRML links:

http://infopark.newcollege.edu/vrmlab/vrmlSites.html

Some 3D creation tools already allow models to be saved in VRML, but others require you to purchase or download separate translation utilities that convert from the vendor's internal format to VRML. Direct VRML output is preferable to converters, since something always gets lost during a translation.

Visit the Caligari art gallery at *http://www.caligari.com:80/lvltwo/2newart.html* to see some examples of great VRML, as shown in Fig. 3-10. (Don't forget to download your MIME first.)

Konstantin Guericke is right. VRML is extremely appropriate for mimicking the way a person normally views a world—in 3D. For example, a site being developed right now by a start-up company called Worldwide Corporate Network is using VRML to mimic a trip through an office park. Visitors will be able to trek around an office park and visit different companies. Once in the company's office, the visitor will be able to move through the office to visit different departments.

3-10 *The VRML gallery.*

All VRML tools are different, but one thing they all have in common is that the "code" contains the description of a series of 3D objects. Some products, like Caligari's Pioneer Pro, provide you with a completely integrated graphical interface for quick builds of 3D objects. Other products make you go through the laborious task of hand-coding using an ASCII editor.

Using cookies

Ever wonder how some sites permit customization of the interface for the user's own palette. It's through something called *cookies*. Cookies are data modules stored on the client (i.e., the user's PC) that give the server specific information. It might be for customization purposes, ordering information, etc. While cookies might be mysterious to some, their creation is rather straightforward.

A cookie is a small piece of information that a Web server (via a CGI script) can store with a Web browser and later read back from that browser. Cookies are useful for having the browser remember some specific information across several pages. For example, when you browse through a "virtual shopping mall," adding items to your "shopping cart" as you browse, a list of the items you've picked up is kept in your browser's cookie file, so that you can pay for all the items at once when you've finished shopping.

To create a cookie, a Web server sends a "Set-Cookie" HTTP header line like this one in response to a URL access from a browser:

```
Set-Cookie: NAME=VALUE; expires=DATE; path=PATH;
domain=DOMAIN_NAME; secure
```

NAME and VALUE are the actual information you're including in the cookie. DATE is the time at which the cookie information expires and will be "forgotten" by the browser. DOMAIN is a host or domain name for which the cookie is valid, and PATH specifies a subset of the URLs at that server for which the cookie is valid. If you include the SECURE parameter in your cookie, then the cookie will be transmitted only over an SSL connection. All of these fields except NAME=VALUE are optional.

Whenever the browser sends an HTTP request for a URL on a server which it has stored cookies for, it includes a line of the form:

```
Cookie: NAME=VALUE; NAME=VALUE; . . .
```

which lists all cookies that apply.

Here is a sample CGI program (a Unix shell script) that sends a cookie:

```
#!/bin/sh
echo "Content-type: text/html"
echo "Set-cookie: MeLove=Cookie%20Monster;
expires=Thursday, 01-Jan-98
   12:00:00 GMT"
echo ""
echo "<H1>Me love Cookie Monster.  Me love cookies.</H1>"
```

This stores "MeLove=Cookie Monster" with the browser. (Note that the space character in the value must be represented as the hexadecimal expression "%20" in the cookie.) Here is a script that reads a cookie:

```
#! /bin/sh
echo "Content-type: text/html"
echo ""
echo "Here is your cookie (munch munch):<P>"
echo "$HTTP_COOKIE<P>"
```

This simple mechanism provides a powerful new tool that allows a host of new types of applications to be written for Web-based environments. Shopping applications now can store information about the currently selected items; for-fee services can send back registration information and free the client from retyping a user-id on next connection; and sites can store per-user preferences on the client, and have the client resupply those preferences every time that site is accessed.

According to the Netscape specification, a cookie is introduced to the client by including a Set-Cookie header as part of an HTTP response; typically this will be generated by a CGI script.

This is the format a CGI script would use to add to the HTTP headers a new piece of data that is to be stored by the client for later retrieval:

```
Set-Cookie: NAME=VALUE; expires=DATE;
path=PATH; domain=DOMAIN_NAME; secure
```

NAME=VALUE is any sequence of characters excluding semicolons, commas, and white space. If there is a need to place such data in the name or value, some encoding method such as URL-style %XX encoding is recommended, though no encoding is defined or required. This is the only required attribute on the Set-Cookie header.

The "expires=DATE" expression specifies a date string that defines the valid lifetime of that cookie. Once the expiration date has been reached, the cookie will no longer be stored or given out. The date string is formatted as:

```
Wdy, DD-Mon-YY HH:MM:SS GMT
```

The expression "domain=DOMAIN_NAME" works like this. During a search of the cookie list for valid cookies, the domain attributes of the cookie are compared to the Internet domain name of the host from which the URL will be fetched. If there is a tail match, then the cookie will go through path matching to see if it should be sent. *Tail matching* means that the domain attribute is matched against the tail of the host's fully qualified domain name. A domain attribute of *acme.com* would match host names *anvil.acme.com* as well as *shipping.crate. acme.com*. The default domain value is the host name of the server that generated the cookie response.

Tip

The full Netscape cookie specification can be found at:

http://www.netscape.com/newsref/std/cookie_spec.html

The "path=PATH" attribute is used to specify the subset of URLs in a domain for which the cookie is valid. If a cookie has already passed domain matching, then the pathname component of the URL is compared with the path attribute and, if there is a match, the cookie is considered valid and is sent along with the URL request. The path */foo* would match */foobar* and */foo/bar.html*. A path consisting solely of the slash character (/) is the most general path.

If the path is not specified, it as assumed to be the same path as the document being described by the header that contains the cookie.

If a cookie is marked secure, it will be only transmitted if the communications channel with the host is a secure one. Currently this means that secure cookies will only be sent to HTTPS (HTTP over SSL) servers. If secure is not specified, a cookie is considered safe to be sent in the clear over unsecured channels.

When requesting a URL from an HTTP server, the browser will match the URL against all cookies and, if any of them match, a line containing the *name=value* pairs of all matching cookies will be included in the HTTP request. Here is the format of that line:

```
Cookie: NAME1=OPAQUE_STRING1; NAME2=OPAQUE_STRING2 . . .
```

Cookies do have their dangers, though. According to a March 13, 1996, article in *MacWeek*, this feature does have some security concerns. Cookies can store information for reuse on particular sites, such as user name, passwords, shopping lists, demographics, and method-of-payment data. When users return to one of these sites, their login information is provided automatically, their shopping list is maintained, and they can purchase items without having to re-enter their credit card number. Sites can read only HTTP Cookie information they create, so users must re-enter information for each site they visit.

That's how Netscape pitches the feature. But researchers and developers said HTTP Cookie can be used to do much more. John Yang, a research assistant in the geology department at Florida International University in Miami, said a cookie program can be built to track the user's every move while he or she is connected to a particular server. This information can be fed into a database that keeps site usage statistics, Webmasters can tailor a site to a particular user's interests.

Combine Cookie with JavaScript and a site's administrator could launch a very effective direct mail campaign without ever having asked the user for permission, Yang observed. In more malevolent hands, these new tools can do far worse. For example, a Webmaster could pretend to be a particular site in order to retrieve a user's Cookie data without authorization. "If you use a server that does not encrypt its information, there is a real problem," Yang said.

HTTP Cookie is not exclusive to Netscape Navigator. Microsoft Corp.'s Internet Explorer, Netcom's Netcruiser, and Quarterdeck's Quarterdeck Mosaic 2.0 are among the browsers that support it.

Indexing your site on the Web

Now that you're HTML experts, you'll probably run right out and develop a really cool page. When you're done with that page, you'll want others to be able to find it. There are two ways to do this. You can actively index your site at one of the many directories, as shown in Table 3-1, or you can use the <META> tag to encode keywords for directory robots.

Most of the major directory sites employ robots (i.e., programs that search the Web looking for pages to index). While these robots get their information from the title and header information tags, you can encode a bunch of keywords that will ensure you get listed in the appropriate place.

The <META> tag is part of the <HEAD> tag. You use the NAME attribute to describe the type of information and the CONTENT attribute to list the keywords themselves:

```
<meta name="keywords" content="word1 word2">
```

Just be sure you don't repeat the same terms in the <TITLE> tag and code it like this:

```
<META  name="description"
content="We specialize in grooming pink poodles.">
<META  name="keywords" content="pet grooming Palo Alto dog">
```

Now that you learned a thing or two about HTML, let's make a bit of a departure and learn a little something about style and graphics. For that, turn the page to start Chapter 4.

Table 3-1 Get Yourself Listed in These Directories

BizWeb	*http://www.bizweb.com/InfoForm/infoform.html*
Open Market Commercial Sites Index	*http://www.directory.net/dir/submit.cgi*
Excite	*http://www.excite.com*
A1's Searchable Directory	*http://www.a1co.com/index.html*
AnnouceNet	*http://www.announcenet.com/*
Magellan	*http://www.mckinley.com*
ALIWEB	*http://www.webcom.com*
Internet Slueth	*http://www.intbc.com/sleuth/*
White Pages of Net Pages	e-mail press release to *np-add@aldea.com*
What's new Too	*http://newtoo.manifest.com/WhatsNewToo/submit.html*
Point	*http://www.pointcom.com/*
Submit-it	*http://www.submit-it.com/*
Free Links	*http://www.mgroup.com/freelinks/*
Global Online Director	*http://www.gold.net/gold/gold2.html*
Go Net-Wide	*http://www.shout.net/~whitney/html/gopublic.html*
WebSight Magazine free listing	*http://websight.com/gridlinks/*
Internet Promotions MegaList	*http://www.2020tech.com/submit.html*
NCSA What's new	*http://www.ncsa.uiuc.edu/SDG/Software/Mosaic/Docs/whats-new-form.html*
InterNic Net Happenings	*http://www.gi.net/NET/*
WebStar	*http://web-star.com/newpage/newpage.html*
W3 new server registration	*http://www.w3.org/hypertext/DataSources/WWW/Geographical_generation/new-servers.html*
Promote-It	*http://www.iTools.com/promote-it/promote-it.html*

4

The graphic connection

The thing that makes the Web so exciting is its use of graphics. Though the World Wide Web had been around for more than a decade, it was only after a young college student named Marc Andressen (now a principal at Netscape) created the Mosaic browser that the Web took off in its current form.

Tip

See an image on the Web you want for your own page (Note: remember copyright and/or attribution?) Use your right mouse button to click on a graphic you want to download from the Web. A drop-down window will appear giving you the option to save the image file to your own computer's hard disk.

From a technology perspective, Andressen did nothing that hadn't been done a million times before by professional programmers: He supplied a graphical front end, or GUI (graphical user interface), to information. What made his GUI, the Mosaic browser, so revolutionary is that he attached it to a global network—the Internet.

By definition, the Internet is a typical client/server graphical system. The server, which is one or more computers storing information, is attached by some means of network to a client, usually a PC, which provides an interface to this information. The part of this network most of us see is the telephone line. Today's corporate intranets are really only graphical browsers tied into server information over an internal network, typically a LAN.

Tip

Want to find a graphic designer?

Graphic Artists Guild
(212) 463-7730

Graphics Arts Service
(816) 421-3879

Society of Illustrators
(212) 838-2560

This chapter will deal with all that's graphical, excluding the HTML tidbits discussed in Chapters 2 and 3, such as imagemaps and body backgrounds. There'll be some surprises along the way. This is meat and potatoes for graphics folks. They do this all the time. But the Web ain't print. To create images using the print way of thinking is a major mistake.

Then there are those of us who are all thumbs when it comes to art. Fear not, my fellow artistically challenged brethren. A scanner, a digital camera, some clip art, and massive amounts of free art from the Web will turn you into a digital Picasso. (Ever notice that Picasso's name begins with the word *pica*?)

But even before we begin delving in the art and science of graphics, I'd like to tackle a more fundamental issue—style.

The elements of Internet style

One thing you won't find on the Web, or even in most books on the subject, is the "elements of style." I don't know why this is, but this latest generation of techno-pioneers seems to have forgotten there is such a thing as good design. As I mentioned in an earlier chapter, the problem manifests itself in the overuse of large graphics. But it also manifests itself in the sloppy layouts, overuse of fonts, and general overcrowding on Web pages (and many Web-oriented magazines as well) that are considered "cool" by today's standards.

Take a look at the magazine *Wired*. While its content is interesting and provocative, its layout is—well, lousy. It's hard to read and, in fact, makes me seasick. There are just too many fonts and the lines are just spaced much too close together. More than one subscription has been canceled as a result.

Tip

Rules of thumb for good home page design:

1 Design for your target audience.
2 Don't use graphics bigger than 50K.
3 Don't use large graphics that force a user to scroll through more than one page at a time.
4 Make sure your graphics look good on the average monitor. Most Webmasters and multimedia designers have high-resolution monitors. Most end users don't. What looks great on a high-res monitor often looks terrible on a low-res monitor.
5 Beware of palette conflict.
6 Design your page around the information, not the graphics.

Tip

Style manuals on the web:

The Web Style Manual of the Yale Center for Advanced Instructional Media

http://info.med.yale.edu/caim/C_HOME.HTML

CERN Guide to Etiquette for Information Providers
http://www.w3.org/hypertext/WWW/Provider/Style/Etiquette

Willamette University HTML Guide
http://www.cs.cmu.edu/~tilt/cgh/

I'm sure that the magazine's graphics designers think they are on the leading edge. But my question is, the leading edge of what? Tom Wolfe, in his searing attack on the art community, *The Painted Word*, decries the pseudo-art of our times. Today talent in the avant garde art community is little more than some broken and bonded crockery, or some politically correct but poorly executed canvas. In today's market, essentially, a lack of talent appears to go a long way. The same appears to be true for the graphic arts community.

Good Web graphics and layout, like good art, are timeless. While the Julian Schnabels (he's the guy with the crockery and bondo) will be scarcely remembered a generation from now, Rembrandt and Picasso will live on forever.

Those targeting Generation X users seem to have a predilection for bad art. The MTV site is a case in point, as shown in Fig. 4-1. I'm sure that the graphic, as it would appear in a print medium, is superlative. But on the Internet it's just too large (about 115K), and unless you have a really good monitor, just too hard to read. In addition, clicking on any of the words located on the imagemap (yes, the image is an imagemap) hyperlinks you to a page with a graphic just as large. More than one Gen-Xer turned 30 before the MTV graphics finished downloading.

Tip

HotNews! Enliven, a plug-in for Netscape, provides streaming multimedia for the Web.

http://www.narrative.com/

4-1 *A kludge of graphics.*

Web pages need to be planned, not just dumped up to a server. Each organization you design for will have its own unique style. That should be reflected in the organization's Web design as well—unless, of course, the organization wishes to alter its style radically. This usually happens in consumer goods companies who try to alter their image frequently to attract new and improved market share.

You also must keep in mind the target audience. Who are they? Kids, teenagers, adults, senior citizens—each of these groups will have a preferred style. Maybe the X Generation really does like the MTV site's too-large and kludged graphics. Some market research might just be in order here.

Before you even get started, particularly if you're going to be working on multiple Web pages for your client firm, it will be worthwhile to develop a style manual.

Different organizations use their WWW sites for different purposes. For some, it's primarily an introduction to their organizations and capabilities. Some use it to capture information about visitors to their sites. Others talk very little about their products and services, and focus instead on generating goodwill for the organization (see the Reebok WWW site at *http://www.planetreebok.com*). Some are even beginning to use their sites as an electronic "storefront" that allows people to place orders for goods and services (Security First Network Bank at *http://www.sfnb.com*). In the end, most WWW sites do a little of all of these.

Tip

Government art usually is in the public domain. If you are interested in old posters, try the National Archives at:

http://www.nara.gov

A sample style guide

The next part of this chapter will focus on the Unisys WWW site, and is written from the perspective of Unisys management speaking to potential Web authors within the organization. The purposes of the site are fourfold:

- *To build Unisys brand awareness and image.* This is Unisys's primary mission. While Unisys is a global company, they don't have the public brand recognition of a Reebok or a Coca-Cola. As in their traditional printed media, they are trying to build the image of Unisys as the information management company. They want to build awareness of that capability.
- *To provide a rich source of information on Unisys and its key partners.* They want their server to present an organized, robust view of Unisys—their services, technologies, markets,

global presence and alliances, etc. People who need to learn information about Unisys and what it can do should be able to find it—or find how to get it—on the Unisys WWW server. And they should be able to find it easily, without having to slog through reams of details that are of interest only to those who work within the Unisys walls.

- *To serve as a proactive marketing and sales tool.* This means actively soliciting feedback from Web surfers who check into the Unisys site, seeking information about them, their areas of interest, their needs, etc. That may involve, for instance, offering token prizes to people willing to fill out an electronic information form. By learning more about visitors, Unisys can know more about what they're looking for and Unisys will be able to market services and products to them.

- *To provide the Unisys foundation for future electronic commerce.* Many people feel that the Internet is not yet secure enough to accommodate financial transactions. That perception is changing as security tools and software quickly mature. Unisys wants to be ready to leverage this important marketing opportunity. For example, Unisys is building its own electronic storefronts that will allow clients and prospective clients to do business with Unisys through the Unisys Web server.

Defining your audience is not easy when it comes to the Web. The tools for measuring specific usage of a given Web site are still primitive, though they are getting better.

In reality, the audience for your Web site could be anyone who's out there surfing on the Internet and happens to bump into your site. That could be a college student, a customer, a prospective client putting out a request for proposal, someone out looking for a job, a government official. When developing your Web site, or your client's, keep in mind how these different audiences may view and react to your message.

Tip

A great resource for those working with communications or graphics arts:

http://www.el.com/ToTheWeb/WebGraphics

That doesn't mean, however, that you should develop your Web site to do all things for all people. Focus is all-important when it comes to the Web. Remember that the Internet is not a traditional "push" distribution vehicle, but rather a "pull" medium. You don't distribute a Web site to a specific set of readers the way you send out brochures to a mailing list. Your material is out there for viewing by anyone. Your job is to attract Web surfers to it. More specifically, your job is to attract the *right* Web surfers to it. That means focusing your material and layout to specific audience.

Planning the site

One approach to planning the site is this four-step scenario:

1 Determine exactly who your desired audience is. It's not enough, for instance, to say you want to reach decision-makers at organizations worldwide. Are you targeting executive decision-makers? Technical decision-makers? Programmers? Are you targeting businesses or government organizations? If you're trying to reach potential employees, are you primarily interested in students coming out of college, or workers with experience?

2 Determine the objective of your Web site. You've seen the mission of the Unisys WWW server above. What is *your* mission? To determine that, consider a few questions. What do your readers want? What do they think about your client? What do you want them to think? What do you want them to know? Use whatever tools you have on hand—customer surveys, focus groups, online questionnaires—to tackle these questions. Then put down the objectives of your Web site on paper. Keep that mission statement in front of you. Pin it on your office wall. It will help keep you focused. (And don't forget to update your objectives as time goes by and your organization changes.)

3 Tailor your Web site material to attract your targeted audience. If you're recruiting consultants from university MBA programs, for instance, you'll want to showcase service lines, service methodologies, job opportunities, training, and developmental programs. If you're selling voice messaging solutions to communications providers, you obviously need much different material, with enough product detail for people to make informed buying decisions.

4 Finally, remember to keep in mind the corporate image. Unisys, for example, is a $6 billion information management company doing business with some of the largest organizations in the world. Your Web site should enhance—not detract from—your client's larger image.

Organizing your site

Once you have determined the audience you want your Web site to attract, and the information you want to present to them, you're ready to create an organizational scheme for your material. This is a critical area in the development of your site. Without a highly structured, easy-to-navigate framework, you'll lose Web surfers right away. Your site organization must be simple enough to get readers quickly to where they want to go, and yet deep enough that, when they get there, they are satisfied with what they find.

The first thing you need to do is situate your prospective Web site within the existing structure of the Unisys WWW server. Bring up the Unisys home page. We have created this home page structure with maximum flexibility to accommodate various Unisys organizations.

Your own home page is the most critical element in your structure. It sets up the organizational scheme for your Web site. Think of your job here as creating a "view" to a rich universe of information that lies beneath your home page. What are the areas your audience are most interested in? Make them the entry points on the home page. Don't make the common mistake of putting too many entry points on your home page. More than seven or eight entry points is probably too many. What you don't want to do is put everything under the sun on your home page, immediately creating the impression that not enough thought has been given to structuring and categorizing it.

Too many items on your home page is a symptom of a shallow organizational scheme. Many Web sites out there suffer from exactly this problem. Shallow Web sites typically arise from one of two reasons: Either their creators have not spent enough time categorizing and structuring their material before putting it out on the Web, or else the site has not been adequately supervised since it was originally created and has grown out of control like an untended bush. Either way, a shallow Web structure overwhelms viewers, turning them off before they ever get interested.

Tip

Your source for 3D:
http://www.3dsite.com/3dsite/

Equally important, don't create a structure that is so deep that it buries information. You'll know you're in one of these Web sites when you keep hitting page after page of menus without getting to any real information. As a general rule of thumb, don't make your viewers dig down more than two or three levels without getting to the information itself. The ideal Web site structure balances on a fine line between too shallow and too deep. You want to guide viewers down logical paths that get progressively more information-rich as they go. If you're marketing technology, for instance, that path will go from product descriptions to feature functionality to detailed spec sheets—not the other way around.

Tip

Read NewMedia magazine online:
http://www.hyperstand.com

You'll find more about Web site organization, including diagrams of too-shallow and too-deep structures, in the *Yale Web Style Manual*.

In creating the pages beneath your home page, stay focused on maximizing ease of navigation and usability of information. A few principles to keep in mind are:

- Every page must stand alone. Don't assume that every Web surfer will enter a given page by first going through the menu on the home page. Unlike a printed document that first presents a cover to readers, a Web site can be entered at any point from any number of other points. Include a header or footer on every page that connects to the original entry point on the home page, and enough contextual information that the viewer knows where he or she is in the general scheme of things.

- If your page includes a menu, make sure every menu item includes an adequate description of what it's all about. Nothing irritates a Web surfer more than starting down a path not knowing exactly where they're going or whether it's worth their time. For instance, don't (as many Web sites do) label a menu item "What's Cool." That's not enough for a viewer to know whether that path is worth following. Be more precise in your title; tell the Web surfer what will be found down that path—for example, "Cool New Technologies to Check Out."

- Likewise, include a short synopsis of every article included in your site. This will let viewers know whether it's something of interest to them. Focus this synopsis on the benefits to be gained by reading the article.

Organizing your articles

Because of the storage power of electronic media compared to printed documents, many of us immediately want to convert lengthy brochures and other tomes into Web site material. Resist that temptation. The attention span of the typical Web surfer is measured in mouse clicks, or number of meteors in the Netscape "working" icon. Make your points up front and then expand on them below for anyone interested.

As a rule, avoid excessively lengthy articles unless appropriate to your audience and the information they are looking for. Wherever possible, limit your documents to one page of text. Consider the popularity of the *USA Today* newspaper that appears under the door of your hotel room when you're traveling. The creators of *USA Today* recognized that people today are pressed for time and want information in short, easily digestible bites.

That doesn't mean everything has to be written this way. Obviously, the *Wall Street Journal* is popular for its substantive articles. But *WSJ* is also extremely well-written, with an easy, anecdotal style that draws the reader in. Let's face it—few of us can write this well. Where longer articles are appropriate and necessary, such as an electronic "white paper" that explains a complex technical subject, include sufficient (and interesting) subheads to retain attention.

Also make use of graphics, charts, photographs, and other appropriate elements to sustain interest and explain the subject you're writing about. Nothing loses a reader more quickly than a dull page of pure text, especially on the Internet, where interactivity and visual excitement is expected.

Creating links

Finally, in organizing your Web site, pay attention to hyperlinks. These are electronic links to other online resources, either within the Unisys server or externally to other sites on the Internet. If you're discussing the use of Oracle software technology on your platform, for instance, allow the viewer to click on the word "Oracle" and launch into the portion of the Unisys server that discusses the Unisys relationship with Oracle and other strategic partners.

Make use of resources outside the Unisys server as well. There's a wealth of electronic resources out there on the Web, and more coming online every day. Go into Lycos (*http://www.lycos.com*) or Yahoo (*http://www.yahoo.com*) and do a search for other servers covering material related to yours. Then, where appropriate, build links in your material that let your readers move to these outside resources to enrich their understanding of the subject.

Obviously you don't want to build so many links that readers go off and never come back, and you probably don't want to link to the page of competitors who offer products that compete with yours. Base your links on the informational value they add to your discussion. For instance, if you're promoting child welfare solutions from Unisys, you might want to link to a U.S. government server that discusses new legislation affecting child welfare. In terms of links to other companies, build on Unisys strategic partnerships with the likes of Intel, Oracle, and Microsoft.

The effective use of hyperlinks can strengthen your own materials dramatically. Equally important, they build the impression that it's easy to do business with Unisys.

Design and layout

Graphics, imagemaps, sound, movies, and hot links provide a wonderful way to show off your creativity. Before jumping into the design and layout of your Web site, however, consider your audience. Whom do you want to impress? How can you best do that? Equally important, how can you make visiting your site a pleasurable experience? How will it help enhance the image of Unisys?

Foremost, you must ensure that visitors to your Web site grasp easily how it's organized and can navigate quickly to the information they are seeking.

Good design seeks a balance between visual sensation that graphics offer, and the text information that those graphics illustrate. Documents that are dense with text, without the visual relief of graphics, will not motivate the viewer to investigate the content. On the other hand, pages that are heavy in graphics may take so long to download that the viewer will move on quickly, maybe never to return. Here are some guidelines for helping you make a cohesive presentation and a memorable experience for whoever visits your Web site.

Web pages are essentially vertical. Users enter at the top and work their way through the page. Each page should be no longer than three screens at 640×480 resolution.

The best Web pages usually conform to a grid. A grid is an invisible set of lines that guide the placement of graphics and text. By using a grid, you can establish how major blocks of text and art appear on the page. This helps a visitor understand how the various pages are organized, and makes it easier for him or her to progress to the information needed. This does not mean that every page must look the same as the preceding one, just that there is an organizing principle. For example, Fig. 4-2 shows two of the many standard Unisys Web page layouts.

4-2 *From the Unisys style guide.*

Unisys standard page specs are as follows:
- Page width no more than 600 pixels maximum
- Home page graphic 600×400 pixels maximum
- Unisys logo on all home pages, and on most following pages
- Navigation graphic (optional)
- Navigation via text links
- Always a link to Unisys home page and top of your section
- Following pages banner 600×250 pixels maximum

As mentioned earlier, each Web page should be designed to stand alone. At a minimum, it should identify Unisys, provide a link to the Unisys home page, and a link to the top of your section. It should also include a date of creation or revision, and links to contacts and the Unisys statement of copyright.

A good practice is to start your page with a banner that relates to the menu that preceded it and/or to the contents of the page. The top-of-page banners can contain graphics; we recommend that these be no larger than 500×100 pixels total, with 600×250 as a maximum. The Unisys logo should be part of the banner of all major pages. Since a Web surfer can jump into our site from many locations, we must let them know that they are in the Unisys site. The banner should be followed by a head that introduces the contents of the page (unless, of course, the head is part of the banner).

Think about navigation

Navigation aids are buttons or links that ensure that users can get to the information they are seeking easily. If you have a multipage section, and provide a link from another section to a topic in the middle of your section, the reader should have an easy way to go to the front of the section and move forward. Here it is a good idea to provide links for "top of section," "previous page," and "next page," as well as links back to the home page, and to other related sections. If users encounter a dead end (a page without links), they will probably leave your site rather than back up through the pages they have already read.

Icons can be fun to create, but we shouldn't make the reader guess what they do. Either provide navigation buttons that state exactly what they do, or provide HTML links. It is best always to include HTML links, whether you have created graphic navigation buttons or not. Many users turn graphics off. Navigation buttons or links should be part of the top-of-page banner or near the top of the page. If a user arrives on a particular page and decides that it doesn't have the information he or she is seeking, we must make it easy to navigate elsewhere. It may also be appropriate to provide navigation links at the bottom of a page, particularly if the page is several screens long. The point is to make it as easy as possible on the user.

Graphics

A picture might be worth a thousand words, but you must ensure that the viewer benefits from having waited for them to download. Graphics can help the Internet reader understand how to navigate through your site, aid in explaining your message, and make visiting your page a memorable experience. But be careful not to overdo them. This medium is not a multimedia CD-ROM. It is typically transmitted over relatively slow lines to your audiences. Any page that takes longer than 20 seconds to download will quickly lose that audience.

Pages that use large graphic image maps as menus will tax the patience of most users. As a rule, each 1K of graphic size requires 1 second to download on a 14.4 modem. Moreover, image maps, while "cool" in letting the viewer click on a point of visual interest, generally take up much more room than a simple listing of available links. Image maps should be used sparingly and kept to a minimum size—but no larger than 600×400 pixels.

Inline graphics should be no larger than 22,500 pixels square (150×150). Though graphics can help break up a page so it's easier to read and more understandable, don't include more than a total of ten individual graphics for a given page.

Color and backgrounds

Most of us who develop pages for the Web work on high-resolution monitors with graphics accelerator cards. Many if not most of our audience are using devices of much lower resolution. Design your pages and select colors that will present your information effectively to *most* of our audience. Test your pages on lower-resolution monitors and through several different browsers before bringing it online.

Be very careful about using backgrounds. While backgrounds can add interest if related to the graphic theme of your pages, they add to the time it takes to download. Excessively textured backgrounds, and some colored backgrounds, can hinder legibility of type. Consider that 12 percent of the population is color-blind. Red type on a blue background (with similar color saturation) is almost indistinguishable to most color-blind people.

Text formatting

The HTML language is constantly being refined, as are the capabilities of the various browser packages. It's very easy to get carried away with special formatting that works with one browser (like Netscape Navigator), but looks terrible when viewed by other software. For this discussion on layout, we recommend that pages include two main heading levels: the HTML H2 heading tag as a main heading for a page, and the H3 tag for subheads. You can set apart the body text of a page using standard HTML text formatting codes, including bold and italics. Please do not use blinking text. It is annoying to most viewers; you can get attention in numerous, more sophisticated ways.

Creating Web graphics

You probably have some of the tools you need to create Web graphics right on your PC. Photoshop, Photostyler, Paint Shop Pro, and CorelDRAW are just a few of the art programs that developers and graphics designers typically have in their arsenals.

Tip

The worst part of color-coordinating your Netscape-enhanced pages is figuring out the hexadecimal representation of your decimals. Now, simply select your red, green, and blue values; Get Hexed! does the rest. It converts to hex, displays the results, and provides a <BODY> tag for you to slip into your next HTML document. Find it at:

http://www.stardot.com/~lukeseem/hexed.html

While you may have the tools at your disposal, that doesn't necessarily mean you have the conceptual wherewithal—even if you are a graphic designer. Designing for print and designing for the Web are two totally different jobs.

Let's look at an example of things that can go wrong, courtesy of Dixon J. Jones at the University of Alaska (*http://zorba.uafadm .alaska.edu*).

4-3
A hard-to-read image.

Most people will find the image in Fig. 4-3 uncomfortable to read or even to look at. A rule of thumb has been violated here, namely foreground and background colors should not be of nearly equal value or grayness.

The image in Fig. 4-4 is a grayscale version of Fig. 4-3. Most people will see this image as nothing but a single gray. This suggests a good way to check images for this problem: Convert the file to grayscale, or change your monitor setting to grayscale if you can, and see if your image is still clearly visible. If it is not, consider changing colors.

The same problem might occur when text color supplied by your Web browser lies on top of a colored background. Solid red text on a solid blue background is a common and usually bad idea.

Tip

Correct Netscape's nagging dithering palette problem. Go to:
http://www.onr.com/user/lights/netcol.html

4-4
A grayscale version of the image in Fig. 4-3.

A drop shadow under a graphic element is a copy of the element in a different (usually darker) color, placed "under" the element (i.e., mostly obscured by it), and moved slightly so as to be visible at the edges of the element. Often a drop shadow will improve the legibility of text on a computer or TV screen.

Tip

Free artwork on the Web:

http://ura1195-6.univ-lyon1.fr/Server/graphics/indexE.html
http://www.cosmicdome.com/graphics/lines/
http://www.cs.cuhk.hk/~ttwong/resource.html
http://www.yahoo.com/text/computers_and_internet/graphics
http://sunsite.unc.edu/echernof/graphics/
http://www.nosc.mil/planet_earth/images.html
http://www2.ncsu.edu/bae/people/faculty/walker/hotlist/icons.html

---

The example in Fig. 4-5 shows a poorly implemented drop shadow. The shadow has been displaced too far from the original text, increasing the visual complexity. A second rule of thumb has been violated here, namely a drop shadow should be displaced no more than the width of the thinnest or narrowest part of the element it shadows. In this example, the thinnest part of the text occurs on the *serifs* (decorative ends of the letters). On the left-hand foot of the letter A, for instance, the width of the letter is only a few pixels at that point. The drop shadow should be displaced only a few pixels from the letter itself.

4-5
A poorly implemented drop shadow.

A common effect, easily created in computer graphics, is the graduated fill, a smooth blend from one color to another. Blends over large distances (i.e., more than about 10 pixels) do not transfer to GIF files very well, because almost by definition they exceed 256 colors. The problem is worse when the blend goes between complementary colors.

Tip

There's a new image format in town. Thomas Boutell, the developer of mapedit, the image map creation program, has created a file format that offers better support for color, as well as better compression. It's known as PNG, or portable network graphics. Netscape does not yet support it, but that's bound to change as PNG grows in popularity. More information is available from Boutell's site at *http://www.boutell.com/boutell/png*.

Figure 4-6 uses an adaptive color table with dithering, an option when converting RGB images to indexed color (the GIF scheme) in Photoshop. As you can see, the print effect simply does not translate well to the Web.

4-6
Using an adaptive color table with dithering, an option when converting RGB images to indexed color in Photoshop.

An easy way to dress up a page is to add a single line of HTML code specifying BODY BACKGROUND to be an image. In Netscape, this image is used to *tile the window* (i.e., repeat to fill the page) under the rest of the text and graphics. Background tiles should not interfere with the legibility of what lies on top of them, as shown in Fig. 4-7.

4-7 *The busy background obscures the lettering.*

Very little tonal variation is needed to create a background tile. The improved version in Fig. 4-8 was created by increasing the brightness drastically and reducing the contrast of the original tile.

4-8 *The effects of increasing brightness and reducing contrast.*

While the HEIGHT= and WIDTH= parameters in the IMG tag allow you to reduce an image to fit a display, this is foolish to do. Not only does it waste time in downloading overly large images, the image itself also can be distorted by the enlargement process.

While it's entirely possible to create a bit of artwork using horizontal rules and tables, (see *http://zorba.uafadm.alaska.edu/Library/impact/rules.html* shown in Fig. 4-9), the best bet is to create images carefully in one of the many draw and paint programs I mentioned at the beginning of this section.

> **Tip**
>
> Some great graphics resources include:
>
> Lview Pro Graphic Program (Windows 3.1
> Lview Pro Graphics Program (Windows 95)
> MapEdit: Clickable Map Editor
> Web Mania
> Map This
> Sample Web Page Graphics: Backgrounds
> Sample Web Page Graphics: Balls
> Sample Web Page Graphics: Buttons
> Sample Web Page Graphics: Lines
> Sample Web Page Graphics: Squares
>
> *http://cspace.unb.ca/nbco/ed5365/flib/graphics.html*

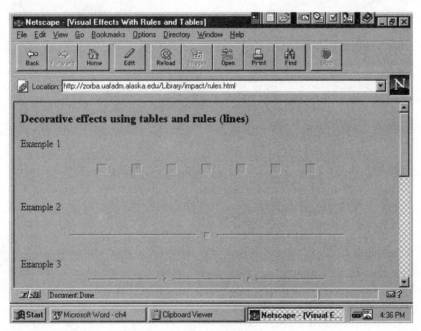

4-9 *Decorative effects using tables and rules.*

A discourse on creating images

Keeping file sizes down is your first consideration when designing graphics for the Web, because the larger the file size, the longer it takes the image to load.

With a 14.4 kbps modem (still the most common connection speed), it takes approximately 20 seconds to load a 20K image or video clip. Because most browsers open to a width of 485 pixels by default, it's best to set your image width accordingly, as shown in Fig. 4-10.

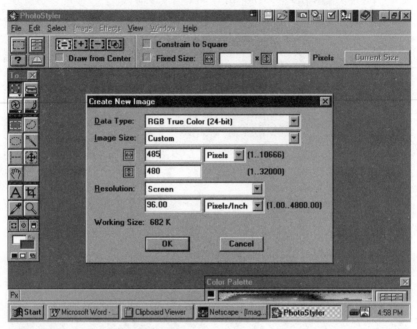

4-10 *Setting your image width.*

There are two common graphics formats on the Web, GIF and JPEG. With the GIF format, you will need to convert your images to *index color* (as opposed to RGB). The term *bit depth* affects the number of distinct colors that can be displayed. Values range from 1-bit (2 colors), through 4-bit and 8-bit (16 and 256 colors, respectively), to 24-bit (16.7 million colors). Few users (other than the aforementioned graphic designers) run their systems in 24-bit "true color" mode all the time, so you'll need to experiment to get the bit depth down to the lowest setting at which the image still looks good. With 24-bit color JPEGs, experiment with the quality settings; the lower the quality, the lower the bit depth.

The GIF format works well with images that have few colors and can be indexed to a low bit depth. Convert images using the "Save As" dialog box in Photoshop or alternate paint program, and give them a .GIF extension.

The image in Fig. 4-11 is about 59,000 bytes. Your task in designing images is to balance successfully the size of the image against the final resolution of the image. The larger the image, the more bytes it uses. The higher the bit (color) depth and resolution, the more bytes the image uses.

4-11 *An image that needs to be reduced.*

One way of making the image smaller is to reduce its size. Most paint programs let you do this rather simply. The Resample function of PhotoStyler lets you change the size of the image in several ways: pixels, inches, picas, points, centimeters, millimeters, and percentage. I've chosen percentage in Fig. 4-12 and reduced the image to 70 percent of its original size. Although the default resolution of most screen prints is 96 pixels per inch, I've decided to reduce mine down to 72. As you can see in Fig. 4-12, the image size is reduced.

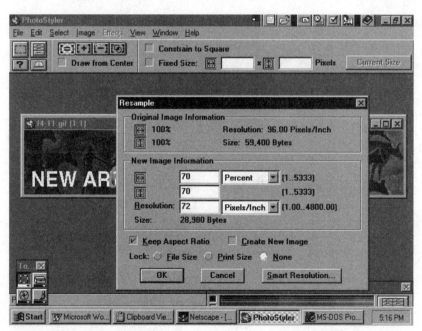

4-12 *Resizing your image.*

PhotoStyler's Resample function tells me that I've managed to reduce the image to 28,900 bytes. By clicking off "Keep Aspect Ratio" and modifying the height to 200 pixels, I've managed to change the image as shown in Fig. 4-13. While the image itself doesn't look too bad, notice that the words look distorted. The secret to imaging success is to keep trying until you get it right.

4-13 *Reducing the image size.*

Paint packages give you the appropriate tool kit to manipulate images. In Photoshop, for example, the Adaptive/Diffusion option creates a custom palette based on the existing colors in your image and the number of colors you've specified. The Dither/Diffusion option dithers the pixels to give an illusion of colors blending. Always try both Diffusion and None options, since results vary from one image to another.

In Fig. 4-14, all four images are in 5-bit color. Image 1 is Adaptive/Diffusion, image 2 is Adaptive/None, image 3 is Uniform/Diffusion, image 4 is Uniform/None. The leftmost image, image 1, obviously looks the best.

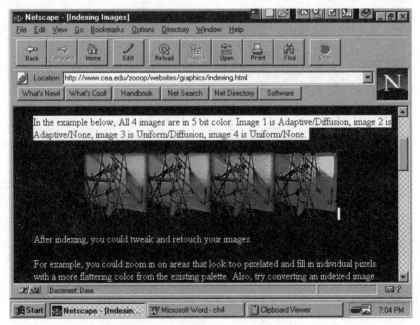

4-14 *An image in different bit depths.*

After an image is indexed, if you go back into Photoshop's Mode menu and choose Color Table, you can replace individual colors from the image. Sometimes creating your own color palette lets you reduce the number of colors even further. You can use the Adaptive/Diffusion option to do this. See if there are any colors that could be replaced with another existing color. Select those colors with the magic wand and fill them in with other existing colors from the palette. Also, tweak colors in the Color Table (from the Mode menu).

Cut out the colors you've eliminated from the color swatches (by pressing Command and clicking on the color), and choose the Save Swatches option from the pop-up menu. When you index the image, choose Palette/Custom and load your new palette!

The JPEG format

The 24-bit color JPEG format (JPEG stands for Joint Photographic Experts Group) are also common on the Web and soon will be supported by most browsers. JPEG usually is a better format for photographs and images with a lot of detail and colors. This format sometimes can compress images to half the size of their GIF counterparts. JPEG compresses about 20:1 before the image is visibly degraded. From a development standpoint, JPEG also compresses rather slowly: about 1–3 seconds for a 1MB image, depending on the computer. The space savings makes this bit of inconvenience worthwhile, however.

Tip

Download LView Pro, Windows-based interlacing and transparency shareware that also lets you convert GIF files to JPEG and vice versa. Get it from:

http://world.std.com/~mmedia

JPEG uses a technique known as *lossy compression*. As its name implies, data is lost during the compression process, which is accomplished through an algorithm that decides what can be discarded safely. JPEG breaks the image down into smaller and more manageable blocks, compresses each block, and then moves on to the next. What this enables is compression-on-the-fly, as well as much higher compression rates (up to 20:1) compared to typical text compression ratios, which hover in the area of 3:1.

Interlacing and transparency

You might have noticed that many images downloaded from a server seem to come in a portion at a time. At first the image is hazy, and then gradually it becomes clearer and clearer as it completes the download process.

For example, a 55,000-byte image on the MTV site looks like Fig. 4-15 within the first few seconds. About 30 seconds later (varying with the load on the system) the image looks a lot better, as shown in Fig. 4-16.

4-15 *Interlaced image when it first starts to download.*

This is quite simple to do, really. It's called *interlacing* and it's done only on GIF files. Unfortunately, most traditional paint programs won't help you out with this one. (Paint Shop Pro is an exception.) There's also a bit of shareware, LVIEW, that not only lets you save the file as interlaced, it also lets you change a background color to transparent and allows you to save a GIF file as a JPEG and vice versa.

Figure 4-17 shows how simple this utility is. Shown is the dialog LVIEW uses to change a background color. Notice the Dropper button at the bottom of the screen. Clicking on this gives you an eyedropper. Placing the eyedropper over the appropriate color on the

4-16 *Interlaced image after it loads.*

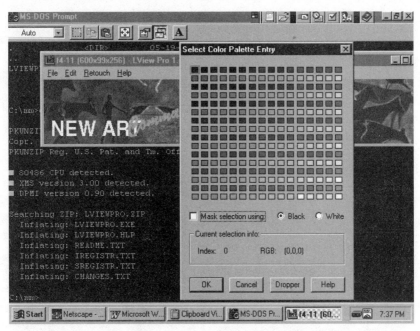

4-17 *Using a tool to select a color for transparency.*

image will "suck the color up." This will become the color that is made transparent.

This means that you can nicely superimpose an oddly shaped graphic logo you've designed, for example, and have that logo seemingly "float" on the background—no matter what color or what background graphics are used. A couple of caveats are in order, though. Transparency does not work in conjunction with interlacing, and this also should always be the last step. If you save the image again in almost any other application, that hard-earned transparency will be lost.

Tip

A great place for audio:
ftp://gatekeeper.dec.com/pub/micro/msdos/win3/sounds/INDEX

Look at the image in Fig. 4-18. Although your version isn't in color, you'll notice right away that the New York Shops & Dines image is the same color as the surrounding area (outside the rectangle). But the image was created with a white background. Since the background on the Web was gray (and could be changed by the user to whatever color he or she wants), the developer wanted to make sure that there was no inconsistency between the color inside the image and outside the image. The dropper was used to select the background color within the image and mark it as transparent. It's as simple as that.

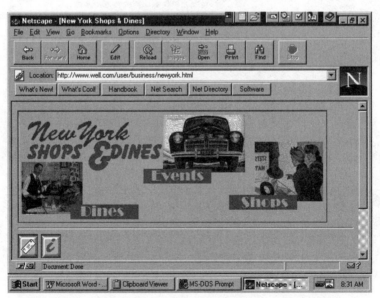

4-18 *The results of transparency. The actual background color is white, although it appears to be gray when displayed.*

Web hot spots for graphics

The Web is a virtual wonderland of free graphic images and tools. Aside from my favorite spots (listed in the Tips boxes), this section will get to the nitty-gritty of using the Web to locate images, buttons, backgrounds, and tools to modify what you find—or even tools to create new ones.

First, make it a point to download PKZIP if you don't already have it. For those of you not familiar with this most popular of all shareware programs, PKZIP is a compression utility. It allows the user to take one or more files (for example, a program file and its associated documentation) and squash it into a single, much smaller file. Depending on the original file format, it's not uncommon for this trusty utility to compress several megabytes into a mere tens of thousands of bytes—a big savings on space. Because of its efficiency, the PKZIP format (known as a *zipped file* or *zipfile* because of its .ZIP file extension), is perhaps the most popular way to store information on remote computers served by the Internet. It's also the utility of choice for most shareware authors who store their programs and images on such proprietary services as CompuServe and America Online.

Many shareware files, including PKZIP itself, are located on ftp (File Transfer Protocol) servers on the Internet. It's possible to use your browser to surf to these locations easily. Instead of typing *http://www.some.name*, you will type *ftp://some.name*. To download PKZIP, surf over to *ftp://ftp.coast.net/Coast/msdos/zip/*. Once there, you will see a file directory that looks like the one in Fig. 4-19.

4-19 *Using FTP to download free images and software.*

Scroll down a bit and then click on the entry for pkz204g.exe, as shown in Fig. 4-20. Your browser will not recognize the file and immediately go into Save As mode. Save this file to a directory, preferably called ZIP. (Note, though, that on other sites the file is called pk204g.exe. What's important is the "204G" part, signifying the most recent shareware release of the software. You should avoid at all costs, at least for now, any file purporting to be version 3.0 of PKZIP, which is bogus and is a destructive Trojan Horse program.)

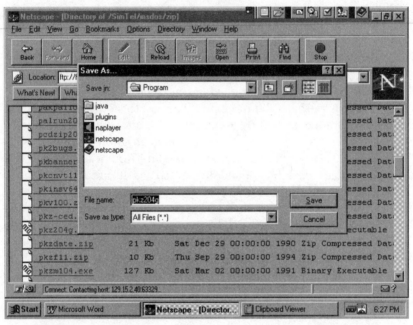

4-20 *The browser's "Save As" dialog.*

pkz204g.exe is what is referred to as an *executable* zipped file, or sometimes as a *self-extracting archive*. PKZIP not only enables you to package multiple files in a single file that takes up less space than the files being compressed, it also lets you turn that zipped file into an executable file that decompresses itself automatically when executed.

PKZIP compresses files into a single file with a .ZIP extension of. When you are confronted with a file such as this, just use the PKUNZIP utility (e.g., *pkunzip yourfile.zip*) to decompress the file. But this presumes that you have the PKUNZIP utility on the computer where you are decompressing the file. The ZIP2EXE utility lets you transform *yourfile.zip* into a self-decompressing file called *yourfile.exe*. See the README files that come with the product for instructions.

PKZ204G.EXE contains all three of the PK utilities just mentioned. It's also the most utilitarian of all shareware utilities, allowing you to unzip easily the literally hundreds of files you'll find on the Web. You'll find this an indispensable tool to deliver files to your clients.

An even easier way to locate excellent shareware is through C I Net Online's *www.shareware.com* site. For those of you not in the know, C I Net airs weekly on diverse cable channels (the Sci-Fi Channel is one of them). Essentially a CNN for computer gearheads, C I Net does serve to keep you informed on subjects relating to the Web. C I Net has invested heavily in its shareware site. Interestingly, though, none of the shareware is physically located on C I Net's computers.

The academic community is the physical host of most of this software. The site *ftp://ftp.coast.net*, shown in Fig. 4-19, actually is the home of the University of Oklahoma. The format shown in Fig. 4-19 is a typical directory listing of files as accessed through ftp. Those familiar with Unix need no introduction, and it should look vaguely similar to DOS for the rest of you (unless, of course, you're an Apple aficionado).

The *www.shareware.com* server grabs all of this information from the various and sundry universities and puts it into a more familiar and easier-to-use HTML format. An alternative to *www.shareware. com* is *www.jumbo.com*, so if you can't find what you want on one, try the other site.

Because the files are located on the university servers and because of the popularity of shareware, you might have trouble accessing the files you are seeking. Some universities have a limit to the number of people logged onto their site at any one time. You may have to keep trying—or go to an alternative site. Many of the heavily accessed sites are duplicated on various computers around the world, the duplicates being called *mirror sites*.

The nice thing about *www.shareware.com* is that you can do a search (keyword, filename, etc.) for the specific piece of software in which you are interested. WinZip is an excellent alternative to the PKZIP utility discussed in preceding paragraphs. Not only does it handle zipped files, it also handles other compression formats such as the arc, arj, gz, tar, sit, Z, and zoo formats commonly used in Unix environments. Figure 4-21 shows the alternatives that *www.shareware.com* gives you.

If you can't download it successfully from one site, try anther site—and another and another. Be creative. My office is on the East Coast, so I get up early to access the sites located on the West Coast. In the evening I try the European sites. I've also downloaded more than one file from Turkey, Japan, and even Australia. My computer seems to travel more than I do. Aside from frequent busy signals, the

4-21 *The* www.shareware.com *server lets you select "mirror" sites from which to download shareware.*

files themselves are volatile. Academic institutions have a tendency to move stuff around, and it's not unusual for the file to be in one spot on one day and another spot on another day. So keep trying.

Information on graphics formats is available from several sources. You also might be interested in sources for icons and images, information on audio editors and converters, and PC utilities.

The rest of this section will point out some choice real estate on the Internet. And, by the way, the same caveat on business and location holds true for the stuff in this section, although everything was locatable when pen hit paper.

Tip

A good example of using a PDF is provided by the Wharton School site, where you can call up a form, fill it in, and send it back without having to print out the form first:

http://www.wharton.upenn.edu

ACDSee
(Get it?) This is a shareware, Windows-based imaging shell that can view BMP, GIF, JPEG, PCX, Photo CD, PNG, TGA, TIFF formats. Find this at *http://vvv.com/acd/acd/acdsys.htm*.

Adobe Systems Acrobat
This is becoming a standard for displaying brochures and other desk-top published documents on the Web. Download the viewer free from the company's Web site at *www.adobe.com*. You'll have to pay for the developer's version, though; information on this is also in-cluded on the site. To see Acrobat in action, surf over to Unisys's ClearPath site at *http://www.clearinfo.com/whatishm.htm* and you'll see a list of documents available. The document titled "ClearPath HMP IX4000 Series Overview" is a PDF file, which is the Acrobat for-mat. Download this (get the viewer first from Adobe), as shown in Fig. 4-22. Then view it with Acrobat (Fig. 4-23).

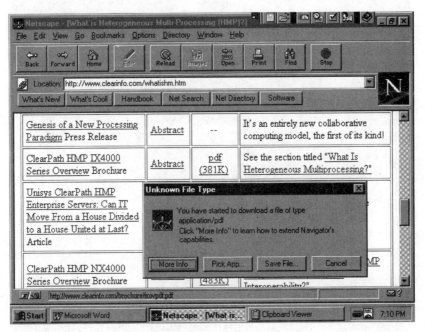

4-22 *Saving a PDF file from an HTML dialog for later viewing with Adobe Acrobat.*

For now, the acrobat PDF extension is not automatically recog-nized by Netscape or any other browser. Given this format's popular-ity, it's just a matter of time before having to download the viewer will be a thing of the past. Even now, using the PDF format is some-

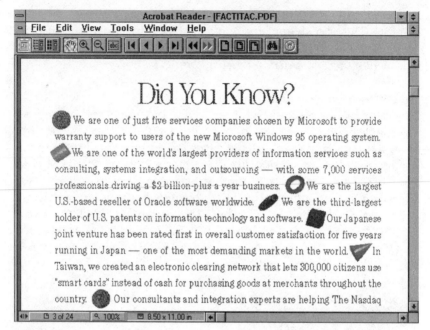

4-23 *The Acrobat viewer.*

thing the Internet consultant should consider if he or she has a client with brochures that will require a home on the Web.

Tip

The sites listed here are a brief overview of what's out there for the asking on the Web. Spend lots of time on *www.share-ware.com* searching through directories, do lots of searches using *altavista.digital.com,* and whenever you visit an ftp site, download the file named *00index.txt,* which invariably is a list of all the files on the ftp site (or the subdirectory you're in).

A little multimedia

There's nothing like it for pizzazz on the Web. One of the more exciting aspects of multimedia is video. The Audio Video Interleave format, or AVI, is Microsoft's entry into the arena. You can download Video for Windows from the Microsoft ftp site, which is located at *ftp://ftp.microsoft.com/developr/drg/Multimedia/.* Look for the file DOC.ZIP.

MPEG tools

MPEG is the professional's choice for digital video. An international standard, MPEG (from Motion Picture Experts Group, who developed it) can be translated from the more common AVI format through a conversion utility. Go to *ftp://x2ftp.oulu.fi/pub/msdos/programming/convert/* for just such a utility, in the file convmpg3.zip.

MPEGPLAY, an MPEG viewer program, can play standard MPEG files and large, 54×288 movie files. It has several display options that include mono, grayscale, and full color. This player has pushbutton VCR controls, a separate Video Window, and displays a wealth of file information. Ftp this gem from *ftp.ncsa.uiuc.edu/Web/Mosaic/Windows/viewers* or *ftp.cic.net/pub/Software/pc/www/viewer.* The filename is mpegw32h.zip.

QuickTime

QuickTime is a multimedia standard advanced by Apple Computer, who practically pioneered multimedia-enabled personal computers. Luckily, you can now get it for the Windows platform. Search for qtw11.zip at *http://ftp.digital.com/cgi-bin/grep-index.*

Tip

Intrigued by multimedia? Join these newsgroups:

alt.binaries.multimedia
alt.binaries.pictures.uti
comp.graphics
comp.graphics.animation
comp.compression
comp.multimedia

SmartVid converts between the Windows AVI format and the QuickTime MOV format. Ftp smartv.exe from *ftp.intel.com/pub/IAL/multimedia/.*

Tip

Some MPEGs to borrow:

ftp://ftp.iij.ad.jp/pub/mail/mime/mpeg/movies/
http://www.cyf-kr.edu.pl/mmedia/movies/
ftp://s2k-ftp.CS.Berkeley.EDU/pub/multimedia/mpeg/movies/
ftp://etlport.etl.go.jp/pub/ccipr/mime/mpeg/movies/

If you have a bunch of PPM, TGA, or RAW files and would like to generate a MPEG file from them, then ftp cmpeg10.zip, a DOS utility, from *ftp://ftp.germany.eu.net/pub/comp/msdos/mirror.garbo/graphics/.*

Hop over to *ftp://ftp.uoknor.edu/SimTel/msdos/graphics/* and download disp189a.zip and disp189b.zip. This is a DOS utility that reads, writes and displays movies and images in many formats, including: AVI, DL, FLI/FLC, GL, MPEG, RAW, BMP, GIF, JPEG, PCX, TGA, TIFF, YUV, and lots more.

Image n' Bits (ima.zip) is a Windows program that lets you tune, smooth, sharpen, flip, and combine images. Ftp it from *ftp://gatekeeper.dec.com/pub/micro/msdos/win3/desktop/*.

Tip

A great place for sounds:

ftp://gatekeeper.dec.com/pub/micro/msdos/win3/sounds/INDEX

Screen snapshots

There are times when you want to capture a screen print right from your PC. The illustrations in this book were captured the simple way. I merely brought up the screen I wanted to capture and pressed the Print Screen key under Windows. This copied the screen display directly into the Windows clipboard. From there, I pasted the contents of the clipboard into a paint program. An alternative, one with bells and whistles, is a screen capture program. Ftp CAPT20.ZIP from *ftp://gatekeeper.dec.com/pub/micro/msdos/win3/desktop*.

The third dimension

If you're interested in generating 3D documents, check out the site at *http://www.geom.umn.edu/apps/cyberview3d/about.html*. Cyberview is an add-on for World Wide Web servers that supports 3D images and imagemaps.

Tip

Animated GIFs are a boon to site developers. They essentially are single files with multiple images overlaid within. Software to help you do this:

http://www.mindworkshop.com/alchemy/alchemy.html

PostScript

Those of you who dabble in desktop publishing know that PostScript files are the method of choice for delivering files to your print shop or service bureau. PostScript, which uses .PS and .EPS file extensions, describes to the output device not only the text in the document, but the formatting and images as well.

If you surf the Net often, you'll often find the PostScript format offered as an alternative for downloading a document file. Sun Microsystems, for example, provides several ways to download some of their manuals and white papers; PostScript and text are but two. Ghostview and GSView are tools that decode the PostScript format for viewing. Without a viewer, raw PostScript (though technically a text file) would be virtually unreadable. Download the programs from *http://www.cs.wisc.edu/~ghost/index.html.*

VRL imaging machine

VRL has graciously provided Internet developers with what they call an imaging machine, located at *http://www.vrl.com:80/Imaging/.* There are online facilities to combine two images with a twist, transmogrify an image, create an animated GIF file, continuously change an image, convert your image to a different file type, combine several images into one index image, and make a particular color transparent.

Morphing

Anyone who watches television will have seen the commercials that employ this popular multimedia technique for transforming one image into another. Even the pop star Michael Jackson used it in one of his music videos. This is a useful graphical technique for Internet developers as well. For example, suppose you have a client who sells real estate. Why not have a morph sequence transform a dowdy home into a newer and more glorious one? You can ftp morph10.zip from *ftp://ftp.coast.net/SimTel/msdos/graphics/.*

Budget photo tools

The Internet consultant's bag of tools need not be expensive. If you can't afford PhotoShop, then download PhotoLab. It's a graphics program that enables you to rotate, mirror, crop, flip, negative, color depth, emboss, edge detect, create wallpaper, etc. Ftp pholab18.zip from *ftp://x2ftp.oulu.fi/pub/msdos/programming/utils/.*

There are many more graphics resources on the Web. Tune into one of the many search engines, such as *http://altavista.digital.com,* enter "Internet graphics" into the search term part of the form, and then surf over to what looks interesting to you. I'm interested in what you find. If you find something you think is great then e-mail me at *newart@panix.com* or *business@well.com.*

Image scanning

Sometimes the Internet just doesn't have the image you need to really jazz up the Web site you are creating. Although there's a plethora of tools that let you design these images yourself, sometimes the best image is a photographic one.

You're lucky. Today there are several economical ways to get a photograph into a computer-readable format. This section will discuss those ways. Be forewarned, though. Photographic images are large. Even after you get it to your PC, you still have to use an image processing program like Photoshop to manipulate it into something manageable and viewable on the Web.

The easiest and least expensive way to get a photograph into a digital format is to process your roll of film in the Kodak Photo CD format. Your local film processing store will have this capability (since they send much of the film out to Kodak anyway). Instead of prints, they return to you a CD. On the outside of the jewel case the CD comes in will be a thumbnail of each photograph on the CD. This makes it easy for you to locate the one of interest.

You will need software that lets you to view images in this format. Kodak provides a viewer that does just this, as shown in Fig. 4-24. Us-

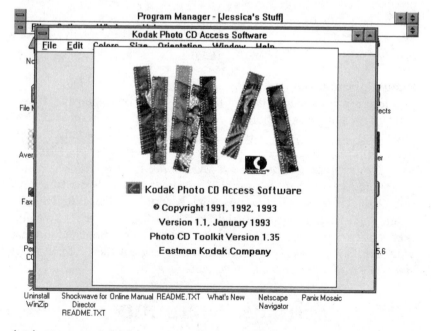

4-24 *Using Kodak Photo CD to select images from photographs.*

ing the viewer, all you need do is choose the image, load it, and then copy it into your image processing program.

The new digital cameras offer another way of getting photographs into your computer. A good example is the Casio QV-10A, which retails for about $499. Those using it think it's stunning. It can hold up to 96 pictures at approximately 320×200 size in 24-bit color. It's downloaded into either your Mac or Windows system with supplied software. Figure 4-25 shows just how compact this device is.

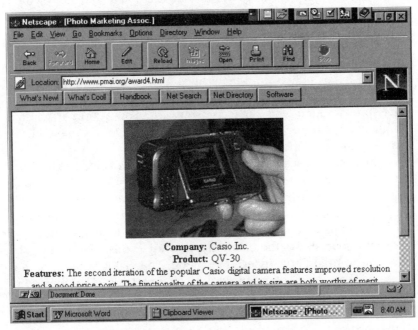

4-25 *The Casio digital camera.*

For those with low cash flow but big ideas, Connectix (*http://www.connectix.com*) just might have a product that fits your particular budget. Connectix QuickCam makes it easy for you to take your own still pictures and video movies.

Tip

Computers and peripherals are hot sellers on the Web: You can order Connectix online from:

http://necxdirect.necx
http://www.eboutique.com/
http://www.gtsi.com/index.htm
http://www.cybout.com/cyberian.html
http://www.creativecomputers.com/

By simply plugging the QuickCam (less than $99) into the parallel port of your PC and easily installing the included Connectix QuickPict and QuickMovie software, you'll see your own images on your computer in minutes. QuickCam uses direct digital imaging to create black and white movies and still pictures. Use the images you create in the programs supplied, or add your movies and pictures to thousands of other Windows applications—virtually anything that supports Windows AVI movies or standard Windows BMP or TIFF images.

Connectix's Color QuickCam (about $225) can take still pictures in millions of colors at 640×480 pixel size. The fast, adjustable-focus lens provides sharp images from less than an inch to infinity, and is optimized for indoor lighting.

The digital scanner was the first device that was able to take photographs, pages pulled from magazines, etc., which were in a paper format, and transform the image to a computer file. Most scanners come prepackaged with imaging software. For example, when I bought my Microtek ScanMaker II several years ago, it came with Aldus (now Adobe) PhotoStyler.

While you can scan directly from the utility provided by the scanner manufacturer, it is far easier to scan directly from the image processing program. While getting the scanner to work with your own image processing program will take a bit of doing (follow the scanner's directions), the end result will be worth the time and effort.

Figure 4-26 shows the dialog the developer sees when he or she selects Scan from PhotoStyler's File menu. The dialog you see here is the same one you'd see if you had run the scanner utility outside of the image processing program. Because the dialog also can be run from within the image program, the image is made available instantly to that program for further processing. Notice that the scan mode is set to color. Color images obviously take up more space than either black and white or grayscale; if you don't need color, use one of the other options.

My Microtek scanner lets me scan up to a resolution of 1200 dots per inch (dpi). While this might be necessary for graphic design using print media, the average computer monitor displays images between 72 and 96 pixels per inch. If you look at the dimensions box in the dialog, you'll see that this image, if scanned as-is, will consume a precious 391,655K. That's 'way too large for the Internet. Downgrading the resolution to 72 dpi reduces disk space consumption to 1409K, still over a megabyte. Of course, this is still too big. But if you take a look at what we're scanning, you'll see that we don't need all the white space and text surrounding the photograph. Using a cropping tool to eliminate this unnecessary clutter pulls me down to 829K, still too big.

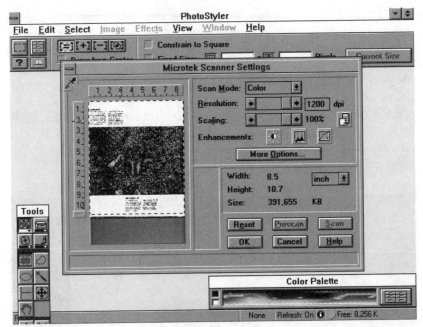

4-26 *Using a scanner to scan an image into a paint program for use on the Web.*

The next step is to consider the dimensions, which right now are a width of 8.4 inches and a height of 6.4 inches.

When designing an image, consider how big it needs to be. By sliding the Scaling bar down to 50 percent, I've now reduced my space requirement to 207K. At this point, I might make the decision to scan and then use the facilities of the image processing program itself to reduce the size to a more manageable and Internet-friendly 50K or below.

Using your image processing program to alter images

Most image processing programs provide a plethora of capabilities. For example, not only does PhotoStyler let me save images in various formats such as GIF and JPEG, it also gives me a bunch of tools to soften, blur, rotate, flip, and otherwise manipulate the image itself.

Since you now have an unsaved image sitting in memory, it's wise to save it before something nasty happens and you lose all the work you did. It's usually best to save in the native format of the acquiring program, if there is one. For example, the ever-popular Photoshop's native file format is PSD. If there is no native format, then try to save in a JPEG format to preserve all the colors.

The goal now is to preserve the integrity of the image while making sure that the file size is small enough to fit on the Web. During the scan process, I mentioned that you crop the image by *scaling* it down to a smaller percentage. *Cropping* is a graphics design term that means to define a portion of the image and then cut out the rest. All image processing programs have a cropping tool. Keep trying it to see the effect of cropping in terms of size and the way it looks. Look at Fig. 4-27. The larger image is the original. It hogs up 732K. The smaller one, which is superimposed on top of the larger one, has the same effect but takes only 376K.

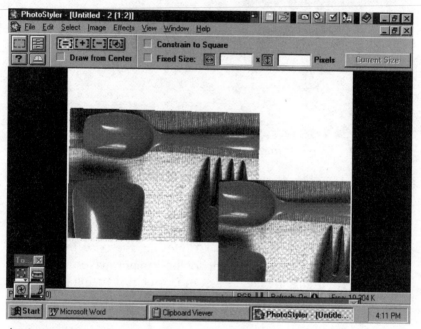

4-27 *Working with an image to reduce file size.*

While cropping might not be a perfect way to reduce the image size, it is a useful tool to eliminate those pieces of the photo you're not interested in displaying.

Because image enhancement is a "trial and error" operation for most of us, be sure you become familiar with the Undo, Revert, Reload, etc., options that allow you to back up a step or more. In order words, don't save until you like the effect.

Keep in mind that the largest image that can be displayed on the smaller, lower-resolution computer displays is an image around 640 pixels wide by 480 pixels deep. If you're going to put the image on the Web, you should strive to keep the final size under 420 pixels wide to allow for browser borders, and for the fact that many users don't run their browsers full-screen. This will ensure that the viewer will not have to use the scroll bars to see all the picture.

Consider 240x250 pixels to be half a screen wide. Thumbnail pictures are usually 75x150 pixels wide. Using the Resize, Image Size, Resample facility of your program, enter just the critical dimension (width or height). The other dimension will be calculated automatically if you make sure that the "Proportional Constraint," Preserve aspect ratio," or similarly named box is checked. This avoids *skewing* the image.

The current "standard" computer color capability (SVGA) is 256 colors. VGA screens only display 16 colors. Representing 16 million colors requires considerable file space. One way to minimize file size is to reduce the number of colors.

For scans done in 256 colors, an Indexed Color mode image was created, and already is reduced to a 256-color table. If you want to reduce this number further, you may need to first convert the image to a 16-million-color format (RGB, for instance).

All image processing programs are slightly different, so you'll have to get familiar with yours to be able to tweak image colors. You can reduce the number of colors in Photoshop by changing from RGB mode to Index Color mode. This brings up the "Index Color" screen, which allows specification of the number of colors or the number of bits per pixel. (You're forced to do this if you wish to do Save As into the GIF format.) Getting the right balance between size and the number of colors displayed is a very difficult problem that will require some effort on your part. This is why traditional graphic designers do not necessarily have the wherewithal to design web graphics. Just like you, they have to learn to adjust images to the Web.

Our objective is to remove as many bits per pixel as possible, without ruining visual quality.

Figure 4-28 shows the PhotoStyler dialog that lets you "convert" the image to an indexed image. Notice that indexed 16-color is 4-bit, while indexed 256-color is 8-bit. The differences between the two are large.

Saving this same image as 256-color (8-bit), with Palette equal to Adaptive and Dither equal to Diffusion, displays the nice, clear image shown in Fig. 4-29. The problem is that this image takes up 244K.

Because the images in this book are obviously not in color, you won't be able to see the degradation in evident in Fig. 4-30. Here we converted the original image to indexed 16-color (4-bit). The file is smaller, but the image looks pretty bad.

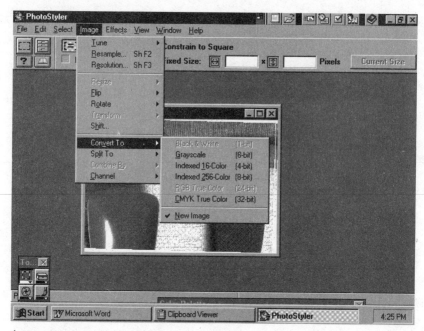

4-28 *Converting a file to a file format for file reduction purposes.*

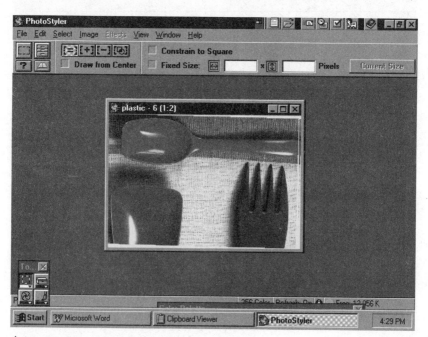

4-29 *Saving to 256 colors, 8 bits.*

One of the reasons why professional Web graphics designers prefer to use custom-designed graphics is that it's far easier to control the color vs. size problem when creating it from scratch, than to try to deal with it after the fact, as is the case with a photograph.

GIF files store colors in an 256-color indexed color map. This means that you can store only a maximum of 256 colors. If you're scanning at 16.7 million colors, something's got to go. JPEG, on the other hand, can represent any number of RGB colors, with size being determined by compression mode rather than number of colors.

One of the reasons why Photoshop is so popular is that it gives you great control over the number of colors in the image. When you save a file in Indexed Color mode in Photoshop, a dialog box appears that gives you multiple resolution choices, from 3 bits per pixel up to 8 bits per pixel. The higher the bits-per-pixel, the better the quality (i.e., colors) of the image, but also the greater the disk space requirement. For example, at 3 bits per pixel only 8 colors are used. At 5 bits per pixel, 32 colors are used, and at 8 bits per pixel, a full 256 colors are used.

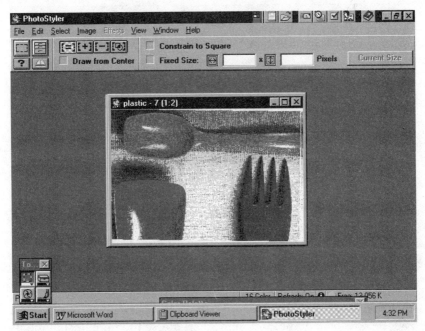

4-30 *Converting to 16 colors, 4 bits.*

Experiment with these choices and see how far down you can go in the bits-to-pixel ratio before you start losing the quality of the image.

Once you have the image saved it's time to test it using your browser. I usually test it right on my PC first, just to get an idea of what it will look like. But this method does not give me any indication of how long it will take a typical user to download the image across the Web into the browser.

My next step is to upload it to our server and then test it out using a variety of browsers, such as Mosaic, Netscape, and Internet Explorer. There are differences, believe it or not, depending upon the browser being used.

Color allocation

If you have more than one image on your page, you might find that the colors don't look quite right. Remember the 256-color maximum? On some systems that's the maximum for the total of all images displayed on a page. So if you have four images and each of those uses 256 colors, you really have a total of 1024 colors—well over the limit.

Tip

Get the ClickArt catalog:

http://www.clickart.com

Photodisc

http://www.photodisc.com

The Stock Solution

http://www.xmission.com:80/~tssphoto

The result will be washed-out or even wrong colors. What's even worse is that this bad effect is not even consistent or predictable.

Color allocation is the province of the graphic designer, but you can use the tools we've been discussing in this section to correct the problem. What we need to do is have the sum of all images on your wayward page use a single color map.

This isn't as strange as it sounds. When you're designing your living room, you probably try to keep the color scheme consistent, don't you? Professional graphics designers often use the same technique in design. If you're not a professional designer, then you'll have to learn to do the same thing. The way to do this is as follows (using Photoshop as our tool of choice):

   1 –Create a very large document, copying all the images on
      your page to this one document.

2 Convert this document to indexed color using a maximum of 256 colors.
3 Select Color Table from the Mode menu. You will now see the color map for the large document.
4 Save that color table.
5 Open each of the individual images (the ones you used to create the one large image) and convert the image to indexed color.
6 Select Color Table from the Mode menu.
7 Load the color table you saved in step 4.
8 Save each of these images using this color table.

All of your images now use one color scheme, and your palette conflict problem should be eliminated.

HTML, graphics, what's next? It's time to learn a bit about the server side of being an Internet consultant.

5

Web server development

There are several ways of approaching the server aspect of Internet consulting. If you are a professional developer, then this task should not be too different from other server-based projects you have tackled in the past. If you're new to the business, you just might want to postpone getting involved in these projects—or at least talk your client into having his server hosted by the ISP. These options, as well as others, will be discussed in this chapter.

Tip

Want to provide concept searches rather than just keywords searches? Try:

http://wizard.inso.com

or how about a distributed search technology using "hives"?

http://www.botbot.com

We'll also discuss the software that needs to be, or can be, installed on the Internet server. It runs the gamut from Web server software to chat, and everything in between. The Internet, as shown in Fig. 5-1, is a loose combination of thousands of servers located on every part of planet Earth. From your Internet-ready PC, you can travel to South Africa, Asia, Europe—even the Arctic Circle.

The device you use to access the Internet is referred to as a *client*. This is a PC, Mac, or other computer (and soon TV!) that has one of several Internet browser packages and a modem. It doesn't really matter how powerful your computer is, but it does matter how powerful your modem is. Most PCs today are running at least 14.4 kbps modems (that is, every second 14,400 or more bits of information are transferred between the modem and some computer). The 28.8 kbps "V.34" modem rapidly is becoming the standard, with a few models running at 33.6 kbps starting to appear.

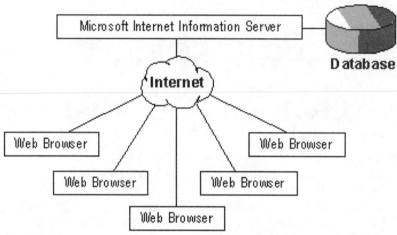

5-1 *The Microsoft Internet Information Server.*

> ### Tip
>
> Redwood City, Calif.-based Zona Research has predicted that the installed intranet base will bypass the Internet base this year. The company predicts that by the end of 1998, revenue generated by the Intranet market will be almost four times that of the Internet: $8 billion versus $2 billion. Interestingly, of the companies that participated in Zona's study, a whopping 85 percent said their networked desktops had Web access. Luckily for consultants (and everyone else), Intranet solutions are much the same as Internet solutions—just inside the firewall. Almost all of the vendors who sell Internet software sell Intranet software too. Aside from Netscape and Microsoft, you might be interested in:
>
> *http://www.netmanage.com*
> *http://www.sun.com*
>
> A good white paper on corporate intranets is located at:
>
> *http://www.process.com/intranets/wp2.htp*

The client does not store information accessed by others over the Internet. Instead, the Internet *server* is the place where the information is stored. Storing and forwarding large quantities of data requires powerful software, as well as powerful telecommunications facilities. If we were to summarize the general attributes of an Internet server, the list would look something like this:

Tip

Sell customers on these intranet features:

- Rapid prototyping (can be measured in hours or days).
- Scalability (start small, build as needs and requirements allow).
- Ease of navigation (internal home page provides links to information).
- Accessible via most computing platforms.
- Capable of integrating distributed computing strategy (localized web servers residing closer to the content author).
- Capable of being tied in to legacy information sources (databases, existing word processing documents, groupware databases).
- Extensible to a variety of media types (audio, video, interactive applications).

- Powerful and fast CPU (central processing unit) with large amounts of memory and disk space
- Very fast telecommunications hookup
- Some sort of security
- Some sort of backup

Sounds simple, doesn't it? But what we're talking about here is no less an effort than installing any new server—except that this server also will be accessed by thousands, maybe millions, of folks outside of the company. This task, then, requires considerable planning.

Case histories of those who have gone before

One of the better ways to introduce you to the problems and pitfalls of Internet server development is through the use of case histories.

In planning an Internet site for your client, you may discover that you will not only have to install a Web server, but also a wide variety of other services. If you read through the glossary at the end of this book, you'll find that organizations also are installing gopher servers, ftp servers, mail servers, mailing lists servers, and Usenet servers. Your client might want all or just some of these services.

The folks in this section have tasted the thrill of victory and the agony of defeat in providing a wide variety of Internet services. Read it carefully, because when you're done with your own project, you'll be a case history, too.

West Virginia University gets connected

The Computing Services department at West Virginia University, located in Morgantown, 70 miles south of Pittsburgh, is just like any other IS department. It's got computers and it's got users. "Servicing over 22,000 students and 5000 employees requires a mixed bag of computers," according to Lew McDaniel, Director of Computing Services.

Tip

Things to do on an intranet:
- Competitive sales information
- Human resources/employee benefits statements
- Technical support/help-desk applications
- Financial activities
- Company newsletters
- Project management
- Documentation

McDaniel's job is to keep West Virginia University's IBM mainframes, DEC VAXen, PCs, and various LANs running smoothly. McDaniel's latest challenge is to connect his site to the Internet.

But once you connect your site to the Internet, a whole set of new issues raises itself. One of these is security. There is no shortage of news articles about people "hacking" their way into an organization's computers. The Internet does indeed provide a formidable access route. Here, conventional mainframe-oriented IS shops actually may have an advantage over the more traditional, workstation-based Internet shops.

"We rely on the normal security of the mainframe. We are using American Management Systems 'Top Secret' to secure our location. By forcing Internet users through their security firewall, the University of West Virginia ensures that its network and data are protected from intruders." (In Internet terminology, a *firewall* is a hardware/software security solution, typically found at the interface between the local system and the Net.)

Tip

The Web Security FAQ is located at:

http://www.genome.wi.mit.edu/WWW/faqs/www-security-faq.html

There's also a mailing list that discusses current security issues. Send the message "subscribe" in the body of your message. *www-security-request@ns2.rutgers.edu*

Aside from the security issue, the other issue that McDaniel is concerned about is access to the Internet itself. The Internet was created, and continues to grow, in a decentralized fashion. In other words, there is no single Internet manager. Therefore, users surfing the Net get the sense that information is sometimes here today and gone tomorrow. At times, sites that have provided an information source pull the plug, leaving users with error messages indicating an unavailable location.

"The problem that we're running into right now is that the pipeline between me and the information source is not controlled by me. It can break. Or intermediate points can decide to do maintenance at 10 A.M., which happens to be when my people want to use it," explains McDaniel. Another difficulty that McDaniel, as well as other users, have encountered is the lack of uniformity from one organization to another. If you're accessing a thousand sites, you have to understand the nuances of a thousand computer systems.

Tip

Need some cybertrivia and statistics to impress potential clients? Surf over to *http://www.cyberatlas.com.* Actually, there's some very serious info on this site, so do check it out.

NSA connects to Usenet and ftp

Network Software Associates is a hardware and software research and development lab that supports the federal government. With offices on both the East and West Coasts, this Arlington, Virginia-based company manages a diverse array of computers that includes IBM mainframes, Unix RS/6000s, midrange AS400s, and a plethora of personal computers.

Network Software Associates needed to find a way to communicate with their staff and their customers, as well as find a better way to keep up to date with the proliferation of software updates and fixes that a shop of their caliber requires.

Since Network Software Associates writes much of the software for the government, and the government is not located on-site at NSA's offices, the Internet is a most valuable tool for user-developer communications.

NSA is one of many who also have opted to start their own Usenet newsgroup. On the Internet, unlike services like CompuServe, you don't need anyone's permission to start your own discussion group. But it does require some special intelligence and some computer resources.

In the tradition of the Internet, the software to manage the mailing list is provided free of charge from the Net itself. "Listserv" software can be downloaded via ftp in the */pub/listserv* directory on *cs.bu.edu.*

Majordomo, another mailing list administrative program, can be obtained via ftp in the */pub* directory at *ftp://Ftp.GreatCircle.com.* Once you've created your group, you can announce it to the world by sending a message containing the list's description to *interest-groups-request@sri.com* and to *new-list@vmi.nodak.edu.*

Tip

Need to provide Web access to customers without Internet access? Try WebPhonic's Web-On-Call Voice Browser, which makes Web pages available to anyone with a touch-tone phone. You need $1000 per telephone line, a Web server and a voice modem: *http://www.netphonic.com*

NSA also has an ftp server that provides tech support to its customers. Government users merely use the Internet to gain access to NSA's ftp server, and download files and fixes. IS managers searching for a better way to provide upgrade information to PC-based customers might want to consider NSA's approach as a model of efficient customer support.

But according to Stan King, Director of R&D, connecting to the Internet is not as straightforward as it would be if one were dealing with a centralized organization, complete with tech support personnel. When connecting to the Internet, you are essentially on your own.

"The way we were able to connect our ftp server to the Internet was to hire someone with Internet experience," says King. The Internet, according to King, is pretty much ad hoc. "We needed this person to understand the policies and procedures and the various standards." King claims that the task of connecting to the Net was difficult and time-consuming, more so because they have a high-speed

(65 kbps) digital link line. "We also made one minor mistake in starting out small. We had our server upload mail on an hourly basis. We outgrew that virtually overnight and had to go through that enormous process again."

That this was so difficult a task is the result of the Internet's reliance on physical numerical addresses, called *IP addresses.* IP or Internet Protocol is the network layer for the TCP/IP protocol suite. It is a connectionless, best-effort packet switching protocol. For example, a server that we know logically as *ns.uu.net* actually has an IP address of 137.39.1.3. Since getting a new line also requires getting a new address, there is a big conversion effort that must be undertaken to change the mapping between logical and physical addresses.

There is a variety of connection options. Factors besides costs may be used to select the appropriate option or series of options. These factors include size and projected use (traffic) of the connection, nature of the use, and purpose of the enterprise driving the effort.

There are three basic categories of IP service connection available at this time. All three support essentially the same set of functions. They support a variety of line speeds (which affects total capacity of the connection), and will run on a variety of hardware platforms. Performance depends on the line speed, the hardware and software used, and the use.

The three basic connection categories are:

- dedicated connection
- dial-up connection
- dial-up access to a connection service

A *dedicated connection* requires a dedicated, point-to-point telecommunications circuit and an IP router (a dedicated networking device) linking the organization to the Internet. Line speeds range from 9.6 kbps to 45 mbps, with the most common connection speeds being 56 kbps and 1.54 mbps. A dedicated Internet connection most commonly connects a campus-wide network with several hosts and workstations.

A *dial-up connection* requires a workstation, which may or may not be dedicated to networking, with appropriate networking software and an attached modem. It uses a regular phone line. When a network connection is needed, the workstation is used to establish a connection over the modem and phone line. At the end of use, the connection is broken. Line speeds range from 9.6 to 56 kbps, with lower speeds being most common. A dialup connection can be used to connect a single workstation or a LAN. If it is used to connect a LAN, however, the workstation must provide some packet-routing functionality. This latter role is increasingly played by a device called a *dial-up router.*

However powerful the computer on your desktop may be, it becomes a dumb terminal on the Internet unless you provide a high-speed connection. There are two types of high-speed IP connections: SLIP (Serial Line IP) and PPP (Point-to-Point Protocol). Both access methods require not only more physical resources, but more financial resources as well.

An organization contemplating a connection to the Internet should be careful to consider not only the physical connection and startup costs, but also the costs of supporting the resulting service infrastructure. This infrastructure includes the development and continued support of a network. In some organizations, this network may only support data. At many other organizations, as the applications and requirements of information technologies supported by internetworking technologies expand, network development must evolve to consider data, voice, and video.

The Internet provides access to a wide variety of resources and a broad set of functions and services that may or may not have been available locally. Support staff need education and training to support, and in turn train, the faculty, other staff, and students in the use of the new technology and new resources that are made available.

This training may mean strategic reorientation and deployment of networking information services. The costs of such added-value services should be planned for in advance. Increased use of the Internet will make additional demands on existing network technical staff. Areas of the organization not currently participating in data network services will want to participate. While not all of these services can be quantified exactly in terms of costs, they must be anticipated and incorporated into Internet planning.

Every organization connecting to the network must have a unique identifier. This identifier is known as the *IP network address*. In addition to a numerical identifier, most organizations also get what is known as a *domain name* (i.e., *whitehouse.gov*). It is through the numerical address and the domain name that the organization's hosts will become known throughout the Internet.

An organization must register with the authority that assigns IP addresses and domain names, but more on that later. The domain name is picked by the organization. It is simply a character string that maps to the numerical IP address. Names are easier for humans to remember than unique sets of numbers.

What King found is that, on the whole, access to the Internet is far less expensive than access to information through other, commercial services such as CompuServe. Although CompuServe charges a flat fee somewhere around $9 per month, the extra charges incurred by "extended services" can easily run to $40 or more.

Signing up for the Internet through an Internet Service Provider should only incur a flat fee, though new service providers are springing up daily and taking advantage of naïve users by charging a per-minute cost.

Of course, setting up your own server negates having to send out a very large check to an ISP (though you'll probably still have to pay a provider for the connection point to the Internet itself). But the cost of hardware, software, and human resources to support the connection can be expensive, as shown in the example below:

Unix workstation (server)	$5000~$10,000 or more
Phone line installation for T-1 line	$2500
Routers	$5000–$6000
Programmer	$60,000 annually

Some Internet experts claim that you can get a server up and running for as little as $14,000 in setup costs and $1000 per month in operating costs.

Beth Israel connects its production system to the outside world

Beth Israel Hospital, which is affiliated with Cambridge-based Harvard University, has all the same problems in supporting its computer installation as any other enterprise organization.

With two data centers running ES9000s, and a host of application programs written in COBOL, PL/I, and CICS, Beth Israel's technical support manager, Rocky Grasso, needed a way to manage the rapid pace of change in the software that he supports, while protecting his environment from interlopers.

"I use the Internet to communicate with people both inside and outside of my organization. I subscribe to various mailing lists, such as ones on CICS and TCP/IP," explains Grasso.

Grasso's method of accessing the Internet is through a protocol called TN3270. Essentially, this permits Grasso and his staff to emulate an IBM 3270 terminal to access IBM or other vendor information. But instead of a direct tie, or a telephone hookup into the vendor, Grasso uses the Internet as his network. "I use TN3270 instead of the Internet's Telnet. It enables me to emulate a 3270 display by executing it under Windows on my PC," he says. (TN3270 is available from a variety of sources. SPRY, located in Seattle, Wash., sells a version called Air tn3270. SPRY can be reached at (800) 777-9638, or on the Net at *info@spry.com/www.spry.com.*)

Beth Israel is representative of organizations who are utilizing the Internet for messaging and research without necessarily hooking up a server. However, according to Grasso, even this level of Internet activity requires an organization to formulate a security plan. Explains Grasso, "When we first got onto the Internet, we noticed that from time to time people would try to get into our system." Grasso's reference is to the propensity of cyber-burglars to program their computers to select IP addresses at random, in an attempt to break into an organization's (any organization's) computers.

Grasso found that many of these attempts were being made by students in such faraway places as Scotland and Austria. If one remembers that the Internet originated as a research- and academic-oriented network, then one can understand why a large number of students are on the network in the first place. If even only a few of these students have cracking on their mind, then the security-conscious organization moving onto the Internet should plan accordingly. Anyone who thinks that the Internet poses minimal security risk to e-mail users is only fooling himself, according to Grasso. He reminds us that the Internet was designed for maximum flexibility and interoperability. Hence the Internet evolved into a decentralized system spread out across thousands of computers worldwide. And each might, or might not, have its own security procedures. As a result, security breaches should be expected.

Most of us can remember the case of Cornell University graduate student Robert Morris, Jr., who programmed an Internet worm that single-handedly brought down 6000 machines. In November, 1991, the United States General Accounting Office reported that computer crackers from the Netherlands broke into military computers and, more recently, a group of students known as The Posse has been taking down systems just for the thrill of it. But, according to officials, hacking/cracking students are being quickly replaced by industrial spies.

Organizations that connect their computer system to the Internet put themselves at risk in two ways. E-mail may be intercepted and read, and the business records stored on their computer system may be viewed, altered, or even destroyed.

Internet security is a hot topic. "At this past IBM SHARE meeting, there were quite a few sessions about Internet security and the building of firewalls," according to Grasso.

The hardware and software that sits between the computer operation and the Internet is colloquially known as a *firewall.* Its specific mission is to examine Internet traffic and allow only approved data to pass through.

One type of firewall is a software-driven filter in the organization's network connection. It is possible to program a packet router to discard any packets requesting information or services that may pose a security threat.

A second approach to building a firewall is to use computers as routers and gateways. For example, Digital Equipment Corporation's SEAL product uses a physical workstation to monitor a network's connection to the outside world. In this way, there is no direct connection between the internal network and the Internet, allowing all network traffic to be monitored before it is passed inside.

Beth Israel has created a software and procedural firewall solution to the Internet security problem. Rocky Grasso provided a copy of a memo that describes the procedures Beth Israel put into place.

Network Services has been asked to provide protection to sensitive corporate data such as personnel information, payroll, and patient account information that reside on the network. In order to limit the potential for attacks from our exposure to the Internet, we are implementing a security system that will screen all inbound Internet traffic. This system is also referred to as a "bastion host" or firewall.

1 All outbound connections from BI (Beth Israel) will still be permitted without restriction (e-mail, ftp, telnet, etc.).

2 To maintain uniformity in username conventions, we will be performing all aliasing for BI on the bastion host machine.

3 Inbound mail will be permitted. However, as part of securing hosts internal to BI, we will strip all host names out of the address before they are sent out of BI. Doing this will require changes to people's sendmail.cf file, as well as a few changes to some other system files. Network Services will be creating a generic sendmail.cf file that will work with the bastion host. This will not prevent mail from arriving into the institution addressed with a host name, but over time we will encourage people to use the username@bih.harvard.edu *standard.*

4 We will permit in-bound telnet, ftp, and netnews. These services will be running on a bastion host and will act as a point of authentication for any inbound traffic. For any other inbound traffic, please contact Network Services so that we can determine if it can be added as a service on the bastion host. Please note that some services will not be offered, such as Mosaic, until software has been written for them to be implemented in a secure manner.

5 *If an individual has the need to transfer files into BInet, we will provide a host with one secure but unrestricted account. That machine will be the bastion host and will have an account where you can place files for immediate retrieval. We wish to emphasize that this will be only a temporary place for files, and therefore a program will delete all files each evening at midnight.*

6 *We will not permit disk mounts, fingering (i.e., an Internet program that displays information about a particular user, or all users, logged on the local system or on a remote system. It typically shows full name, last login time, idle time, terminal line, and terminal location. It may also display plan and project files left by the user), file transfer or remote logins from outside of BI to any BInet-connected host.*

Organizations requiring an extremely stringent amount of security, says Grasso, should use encryption, both in e-mail and in data stored on disk. Most commercial messaging products, such as Lotus cc:Mail, incorporate encryption. Unfortunately, there is nothing so exotic built into the Internet itself. That may change in the future, however. Secure HTTP, discussed later in this chapter, is designed to bring data encryption, authentication, and digital signature technologies to the Internet.

The business of running a server

I think that there is no better example of what it takes to run a server than the ISP. Internet Service Providers are in the business of running Internet installations. Not only do most of the larger ones run their own, off which many of us hang our Internet clients, they also are in the business of hosting your web server—at their site.

The market for Internet access services is extremely competitive. There are no substantial barriers to entry, and it is expected that competition will intensify in the future. The ability to compete successfully depends on a number of factors: market presence, capacity, reliability and security of network infrastructure, ease of access to and navigation of the Internet, pricing policies of competitors and suppliers, introduction of new products and services, ability to support standards, and industry general economic trends.

There are three groups of competitors:

- Internet Access Providers such as Bolt, Beranek & Newman Inc. (BBN), NETCOM, and PSI
- Telecommunications companies such as AT&T and MCI
- Online service providers such as America Online and CompuServe

Although most of the established online services and telecom companies currently offer only limited Internet access, many have announced plans to offer expanded Internet capabilities. Most long-term ISPs believe that all of the major online service and telecom companies will compete fully in the Internet access market. Most also believe that new competitors will enter the market, including large computer hardware, software, media, and telecom companies. This will result in even greater competition for the current market leaders.

Many of the companies, including AOL, BBN, and PSI, have obtained or expanded their Internet access products or services as a result of acquisitions. This trend will continue and ultimately accelerate. As a result of increased competition, Internet companies will encounter significant pricing pressure.

The most significant challenge, and risk, is the dependence upon suppliers—primarily the telecommunications companies. In addition, most Internet companies utilize the same companies from which they purchase routers, switches, and modems (e.g., Cisco, Cascade Communications, and Ascend Communications). There is no assurance that these companies will not enter the arena on their own—to significant competitive advantage.

Internet companies have captured the attention of venture capitalists. Menlo has $800,000 invested in UUNET, and Geocapital has $2.5 million invested in Netcom. Acquisitions have played a major role in shaping the competitive landscape of the market. CompuServe purchased SPRY for $100 million; Microsoft has taken an equity stake in UUNET for $15 million; America Online has acquired GNN for $11 million; and AT&T has taken an equity stake in BBN for $8 million.

The most popular route for raising money remains going public. During the last half of 1995, UUNET raised $66 million, Netcom raised $63 million, PSI raised $45 million, and Netcom raised $14 million.

The Internet companies that have gone public have been experiencing a bull market. Goldman Sachs analyst Michael Parekh likens the Internet to the investment opportunity represented by the personal computer industry in the early 1980s. One of the larger and most reliable of all ISPs is UUNET. The company, based in Fairfax, Va., was acquired recently by MFS, a large telecommunications concern.

UUNET was formed in 1987 to provide dedicated communication services for its customers. In January, 1990, UUNET Technologies launched AlterNet, the first commercial TCP/IP network. UUNET's customer base has grown to over 4000 commercial and professional accounts.

UUNET is a founding member of the Commercial Internet Exchange (CIX), the Metropolitan Area Ethernet and the SMDS Washington Area Bypass. UUNET's founder, Rick Adams, created and developed the popular Serial Line Internet Protocol (SLIP) and engineered its first implementation. UUNET's backbone planning group has more than 75 years of aggregate experience, and has staff members whose experience with the Internet predates the introduction of TCP/IP.

The UUNET network

UUNET's core backbone (AlterNet) consists of redundant, fully meshed 45 mbps connections for routing efficiency and reliability. The underlying physical network is a series of bidirectional 45 mbps links, forming a circle around the country. The loss of a single 45 mbps link causes traffic to be rerouted, resulting in no customer-visible outage. UUNET hubs are connected to the backbone primarily by 10 mbps links and, in some cases, multiple T-1 lines. Since UUNET has operated its own backbone since the beginning of the commercial service, traffic on AlterNet is not subject to usage restrictions imposed by some other providers.

By the end of 1996, UUNET's network infrastructure will allow local access to users in over 200 cities, including 20 international sites.

The company has agreements with WilTel and MFS to provide the company with data communications facilities and capacity and physical space for network equipment. UUNET receives substantial discounts in exchange for minimum usage commitments. UUNET's backbone connects to a wide variety of regional, national, and international networks directly, over private facilities. Notable networks include Advantis, ANS, BARRNet, CERFnet, NEARnet, NETCOM, PSINet, and SprintLink.

UUNET's Network Operations Center is staffed and operational 24 hours per day, 7 days a week. NOC engineers monitor customer and backbone links at all times. Their dedicated connections are checked every 5 minutes by their network monitoring systems. UUNET guarantees that a person at NOC will answer the phone via its 800 number no matter what time the call is placed. The NOC team always consists of at least one senior engineer, in addition to several staff engineers, to guarantee that the level of expertise required is always at hand.

UUNET's switching equipment typically is kept in telephone company switching centers. Support hosts are kept away from backbone links in case of a security breach. UUNET maintains a staff of experienced engineers who plan and secure backbone routers and internal hosts to provide maximum security. Other security options include firewalls and the LanGuardian encryption facility. LanGuardian, developed by UUNET, is a combination of hardware and software that provides encrypted IP network security. Security packages used are Gauntlet and LanGuardian.

Turnkey Web server service includes content development, graphic design, facilities management, T-1 or 10 mbps connectivity, and monitoring user connection times and usage patterns with monthly reports.

UUNET's current network infrastructure includes Cisco 7000 routers and a 45 mbps, ATM-based network backbone. This network infrastructure enables customers to access the Internet through dedicated lines or by placing a local telephone call (dial-up) through a modem to the nearest UUNET point of presence (POP). In response to the increase in the number of customers, UUNET plans to implement a high-performance network that includes a new, higher-capacity network backbone based on frame relay.

A dial-up customer calls into the ISDN/28.8 access router via ISDN or analog modem service provided by their local exchange carrier. The ISDN/28.8 access router replays the data via the customer access switch to the routing engine for further processing. Dedicated customers connect directly to the customer access switch, which relays the data to the routing engine. The routing engine relays the data to the appropriate backbone switch for delivery to the destination. The DS-3 bandwidth manager will be used to connect the DS-03 frame relay circuits from other hubs to the local backbone switch.

Tip

Frame relay describes an interface standard. As such, it is a technology that has been optimized for the transport of protocol-oriented data in discrete units of information (generic packets). Its ability to statistically multiplex provides the same bandwidth-sharing and efficiency as X.25.

Transport technology is frame relay, the transport providers being Wiltel and MFS (in a purely customer relationship). UUNET's backbone speed is T-3 with full routing. Connection equipment is Cisco 2501 Router and Kentrox CSU/DSU, which are configured before shipment. Other equipment includes U.S. Robotics and Telebit modems, Ascend dial-up routers, and Ascend MAX ISDN adapters.

Major customers include AT&T, Microsoft, MCI, SkyTel, Southwestern Bell, America Online, CompuServe, Dow Jones, General Electric Information Services, Reuters, American Express, Morgan Stanley, Nomura Securities, Microsoft, Lockheed, Boston Edison, Chicago Tribune, Knight-Ridder, New York Times, Digital Equipment, IBM, Intel,

Citicorp, Swiss Bank, John Wiley & Sons, Time, Paramount, the U.S. Federal Reserve, the United Nations, DHL, and Kaiser Permanente.

Where should your client host its Web server?

After reading the particulars of UUNET, by now you realize that hosting and running any kind of server that can be accessed reliably and securely by potentially millions of users is not as easy as you might have thought. And unless you have a lot of financial backing to be able to duplicate at least part of what UUNET has accomplished, get those thoughts of cashing in on the ISP market out of your head right now—especially since there will be a shakeout in the industry and only the strong will survive.

For the most part, your client will not want to become its own ISP. The information presented above was provided to explain both to your client—and to you—what's involved in this business.

Your client, no matter how big or small it may be, will want to provide some content over the Internet. This will always entail providing server capability. There are several alternatives for hosting content. If the company is small, does not want to spend a lot of money, and does not require any fancy services, then the best bet would be to utilize the services of an ISP. This is where it gets tricky.

UUNET epitomizes the top of the line in terms of service providers. It has many POPs, so you can dial in with a local telephone call. It provides a 24-hours-a-day, 7-days-a-week command center that monitors its equipment. It provides high-speed telecommunications links into its servers. But all of this comes at a price. For example, a 56 kbps hookup is $595–$695 per month, with a $495–795 startup fee. T-1 capability will cost you $995–$3000 per month, with a $3000–$5000 startup fee. The ultimate, High Bandwidth bandwidth will soak you for $1500–$42,000 per month, with a $5000–$9500 startup fee.

Tip

A good place to start looking for your new ISP is:
http://thelist.com/

If your client is the Federal Reserve, these prices may or may not mean much, but if your client is Small Firm, USA, there has to be another option. Options for Internet service include (from least expensive to most expensive) include the following:

- Rent space from a reliable but inexpensive ISP, and display pages for your clients.
- Establish a domain for yourself with an ISP, and then rent space to your clients.
- Place a full-featured server for your client at the ISP's premises.
- Place a full-featured server for the client at the client's premises.

Displaying client pages

In this option, you rent space from an ISP that is reliable but inexpensive, such as The WELL (about $15 per month plus charges for space utilized over a certain amount). You then build pages for your clients under your own ID.

Tip

The WELL offers virtual Web site hosting at low prices. For a $150 setup (which includes domain name registration), you can choose between several low-cost plans ($99/month to $225/month). Small additional fees are charged for RealAudio streams and Chat Server. They have a T-3 line, run on a Sparc, and support CGI scripting, Java, VRML, Shockwave and more. It's a bargain.

This alternative does not provide a separate domain name for each client. Instead, each client is identified by either a subdirectory name or some other creative naming mechanism. For example, some of our really small clients rent space under our ID on The WELL, as shown in Fig. 5-2. Under one of our WELL accounts we are known as *business*, which makes our domain name *www.well.com/user/business*. Rafferty Associates, a commodities firm, can be accessed under our ID as *www.well.com/user/business/rafferty.html*. While this scheme does not have the panache of a separate domain name, it is inexpensive and effective. The majority of users surf over to the site not by keying in the domain name, but by performing a search and hyperlinking from the results page (Fig. 5-3).

From the consultant's perspective, the only computer charge that needs to be passed along to your client is the one for disk space used. The WELL charges $15 a month on its basic plan, which gives you your first 5 hours of time, with additional hours at $2.50 per hour. All WELL clients are entitled to half a megabyte (512K) of disk storage. Excess storage from 512K to 2 megabytes is $5 per month; more than 2 megabytes is $1 per month per megabyte. Prices for transfer (throughput) in excess of 1 gigabyte per month is $0.20 per megabyte. Of course, this does not take into account your particular profit motive. There's nothing to stop you from charging each of your clients some set fee per month for disk usage and access.

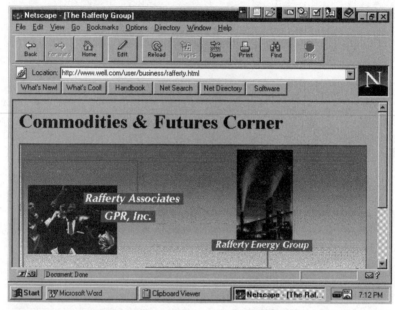

5-2 *Using an ISP's server.*

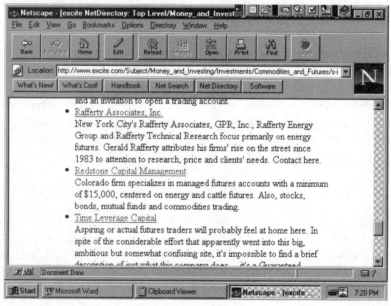

5-3 *You don't need to type the full URL if you use a search engine.*

Subletting your domain

As a consultant, you may decide to go one step further by arranging for an ISP to host a domain for your own firm. You then can rent out space on this to your clients. This is known as a *storefront*. If you're consulting firm is named W.W. Associates, rather than serving up a domain name of *www.ww.com*, try to secure a name that gives the impression that many people are behind the doorway. For example, *http://www.malls-ltd.com* lets you know exactly what it is, as shown in Fig. 5-4. Just like a real mall, retailers can take comfort in the fact that they're bound to get visitors just by virtue of "location, location, location."

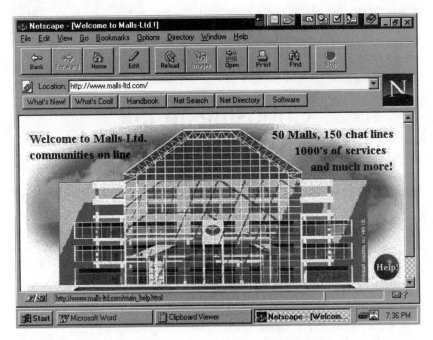

5-4 *Using one of the many storefronts to host a client's page.*

Full-featured server, type 1

Your client's requirements might call for a server with all the bells and whistles. Your client, however, might not have the technical capacity to host it. The solution to this problem might be to locate an ISP to host a server for your client—at the ISP's site. This solution calls for separate hardware and software located in the ISP's network operations center.

Full-featured server, type 2

The most technical and complex of all solutions is to set up the server, and all its attendant hardware and software, at the client's site.

Even if this is the ultimate solution, you still will need to deal with an ISP to link the server physically to the Internet.

> ### Tip
>
> You're going to have to try many domain names before you find one that's not already in use. Once you find an available name, you'll need to register it with InterNIC, which requires the domain name, an IP address (computer address), and a $50 fee. Your ISP will do it for you for free. If you have not chosen an ISP, you can register your domain name through one of the many service bureaus on the Net. You also can register your name directly on line. Each of the following locations provides you with the ability to check whether the name you want is available:
>
> *www.tabnet.com*
> *www.entrepreneur.net*

Choosing an ISP

One of the first things you should do as an Internet consultant is determine the membership of your list of preferred Internet Service Providers. Obviously, UUNET is high on my own list, but it's not the only one. I also use Panix (*www.panix.com*) in New York City, and The WELL (*www.well.com*) in Sausalito, Calif. Both are low-cost alternatives. Both are well-established, reliable ISPs who provide cost-efficient services.

In choosing one or more ISPs, the following should be considered:

- How long they've been in business.
- What their customers think about them.
- Does the ISP provide domain name registration?
- Does the ISP provide file upload and maintenance tools?
- What kind of server-side capabilities does the ISP provide?
- Can the ISP host a separate server for your client at their facilities?

A track record, with some longevity in the business, says a good deal about a provider. More than one fly-by-night operator has disappointed customers and hurt client businesses. Obtain customer references and then e-mail the Webmasters to find out the pros and cons of the ISP. Most ISP home pages provide a list of their customers, so it should be an easy matter to contact a few of them for references.

Regarding domain names, most organizations will want to have their company name or trademark as their domain name. The name *www.microsoft.com* is typical. The *www* (World Wide Web) is a server naming convention, *microsoft* is (obviously) the name of the company, and *com* stands for "commercial." Your client will no doubt ask for your assistance in determining whether its name is available. Domain name registrations are being done at a rate of about 1500 a day and, from what I hear, most of the original names are gone. The Wild West days of domain name registration are gone, too. These were the days when it was done for free and folks could make a land grab for any name. For example, some enterprising fellow made a grab for the *mcdonalds* name, intending to sell it to McDonald's. This sort of ploy inevitably leads to litigation, so try to register a name that can be used legitimately by your client. Most ISPs will register the domain name for free if you use their service.

Easy file uploading and maintenance on your Web server is important. The WELL's server is Unix-based but provides an easy-to-use, menu-based approach, as shown in Fig. 5-5. You may not realize how important this is. There are many ISPs out there who will provide only the most rudimentary of services.

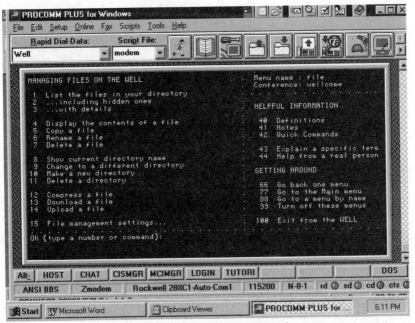

5-5 *Make sure you have some good utilities to manage your Web files.*

For example, one client of mine had already chosen an ISP who provided no Unix shell for upload, etc. Their mode of upload and download was through the use of ftp. While ftp does have facilities for deleting, renaming, etc., you need to have two computer accounts to get this to work: one to ftp the files to, and one to ftp the files from. Needless to say, this was a time-consuming, painful, and expensive task.

Imagemap and mailgate are two server-side CGI scripts your ISP should provide. These are standard fare, and without these capabilities you won't be able to create any worthwhile HTML documents. If you intend to create complex documents, you'll want to find out if your ISP will support your use of CGI scripting. Can you write your own and upload them? Can you use relational or other type of databases? Will the ISP allow robots ("bots"), spiders, and other software that you may need to upload and run from your server?

Tip

Shareware servers:

World Wide Web Consortium maintains a site of free software including server software:

http://www.w3.org/pub/WWW/Status.html

A great jumping-off place to find other server shareware:

http://union.ncsa.uiuc.edu/HyperNews/get/www/httpd.html

Setting up your own server

A World Wide Web server is simply a program that answers requests for documents from Web clients over the Internet. All Web servers use a language, or *protocol*, to communicate with Web clients. This protocol is called the HyperText Transfer Protocol—which is where the *http* in a Web URL comes from. All types of data can be exchanged using this protocol, including HTML, graphics, sound, and video.

Tip

Popular MIMEs:

HTML	.html	.htm		
text	.txt			
PostScript	.ps			
GIF	.gif			
JPEG	.jpg	.jpeg		
audio	.au	.snd		
video	.mpeg	.mpg	.avi	.mov

Data types are identified by the server and preceded by a MIME header (MIME is Multipurpose Internet Mail Extensions). Web clients convert "open" URL commands into HTTP "get" requests. In response to a URL such as

http://www.well.com/user/business/hotspots.html

a browser like Mosaic or Netscape would convert this to a "get *hot spots.html*" command, connect to the Web server running on *www .well.com*, issue the command, and wait for a response. The response can be the requested document or an error message. After the document or error is returned, the connection is closed.

HTTP is a stateless protocol, meaning there is no continuous connection between the client and server, as there is with, for example, telnet. You may be starting to realize that a Web client does a lot of work. It receives only raw HTML or other data and, after determining what type of data it has received, has to perform formatting or launch a helper application such as a sound player. The server only sends the data and goes away. Web clients are responsible for interacting with non-Web servers such as gopher or ftp directly, and they create a virtual HTML document while doing so.

So what else do Web servers do? They can log activity. Servers can record the Internet address, time, and request made for each connection. Servers also can protect certain files from non-authenticated users. Finally, servers can forward requests for data that neither the client nor the server can access, directly to applications called *gateways*. With gateways, the Web can support data types and resources not even conceived of when it was invented. Data is gathered by the Web client, usually using an HTML form, and sent to the server along with the name of a gateway program to be run. Then the gateway reformats the data and sends it to an information server, receives a response, and reformats that response as an HTML document which is delivered to the Web client. Gateway support, logging, and user authentication are important features to look for when selecting a specific Web server. Logging is an absolute necessity, both for usage statistics and security.

While you may download server software for free from several sites on the Internet, the lack of support and documentation inherent in shareware makes this risky business for a consultant.

Fortunately, the popularity of the Internet has spawned some excellent, not particularly expensive, well-documented, and support-intensive server software. Since the installation, configuration, and general overall running of a Web server differs among vendors, what this section will discuss instead are the criteria that should be used in selecting server software. It should come as no surprise that both Microsoft and Netscape are in this market segment in a big way. Given the reliability of these companies, it also should come as no surprise that I'd recommend researching these companies' server solutions.

Microsoft's Internet Information Server (*http://www.microsoft.com/INFOSERV/*) can be downloaded free as of this writing. There's a war between Netscape and Microsoft, with the consumer happily being the benefactor.

Of course there's a catch here. While most Web servers that live on the Internet today are Unix-based, Microsoft naturally will impose its own operating system as a base. The IIS (Internet Information Server) was designed to be run under the Windows NT operating system.

This, of course, gets us squarely into what I like to refer to as the "clash of the titans." There have been arguments for the last couple of years, over whether Unix or Windows NT is the better production-oriented operating system. Even Unix Expo, the most famous of Unix trade shows, has been drawn into the fray, this year renaming their massively attended conference to UNIX Expo Plus—and we all know who the plus is.

This book is not really the venue to discuss the pros and cons of each particular operating system. Unix is a mature, stable operating system that's been in use for a long time. Most professional Webmasters and HTML programmers in the market work in this environment. Windows NT, on the other hand, has matured greatly since its entry into the market. It's now the operating system of choice for production-class client/server systems.

Tip

Yahoo is a great point from which to begin your evaluation of servers:

http://www.yahoo.com/Computers_and_Internet/Internet/World_Wide_Web/HTTP/Servers/

As a consultant, you will no doubt find that some of your clients' shops will be Unix-based and some will be NT-based. My suggestion is to go with the flow, so that you don't have to tackle retraining and other assorted difficult issues. There will be other times, however, when your client will require your assistance in determining both the server and the operating system to be used.

Microsoft's Internet Information Server

According to Microsoft, the IIS graphical setup installs and runs all services (Web, ftp, gopher) on an existing Windows NT Server in less than 10 minutes, so you can create powerful Web servers on existing hardware almost instantly. If this is true, then Microsoft certainly has my vote.

The use of what they refer to as "Virtual Directories" and "Directory Browsing" lets you publish existing files from current servers, turning your file- and printer-sharing network into a corporate Web.

The Internet Service Manager simplifies operational issues by displaying all options in a graphical menu, helping find all IIS servers on your network and allowing management of remote servers over the Internet. It also optimizes site management and analysis by logging information directly to SQL Server for further analysis.

You can use its Performance Monitor to measure all Internet events in real time, and later review for comparison and analysis, to optimize capacity planning. SNMP is included for reporting to a management console.

Internet Information Server comes with free use of the Internet Explorer browser as well as support from Microsoft Product Support Services and authorized support partners.

Windows NT Server's protected memory and micro-kernel architecture provide a highly reliable platform to minimize Web server downtime. Advanced fault tolerance is built into Windows NT Server; information is protected with disk mirroring, drive duplexing, and RAID Level 5.

Web server security is provided via the option of requiring user IDs and passwords to access "privileged" areas of the Web site. Windows NT Server access control lists and user security manager provide a way to share information safely with specific users or groups of users over the Internet, or on your own network. Built-in Secure Sockets Layer support keeps secure communications private by encrypting the conversation between IIS and all browsers that support SSL; these include Microsoft Internet Explorer, Netscape Navigator, and others.

The IIS virtual server capability also provides a way to host multiple sites securely. Multiple Web sites can be hosted on a single server and administered from that server, as shown in Fig. 5-6

The Internet Server Application Program Interface (ISAPI) is designed for custom server extensions like content indexing, log analysis, data input forms, bulletin boards, database access, and third-party applications such as document management, accounting systems, and Web-site creation and management tools.

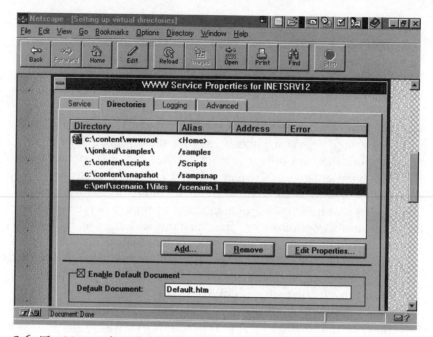

5-6 *The Microsoft IIS has abilities to manage files and multiple Web sites.*

IIS provides easy integration with existing databases. The Internet Database Connector is a simple way to publish information on the Internet. IDC connects to a variety of industry-standard databases such as Microsoft SQL Server (the connection drivers are included with IIS), Microsoft Access, Oracle, Informix, Sybase, and other ODBC-compliant databases.

IIS supports the industry-standard Common Gateway Interface (CGI) and Perl, the most common language for developing simple Web applications such as data input forms and log analysis routines.

Microsoft has a way of becoming a standard in whatever segment of the market it enters. The following list of server features, therefore, can be used as a benchmark which you can use to judge competitive server software:

Tip

Want to find out whose server is linking to your server? Use the *altavista.digital.com* search engine with the following query:

link:http://www.site.com/

- Security
  - Controlling anonymous access
  - Controlling known users and groups
  - Setting document permissions
  - Auditing document access
  - Controlling access by host or network
  - Setting up SSL (Secure Sockets Layer)
- Service management
  - Managing services with Windows NT
  - Managing service views
  - Configuring logging
  - Setting up virtual directories
  - Controlling bandwidth utilization
- Performance monitoring
  - SNMP integration
  - Counter definitions
  - Performance Monitor details

The Netscape line of servers

Netscape's productivity never ceases to amaze me. Just how do they turn out all of that software in such a short period of time? As the author of more than one book on productivity, I just have to find out.

Netscape (*http://home.netscape.com/comprod/server_central/index.html*) provides a series of server solutions, rather than one solution that must be shoehorned into every situation. SuiteSpot is an integrated package of Internet server software. The customer chooses which products actually make up the suite. With SuiteSpot comes Netscape's LiveWire Pro, a complete integrated visual development environment (see Fig. 5-7) that includes support for Javascript, plus the choice of any combination of five Netscape servers:

- Enterprise, for high-performance HTML delivery and management
- Proxy, for Web replication and site access control
- News, for Usenet-compatible, collaborative computing
- Mail, for efficient messaging based on open standards
- Catalog, for Yahoo-style directory services

Because consultants take on more than their share of small businesses, Netscape's FastTrack Server, shown in Fig. 5-8, might be worth considering. It's easy to use, cheap ($295, with 30-day free trial), has tons of functionality, and requires little or no programming. It requires NT or Unix as an operating system.

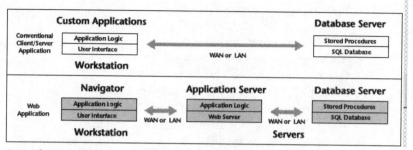

5-7 *The Netscape application development tool suite.*

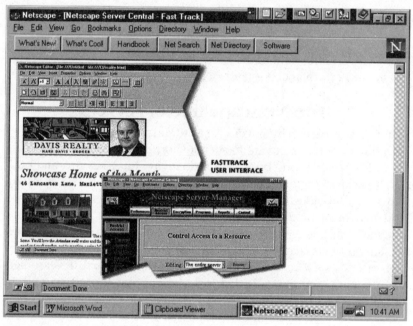

5-8 *The Netscape FastTrack server.*

FastTrack, which includes Netscape's popular Netscape Navigator Gold as a browser, also might be a solution for the Internet consultant looking to set up his or her site. FastTrack features include:

- Setup
  - Automated installation guides the user through a set of questions to install and configure the server quickly for optimum performance.
  - Configuration agent detects network settings and automatically configures the server to work with the network.

- Server Management
  - Users manage the server with Netscape Navigator Gold 2.0 and an easy-to-use user interface that integrates all the server's administration tools.
  - Remote management allows users to manage the server from any desktop on the network.
  - Online help provides context sensitive help using HTML documents accessible from any desktop on the network.
  - Detailed reports, featuring one-click access to site-wide statistics such as total hits, number of unique clients visiting this site, total number of unique hosts, total traffic transferred, and most popular documents served.
- Authoring
  - Includes Netscape Navigator Gold 2.0.
  - FastTrack server allows authors to publish documents onto the server from their desktops with the click of a button.
- Security
  - Security tools are available to restrict access to information stored on the server and to encrypt communications between the server and a Web browser.
  - Access to documents, directories, and applications may be granted or permitted to particular username/password pairs, groups (collections of users), IP addresses, host names, or domain names.
  - Incorporates Secure Sockets Layer 3.0, the latest version of the widely accepted Internet channel security standard.
- Other
  - Supports the Open Internet Framework, a flexible and powerful applications development platform.
  - Supports Java and JavaScript, the leading languages for writing cross-platform Internet applications, offering developers the ability to write code to execute on the server or client.
  - Allows the developer to maintain information about the client across HTTP connections.
  - Netscape Server APIs (NSAPI) allow developers to extend or modify the server behavior by writing high-performance extensions.
  - CGI support allows applications in popular languages such as Java, JavaScript, C, and Perl to communicate with the server.
  - WinCGI support allows Visual Basic applications to communicate with the server.

> **Tip**
>
> See App. C (Annotated resource guide) for a list of Web servers.

> **Tip**
>
> The latest and greatest shareware Web server is Apache. Although we haven't tried it out, I know others who have, and they have nothing but praise.
>
> *http://www.apache.org/*

In the end, you'll have to do what you've done a thousand times before: create a checklist of options you will need, pick several competitive products, and then evaluate the heck out of them. As you can see from the descriptions of the products offered by Microsoft and Netscape, there's a lot of functionality at low, low, low prices. But the "Big Two" do have their competitors—and for all you know, one of these smaller companies might just have the exact feature you need.

As an aside, note that VISA International and Microsoft had just announced (at the time I wrote this page) a new Web transaction protocol called Secure Transaction Technology (STT). Although Secure HTTP (S-HTTP) currently is the favorite, the VISA endorsement throws a crimp in the acceptance of a single, uniform standard. So when you go out there in the search of a perfect secured server, check to see what the current standard is.

Things you'll want your server to do

The reason you've taken the painful step of buying and installing a server for your client (or yourself) is to have better control over the way the information is served up to the user. Those of us who are limited to ISP-maintained servers are limited indeed. Many ISPs do not permit the installation of nonstandard software or even the implementation of CGI scripts. ISPs like The WELL, who charge low rates (and do give fantastic service), sometimes severely restrict the tools that can be used to create the ultimate deliverable product. This is why earlier in this chapter I recommended such ISPs only for clients who have limited requirements and are looking to save money.

So as long as you've taken the steps to implement a server, you should be aware of some of the nice bells and whistles you can add to it. Computer professionals know that anytime you add a new computer to the mix, the opportunities are endless. What you can do is limited only by the available software out there—or your own (or your staff's) programming prowess. In this section, therefore, I will not talk about custom programming. I will, however, talk about some of the great things that are available.

Streaming media

Streaming is fast becoming the technique *de rigeur* of sites that want to be considered cool. The Sci-Fi Channel (*http://www.scifi.com*) and the Discovery Channel (*http://www.discovery.com*) are but two of the sites that have chosen to broadcast live audio and video.

During Net Day '96, in March of 1996, technicians used CUSeeMe software (*http://www.cuseeme.com*) to arrange a real-time "cybercast" of remarks made by President Clinton at a high school in California. Here's how it worked:

Tip

Macromedia's Shockwave for Director enables Web servers to stream entire interactive movies consisting of scripts, audio, video, images, animations, and other multimedia elements.
http://www.macromedia.com

---

1 A video camera recorded the President. The audio and video signals were connected through a standard RCA jack into a capture card on a 75 MHz Pentium PC.
2 CUSeeMe software (which can be used for point-to-point videoconferencing as well as cybercasting) running on the Pentium compressed the digital video and audio signals to a tiny fraction of their original size.
3 Compressed video was then transmitted over an ISDN line to approximately half a dozen Internet nodes outfitted with "reflector" software supplied by the same company that makes CUSeeMe.
4 Users equipped with CUSeeMe client software and at least a 28.8 modem could connect to one of the reflector sites, decompress the data, and see the president in action.

Given the low speed of the modems involved, you can imagine that the final product was less than perfect. Not only was there a slight delay between transmission and reception, there was some slight jerkiness in the image, the latter a result of the viewer seeing only 10–12 frames per second, instead of the 24 or 30 frames per second speeds that are normal in film or television.To see what this looks like without having to have CUSeeMe installed, hyperlink to *http://www.live.net/sandiego/* to get a bird's-eye view of San Diego. A still view is shown in Fig. 5-9.

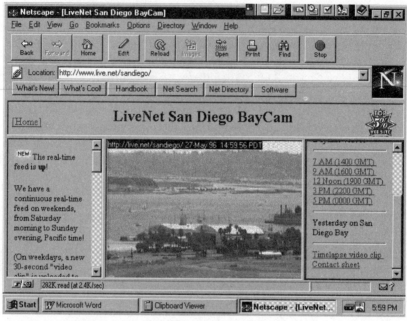

5-9 *CUSeeMe real-time view of San Diego.*

> **Tip**
>
> Need to encode video?
>
> *http://www.vdolive.com*

If streaming is part of your plans, expect to do a lot of work. Although CUSeeMe encodes camera video on-the-fly, video on tape (from a TV performance, for example) has to be encoded manually. This process is quite time-consuming. David Meharg, assistant operations director at KPIX-TV, says that the encode ratio is about 10:1, meaning it takes half an hour to encode a 3-minute video. Moreover, video and sound take up a lot more bandwidth than other types of information. Even using a T-1 line, 5 fps (frames per second) of CUSeeMe is about standard.

> **Tip**
>
> Download the RealAudio player and then try out National Public Radio:
>
> *http://www.realaudio.com/contentp/npr/atc.html*

RealAudio

If video isn't an absolute requirement but you need something to make your client's site more "real," try RealAudio (*http://www. realaudio.com*).

> **Tip**
>
> One second of audio takes up approximately 1000 bytes. At this rate:
>
> 1 minute   = 60K
> 30 minutes = 1.8MB
>
> Fortunately, RealAudio doesn't wait until the whole file is downloaded before beginning playback. Compare this to the download of an 8.9MB WAV file, which takes upwards of 1.5 hours to download and play.

Since the product won a spate of awards in early 1996, over 4 million users have hyperlinked to the RealAudio site to download the free RealAudio player. To access a site hosting RealAudio, all a user need do is click on the appropriate hyperlink; because he or she presumably has already downloaded the RealAudio player, the controller appears to control the playback (Fig. 5-10).

RealAudio Server 2.0 (about $495) makes your server an audio server. It provides seamless integration of live and on-demand audio into your Web site or company network. It delivers audio to your audience in real time, without download delays. HotWired, C I Net Online, and ESPNET SportsZone use RealAudio extensively to attract audiences.

It's not particularly difficult to incorporate audio into your Web application. The RealAudio Playback Engine API provides direct access to RealAudio Player functions, so that commercial Web authoring tools, productivity applications, and in-house custom applications can manage RealAudio streams.

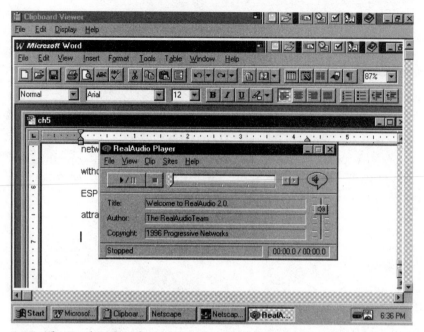

5-10 *The RealAudio player. Users must add this extension to their browsers.*

Tip

Want to install a shareware message forum on your server? Get NetForum for Unix from:

http://www.biostat.wisc.edu/nf_home

Agora Web for Windows:

http://www.ontrac.yorku.ca/agora

The Encoder API allows RealAudio to be used as a delivery system for a wide variety of audio compression algorithms. New algorithms are easily adapted to RealAudio as they become available. SoundEdit 16 from Macromedia (*www.macromedia.com*) is one of the earliest applications of the RealAudio Encoder API.

Tip

Download the ichat plugin:

http://www.ichat.com/ichat2/download.html

Chat on the Web

Chat is text-based electronic communication. Individuals and groups of users talk (type) to each other in virtual spaces (chat rooms) on the Internet. Users run programs (clients) on their computers that let them connect to server software on network computers.

Tip

Start your chat research here:

http://www.yahoo.com/Computers_and_Internet/Internet/Chatting/Products/

The importance of chat lies in its ability to bring large groups of people together in an engaging way that makes it easy to communicate. Many use chat technology to connect worldwide for less than the cost of a local phone call. Individuals can chat one-on-one or with groups of users. The latter is comparable to a conference call, but without the confusion about who is speaking.

On the Internet, the two most popular forms of chat are text-only and are not easily accessible to a novice. These are MUDs (Multi-User Dungeons) and IRC (Internet Relay Chat). While MUDs often have game components in addition to chat, IRC is a chat-only system. The main IRC network often has over 10,000 users online at any given time.

Until recently, there were very few programs for PCs that allowed easy access to IRC and MUD sites. Most users had to log in to Unix accounts and run Unix clients. And the Web—though a powerful solution for information delivery to a wide variety of client platforms—did not have a mechanism for real-time chat.

Tip

Microsoft intends to integrate NetMeeting into Windows. For now, you can download this data-conferencing software for free from the company's Web site:

http://www.microsoft.com/ie/conf

The product ichat (*www.ichat.com*) provides a much easier access channel to existing Internet chat resources, and provides tools for creating robust and professional chat servers that are integrated with the World Wide Web. It is a plug-in for Netscape Navigator 2.0 that permits users to communicate in real time over the Web without learning new applications. With ichat installed, Web pages become chat rooms and Web browsers become chat clients.

When users visit a chat-enabled Web page, the plug-in opens a frame in the lower part of the browser window. Within that frame, ichat displays a real-time, ongoing chat session among all the visitors on that Web page. Users can enter the conversation and communicate with one other simply by typing, as shown in Fig. 5-11.

Tip

The ichat company is but one of a growing number of enterprise-quality chat vendors. Also research Quarterdeck.

http://www.qdeck.com/chat
http://www.cuseeme.com
http://www.picturetalk.com

You also might be interested in the Virtual Places site, which uses chat and is just darned interesting (see the business header):

http://www.vplaces.com

5-11 *Adding chat conferencing capabilities.*

By adding two-way communications to a Web site, that site is transformed from a static source of content to a highly interactive community.

Ichat's event moderation package provides another powerful tool for attracting and keeping large audiences. Event moderation allows large numbers of users to sit in on a chat with special guests, such as sports, entertainment, and industry personalities. Moderators forward questions from the audience to guest speakers, with text-based replies sent to all.

Tip

Chat, fax, etc., etc., etc. That's a lot to do to create a great Web site. It might be wise to borrow a tactic from professional object-oriented developers. These folks basically plug modules together to create interesting applications. The same technique can work for Web development. One company that sells these plug-ins is Galacticomm, long a fixture on the BBS circuit. Plug-ins include:

- multimedia databases
- catalog order entry
- groupware discussion areas
- video conferencing
- search engines

http://www.gcomm.com

To serve up ichat, the ROOMS (Real-time Object Oriented Multimedia Server) software must be purchased (between $495 and $9000, plus a maintenance fee) and installed. Each ichat server supports up to 1000 concurrent users, although an unlimited number of users may hold accounts. More concurrent users can be supported on a single site by adding ichat servers. Chat rooms may be associated with a single page, multiple pages, or even an entire site.

Spiders, robots, and search engines

There will come a time, and it will most definitely come, when one of your clients will want to add a search engine to its site for one of several reasons:

Tip

IBM has posted an Internet search service called InfoMarket Search. It is based on a Cold War technology called Minerva, which uses infodroids to search different types of databases such as Oracle, Sybase, and Basis Plus. InfoMarket Search is available at:

http://www.infomkt.ibm.com.

- The client needs to provide a way for visitors to search through a very large site to find a specific topic.
- The client wants to host a Web search service to attract visitors to the site. Just look at how much great free publicity Digital's AltaVista search engine generated. (See *http://altavista.digital.com*)

Unless you've got some remarkable programming talent in your shop, I wouldn't advise even tackling the project or writing your own search engine. Digital's is just too good. Its Web index contains 30 million pages found on 225,000 servers, and 3 million articles from 14,000 Usenet newsgroups. It is accessed over 12 million times per weekday. It's fast too. That's because it runs on Digital's own super-fast, 64-bit AlphaServer. Don't even try to compete unless you have something so fanstastic it'll blow AltaVista away.

Of course, there are other search engines out there that you probably use in your own research. InfoSeek (*http://www.infoseek.com*) and Excite (*http://www.excite.com*) are two of the dozens out there on the Web. Table 3-1 lists more than a few directories in which you should get yourself noted. Most of these sites utilize search engines that access a database into which you have put your directory entry.

A database, usually either relational or object-oriented, is the medium used to store these directory entries. Sites that host search criteria store information concerning a wide variety of Web sites. Information stored is usually the title of the homepage, URL, keywords, and a short description.

Other sites use their search engines for other purposes. For example, Unisys uses a shareware search engine called SWISH (*http://www.eit.com/software/swish/*) to grant visitors to their homepage the ability to search for a topic of interest, as shown in Fig. 5-12.

Unisys has a wide variety of pages on their site; each is written in HTML. The SWISH search engine reads through all of these pages, collects its information, and then updates a Unisys database. This process takes place on a weekly basis. The output as seen by the user (Fig. 5-12) is a result of a query to this database.

To implement a search capability, therefore, you need to be concerned about both a database to store the index or directory and a facility, referred to as a *search engine*, to retrieve and display the information. Readers who are also programmers will be very familiar with this, since it is no more and no less than a typical database query and retrieval function.

Spiders and *robots* are typically Web-sexy terms for programs that read through the millions of pages, either searching for new ones or following other particular criteria. The information returned is then updated automatically in the database discussed in the last paragraph.

5-12 *The search form.*

Tip

NetCarta's CyberPilot Pro for users and WebMapper for Web-masters are socially responsible spiders:

http://www.netcarta.com

Robots and spiders are not always looked at favorably, though. These programs have the ability to bring servers to their knees. Robots designed to do a "breadth-first" search of the Web (i.e., exploring many sites in a gradual fashion instead of aggressively rooting out all of one site's pages at a time) are the preferred medium. The alternative, depth-first searches, can gum up the works in minutes by recursively downloading information from CGI script-based pages that may contain an infinite number of links.

So spiders, robots, and search engines are really part of a team of software tools that can be used to enhance your site—but you need to learn a little spider etiquette first. The following rules of good behavior are courtesy of NetCarta:

- Use the spider during off-peak hours.
- Don't crawl a particular site more often than necessary.

- Use default settings on the spider, which are designed to minimize server load by limiting pages examined or spider operating speed.
- Map only sites that you'll actually use.
- Respect the robot exclusion protocol, which lets Web sites bar spiders.
- Don't let spiders run unattended.
- Identify your spider so you can be traced.
- Respond to a Webmaster's queries about what you're doing on their site.

Martijn Koster, now on AOL's webcrawler team, wrote a fine standard and methodology for excluding robots from your site. Essentially it calls for a "/robots.txt" file, which provides instructions on what's permissible and what's not for a robot entering a site. Link to Koster's instructions at *http://info.webcrawler.com/mak/projects/ robots/norobots.html*.

If you want to make your client's site searchable by the user and don't want to build your own search engine, the Web itself again holds the answer. DEC now makes its AltaVista search engine available for a fee, but there are quite a few free search engines available as well.

The University of Arizona provides the Glimpse search engine, which can be used to search large numbers of HTML documents easily. Find it at *http://glimpse.cs.arizona.edu:1994/index.html*.

Tip

Take home a spider or robot for a pet from:

http://info.webcrawler.com/mak/projects/robots/active.html

Excite (*http://www.excite.com/navigate*) provides a free search engine, but the toll is that your users will see Excite's customers' advertising banners.

SWISH is downloadable from *http://www.eit.com/software/swish/*.

Using a database on a server

Unless all the sites you develop are purely text and images, there will come a time when you need to store information into a database and then get that information back out again.

Databases have been around a long time. Most of today's databases use the relational model. These run the gamut from the heavy-duty Oracle, Informix, and Sybase databases, to the lighter ones such as Microsoft Access, which comes as part of the Microsoft Office suite of tools. In theory, you should be able to attach to any database present on your server (or to a server which connects to your Web server). But you need programming prowess to do it.

Database access is a three-part task. Part one entails some HTML, usually in a forms format, where the user or visitor makes a request to see some information. Part two involves some sort of CGI, Perl, or Java code that interfaces between the HTML form and the physical database. Part three is the database itself.

Parts one and three are straightforward enough. It's the part in the middle, the gateway between the HTML and the database, that presents the challenge.

Figure 5-13 shows an example of a Web-to-database call. The product used here is WDB (*http://arch-http.hq.eso.org/bfrasmus/wdb/*

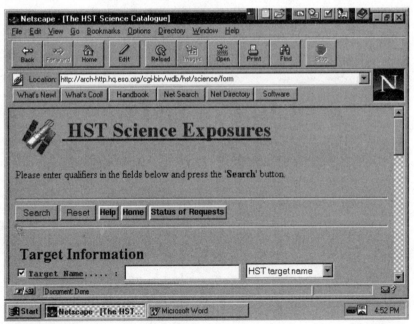

5-13 *A Web-to-database information request.*

wdb.html), a software tool set developed by the European Southern Observatory (ESO), a multinational astronomical organization headquartered in Munich. WDB tremendously simplifies integrating relational databases into the World Wide Web. WDB lets you provide WWW access to the contents of databases without having to write a single line of code.

At the moment, WDB supports Sybase, Informix, and mSQL. It is relatively easy to port to other SQL-based databases, however.

Tip

There's a trade show for every industry, business, and type of product. Find out when they are at:

http://www.tscentral.com/

All that's needed to use WDB is the WDB script (written in Perl) and a set of high-level form definition files, each describing a different view on the database. WDB automatically creates HTML forms on-the-fly to allow the users to query the database, and, given the user's query constraints, it will search the database and present the result. WDB even comes with a utility to extract information about a table from the database automatically, and create a working template form definition file.

A number of conversions on the data coming from the database are possible, before they are shown to the users, such as formatting coordinates into hours, minutes, and seconds, or formatting dates into the normal conventions.

The most notable feature is the possibility of converting data from the database into hypertext links, and (because it is possible through WDB to access any database element directly via a WWW URL) turning the entire database into a huge hypertext system. These hypertext links can be links to other elements in the database, thereby providing a simple way of jumping between related information.

They could also be links to other documents on the Web, providing easy integration between data in the database and related documents on the Web. Or they could be links to other databases with a WDB or similar interface, thus providing a simple mechanism for cross-database links.

WDB is a CGI script written in Perl for NCSA's HTTP server for the World Wide Web. WDB was written at European Southern Observatory for the ESO and ST-ECF science data archive. The best thing is that it's free.

> **Tip**
>
> The major database vendors are hot on the Web scene. They've all got products under wraps (or already on the market) that will let you generate Web pages directly from their databases. Oracle is a case in point, with its new World Wide Web Interface Kit.

Those who want the comfort of a "name" big in the PC arena would do well to take a look at Corel's WEB.DATA, a program that's basically a middleman between your database(s) and the Web. It supports Microsoft Access, Microsoft FoxPro, Borland dBASE, Lotus 1-2-3, Microsoft Excel, Borland Paradox, Oracle, text files, Microsoft SQL Server, or any other ODBC-compliant database. You can access several of these databases simultaneously. You even can format your output to be browser-specific—so Internet Explorer can have one display and Netscape Navigator another. At $149 it's something of a bargain.

Security on the Web

There's been a lot of publicity about how unsecure the Internet is. While open access to your company's computer is not recommended, there still are ways you can have a presence on the Internet and not open the door to cyber-vandals and other unsavory characters.

Secure Hypertext Transfer Protocol (S-HTTP) and Secure Sockets Layer (SSL) provide the greatest flexibility for companies who want to conduct secure operations over the Internet. This genre of server software employs various methods to ensure security, including cryptography as well as something as simple as requiring passwords. Surf over to *http://www.rsa.com* for some interesting info about their secured product line.

There's no reason why you can't have a variety of servers attached to the Internet, as shown in Fig. 5-14. In the example, this fictitious company has a public server (non-secured) as well as a secured sever. Secured servers are popular in sites that require the transfer of checking account numbers, credit card numbers, and other personal information.

In addition to the secured server, organizations might want to utilize a firewall. I personally consider *firewall* to be a broad term, covering both hardware and software products, including secured servers. Passwords and security procedures, long the mainstay of enterprise computing environments, do have a place in the world of the Internet. An the beginning of this chapter we read about Beth Israel Hospital's procedure to maintain security between the Internet and their production systems.

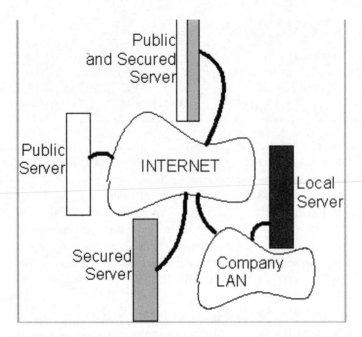

5-14 *A multiplicity of servers from one organization are attached to the Internet.*

While computer departments, as a matter of standards, usually implement security procedures like those instituted at Beth Israel, smaller firms have a tendency to just throw up a Web server—and hang the security. If this server also contains, or is connected to, the firm's sensitive data, then watch out. As a consultant, even if you're no computer guru, you're obligated to warn your client of the dangers inherent in designing an unprotected site.

Well, that's it. We've completed the first part of this guide. You now know how to write HTML, can create a graphic or two, and understand the intricacies of Web servers. It's time to print those business cards and go out on the prowl for the elusive part of the Internet business—your client. The second part of this book is a detailed guide to the secrets of being a successful businessperson.

6

Hanging out your shingle

There are different flavors of Internet consultants. Some are bona fide organizations with employees, office space, and a stellar list of clients. Some are independents who conceive and then design the site, but ultimately outsource the actual creation of it to others. And then there are the graphics designers, programmers, and assorted other folks who work entirely on their own. All of these people compete in the great marketplace known as Internet consulting.

> **Tip**
> Our very first tip for marketing your business: List your business for free in the SBA's business card database.
> *http://www.sba.gov/buscard/*

With about 1500 domain registrations per day, there's more than enough work for all. Getting that work is tough, however. You've now entered the (shudder) business side of the Internet business.

You can be blessed with all the talent in the world—be the greatest graphic designer, have the best programming skills, write with a golden quill—but if you don't somehow get the word out, you won't generate business. And if you don't generate business, soon you'll be out of business.

I'll warn you right up front that the process of staying in business will consume a minimum of 20 percent of all of your resources. That's 20 percent of your time. That's 20 percent of your money. If you're not willing to invest this level of time and money, then you'll probably be more successful as an employee than employer.

Tip

When you start your own business, you lose the safety net of your old company's health insurance. And it's not so easy getting health insurance if you're a small business. Review the following:

http://ww.buyerszone.com/hmo/hmoindex.html

You'll probably have to join an association or group to get the best rates. Look into the Small Business Service Bureau, (800) 472-7199. They're our choice.

Also check out Alliance for Affordable Health Care, which offers health insurance plans for the self-employed.

1725 K Street, NW, Suite 310
Washington, DC 20006

It's amazing how naïve people can be when starting a business. They add a phone line, get a post office box, print a couple of hundred business cards, and they think they're in business. If it were as simple as that, we'd all have bank accounts as thick as Bill Gates's by now.

Now if your expectations are low, or you're just doing this for a hobby, you'll be able to pick up some spare change this way. But if you want to earn substantially more, maybe pay off that mortgage and retire in style, there are a few more things you'll have to know to get into business and stay in business.

That's what the second half of this book is all about: how to stay in business. Or better yet, how to stay in a lucrative business.

Getting down to business

You've probably heard this all before. Don't quit your day job unless you have enough money to live on for about 6 months. I'd like to amend that. Don't quit your day job unless you have enough money to live on for 6 months, plus 20 percent over that amount for marketing yourself, and have two customers lined up.

Tip

Resource for home-based businesses:
http://decit.if.uidaho.edu/HBB/homebus.html.

It's no secret that many of us started out by moonlighting. You work your 9-to-5 (or whatever) job by day, and at night you take on some freelance work. The problem with this is that you get the wrong impression of what it means to be in business. Moonlighters don't always good business people make. First of all, you're living comfortably off a very secure salary. Second, you probably didn't actively go out in search of the freelance work you're now doing. You got it through a friend of a friend, a relative, a coworker. You moonlight sporadically, when the opportunity arises. If there is no work on the horizon, you just shrug your shoulders and go to a ballgame instead. This is not a business. These are odd jobs.

Business people are aggressive about securing business. If they have one client, they're actively working on getting a second. From the time they wake up until the time they go to sleep, they're thinking of ways to increase business. When they're at a ballgame, they're thinking of business. When they're out on a date, they're thinking of business. When they're on vacation, they're thinking of business. And they don't think of it as work. They think of business as fun. I know I do.

I enjoy thinking of new ways of going after customers. The promotions I design are every bit as invigorating for me as my vacations are. The newsletters I write to send to current and prospective customers are every bit as much fun as going out to that new movie. Even when I find myself stuck sticking on the last of 10,000 stamps on a direct-mail letter, I'm having fun. You should think of it as fun, too. If not, maybe being in business for yourself is not for you.

The first thing you should do, before you set off in the great unknown of working for yourself, is determine if working for yourself is something you really *want* to do, and something you *can* do.

The Small Business Administration's "Checklist for Going into Business" (*http://www.sbaonline.sba.gov/gopher/Business-Development/ General-Information-And-Publications/chklist.txt*) has a great test that you can use to determine if you have what it takes to go into business. Give this excerpt a whirl. If, at the end, you still want to go into business, keep reading. If not—well, it was nice to have your ear for a while.

Tip

Dealing with the federal government has gotten easier, thanks to the U.S. Business Advisor. Use this new online clearinghouse access government forms, business development software, and business information from the Small Business Administration. The address is *http://www.business.gov*.

1 Are you a leader?
2 Do you like to make your own decisions?
3 Do others turn to you for help in making decisions?
4 Do you enjoy competition?
5 Do you have will power and self-discipline?
6 Do you plan ahead?
7 Do you like people?
8 Do you get along well with others?
9 Are you aware that running your own business may require working 12–16 hours a day, 6 days a week, and maybe even Sundays and holidays?
10 Do you have the physical stamina to handle the workload and schedule?
11 Do you have the emotional strength to withstand the strain?
12 Are you prepared to lower your standard of living temporarily until your business is firmly established?
13 Is your family prepared to go along with the strains they, too, must bear?
14 Are you prepared to lose your savings?
15 Do you know what basic skills you will need in order to have a successful business?
16 Do you possess those skills?
17 When hiring personnel, will you be able to determine if the applicants' skills meet the requirements for the positions you are filling?
18 Have you ever worked in a managerial or supervisory capacity?
19 Have you ever worked in a business similar to the one you want to start?
20 Have you had any business training in school?
21 If you discover you don't have the basic skills needed for your business, will you be willing to delay your plans until you've acquired the necessary skills?

If you answered yes to most of these questions, then roll up those sleeves. You're in for the long haul.

> ### Tip
>
> Inevitably, you're going to use a lawyer. Know your rights. HALT is a 100,000-member public-interest group, whose mission is making the legal system work fairly. They publish a legal consumer's guide, *Using A Lawyer and What To do if Things Go Wrong,* by Kay Otsberg. It is available as part of the membership fee, or can be purchased separately.
>
> 1319 F Street, NW, Suite 300
> Washington, DC 20004
> (202) 347-9600
>
> For a legal reference on-line go to:
> *http://galaxy.einet.net/gopher/gopher.html*

What you need to know

The SBA site lists more than 40 publications in its "Starting a Business" section. Highlights include:

- How to Start a Small Business
- Planning—The Most Important Ingredient
- Knowing Your Market
- Information—The Key To Success
- How to Price Your Products and Services
- How to Start a Home-Based Business
- Cash Flow Analysis
- Small Business Health Insurance
- Advertising Your Business
- Financing for the Small Business

> ### Tip
>
> Computer software can help with contract preparation. One example is *It's Legal* ($40), by Parsons Technology.
>
> One Parsons Drive
> P.O. Box 100
> Hiawatha, IA 52233-0100
> (319) 0395-9626 or (800) 223-6925

> ### Tip
>
> Some national links to other home-based business people in your region include:
>
> The Network
> (800) 825-8286 or (909) 624-2227
>
> LeTip
> (800) 255-3847
>
> Leads Club
> (800) 783-3761 or (619) 434-3761

If you're serious about running a business, it's a good idea to read them all, because I'm not going to reiterate much of this information here. They're all downloadable or, if you prefer, you can visit one of the many government bookstores and get these publications on paper.

It's also a good idea to visit your local public library or Barnes & Noble (which I consider to be my very own personal public library). Visit the business sections, grab a few dozen books, and sit down to read.

I must have read what feels like a thousand books. Believe it or not, I still hit the business section of bookstores before I go over to the computer section. Call it survival instinct. But I've been in business, and quite successfully I might add, for close to a decade. Given the sad statistic that four out of five businesses fail within the first 3 years, I'm pretty proud of myself.

> ### Tip
>
> Executive Book Summaries provides monthly, eight-page summaries of leading business books on a subscription basis.
>
> 5 Main St.
> Bristol, VT 05443-1398
> (800) 521-1227

Along the way I've picked up dozens and dozens of tips, techniques, and methodologies for making my business work. Although I want you to invest the time and effort in doing your own research (your nightstand should always include at least one computer book and one business book), this chapter and all those that remain will provide short, sweet, and successful tidbits of business advice.

> ### Tip
>
> Fax response systems for replying to requests for information are available. To see how they work, try Biz FAX at (800) 227-5638.
>
> FaxQuest
> (415) 771-0923 or (800) 995-9141
>
> Ricoh Corp.
> (408) 432-8800 or (800) 524-1801

The first order of business, then, is to figure out just what your business is. It's not enough just to say "Internet consulting." There are lots of Internet consultancies out there. How is yours different? Do you bring something to the table that no one else has? A new tool or a new technique? Or perhaps your chief selling proposition is that you do fabulous art. Or maybe it's that your prices are lower than everybody else's.

Your first order of business, therefore, is finding out what everybody else is offering. It's called *competitive intelligence.*

Find out what the competition's up to

Your mission, should you choose to accept it, is to find out all you can about your competitors and, along the way, get the following:

- Ideas for advertising
- Ideas for brochures and direct mailings
- A handle on what fees to charge
- Possible networking contacts (competitors can be friends, too!)

> ### Tip
>
> Time share offices:
>
> Alliance Business Centers (locations nationwide)
> (800) 869-9595
>
> INterOffice (nationwide)
> (800) 776-8330

If the research you were doing were on public companies, you'd be able to get a plethora of information. These companies are required to make public everything from annual reports to financial figures. Most of the companies you will be competing against, however, are not public companies, so information is a bit trickier to get. Lucky for you, there's an Internet around.

Datamax (*http://www.dmax.com*) is an Internet consultancy based in Washington, D.C. It provides a good example of what you're going to be up against in the creativity area. Figure 6-1 starts off pretty tame, but as you scroll through the site you begin to realize that these folks have used it as a sample of their work.

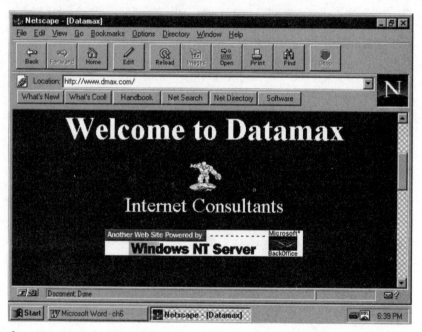

6-1 *The Datamax portfolio.*

Figure 6-2 shows an amazing amount of creativity. You can't see it, but there's lots of animation created using Java applets—everything from weather forecasts and news briefs to little twirling balls. What these folks have done is provide a sample of their wares right online. A potential customer surfing the Internet would most certainly, if the price is right, pick this company over one with a duller home page. Also notice that the Datamax site owns its own domain name (i.e., *www.dmax.com*).

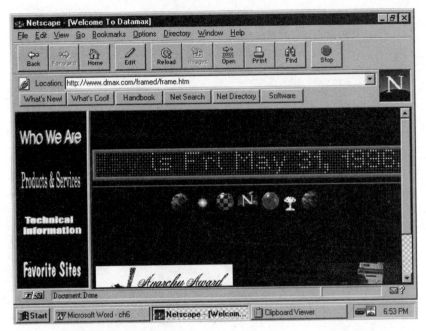

6-2 *A site with Java animation.*

Tip

If you don't have one already, buy a file cabinet. In it, create a folder and label it "Ideas." Once you start your business, you're going to be on a lot of mailing lists. Don't just toss out your mail. Look at it. See if there is any mailing that you actually like (artwork, writing, etc.). Save it in your Ideas file. It'll come in handy as an idea generator when you have to do a mailing of your own.

It's hard to tell exactly what our friend at *http://www.monmouth.com/~rallan/index1.html* does. Either Mr. Allan is a moonlighter for an unnamed computer company in central New Jersey, or he works directly for Monmouth Computers.

His site is interesting for two reasons. It provides some prices and it gives customer testimonials, as shown in Fig. 6-3. This is an excellent technique for proving how good your company is. Of course, you have to have some real testimonials before you can use them. You also need permission to attribute each of the quotes to a customer. If you can't get permission, don't bother to use the quote. Unattributed testimonials, or those signed with initials, look fictitious.

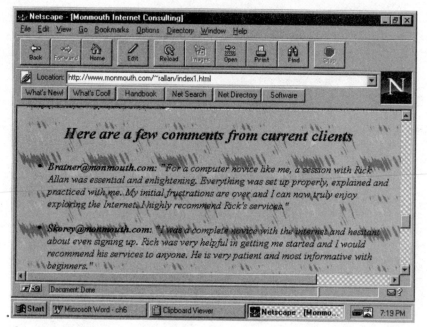

6-3 *Using customer testimonials.*

This site also gives us some insight into pricing (see Table 6-1), although keep in mind that this fellow just might be moonlighting and his prices are artificially low.

Tip

Consultants National Resource Center has books, periodicals, software, etc., for consultants and small business owners.

P.O. Box 430
Clear Spring, MD 21722
(301) 791-9332

Our last example, Reality Communications, shows the depth and breadth of services that an average professional Internet consultancy offers. As shown in Fig. 6-4, Reality offers a variety of services including Web page design, hosting, and scanning, as well as audio and movie capture.

Reality provides a feedback form for interested potential customers. It's here that you enter your contact information, describe your project (I've cut that part out of the figure to save space), and ask for pricing.

Table 6-1. One Consultant's Fee Structure

Introductory Internet Setup Special: $49.95 (Residential Accounts Only)

Install and set up the latest Web Browser including FTP, email, IRC and Newsgroups. Provide an Internet tutorial to familiarize the client with the new software. Provide free telephone support with using the new software. Includes only software setup, all hardware installations are extra. For all dialup accounts up to 28.8 baud.

Internet Tutorial: $50.00 first 90 mins. $50.00 per hour thereafter (Residential Accounts Only)

Provide onhand teaching of using the Internet including Web Browsing, IRC chat, FTP transfers, real-audio, real-video, newsgroups , email. Anything dealing with the Internet can be learned in a friendly 1-on-1 training session.

All other Internet Computing Needs: $50.00 per hour (Residential Accounts Only)

Any other Internet need not previously listed such as installing and configuring modems, installation of larger hard drives, or anything dealing with hardware for the Internet.

Introductory Internet Setup Special: $75.00 (Business Accounts)

Install and set up the latest Web Browser including FTP, email, IRC and Newgroups. Provide and Internet tutorial to familiarize the client with the new software. Provide free telephone support with using the new software. Help business clients develop a webpage and give information regarding webpage rates. Includes only software setup, all hardware installations are extra. For all dialup accounts up to 28.8 baud.

Internet Tutorial: $75.00 first 90 mins.
$75.00 per hour thereafter (Business Accounts)

Provide Businesses with the information they need to use the Internet to their fullest potential. Business web page publication can be explained as well as using internet applications for web browsing, IRC chat, realtime audio and video on demand. All in a friendly 1-on-1 discussion.

All other Internet Computing Needs:
$75.00 per hour (Business Accounts)

Any other business need not previously listed such as installation of Internet related business hardware. Advice and consultation on what hardware to use for the needs of your business.

Tip

Some organizations for you to look into:

National Association for Self-Employed
Newsletter, insurance, etc., membership fee $48.
2121 Precinct Line Rd.
Hurst, TX 76054
(800) 827-9990

National Business Incubation Association
One President St.
Athens, OH 45701
(614) 593-4331

National Small Business United
Newsletters, seminars, etc., membership fee $75 and up.
1155 15th St., NW
Washington, DC 20005
(202) 293-8830

Independent Computer Consultants Association
933 Grandview Office Parkway
St. Louis, MO 63141
(314) 997-4633

American Association of Professional Consultants
9140 Ward Parkway
Kansas City, MO 64114

United States Federation of Small Businesses
(800) 637-3331

The Internet can provide you with a wealth of information, but there's still more to be had. Even though you're an Internet consultant, where your world is the Web and the Web is your world, you're still going to have to do earthly things like send a literature pack to prospective customers.

While desktop publishing packages have the ability to produce professional graphics, unless you're a graphic designer and have access to a color printer, you're going to have to find a better way to produce your marketing communications literature.

One way to get a handle on what this literature should look like is to get some from competitors. You now have a list of interesting sites on the Web. Another source of Internet companies is *AdWeek.* This is a weekly publication that's the bible of the advertising community. The classifieds section, located at the back of the publication,

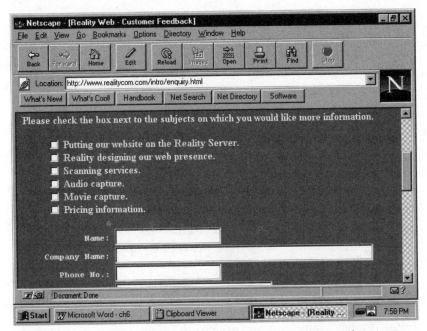

6-4 *Using a questionnaire to find out your customer's needs.*

lists a good number of Internet companies. Call these folks up and ask them questions about the mission and scope of their companies: How many people do they employ? Who are their biggest clients? How long they have been in business? Then ask them to send you their brochure.

Tip

If you can't afford professional stationery and brochures right now, try using a combination of desktop publishing software (many word processors have these capabilities, too), a good quality laser printer, and preprinted paper. Paper Direct has hundreds of varieties of full-color letterheads, business cards, tri-folds, and lots more. Get a free catalog from:

(800) APAPERS

Of course, telling them you are a competitor will get a polite hang up, so you have to be creative in your approach. I usually tell people that I am a computer consultant (true) who's working with a large un-named client (usually true), and I am looking for a company with their product or service for a project with this particular client. I get lots of literature this way and, while I'm not really considering this company at the present time, over the years I've probably steered business towards 95 percent of them. So even if the act of competitive intelligence doesn't make you feel quite comfortable, it's a critical task for your business, it's done all the time, and nobody really comes out a loser.

Tip

MyBrochures Mailers & More is Windows-based PC software that includes preprinted paper, all for around $59.95. Call MYSoftware Company (800) 325-9095.

Examine carefully what these companies send you. Examine even more carefully your competitor's Web sites. What are they selling? How are they differentiating themselves from their competitors? Are they servicing both residential and business? Are their fees reasonable or not? Can you make money (remember that mortgage) if you offer the same fee structure? Is their Web site both content- and graphic-rich? Do they own their domain name or do they rent out space from an ISP? Do they appear to make their own literature, or have they invested the money to do it professionally? How many competitors are in your particular region and how do your skills stack up against theirs?

Your business plan

It's time to write your own mission and goals statement. As mentioned, the SBA has some very fine documents, some of them on planning. Read them and anything else you can get your hands on. You really should write a business plan. The sad fact is that 95 percent of all businesses do not have a business plan. I didn't even have a business plan until a few years after I started in business. Even if you dispense with the plan, you really should write down at least your mission and goals.

Tip

Automation comes to the rescue again. Check your local software store for Business Plan Writer, which retails for about $99, or surf over to the Smart Business Plan at *http://www.aifr. com/plantips.htm.*

The mission is a written statement detailing what your company does. For example, World Wide Webport (*http://www.wwwebport. com/mission.html*) has the following mission statement right on their home page:

The World Wide WebPort is an eclectic collection of Internet "Web sites" and portal into another world. Locations are tied together under one WebPort roof, as part of a growing global marketing engine with two purposes:

1 To maintain a user-friendly interface that will attract an online "mass market" of members, through a number of mediums. Novice users can learn about online capabilities and terminology in a fun and rewarding environment. Seasoned users can participate in helping develop this interactive graphical community.

2 To give space for "local" businesses and multinational corporations to market their goods and services online, worldwide.

Your mission should include specifically what you will be doing and who your market is. For example:

The mission of the Webbed Foot Company is to build, maintain, and train in the area of interactive systems for the Fortune 1000. By definition, interactive includes both multimedia and Internet-related activities.

This very specific and very short mission statement will serve to identify exactly what you do. It makes it clear, not only to your prospective customers, but also to your employees or subcontractors, exactly what is your specialty. Of course, if your own mission statement is broader, then by all means include the specifics of your additional skill sets. Depending upon your background, this can include software development, graphic design, and even video production. Although most experts advise that the mission be short and sweet, the computer field is anything but. It's perfectly okay to have a mission statement and then some bullets that further clarify what it is you do, as shown in the Avanti mission statement (Fig. 6-5).

Tip

Need some marketing research?

CACI
(800) 292-2224

Find/SVP
(212) 633-4510

Information Resources
(312) 726-1221

R.R. Donnelley
(203) 353-7223

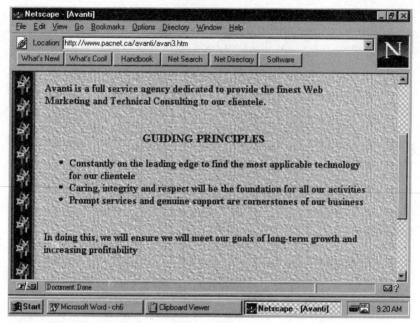

6-5 *Displaying your mission and goals.*

Once you've identified exactly who you are, you can tackle your organization's goals. Goals have to be actionable and measurable. This usually takes the form of making the goal active, providing a date by which this event will happen and then having a way to measure whether you've met your goal. For example:

- Get 10 new clients by October, 1997. This is actionable and measurable. We've supplied a realistic goal of 10 (not 100, which is unrealistic) and provided a date by which this action should happen.
- Produce a marketing plan with up to five ideas and/or concepts by May, 1997. This, too, is actionable and measurable. Here we've designated a goal of developing a marketing plan with up to five great ideas to market our company, by a specific target date.

Tip
Go to your local Barnes and Noble and get a copy of this year's *Information Please Business Almanac*. It lists tons of interesting information.

By now you're probably beginning to understand the process. You need to be able to specify exactly what it is you want to do (mission), and then devise a framework (your goals) for getting you there.

Your mission and goals are a very important subset of the written business plan. A business plan describes what a business does, how it will be done, who has to do it, where it will be done, why it's being done, and when it has to be completed. Here are the typical parts of a business plan:

Tip

The SBA remains the best single source of assistance (check your local white pages). Offline sources include:

Small Business Development Centers (SBDCs)
Service Corps of Retired Executives (SCORE)
Small Business Institutes (SBIs)

The SBA also has an online Developing your Business Plan Workshop:

*http://www.sbaonline.sba.gov/gopher/Business-Development/
Business-Initiatives-Education-Training/Business-Plan/*

- **Business Description** includes the business name, address, and owner identification. It identifies goals and objectives, and clarifies why you are or why you want to be in business.
- **Products and Services** is a very descriptive explanation of all products and services, describing what you are selling, and why.
- **Sales and Marketing** describes the composition and size of your market, how you will be competitive, what pricing and sales terms you are planning, and how you will market your products and services.
- **Operating Requirements** identifies and describes the equipment, facilities, and people necessary to generate your products and services, and how your products and services will be produced and made available to the customer.
- **Financial Management** (for start-ups) gives projected start-up costs, expected profit or return on investment (ROI) for the first year, projected income and balance sheet for 2 years, and a projected monthly cash flow statement for 12 months.
- **Financial Management** (for established companies) gives income statement and balance sheet for the last 2 years,

projected income statement and balance sheet for the next 2 years, projected monthly cash flow statement for 12 months, and an explanation of all projections.

- **Concluding Narrative** summarizes your business goals and objectives, and sends a message that you are committed to the success of your business.

Writing a business plan is not a once-in-a-lifetime effort. The business plan is an evolving document. It needs to be changed as circumstances change. It should become an active part of your marketing plan.

Just how do you know when to modify your business plan, hence the way you do business? The consultant, like any business owner, must keep one ear to the ground. Researching competition never stops; finding out what your customer needs never stops either. Here are some methodologies you can use to keep your business in top form, and some concepts to consider:

Tip

Just starting up? Subscribe to AT&T's Resources for New Business, at (800) 537-8700. You get lots of information, discounts and a fax-back service.

- Sample survey
- Focus group interview
- Brainstorming
- Complaint analysis
- Customer analysis
- Trade journals and trade shows
- Sales representatives
- Advertising notebook
- Exit interviews
- Entrance interviews

Canvass and survey your prospects to gather data. If you wish to remain anonymous, line up some marketing students to perform the survey, or engage a local marketing agency. Be sure you establish a technique for getting a random sample, because the natural tendency is to attempt to attract respondents with whom one feels comfortable. Be sure to test your questionnaire to see that the questions are easily understood and are meaningful.

To run a focus group, get 10 to 15 people together in a relaxed setting and encourage them to talk about products or services they like or dislike. Use a moderator who can lead the group discussion without inhibiting the thought processes or limiting the expression of ideas and opinions. Tape record the session for later analysis.

Brainstorming is a variation of the focus group in which participants are encouraged to freewheel in their thinking, to produce as many suggestions as possible without stopping to analyze them. Here, too, a trained moderator will obtain the best results.

Encourage your customers to contact you directly if they have complaints. Study those complaints. Respond to every one with a courteous letter assuring that you will correct the situation. A few disgruntled customers can be harmful. If your customers feel that they can work with you to solve their problems, you are sure to be successful. Tabulate information about customers regularly to determine future requirements. If there is enough commonality, you can launch a new product or service—and beat your competitors to the punch. In addition, keep track of the magazines they read, TV shows they watch, and other indicators that will help you make future marketing decisions.

Subscribing to trade journals and attending trade shows keeps you current on marketing developments. Keep an active file of advertisements and literature that caught your eye. Many of these ideas can be reused in your own marketing campaigns.

Representatives who call on other, similar businesses in your area can provide valuable information on business trends, new items, and changes in the industry. Be sure the information is reliable.

Each ad that you run represents an investment. To make sure you maximize your investment, cut out each ad and tape it to a page in a three-ring notebook. (For a radio or TV ad, write a short description.) Enter the date, medium, and cost of the ad. Record the results of the ad in sales, inquiries, or coupons redeemed. Divide the cost by the results to get a cost-per-inquiry factor that you can use to compare your ads and the media in which they appeared.

Tip

If you want to try to sell to the government, a good source of leads is Commerce Business Daily. "Go CBD" on AOL or *http://www.sba.gov/hotlist/cbd.html.*

Try the Federal Web Locator to find other government agencies: *http://www.law.vill.edu/fed-agency/fedwebloc.html*

Government Contractor Resource Center: *http://www.govcon.com/*

When someone leaves your employ, be sure to spend enough time to find out exactly why he or she is leaving. Probe deep to learn what may be occurring in your business that causes hard feelings, employee conflict, or customer dissatisfaction. It is important that your employees leave with a good feeling about you and your business, so they will not spread unfounded rumors. You also might wish to keep them as customers. Employee turnover and training can be expensive to a business, so try to find out what you must do to keep employees, and then decide if they are worth the price.

You should personally welcome new employees. If they've come from a competitor, they can provide a wealth of inside information.

The Wharton Small Business Development Center came up with a list of surefire ways to make certain your business fails:

- Fall in love with your product instead of finding a customer who has a need for it.
- Think you're smarter than your competition, or try to beat big competitors on price.
- Don't seek out or listen to outside advisors.
- Mismanage your cash flow.
- Pay no attention to how your competition is changing.
- Fail to respond to changes in your marketplace or customer base.
- Have your biggest (or only) customer go out of business.
- Think you don't need a business plan.
- Run out of money.

Always keep your eye on the ball. Make a large sign and hang it over your computer. On it state:

- What are your company's objectives?
- Who is your market?
- What are the strengths and weaknesses of your firm and product? Your competitor's firm and product?
- How do you plan to grow aggressively but safely?
- What are your alternative plans if conditions change?

Tip

If you're trying to market your services to marketing professionals, you might be interested in being included in the Marketing Bulletin Board card deck:

(805) 682-5094

Starting out on the right foot

The literature your competitors send you, if you've done your job right, will be an eye-opener. While some of it may be homemade, far more of it will have been professionally created. Set aside the most professionally created and save it in your "Ideas" folder. Notice what these all have in common:

- A folder with the company name printed on it.
- An envelope large enough to mail the folder with its contents.
- A business card.
- The literature pack.

When I started out, I bought white glossy folders from a stationery supply store and then used a clear Avery label laser printed with my company name and logo. While it didn't look bad (in fact you could hardly see that my company name was on a label), I didn't wait long before I invested in something better. My current folder, and one that I've been using for years, is a nice grainy gray with my company name embossed (that means raised lettering) on the front. I bought 20,000 from the printer to reduce the price paid per unit, but the expense was worth it. I'm still using these folders, and I've looked professional since the days my company was quite small.

Since the envelope is the first thing the prospect sees, you want to take extra care here. Throwing a great folder into a manila envelope sort of defeats the purpose. Most companies will have envelopes printed with their logos. If you want to watch those dollars and cents, then invest in professionally printed shipping labels that can be adhered to plain envelopes. If you look in your business-to-business yellow pages under "Envelopes," you'll probably be able to find one or more dealers who will sell you envelopes in quantity at a really good price. Since my folder and my shipping label are gray, I invested in a classic black linen envelope.

Another ploy, and one that really works, is if you're sending out some information unsolicited and you want to get the prospect to open it, is to use a Priority Mail envelope that you can get at your local post office. Chances are good that, by the time you fill your folder, it will cost about $3.00 to mail anyway. Since that's the Priority Mail rate, you might as well use this service and benefit from its full-color envelope. No one tosses out such a letter unopened.

Tip

Want a plastic business card but can't locate a manufacturer? The folks that did my card can ship. Call Brooklyn (NY)-based Direct Promotions at (718) 627-4070.

A business card is the first thing that most new companies invest in. While you can make them yourself, I would strongly advise against it—it usually looks homemade. People are given many business cards, so you want yours to be a bit different. Whether it gets this way via color or design is up to you. I've changed my card over the years. Originally my business card was a bi-fold. It had four surfaces to print on. On the top was the logo, name, and address, and inside I listed the services of my firm. I still like this idea, but over the years (probably from boredom) I changed my card several times.

My current card is made out of gray transparent plastic. It's certainly a conversation piece. I had gotten a sample from a company that did this sort of work (most printers don't do plastic), but by the time I called they were out of business. So back to the trusty business-to-business yellow pages I went. I happened on a company that had the word "promotions" in their name. I was lucky. It turned out that they could do exactly what I wanted.

No matter what type of business card you use make sure you include your e-mail address and Web URL.

The actual contents of the folder are variable, depending upon what you do and who you are. Larger companies will have a professionally printed, eight-page (or more) color brochure—which can't be done for less than $10,000. (This translates to about $1 per copy, more if you're printing smaller quantities.)

If you can't afford this, don't despair. Just put enough information in your folder to keep the prospect interested. This should include, at a minimum:

- An information sheet about your company, its missions and its goals
- A list of services
- A client list
- Any customer testimonials
- A price list if you publish it
- Your bio, if you have a fabulous resume
- Copies of any articles you've written
- Samples of your work

Since I've written nine books, if the prospect is important enough, I include a book in the package as well. If you have access to a color printer, print some of your choice home page designs and include this in the package as well.

Boosting your business with a marketing plan

You've now got your foot in the door. You have a mission and a set of goals, you've researched your competitors, and have an idea or two about the way you'd like to present your company to the world.

If you recall, one of the sample goals I listed in the last section was creating a marketing plan. Like I keep telling people: You can have the very best product or service in the world, but if nobody knows about it. . . .

Unfortunately, there still is a misunderstanding about the word "marketing." Many people, including top executives, use it as a so-phisticated term for selling. "Marketing representative" is commonly used in ads to recruit salespeople. Marketing actually is a way of man-aging a business so that each critical business decision is made with full knowledge of the impact it will have on the customer. There are some specific ways in which the marketing approach differs from the classic, or sales, approach to managing a business.

In the classic approach, engineers and designers create a product, which is then given to salespeople who are told to find customers and sell the product. In the marketing approach, the first step is to de-termine what the customer needs or wants. That information is given to designers who develop the product, and finally to engineers who produce it. Thus, the sales approach only ends with the customer, while the marketing approach begins and ends with the customer.

The second major difference between the sales and marketing ap-proaches is the focus of management. The sales approach almost al-ways focuses on volume, while the marketing approach focuses on profit.

In short, under the classic (sales) approach the customer exists for the business, while under the marketing approach the business exists for the customer.

The marketing concept is a management plan that views all mar-keting components as part of a total system that requires effective planning, organization, leadership, and control. It is based on the im-portance of customers to a firm, and states that:

- All company policies and activities should be aimed at satisfying customer needs.
- Profitable sales volume is a better company goal than maximum sales volume.

The marketing plan is an essential ingredient for success. It details the steps you will take to market your business. There are different facets to marketing. They include:

- *Marketing communications* is your literature package, which may consist of brochures, newsletters, letterhead, etc.
- *Advertising* can be print, radio, television, or Internet ads.
- *Direct Mail* includes sales letters, promotions, etc.
- *Public Relations* is coverage by the media.
- *Trade Shows* are your chance for a presence at industry events.
- *Telemarketing* means sales phone calls.

Ideas for all of these areas will be discussed in later chapters. What I want to emphasize here is that there really has to be a process performed, at least once a year, where you decide the type of marketing events you will participate in, how many of them you will participate in, how much each costs, and when each event will be launched. For example:

June 1996	Publish newsletter	$900
August 1996	Direct mail full-color postcard	600
October 1996	Telemarketing effort	2000

This example shows that three marketing events will be undertaken at a total cost of $3500. The process of writing this plan, which would be far more descriptive of the marketing event than I have shown here, serves to tell me how much money I need. It also helps me budget my time by indicating when these events are going to happen.

Tip

Give your client this list of reasons for using a Web site:
1 Advertising.
2 Communicating to new and existing customers.
3 Displaying online catalogs.
4 Ordering online.
5 Putting itself in a positive light by using the Web for marketing.
6 Developing a following by running contests, etc.
7 Publishing newsletters, press releases, brochures, and other marketing communications.

As an Internet consultant, the majority of assignments you will get will be marketing-oriented. When Pepsi-Cola puts a site online, it's for marketing purposes. When Nike puts a site online, it's for marketing services. By now you've probably honed a sales pitch that includes all of the reasons why the company in question needs a Web site. It makes sense, therefore, that you should have a site yourself. Your very first marketing task, therefore, is to create the best of all Web sites for yours truly.

Developing your own site

The first five chapters of this book detailed everything you need to know to start a career as an Internet consultant. Perhaps you've already taken what you learned and turned it into a "cool" Web site for yourself. If you haven't done so, then do it now. Your Web site should be:

- Visually pleasing
- State-of-the-art in its HTML
- Content-rich
- Updated regularly
- Indexed in all the major directories

Part of what you're selling is graphical. So if you're not a graphics designer, get the help of one. If you can't afford one, then spend some time on the Web finding what you consider to be the most artistically pleasing of all Web sites. Let these sites be your tutor. Copy their style. Do not use clip art, use photographs or professionally created graphics instead. Much of this can be secured either through the Internet itself, or in one of the larger computer stores. Corel and other vendors sell CDs stacked high with images, at a low cost. There's simply no excuse for a boring page today.

Your page is your sample book, so strut your stuff. Don't clutter up your page or use techniques without reason, but do show your potential customers how creative you are. This means adding graphics, animation, frames, forms, and whatever else turns you on. There's nothing worse than a boring site. Most Internet consultants are guilty of this. They may spend lots of time showing off their wares, but they provide nothing but their own marketing message. You need to create a reason for people to come to your site. Many of the Internet consulting sites I visited when writing this book were visually interesting, but there was really no reason for me to be there—except that I happened to be looking up Internet consultants.

What you really want is for prospects to find your site, keep coming back to it, decide you're an interesting company, and then hire you for a fat fee. You can't do this if your site provides no value added. For example, my site offers a newsletter as well as a jumping-off site for business-related places on the Web. Some sites offer free shareware, some offer free Java applets, some offer photos and other artwork. These are the sites that keep you coming back. By the way, this is the same advice that you will be offering your own clients.

If your site never changes, there is really no reason why someone should come back more than once. Keep it stimulating. While directory robots will find your site eventually, it's best to spend a couple of hours indexing them yourself. Table 3-1 lists the best directories to index your page, I'm repeating it here in Table 6-2, so you can get started right away.

Tip
Look up zip codes online:
http://www.usps.gov

We've set the tone, now let's rev it up. On to Chapter 7, where we'll talk about ways to auto-market your business.

Table 6-2. Get Yourself Listed in These Directories

BizWeb	*http://www.bizweb.com/InfoForm/info-form.html*
Open Market Commercial Sites Index	*http://www.directory.net/dir/submit.cgi*
Excite	*http://www.excite.com*
A1's Searchable Directory	*http://www.a1co.com/index.html*
AnnounceNet	*http://www.announcenet.com/*
Magellan	*http://www.mckinley.com*
ALIWEB	*http://www.webcom.com*
Internet Slueth	*http://www.intbc.com/sleuth/*
White Pages of Net Pages e-mail press release to	*np-add@aldea.com*
What's new Too	*http://newtoo.manifest.com/ WhatsNewToo/submit.html*
Point	*http://www.pointcom.com/*
Submit-it	*http://www.submit-it.com/*
Free Links	*http://www.mgroup.com/freelinks/*
Global Online Director	*http://www.gold.net/gold/gold2.html*
Go Net-Wide	*http://www.shout.net/~whitney/html/ gopublic.html*
WebSight Magazine free listing	*http://websight.com/gridlinks/*
Internet Promotions MegaList	*http://www.2020tech.com/submit.html*
NCSA What's new	*http://www.ncsa.uiuc.edu/SDG/Software/ Mosaic/Docs/whats-new-form.html*
InterNic Net Happenings	*http://www.gi.net/NET/*
WebStar	*http://web-star.com/newpage/newpage.html*
W3 new server registration	*http://www.w3.org/hypertext/DataSources/ WWW/Geographical_generation/new-servers.html*
Promote-It	*http://www.iTools.com/promote-it/promote-it.html*

7

Auto-marketing your Internet business

You have the skills, the will, and are raring to go. So how do you get your first customer? If you're like most of us, you probably already had a client lined up before you threw your hat into the competitive ring. But one customer does not a company make. If your sole client fires you, then you've lost 100 percent of your business. Foolish.

Tip

To keep up with the latest developments on the Internet, there is now Netrepreneur News. This online publication contains abstracts of articles on Internet commerce and marketing from more than 70 consumer publications and trade magazines, with hypertext links to original sources.

http://www.conceptone.com/netnews/netnews.htm

Marketing is the act of securing a steady stream of business. It is a variety of methods that you will use continuously (if you're smart) to ensure a consistent cash flow. Even with two customers under your belt, and up to your ears in work, you should reserve part of your time for the effort needed to find your next customer. And your next. This chapter will provide the best of the best in automated marketing techniques. It will cut to the chase, dispense with the philosophy, and present a businessperson's tutorial on how to deploy each of these techniques. So catch your breath and hold on for quite a ride.

One note before we depart: These techniques are not presented in any particular order. Read 'em and choose the one, two, or five that you like and then reorder them to suit your own palate and your own budget.

Dialing for dollars

There are certain areas where marketing and sales overlap. Telemarketing is one of them. Here both marketing and sales pitches combine in the guise of a faceless voice on the other end of the telephone.

Tip

SalesDoctors is an Internet-based sales newsletter:

http://salesdoctors.com

Telemarketing is an inexpensive alternative to a combined marketing and sales effort. The cost of the average sales call (that's when a salesperson meets and greets a potential customer) has increased from $137 in 1979 to $260 in 1994, and the number of sales calls needed to close the sale has increased from 4.3 to 6.5 in the same time period. Compare this to the average price of a telemarketing call which is $5–$15.

There are two types of telemarketing: inbound and outbound. Inbound telemarketing comprises the procedures you put in place for those times when potential customers call you. This may be as a result of an advertisement, direct mail piece, or even the simple process of handing out business cards.

Tip

The best jumpoff place for entrepreneurs is our very own:

http://www.business-america.com

Customers will call. Ask yourself what response they will get. If you're just starting out, you should consider this carefully. If you're in the office, how will you answer the phone? A "hello" is insufficient. You're in business now. Most organizations answer with the name of the company. If you call yourself "The Internet Store," then answer with this salutation. Working the phone is an art form. A survey by Communications Briefings, based in Alexandria, Va., had this to say about the subject:

How much does the way the phone is answered influence your opinion of the company you're calling?

82 percent	*a lot*
17 percent	*some*
1 percent	*not much*

Which of the following company phone practices bother you the most?

42 percent	*long automated menus*
25 percent	*not answering by third or fourth ring*
21 percent	*busy numbers*
7 percent	*playing music/ads while you wait*
5 percent	*other: no after-hours answering machine*
	no etiquette for timely call return
	no policy for placing on hold

Which of the following employee phone habits bothers you most?

34 percent	*using hold button without asking*
30 percent	*being uninformed*
15 percent	*poor grammar*
11 percent	*failing to identify themselves*
6 percent	*mangling the company name*

When your line is busy, are you losing customers? Invest in more than one line and a telephone system capable or answering these multiple lines. Call your local phone company for information.

Tip

Instead of playing on-hold music, market to your callers. Information-on-Hold, a company specializing in this service, will readily assist. (408) 980-8282

An alternative to expensive phone systems is a combination of a digital, multiple-mailbox answering machine (try a Bogen Friday, available at Staples) and your local telco's voice messaging service. If you're on the phone, the line will never be busy. The phone company routes it over to their voice messaging computer, which is capable of taking about 100 messages simultaneously. At about $11 (NYC business rate) per month, this is a great bargain.

Tip

Suppliers of voice mail systems suitable for home offices:

Bogen Communications
50 Spring St.
P.O. Box 575
Ramsey, NJ 07446
(201) 934-8500

ImageVoc Communications
13610 N. Scottsdale Rd., Suite 10
Scottsdale, AZ 85254
(800) 578-8424

Venture Communications
808 W. Vermont Ave, 2nd Fl.
Anaheim, CA 92805
(714) 635-2000

If you have a multiple-mailbox answering machine like the Bogen Friday and you're a tiny company, use the mail boxes efficiently. Reserve one box for your personal use. Change the message frequently. If you're out of town, let people know so they won't expect a call back right away. Use another mailbox to solicit names and addresses for your literature. If your message tells callers that they can get your company's Internet services literature pack by leaving their name and address, you probably have saved yourself a phone call back.

Use another mailbox to provide the company's name, address, phone, fax number, e-mail, and URL. If you have any leftover mailboxes, use them as generic "departmental" boxes, such as Marketing or Research and Development or Systems Engineering. You might not have a staff and might be operating out of your bedroom, but nobody needs to know that. Always foster the illusion that you are bigger than you really are.

Tip

If you're tight on cash and need a copier, fax, scanner, and answering machine for a low-price, try a Brother EF-1550. It can be purchased at your local Staples.

Or call Small Office Home Office (SOHO) for their catalog:

(800) 570-SOHO

Develop a company procedure guide for answering phones. In it should be detailed how your staff should answers the phone, the policy for putting people on hold, etc. Basically, address all the points in the Communications Briefings survey discussed above.

Tip

Entrepreneur sites on the Web:

CEO Access
http://www.ceo-access.com

Entrepreneur's Association
http://www.tpoint.net/EA

Entrepreneur's Exchange
http://www.astranet.com/eechange/jc00indx.htm

Entrepreneurs on the Web
http://sashimi.wwa.com/~notime/eotw

Business Opportunities Online
http://www.netcap.com

Entrepreneurs Online
http://entreps.com/eol/index.htm

If you're a sole proprietor and use the answering machine, check for messages frequently and always return all phone calls by the end of the day. As an alternative, you can add your beeper number to your phone message for those clients who just can't wait for you to pick up your mail.

If you're getting disgruntled signals from customers and many hang-ups, it could be for a number of reasons noted in the following paragraphs.

- *Whoever picks up your phone doesn't seem to know anything about your company.* This is the reason why I would never use an answering service.
- *The person answering the phone is not friendly, or seems to be resentful over having to take a message.* I cannot tell you how many times I have been turned off by a company because the person picking up the phone made me feel that they were doing me a favor by taking my message. No, I am doing your company a favor by calling.
- *The person answering the call is not persuasive.* Every staff member should consider a telephone call to be a marketing opportunity that doesn't cost anything. The prospect is calling

you. Answer his or her questions and stimulate interest in your company.

- *The person called did not close.* "Closing the sale" is the most important part of the sales process. You have to ask for the sale. It's not enough to say all the right things about the service, get the customer interested, and then never get to the next step. If the person is calling to get more information about the company, then the person answering the phone should strive to answer all the questions. At the end of the call, a closing pitch should be made. This might be to set up a personal sales call—or even to try that special offer of a two-page Web site for only $250.
- *The person answering did not take call-back information.* At minimum, you need the name, firm, and number of the person calling. You can't call back people for whom you don't have telephone numbers.

Tip

More Net Resources:

The Better Business Bureau
http://www.bbb.org/bbb

IOMA
http://ioma.com/ioma

MicroPatent Server
http://www.micropat.com

Outbound telemarketing is a bird of a different feather. Here you are aggressively seeking sales. Just like any other marketing activity, this one requires planning and a methodology. Here are some questions to ask yourself:

- Who am I going to call?
- What am I going to say?
- How am I going to say it?
- How is my phoneside manner?
- Voice mail is a pain, right?
- How do I evade the dreaded secretary?

If you're reading this book, you are or want to be an Internet consultant. That means you're probably not going to call the local pizza shop (or maybe you are). The point is that the first thing you must develop is a list of prospects. Rather than go off on the tangent of finding suitable prospects, I'll cover that in the next section. Suffice it to say that you need some kind of organized prospect database to mount a successful telemarketing program. Most telemarketers work from a script. Even if you're going to perform this task yourself, it's a good idea to jot down what you're going to say. Keep it brief. You have about 20 seconds to pique someone's interest. It's also important not to do all the talking. Experts recommend that you get the prospect to conduct at least half of the conversation.

Always create a visual image of what you're trying to sell. Offer features and benefits concisely and persuasively. If the prospect says no, then try to offer options. For example, if they're not interested in a large Internet development effort, try to sell them on a more inexpensive trial period.

Expert telemarketers adapt to the prospect's pace and way of talking. It's essential to create a dialog. Ask about the person's needs and problems, likes and dislikes. Always start your conversation by asking if you could borrow a few moments of that person's time. If he or she says no, then ask when you might call back. Don't be insistent or huffy. If you reach voice mail, take advantage of the opportunity. Most people hate voice mail. But it does provide the opportunity to make at least a 60-second uninterrupted sales pitch. If you can't get through the dreaded secretary, go around. People with titles usually have secretaries, part of whose job is to protect the boss from unsolicited phone calls. There are several ways of handling this. You can try calling around 8:30 A.M. or after 5 P.M. You'd be surprised at how many people pick up their own phones when the secretary has gone home.

You also can try to befriend the secretary. When you call, make a point of getting his or her name. When you call again, be sure to use that name and engage in some idle chitchat. It might take some time, but after a while the secretary will feel comfortable with you—and might even put in a good word for you with the boss.

Always try to close. The nature of the closing depends on the reason you're calling. It might be to get an appointment to see the person, or it might be to sell advertising space on your new Web server. Whatever it is, always ask for the business.

Developing a prospect database

People who surf the Web and contact you through your home page represent only about 5 percent of your potential customer base.

There are a lot more companies considering getting on the Internet than are actually on the Internet. This is the major reason to develop a prospect database. With it, you will perform all the tasks of marketing, including telemarketing and direct mail.

Tip

Use a computer as your smart assistant for all your telephone needs. For a demo, call (800) WILDFIRE.

Your prospect database is one of the most important things you can develop. With constant care and feeding it will treat you well. But how do you start? First you have to decide with what segment of the market you want to do business. Since you are an Internet consultant, the primary focus of your business will be other businesses. But there are many types of businesses out there. Are you interested in working with small businesses? Large businesses? All businesses?

I personally find it much more lucrative to work with midsize to large companies. Small companies usually want a lot of effort, but don't want to pay the price tag for this amount of labor. In addition, you'll find yourself in competition with every teenager with a computer. We stopped working with very small businesses after I heard for the umpteenth time, "But my nephew can do my home page for $50." Fine. Let him.

The next thing you have to determine is who in the company would be most likely to make the decision to develop a Web presence. In a small company (fewer than 100 people) it's probably the president, unless there's a marketing function. If it's a larger company, then it's the marketing department. Many large companies have multiple marketing managers, one for each product or service. You'll have to contact each one. And there are a variety of ways you can get the contact information on people of authority in companies.

Mailing lists

Trade magazines are a good place to start. If the people you want to contact read one or more of them, then contact the lists department of the magazine. Many magazines outsource the renting of their lists to list brokerage companies. If you get to speak to a list broker, ask them what other magazines in your industry they handle.

The magazine or the list brokerage rents a one-time usage of the list for a certain number of dollars per thousand names. The usual minimum you can rent is 5000 names, with an average cost per thousand between $95 and $150. For an extra charge, the magazine or list broker should be able to select (they use a database) names by region, type of business, and by title. For example, you might ask for all readers who have a title of CEO or marketing manager in the New York area. The magazine or list brokerage usually will supply a list of the selection criteria available. Because the readers are the ones who write down their job titles, you'll have to be flexible in your list selection. Marketing manager, marketing communications manager, and advertising manager might all be valid marketing titles. While phone number doesn't usually come with the list, you should be able to pay extra to get it.

Tip

Keep up to date on the software that's available for business. Get these free catalogs:

MacWarehouse (800) 255-6227
Mac Connection (800) 800-1111
Mac Zone (800) 248-0800
MacMall (800) 222-2808
Club Mac (800) 258-2622
Mac Wholesale (800) 531-4MAC
Computer Discount Warehouse (800) 656-4CDW
Tiger Software (800) 888-4437
Tiger Software CDROM Buyers Guide (800) 238-4437
Egghead (800) 344-4323
Publisher's Toolbox (for digital artists & designers) (800) 390-0461
Image Club Graphics (software catalog from Adobe) (800) 661-9410

You will have to sign a legal agreement to use the list no more than once. The magazine or list broker peppers the list with names only they know about, so if you try to mail to the list more than once, they will find you out. The magazine surely will ask to see a sample of what you're mailing, so have a mock-up available.

The list will be delivered in one of several formats, including pull-off labels, magnetic tape, diskette, and sometimes index cards (usually used for telemarketing). If the format is Cheshire labels, you'll need to deliver them to a printer who has the equipment to cut the large green and white sheets down to labels.

By the way, you own all the names that respond to your mailing or telephone call. You can put these guys in your own prospect database and never pay a fee on that name again.

> **Tip**
>
> If the computer industry is your market, or you're just interested in the industry itself, get a copy of the *Computer Industry Alamanac*. It has 3000 company listings, directories of assocations and conferences, and technology trends. At your local bookstore, or call (800) 486-8666.

Directories

If the mailing list route is too expensive for you, try one of the directories you can purchase at the bookstore. For example, my company markets heavily to the computer industry. At my local Barnes and Noble I found a book titled *Hoover's Guide to Computer Companies* (Reference Press). In it is a list of over 1000 key computer companies, including the names of many of the officers. The best thing is that the book came with free Windows software that let me import the list to my own database program. All this cost a mere $34.95. Contact Reference Press at (512) 454-7778.

ProCD's Select Phone contains the names and addresses of every business in the United States. While there is no contact name or description of the company, there is an SIC (Standard Industry Classification) number. Select the SIC you want (the software tells you the English translation for each code) and generate a list. The results can be exported to your database. ProCD can be reached at (800) 560-3526 or at their Web site: *http://www.procd.com*. The product retails for less than $160.

> **Tip**
>
> American Information Exchange Corporation is an online service on which you can market newsletters, business information and software for a fee.
>
> 1881 Landings Dr.
> Mountain View, CA 94043
> (415) 903-1000

Dun & Bradstreet keeps tabs on all businesses in the United States—maybe even you. If you get the Tiger Software catalog, you've probably seen an advertisement for D&B's Marketplace. This product is a CD with extensive information on over 10 million U.S. businesses, including primary contact name. While D&B sells it for $849, you can get it far cheaper from Tiger. Call them at (800) 888-4437.

The way Marketplace works is that you pay your money and get about 3000 selections for your dollars. You can use these 3000 names as many times as you want. If you want more, just call up D&B and pay about 35 cents maximum per company for full demographic and contact information; D&B will give you a numeric key to unlock the Marketplace database. For more information surf to *http://206.240.110.11/icon/bzone/br.html.* Demand Research has compiled diskettes full of good contacts (e.g., DRC's *Directory of Corporate Officers,* and *The Executive Desk Register of Publicly Held Corporations*). They can be contacted at (614) 891-5600. DRC is reliable and efficient. They are also very inexpensive.

Other sources

You've probably noticed the advertisements in some business magazines for mailing lists. Many of these are fly-by-nighters. While they do provide names, these lists may be out of date or just don't get results.

Tip

If you absolutely must market via e-mail, get a good mailing list. I don't know whether these folks are good, but they do sell e-mail lists:

ICON
http://www.iconinc.com/icserv/icserv.html#email

You also can go online to get names of prospects, about which there's more in the next section. While *spamming* (the act of sending out the same e-mail message to multiple mailing lists or newsgroups) is still not an acceptable practice on the Web, the mailing lists involved in business might be more lenient. I still wouldn't advise spamming. Instead, join these lists and work them like you would work a cocktail party. If it turns out that the list doesn't mind a solicitation, then go right ahead.

Surf over to *http://www.nova.edu/Inter-Links/cgi-bin/lists.* Here you will find a form where you can enter a word you would like to search for. If you enter the word "business," you will get a list of all mailing lists that dabble in business-related topics. Note, however, that a goodly number of these will be academically oriented. These are not good prospects. Another source of online mailing list is *http://www.NeoSoft.com/internet/paml/.* One or all of these sources might work for you. One or all of these sources might not work for you. Keep looking for new sources, and keep the database you create up to date. It's your lifeline to new business.

Going online to generate business

We've already talked about your Web site, so I'll not belabor the point here. What I would like to talk about is the use of the Internet, as well as the proprietary on-line services, to generate leads.

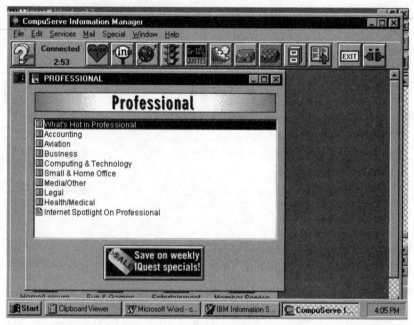

7-1 *The proprietary online services have forums which you can use to "soft" market yourself.*

As shown in Fig. 7-1, mailing lists (sometimes called *Listservs*) on the Internet and forums on the proprietary services such as America Online and CompuServe are like networking cocktail parties. People with like interests gather together to discuss topical issues.

This can work to your benefit. For example, suppose you specialize in Internet sites for accountants. If you join all the Internet mailing lists that serve accountants, as well as the forums for accountants (Fig. 7-2) on the proprietary services, you'll have an audience of thousands of potential clients. (Type the keyword "accounting" on *http://www.nova.edu/Inter-Links/cgi-bin/lists.*)

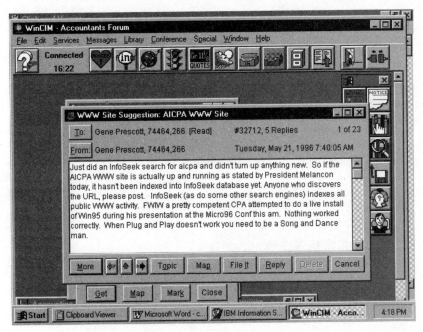

7-2 *An e-mail on CompuServe.*

So how does this work? While Usenet (the newsgroups part of the Internet) often permits aggressive posting of business messages, I don't recommend it because it seems to be more like a flea market than a forum of legitimate business opportunities. The other venues require a more subtle approach known as *soft marketing*.

Monitor mailing lists and forums frequently, at least once a week. Become an active participant rather than a lurker (someone who reads the messages but does not join in). Offer advice frequently to develop a reputation as someone who is an expert in the field, as shown in Fig. 7-3, but do not pitch your products or services unless it comes up in the course of answering a question.

Append your *signature file* to each one of your messages so people will know how to contact you. Your signature file is a text file containing your name, company name, and whatever else you need to pitch your business. Most mail reader software will append the sig file automatically to all outgoing mail.

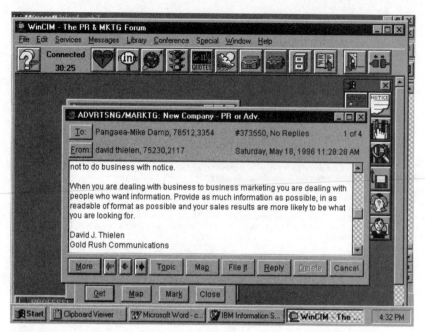

7-3 *Use forums to provide advice, but be sure to let them know who and what you are.*

The take-away Internet CD

There will come a time when a prospect will ask you for some information about your company. This was discussed in Chap. 6, but one thing was omitted: the interactive CD. While printed literature is an absolute necessity if you want to demonstrate the professionalism of your business, the interactive demo CD is the mark of a true online professional.

Yes, you're an Internet consultant, but most of your prospects are not necessarily Web-literate. How do you convince them that you're capable of designing fabulous Web sites when they don't know how to get online to see your samples? There aren't many businesses in America that don't have one or more PCs. Since CD-ROMs have been standard on PCs for the last several years, an interactive CD is a viable delivery method for showing off how talented you are.

You can use diskettes, of course, but your "interactive brochure" will be brief and might even do you more harm than good. CD creation is not particularly expensive, and you might actually find a second line of work in multimedia as you learn how to create CDs.

Tip

Need to duplicate and label your CD?

Media Control
(212) 924-4021

What to put on your CD

Your CD is your interactive brochure. The creativity you use to craft Web sites should be used to create this CD. As on a Web site, use vivid graphics, animation, audio, and video. Unlike the Web, however, you don't really have to worry about the time it takes to download a large image. You can apply extra creative here and, because you have about 650 megabytes to play with, you can add all sorts of bells and whistles.

There are two schools of thought on the subject of creating interactive brochures:

- Mimic the look and feel of the Internet exactly by using Netscape or some other browser as the graphical interface.
- Use an authoring tool to create a bona fide, interactive, multimedia CD.

The first method is probably the easiest. Both Netscape and Microsoft are giving their browsers away free, so why not copy it to the CD and then configure it to play directly from that medium? Then you can build your home page directly on the CD. It's really no different than building for online delivery. Instead of coming from a distant server, your text and graphics, animation, etc., will be served directly from the CD. You can copy your own site, your customers' sites, or both. You also can add some additional information about your company. In fact, if you have gone through the trouble of creating a paper brochure for your company, you can add that, too.

Make the CD easy to install. Remember that your prospects may have limited expertise with the PC. Your prospects should be able to start the process by merely typing something like

File, Run d:\netscape.exe

or whatever browser you are using. This means loading everything under one directory on the CD so that your prospects don't have to change directories.

Make sure you modify the browser's options so that it displays your home page automatically on startup, as shown in Fig. 7-4. Make

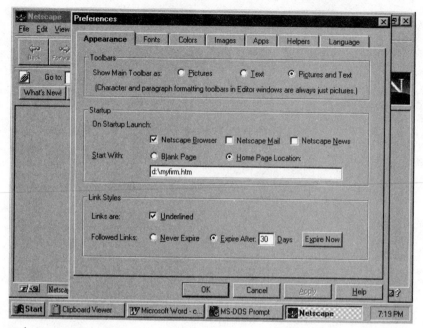

7-4 *You can set the start-up homepage to any location you want including a CD or hard disk.*

sure you add to the CD any plug-ins, such as Shockwave or RealAudio, that you have elected to use.

Supply an instruction sheet. Make it no more than one page. If it's longer than that, your prospects will lose interest as they grow more and more confused. After all, this might be the first time they've used an Internet browser. Make sure you provide a contact name and telephone number for the inevitable questions. And make sure you label the CD itself with title, contact information, and a copyright notice.

Show the prospect all your stuff. You've got 650 megabytes and the attention of your prospects. If your own site or your samples don't contain all the latest whizbang features, take the time to add them now.

If you have paper brochures and other literature that were created on a desktop publishing system, invest in the Adobe Acrobat development environment (*http://www.adobe.com*). The PDF Acrobat extension is a plug-in that will show your prospects your brochures in all their full-color glory, directly online.

The alternative to a browser-based CD is a multimedia CD. In my book, *The Ultimate Sourcebook of Multimedia* (McGraw-Hill, 1996), the topic of multimedia development is covered more in 70 chapters and 1100 pages. Obviously, I can't cover the topic here in depth.

What I can do is recommend you take a look at some of the tool sets that multimedia developers use to create their products.

Multimedia authoring packages run the gamut from tool sets that work the same way as desktop presentation software, like Lotus Freelance and Microsoft PowerPoint, to scripting/programming languages closely related to Java.

All of these tools give developers the wherewithal to create incredible tutorials, presentations, catalogs, and more. I'm sure you've received a CD or two or three in the mail. All of these were created with one or more multimedia tool sets. And all of these tool sets, whether they're easy to use or hard, have one thing in common: They let you embed multimedia elements such as audio, video, animation, into your production.

Tip

Multimedia authoring is a good adjunct business for Internet consultants to get into. Find out more about the tool sets of the business at:

http://www.yahoo.com/Business_and_Economy/
Companies/Computers/Software/Multimedia/Authoring_Tools/

If you're not familiar with, and don't have the time to learn, a new tool set like Asymetrix Toolbook (which has just been enhanced to operate on the Web), then use a package like Asymetrix Compel, Oracle's Media Objects, or Microsoft's Viewer (Fig. 7-5).

Those of you who invested in Lotus Smart Suite (mine came free with my IBM Aptiva) will get a fabulous surprise. Not only does Smart Suite have Lotus 1-2-3, Freelance, and a word processor, it also has ScreenCam.

Tip

TipsScreen capture your way to a presentation with:

http://www.c-star1.com/
http://www.techsmith.com/
http://www.beale.com/
http://198.207.242.3/authors/gregko/snap32.htm

Also type "capture" as a keyword on *http://www.share-ware.com* to locate shareware screen capture utilities.

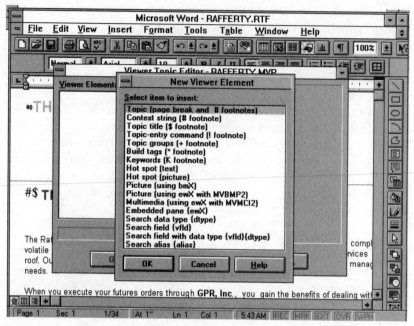

7-5 *Using a multimedia tool to create an interactive demo.*

ScreenCam runs in the background on your PC, as shown in Fig. 7-6, and records every action you take. If you have a sound card and a microphone, it lets you record voice-overs. Let's say you have a bunch of home pages you want everyone to see. Write a script and then turn on ScreenCam. Move from home page to home page while recording your comments. When you've finished, you have a video demonstration of your Internet consulting prowess.

If you choose to use a multimedia-based tool, the creative demands involved in making this CD production are squarely in your ballpark. You can add elements of your Internet-based productions by making screen prints. (The Print Screen key plus a paint package are good enablers, or you can try one of the screen capture packages available.) Add a voice-over. Use your video camera to create a video, then pull it into your computer with a video capture card. Unleash your imagination. Packages like Asymetrix Compel even provides the tools to do some minor animation directly within the software.

Manufacturing the CD

If you've invested in a CD-R (recordable CD-ROM) drive, then you can load the entire production to a single CD and send it off to a reproduction house—or run them off on your own. CD-Rs have come down in

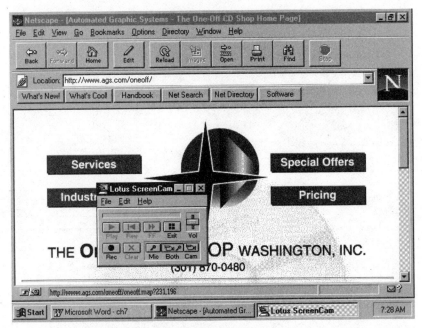

7-6 *Using Lotus ScreenCam to make a "movie."*

price dramatically. Just a few years ago you couldn't buy one for under $5000. Now a CD-R can be had, with packaged software, for $900–$1200. It just might be worth investigating. Not only can you use it to produce multimedia CDs, you can use it as a backup device as well.

The CD-R I use is a Pinnacle RCD 5040 for the PC. You can contact Pinnacle at (408) 720-9669. The drive came with backup software and Corel's CD Creator (Fig. 7-7). CD Creator is an easy-to-use package that lets you copy files from your hard disk to the CD. You only get one shot at creating a CD-R; the slightest glitch means you have to start over with a fresh blank. It's a read-many, write-once technology. Make sure you've got it right the first time.

If you don't want to spend the money to buy a CD-R, then you'll have to copy your 650 megabytes to a bunch of diskettes, a tape, a cartridge, or some other medium to get it out the door to a service bureau that will create a master CD for you, and then make as many duplicates as you want.

Recordable CD blanks cost about $15 each when you don't buy them in quantity. If you are going to be giving just a few out to prospects, then by all means reproduce them yourself. If you intend to mail them out to lots of folks, however, send your work of art to a company that does CD mastering (see the Appendix of this book). This should reduce your cost, in quantity, to about a dollar per CD.

These companies will even save you the trouble of printing a CD label for the jewel box, by printing your information directly on the surface of the CD itself. It gives it that professional touch.

Tip

You can get a quote right online from some of the companies that do mastering. Try The One-Off CD Shop at *http://www.ags.com/oneoff/*.

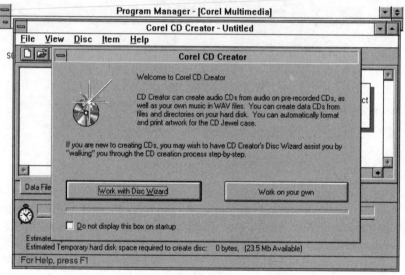

7-7 *Using Corel CD Creator to create a CD.*

Not all CD manufacturers are created equal. Before you turn over any serious money ask these questions:

- How much experience does the manufacturer have in making CDs?
- How many customers does the company have and who are they? Get references and call them.
- Is the work done in-house or are they outsourcing it?
- What are the lead times necessary for scheduling?
- What is the minimum quantity run available and the cost per disc at several levels? What kind of quantity discounts are offered?
- What input media does the manufacturer accept?
- What are the label, jewel case, and insert requirements and capabilities?

Some more interactive CD hints

Once you get the hang of the interactive CD medium, you'll probably want to use it as a mainstay of your marketing effort. There are a number of points to keep firmly in mind, the first of which is: Keep it easy to use.

Make sure to include as much information as you can about your company and its staff (even if it's just you). This means you should include magazine articles you've written, ads that you've run, and all the other items listed earlier, in the printed-materials discussion. Show essentially everything you have in your arsenal.

Provide some means for the prospect to interact with you. Supply a requirements form that the prospect can fill in, print out, and then fax or mail back to you. On this form he or she can fill in what it is he wants from the Internet, and any other information deemed important.

Before you spend any money on mastering, beta test your production by showing it to current customers. Get their feedback.

Produce just a few in the first go-round. See the reaction of your prospect database. Are they buying it or not? If not, find out why by doing a mini-market survey. Call a few prospects up. Ask them if they've seen your CD and what they thought about it. (This is also a great ploy to get the prospect on the phone.) Change your production accordingly.

Measure your sales from this medium. If you don't get any, then stop and figure out what's wrong. Don't waste money.

The secrets of fax marketing

Whoever said that fax is dead was wrong. More businesses use fax than use the Internet. Fax marketing is tricky business, however. Many states have laws against sending unsolicited marketing faxes. Faxes also eat up relatively costly paper, so a business on the other side may be less than appreciative of this technique. Still, it has its merits if done correctly.

There are three forms of fax marketing:
- Faxmail marketing
- Fax-enhanced ads
- Faxinfo services

Faxmail marketing is essentially doing by fax what you would have done by direct mail. *Fax-enhanced ads* are advertisements designed especially for a faxed delivery. *Faxinfo services* use the technology to send information of interest, with just a small plug given to your firm.

Of the three, I recommend only the last. The first two are in clear violation of many laws against it, are a nuisance, and are less than professional. If you insist on trying it, then I recommend you start with faxinfo. Then branch out into the other two only when you develop a database of those who have indicated they would be willing to receive special offers and other paraphernalia from you via fax.

Faxinfo is a technique similar to what you probably already use on the Internet. To get people to come to your site, you try to offer them a value-added home page. If it's just marketing, marketing, marketing, your prospects soon will be turned off. If you provide them with important (or at least interesting) information, however, your company will gain a reputation as a resource.

Tip

Your local telephone directory publisher has more directories than you think. One of these is a fax directory. You can order by phone with a credit card or charge it to your telephone.

The first thing you need to do is add the contact's fax number to your prospect database. As you build the database, this is one piece of information you definitely want to track. While directories such as Hoover's do list fax numbers, large organizations have lots of fax machines; the chances of the one listed being the right one are remote. Faxes sent to the wrong fax machine are thrown out. Faxes sent to the wrong person gets thrown out, too. My suggestion is to hire a temporary worker to call each of the numbers in your prospect database and get the right fax number.

Once you have a list of fax numbers, you need to have a way to get your faxinfo sent to them. Today everybody's PC probably has some sort of fax broadcasting service on it, or at least a fax driver that takes the place of the printer. My new Aptiva has a built-in communications center. All I need do is select one or more entries from an address book, as shown in Fig. 7-8, and off goes my fax.

The company that started this revolution was Canada-based Delrina Corporation, (206) 628-8080. Their WinFax Pro has become something of a standard in the industry. WinFax Pro lets you organize your address book by group. If you want to send separate faxinfos to prospects in separate industries, you can group them by industry. Once you've created the document, you can select the appropriate group easily, schedule it for after 9 P.M. when the rates are lowest, and go home and get a good rest.

Tip

Try these companies for fax broadcasting:

http://www.delrina.com/product/idxserv.htm
http://naples.com/spectrafax/sfxbjob.htm
http://www.greattv.com/
http://www.anawave.com/~cca/fax.htm
http://www.sirius.com/~mast-ent/fax_tel/

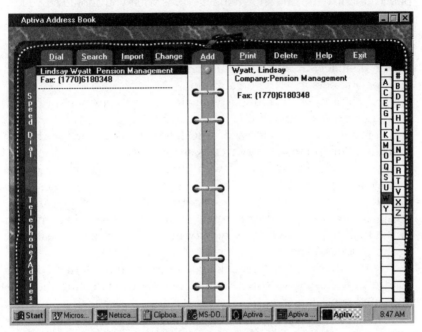

7-8 *Your modem software probably has a built-in fax broadcasting system.*

If you have fewer than 100 hundred prospects, then you can fax them yourself. Do it overnight, both to save on telephone costs and to make sure that your computer and your prospect's fax (or computer) aren't otherwise occupied. Just be sure to check your fax log in the morning. More than a few businesses turn off the fax machine overnight, and there will be busy signals and other errors. If you have more than a 100 prospects, or don't want to bother with doing it yourself, you can contact a service bureau that specializes in fax broadcast.

Now it's time to create your faxinfo. Because you can fax anything you can print, make it a point to create your faxinfo with a desktop publishing package like QuarkXPress, which is the one most graphics designers use.

> ## Tip
> Need some DTP resources? Jump to:
>
> *http://www.teleport.com/~eidos/dtpij/dtpij.html*

Your faxinfo should be well-researched. It should be something interesting to read, hard to throw out, and make you look like an expert. If you are trying to attract small business owners, for example, then a publication like the one shown in Fig. 7-9 is what you should strive for.

The faxinfo should be no more than one or two pages in length, maximum. It should be well-designed. Just because it's a fax doesn't mean that good graphic design can't be seen. It should contain information definitely meaningful to the prospect, and *must* be addressed to a specific person at the organization.

Include a brief pitch about your firm at the very bottom of the first page. For example, it could be a tagline such as, "This newsletter is brought to you courtesy of ABC Internet, your guide to the Information Superhighway. Contact us at 555-6789."

If you get stuck coming up with ideas for what should be in the faxinfo, then go directly to the Internet to find those ideas. These can include screen prints and descriptions of what others in the prospect's industry are doing, tidbits of industry news, hints on how to use Internet, or some other type of information. There's really no dearth of ideas, especially for a mere 1–2 pages.

Okay. You've faxed, telemarketed, forumed, and Internetted your way to new business. Now let's find out about marketing the old-fashioned way. Paper.

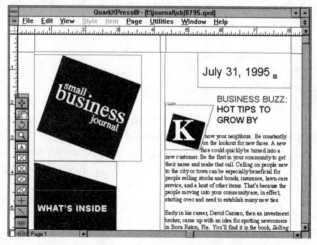

7-9 *A formatted newsletter ready for faxing.*

8

Master marketing for Internet consultants

Marketing and sales are age-old professions. Some traditional techniques have withstood the test of time. This chapter contains a wealth of marketing tips I have picked up over the years. They've all been tested and proven to be reliable sales boosters.

> **Tip**
>
> If sales is not your game, rent a sales expert:
>
> Sales Staffers International
> (508) 777-5400

Remember that Internet consulting is a business like any other business. To market yourself, you must get the attention of a prospect, make a favorable impression, and then close the sale.

Guerrilla marketing techniques

There's a slew of books at your local bookstore on "guerrilla" techniques for marketing your business. Buy them. They're worthwhile. They might restate common sense, but you'd be surprised at how we forget the common sense when it comes to marketing and sales. Here's a sampler of guerrilla-in-the-forest tips and tidbits to whet your appetite:

> **Tip**
>
> Guerrilla Marketing Newsletter
> P.O. Box 1336
> Mill Valley, CA 94942
> (800) 748-6444
>
> *http://www.gmarketing.com*

- When you talk to a prospect, especially on the phone, use short sentences. Your voice should project authority and warmth while instilling trust. Don't read from a script, but do memorize one.
- Objections are really opportunities in disguise. In fact, "close on the objection" is a sales credo for many professional sales people. For example, if a prospect says they're already using another consultant, ask if they're completely satisfied or if there's room for improvement.
- Establish alliances with other consultants to pick up the slack when you're overworked. Since turnabout is fair play, make sure they return the favor.
- It doesn't matter what your billings are, or how much you make. The only thing that matters is how much you keep.
- Always investigate the reasons why a proposal you've submitted is not accepted.
- Following up in 6 months or a year provides the client with a sense of continuity and long-term interest.
- To grow, you must fail periodically, so that you are continually aware of opportunities for improvement.
- A consulting firm's image, or lack of it, will play a key role in influencing a buyer one way or another.
- If you never accept an assignment that calls for doing something you've never done before, you'll never earn significant amounts of money.
- Consulting is a relationship business. Join networks, associations, chambers of commerce, advisory boards, and whatever else comes your way.
- Successful consultants differentiate their services so that they can convey some distinction to the client.
- Never take a job at a reduced fee just to get in the front door. You'll lock yourself permanently into a no-gain situation. Clients do talk among themselves about fee structures, so keep one fee schedule for all and make it worth your financial while.

Tip

National Mail Order Association provides help at a minimal cost to small businesses wishing to market through mail order and direct mail.

2807 Polk St., N.E.
Minneapolis, MN 55418
(612) 788-1673

Tip

MCI maintains a list (not a complete one) of associations with hyperlinks to their homepages.

http://www.mci.com/resources/sites/

Face to face with your customers

Most of us who spend a lot of time on the Internet tend to forget that there are such things as other human beings. Going into business for yourself means you'll be interacting with a lot of these folks. This is an art form in itself.

Tip

National Mailing List Firms include:

Hugo Dunhill
(800) 888-8030

Americalist
(800) 321-0448

Bell Atlantic
(800) 333-7980

TRW
(800) 527-3933

The first thing a prospect will see is your company name on some piece of literature. While we discussed what should go into your literature pack, and what it should look like, we never discussed your company name. Millions of dollars are paid annually to consultants who specialize in picking names. Most agree that a name that's right on target is a marketing necessity. ABC Internet Consulting, which describes the company in detail, is far better than ABC Inc.

I didn't know this, unfortunately, when I selected my own company name, New Art Inc. When I started in business, it was in the area of artificial intelligence—hence the word *Art*. This name actually gives the wrong impression of what we do. The only positive aspect of this name is that I do get in on a trade pass to lots of art shows (where I get 40 percent off!). Since I'm a corporation in the state of New York, it's too much of a bother to change my name at this point. Since many people know who we are after 9 years of business, I think I'll keep the name.

Tip

Three programs offer interesting ways to tackle business problems such as marketing strategies:

The Idea Generator Plus *[MS-DOS, $97.50]*
Experience in Software, (800) 678-7008

Inspiration *[Win/Mac, $195]*
Inspiration Software, (503) 297-3004

MindLink Problem Solver *[Win/Mac, $199/$99]*
MindLink Software, (802) 253-1844

I won't get into a discussion of whether you should go into business as a sole proprietor, a partnership, or corporation. Go to your attorney for that. I will say that there are certain advantages to being a corporation. If you're a small firm with a small number of potential shareholders, then look into becoming a "Subchapter S" corporation.

Tip

You can incorporate your company rather inexpensively—and quickly:

http://www.abbi.com/
http://www.corporate.com/online.htm

If you become a corporation, you'll have to have a unique corporate name. If you're a sole proprietor or partnership, you'll probably have to file a "DBA" (doing business as) form with your state agency if you do business under a name other than your own.

Once you have a good name and some literature, you'll probably use some of the techniques listed in this and the next chapter to start luring customers your way. Eventually you're going to have to meet them. I hate to mention this, but appearance does matter. Your personality does, too. Follow these guidelines:

> **Tip**
>
> Karras is a leading training organization devoted to negotiating. Two-day seminars are scheduled in major cities around the world, costing between $500 and $600. The multimedia package for people who cannot attend costs about $330.
>
> 1633 Stanford St.
> Santa Monica, CA 90404-4163
> (310) 453-1806

- Smile.
- Radiate charm.
- Project enthusiasm.
- Be courteous.
- Dress appropriately for the business you are visiting.
- Remember that good clothes are a salesperson's best friend.

You can project success by dressing like a successful person. I hate to sound materialistic, but showing your wealth has a subtle psychological effect. If they think you're doing well, then they think your business is successful. That means you probably offer a good service. Success begets success.

You're going to have to understand your customers, too:

- Understand what makes your customer tick, what he or she needs in order to feel secure, to be appreciated, to receive affection, to have new experiences.
- Understand the secrets of using psychology. People are highly amenable to suggestion; they're easily swayed if an advantage is evident. They do not need to be pressured if the proposition appeals to their ego and boosts their self-esteem.
- Analyze the customer's buying motive. Who is the buyer? What is it he or she requires? When does he or she wish to use the service? Why should be or she buy the service?
- Analyze each need and desire: gain, to obtain financial advantage and increase worth; pride, to satisfy the ego; fear, to stem competition; and imitation, to increase social standing and enhance self or business image.

Once you get in the front door, it's up to you to carry the first part of the conversation. Just how do you start a conversation?

- Use a current event to begin the conversation neutrally.
- Describe a situation you witnessed.
- Discuss a common acquaintance.
- Offer assistance in some way.
- Make a complementary remark.

Chances are good that you are going to make some sort of presentation. Since you're an Internet consultant, I'd strongly recommend bringing your laptop along (with some projection equipment if the audience is more than two people). It's times like these when your interactive CD can come in handy.

Of course, feel free to create a presentation using the traditional tools of presentation graphics, such as Freelance or PowerPoint. Just make it exciting. The idea here is to hold the prospect's interest, arouse curiosity, support your claims, and supply buying reasons.

In all cases, use affirmative suggestion and repetition techniques to make the point—and don't oversell. I'm reminded of a commercial that aired in the metro New York area, offering tax amnesty for New Jerseyites. The background music was the compelling part of the commercial. It was a rock song with the lyrics, "Some day or another I'm gonna get you, gonna get ya, get ya, get ya, get ya—" I heard it so often and was so hooked by it that I wanted to turn myself in. Problem was, I don't live in New Jersey, nor run my business from there.

Before we start, get some help

If you are short-staffed or have no staff, you might need some assistance from time to time. If your spouse, children, or assorted friends and relatives won't pitch in, then you're going to need some outside help.

Tip
The Association of Part Time Professionals, (703) 734-7975, may be a good source for you.

Consider using high school or college students. They can make telephone calls, buy supplies, answer phones, stuff envelopes, work the computer, write HTML, create DTP documents, survey customers, survey competitors, and make research trips to the library. You can locate them through local bulletin boards at the schools themselves.

The sales letter

There is a variety of marketing communications techniques used to solicit business. The preceding chapter discussed creating a prospect database. It is to these people that you will direct your marketing communications efforts.

Tip

Need pointers on sales techniques? Try *Dynamic Selling* newsletter, (800) 526-2554.

One of the major mistakes a newbie business owner makes in a marketing effort is to mail too infrequently, and to too small a base. The average response rate to a solicitation is 1–3 percent. If you mail a hundred letters, you might get from one to three bites.

Mailings should be done in threes. For example, send out a sales letter this month, a newsletter 3 months later, and then a postcard several months after that. Conventional wisdom is that the first correspondence will be tossed, and the second one read and then tossed. By the third missive, your company will sound sort of familiar. The prospect might call right away, or save it for when the need arises. Words of wisdom: Don't give up after the first mailing.

The sales letter is the easiest and least expensive paper-based way to generate business. You've probably already invested in stationery, so all you need to do is write the letter and then send it, right?

Tip

These printers specialize in inexpensive color printing by mail:

Color Impressions
(800) 626-1333

Multiprint
(800) 858-9999

Scangraphics
(708) 392-3980

The process is really far more complicated than that. Look at your own mailbox. Isn't it overflowing with letters? I know that I open my mail over my garbage pail. I'll bet you do too. And so do our prospects. The key is to get the prospect to open your letter. There are several ways of doing this:

- Make the letter a self-mailer.
- Use an envelope that begs to be opened.
- Mail first class if you can.
- Add color to the envelope.
- Consider professional printing.
- Try creative addressing.
- Use the element of mystery.

You can mail without an envelope. Fold the letter in threes and make sure that some interesting message is printed on the part that can be seen. Close the tri-fold with cellophane tape, an Avery sticker made just for this purpose, or a staple (the post office will hate you). Paper Direct and Queblo sell preprinted tri-fold mailers (which can also be used as self-made brochures) in a variety of themes. They also sell a word processing plug-in that helps you automatically format the document, as shown in Fig. 8-1. Contact Paper Direct at (800) 272-7377, or Queblo at (800) 523-9080.

Tip

Those faux Express Mail envelopes are a great gimmick to get people to open your mail. Mega Direct prints a complete line of them—matching letterheads too. They'll even print your letter and mail it for you. (800) 826-2869

If you use an envelope, make it one that screams "Open me!" To do this, you'll have to learn the art of the enticing tag line: Free Gift! Money-saving offer inside! Wealth-building hints enclosed! For your eyes only!

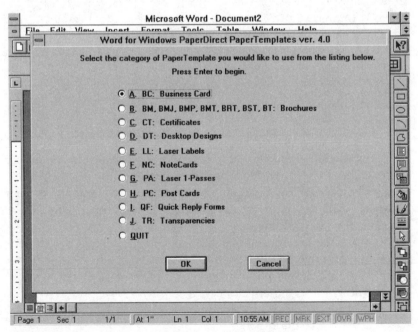

8-1 *Paper design template from Paper Direct.*

While you can save money mailing bulk rate (about 19.8 cents per ounce vs. 32 cents), people now usually toss out this form of mail instinctively. In addition, bulk takes much longer to deliver. Never mail bulk when the catalog retailers are sending out their millions of catalogs, usually around holidays. Mail first class if you can afford to do so.

Add a splash of color to your envelope, either by adding some artwork or by printing the tagline in a different color. Better yet, use oddly colored envelopes. Bright colors stand out from the rest of the mail. And consider using oversized addressing. Printing someone's name in 36-point type appeals to the subconscious need to see one's name in print.

You might want to consider having your letter and envelope professionally printed. Call at least three printers from your phone book. Fax them what you've created and ask them to give you a quote. We do a lot of our own custom graphic design right here using QuarkX-Press. Using Quark, you can add colors, special fonts, and other effects. Send the file either via modem or on a diskette to your printer.

If you choose to work only in black and white, point out the words you want in spot color. Tell the printer what color you want. Printers usually use a swatch book of colors known as PMS, short for Pantone Matching System. Each color has a number. If you want the words "FREE REPORT" to print in a particular color, for example, you'd have to select the color and then get the appropriate PMS number from the swatch. There are lots of colors from which to choose, as shown in Fig. 8-2.

Finally, note that a white envelope with no return address and a first class stamp always gets opened. Is it a bill? A check?

Tip

Need an extra edge to get to that customer? Try a greeting card just for sales.

IntroKnocks
(212) 967-6185

A good printer can help you in many other ways. Not only can printers provide advice on what makes a good design, they can fix some of the errors you put into your work (you're not an expert—yet), and locate a mailing house to do the onerous task of affixing labels and stamps.

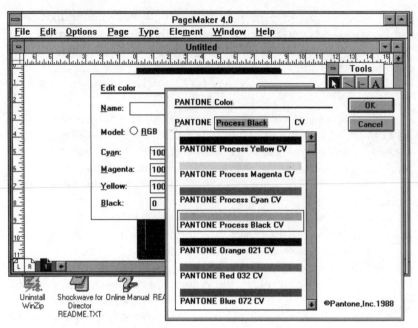

8-2 *Designing with color. You need to let your printer know the color you're using.*

Tip

I don't want to make you paranoid, but if you entrust your money mailing to an outside organization, get proof of mailing. This is supplied when you do a bulk mailing by the post office. Get a copy of it.

Also add your name and one or two others to your mailing list. This way you'll know if it's really been mailed and when people receive it.

If you've decided to go the bulk rate route, you'll probably want to use a mailing service. You really don't want to apply for a bulk permit, and then go through the trouble of putting the letters in Zip order and drag the bag to the main post office. While there is such a thing as a bulk mail stamp, most printers will print the bulk mail indicia (the box with a permit number inside), and assorted bar codes as part of the job.

First class permits work the same way. Instead of paying for the licking and sticking of stamps, you can have your own first class permit number printed on the envelope, or the indicia of the mailing house.

Once you get the prospect to open the envelope, you have to make sure your letter does a good job of selling:

- Always use the prospect's name. "Dear Mr. Thomas" is a lot better than "Dear Marketing Manager."
- Don't print on the reverse side of the letter to save money. People might not turn it over.
- Print the most important points first. Don't build up to the climax. If you don't grab them in the first few sentences, you've lost them.
- Incorporate graphics and good design.
- Always discuss the reader's needs, service benefits, features, and endorsements, and provide ways to respond.
- Include a response form that can be faxed back or mailed; it can be on the bottom of the letter. Always repeat your offer on the response form.
- Don't cram tons of text into a tight area. Leave plenty of white space. Keep your paragraphs and sentences short.
- Use noticeable graphics. Bold it. Italicize it. Underline it. Even hand write it. Do anything to grab your reader's attention.
- Include a P.S. For some bizarre reason, people always read these.

Tip

Subscribe to *MARKET YOUR BUSINESS!*, New Art's very own faxed newsletter. Great advice. Great price: just $37/52 issues a year for the readers of this book. Mail your check, name and fax number to:

New Art Communications
200 West 79 Street, 8H
New York, NY 10024

Tip

Call lots of printers to get quotes. You'll be surprised at the wide variation in prices.

One of the major U.S. postcard printers is Lawson Mardon Post Card. The "Mirror-Krome" division can be reached at (800) 347-2723.

Print your TIFF file to a transparency using a service bureau. Look in the yellow pages under Graphics Services, or in the classifieds of any magazine dedicated to desktop publishing for one in your area.

The postal card

What costs only 20 cents but packs a lot of weight? It's the lowly post-card. When we do a set of mailings (remember three is the lucky number), I like to follow a long sales letter or newsletter with a post-card. Prospects are almost forced to read them as they drop them into the wastebasket.

The 20-cent rate gets you a 4.25×6-inch area to work with. (You can create a larger postcard, but you will have to pay the full 32 cents to mail it.) One side should be some colorful attention grabber. Though this will be a graphic, you can embed some taglines in it using PhotoShop or some other graphics package. The flip side will contain your marketing message.

Tip

Need a graphics designer but want to see his or her portfolio first?

http://www.portfolios.com/

Here, too, you can use a desktop publishing system like QuarkX-Press to create the postcard. Just draw a box with the right dimensions and then proceed to fill it in. Because the front of your card will be in full color, you'll have to embed (paste or link) some kind of TIFF file to the document. If creating TIFF files with your trusty paint package is not your forte, then you might want to download some freeware graphic images from the Internet (see the tips boxes in Chapter 2), or buy one of the many graphics libraries at your local computer store. Use some of Corel Gallery's 10,000 images, or try PhotoDisc at (800) 528-3472 or *http://www.photodisc.com*. Or hire a graphic designer.

The newsletter

Though longer, the newsletter is a paper version of the faxinfo, discussed in the preceding chapter. It can be sent out either alone as a direct mail piece, or as a fulfillment piece to a sales letter. The newsletter should contain information of interest to your prospect. It should be well-designed and contain subtle sales images that gently persuade the prospect to give you a call.

Tip

It's hard to print a multipage newsletter on your laser. Fortunately, there's a company that specializes in just printing newsletters.

Newsletter Services
(301) 731-5200

Although Lead Story, the AT&T newsletter shown in Fig. 8-3 is not paper-based, its design is so good that I wanted to provide it as an example of how to design your own newsletter. An aside: It's not necessary to print your newsletter in color. Most printed newsletters are in black and white; color printing is expensive.

8-3 *AT&T online newsletter.*

Here are some tips for writing newsletters:
- Research news items directly on the Internet and proprietary services.
- Ask current customers to provide written articles.
- Ask prospective clients to provide written articles. (What a way to meet them!)

- Ask non-competing associates (e.g., lawyer, accountant, telemarketer) to write articles. You may be able to split costs, since they could get some business out of the mailing, too.

Send out your newsletter on a regular basis, at least twice a year, if not more. Make sure you distribute copies when visiting prospects and current customers, attending trade shows, and making speeches.

I'm a strong advocate for self-mailers. Design half of the back page with your return address as shown in Fig. 8-4, leaving room for the address label. Put a sticky to seal it, stamp it, put the address label on it, and put it in the mailbox.

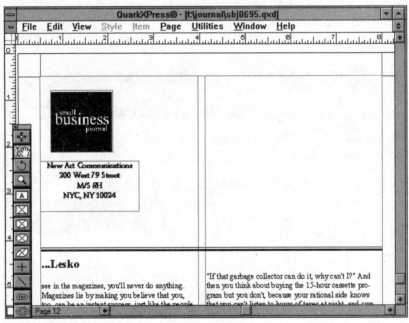

8-4 *Creating a newsletter self-mailer.*

If a self-mailer is not to your taste, then have a large envelope printed with the words "NEWSLETTER INSIDE." Better yet, open your yellow pages and call a company that sells envelopes. Ask for a quote on *presentation envelopes*, which have a glassine or vellum (see-through plastic) cover on one side. They come in several sizes and colors. You can put your newsletter in one of these envelopes so that prospects can see what they're getting. The label goes on the backside.

Your brochure

Your brochure consists of two parts: the writing and the graphics. If you're not good at one or both, get help. Writing for marketing purposes is a very different ballgame than writing for technical manuals or other pursuits.

If you decide to write your own, collect samples of other brochures first. This is where your competitive intelligence activities pay off. Find out what your competitors are saying, then say more of it and more powerfully. Here's how.

Start off by describing the business environment for your services. It's a tough world out there. There's tons of competition, both American and global. Write the opening in short pithy sentences like this:

Issues. Trends. Techniques. That's what you have to know to get ahead and stay ahead in this business. You really are what you know. But like everyone these days, you have so little time. And even if you did have the time, where could you go to learn all the things you need to know to get on top and stay on top? In just a few days?

Then tell them what they need, and the services you offer to fulfill them. Here again, say it in short pithy sentences:

To compete in today's competitive, dog-eat-dog world you need all the help you can get. And the help that business people like you are turning to is the Internet.

ABC World Internet is your roadmap to the Information Superhighway. Don't be fooled. There are detours. And roadblocks. Only ABC can guide you there safely—and cost-effectively.

Now list your credentials, including your mission. Next, enumerate your services, including newsletters, training, and anything else you offer. Provide a list of customers. Better yet, provide taglines with customer quotes and an attribution.

Provide a "call to action" that includes whom to call. Finally, close with a bookend that matches your opening. Make it dramatic:

The next several years will decide who will win and will lose in this age of information.

The look and feel of the brochure is just as important as the words. Break up the monotony of lots of text with compelling headlines—but make these headlines meaningful. Use appropriate fonts and spacing to make it easy to read. Serif fonts, i.e., ones like Times New Roman that have the little ornaments hanging off the letters, are much easier to read from a printed page than sans-serif ones like Arial (which is the standard Windows on-screen font). And please, please, stick to appropriate, mixed-cased capitalization. There's nothing worse than all-caps, which is impossible to read. (You're not e.e. cummings, either, so don't try all lowercase.)

If you're going to create a literature pack (e.g., brochure, letterhead, tri-folds), try to create a consistent image. If your brochure is pink and green and your letterhead is red and white, you simply won't match. If you do it yourself, you're in luck again. Paper Direct, at (800) 272-7377, sells sets of preprinted papers. You can match your business card to your brochure to your letterhead.

Whatever you do, don't put dates in your brochure. To save money, you'll have to print the brochures in quantity. If you have 5000 brochures that say, "In 1996 we were the most popular Internet . . .," you'll have to dump a lot of them in 1997.

Technology brochures are usually visually exciting, as shown in Figs. 8-5 and 8-6. Some interesting design techniques are:

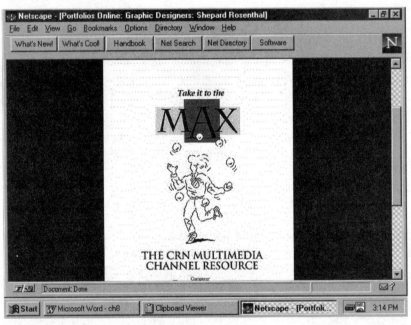

8-5 *Portfolios online.*

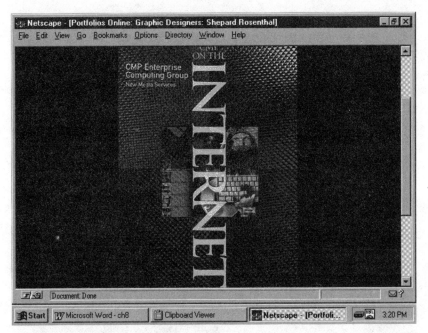

8-6 *A good design example.*

- **Bleeds.** This is ink coverage that goes all the way to the edge of the paper. Notice that you simply can't do bleeds on a laser printer. There will always be some white space to the left and the right.
- **Embossing.** Remember my folder? The name of my company is raised. It looks quite professional and very elegant.
- **Ghosting.** Shown in Fig. 8-7, ghosting is a neat way to print your customer list without appearing obvious.
- **Unusual bindings.** Most brochures are perfect bound. That means they are stapled together in the center. If you plan to create a few brochures, try to be creative. I'm somewhat partial to ribbon binding.
- **Gloss.** I love those glossy brochures. Did you know that you don't have to cover the whole page with it? You can do just a portion. You can use this to great effect to make something stand out.
- **Die cuts.** You probably notice literature that's cut unusually. Maybe the front opens along a jagged line, or maybe the center is cut out.

- **Unusual fonts.** Your word processor probably came with dozens of fonts. Try them out to see how they look. An advanced graphics package like CorelDRAW provides the ability to twist and turn words to create unusual designs, as shown in Fig. 8-8.

Tip

Want to imprint your company name on something and give it out as a promotion?

http://www.vcnet.com/think/

Tip

Go to your local bookstore and spend some time in the Graphics department. There are lots of great books on the subject of promotions; here are two of my personal favorites:

Fresh Ideas in Promotion (Lynn Haller, North Light Books)
Direct Mail Marketing Design (Day and Evans, Rockport Publishers)

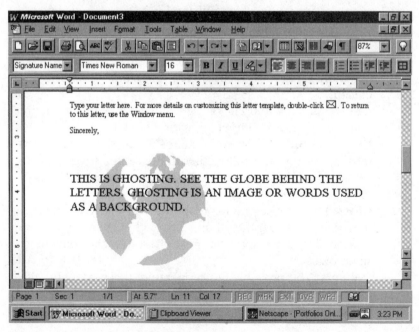

8-7 *Use ghosting for good effect.*

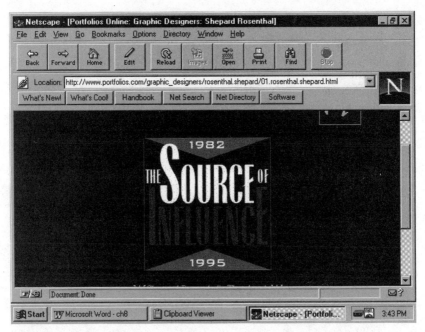

8-8 *Creative use of fonts.*

Internet consultants use promotions, too

Promotions are a form of direct mail. I like to think of them as a fun form of getting yourself known. It's here where your creativity can run rampant. The goal here is to catch your prospects' attention.

Sending greeting cards (especially calendars) during various holiday seasons is a form of promotion. Giving out free pens, totes, and pads emblazoned with your logo are promotions, too.

Promotions can be used separately from or in conjunction with other forms of direct mail such as sales letters. It is common to include as an enticement a free newsletter, report, or consultation as part of your call to action.

But you don't have to stay with the tried and true. All of the following make good promotions.

Send packaged seeds to your prospect and tell them that you can help make their company grow. Print on a book of matches the fact that you can make their company "hot." Or put a small light bulb in a box with a note that the Internet can make their company glow.

Tip

Sources of premiums:

Promotional Products Association
(214) 252-0404

Promotion and Marketing Association of America
(212) 420-1100

Cut rectangles out of a cardboard box. Affix address labels and a stamp (get it weighed first). Hand-print the message with felt-tip markers. Tell your prospects that if they are not marketing on the Internet, their marketing messages are going to be as effective as writing on a box.

Tip

Dial-a-promo:

Dial-A-Gift
(800) 453-0428

800 Spirits
(800) 238-4373

Petersen Nut Company
(800) 367-6887

Popcorn World
(800) 443-8226

Design and print a t-shirt with a quirky image and saying. The Canon color printers will print to a transfer sheet, which you then can iron on a t-shirt. Or use your yellow pages to locate a t-shirt maker or promotions house.

Have fortune cookies made up with the message that your company will be in the prospect's future. Or send a bag of peanuts, with a note saying that it costs only peanuts to reach 27 million potential customers through the Internet.

More simply, you can send prospects your audio tape or videotape, or a special research report.

There are literally thousands of ideas. If you have one that works, why not let me know? Send e-mail to *newart@panix.com*. I'll post it on my home page with other information from this book.

Speaking your way to success

This last topic we're going to discuss might not be up your alley. Most people are afraid of speaking in public. I don't know why. I personally get a big kick out of it.

If you have a fear of getting in front of a large group, grow out of it. Check out your local college adult continuing education catalog. Take a course in public speaking. You'll be glad you did.

Tip

Chambers of Commerce are good organizations to join. They have lots of meetings with chances at networking and a venue for public speaking:

Try *World Chamber of Commerce Directory,* published annually in June.

World Chamber of Commerce Directory
P.O. Box 1029
Loveland, CO 80539
(970) 663-3231

They used to call speaking engagements the "rubber chicken circuit" because lunch or dinner, usually bad, came as part of the package. Whether the chicken is rubber or not, this is the best of all possible ways to strut your stuff. You've got a captive audience, after all.

Tips

Trade shows are a great place to speak.

Trade Show and Convention Guide
Amusement Business
(615) 321-4250

There are two different types of "seminars." One is specifically geared to market your services. It's relatively simple:

- Take out an ad in the trades or other publications that your target audience reads.
- Send out a sales letter or invitation.
- Run a radio advertisement if you have the budget and you can target your audience in this way.
- Rent a room (or use your own office if you have the space).

- Arrange for refreshments. In the morning provide coffee, tea, and pastry. Afternoon seminars can get away with cans of soda and cookies.
- Have someone sign guests in and provide name tags.
- Use 35mm color slides rather than overheads. Create the slides with a presentation graphics package. Find a graphics firm in your yellow pages that can print 35mm slides from your files. If there aren't any, see if any of the inserts that came with your software is for one of these service bureaus. If not, check your manual or call tech support.

Tip

Need to have 35mm made out of your computer file?

Perfect Presentations
(800) 991-4465

Computer Imaging
(800) 883-6537

- Don't give live demos. Murphy's Law will kick in. The computer will break. Or hang. Run your Internet demo from your CD or hard disk.
- Hand out a promotional item like a free tote bag or pen and pad.
- Hand out a copy of what you will say, as well as literature about your company. Attach your business card.

There are variations on the theme. If you do everything I mentioned above, your total cost will be about $15,000. (This was the price for the last one we did in expensive New York City, but we had an evening event and an open bar.) You can split the costs with others in your industry. If you do only Internet and an associate firm does only multimedia, you can team up to deliver a seminar on using interactive technologies. This will cut your costs in half.

Tip

Go on-line to find a speech trainer:
http://www.catalog.com/seminars/tpd.htm
http://www.walters-intl.com/

Others who might want to get in on the act are newsletter and magazine publishers, educational institutions, and attorneys. In fact, a multi-organizational seminar is often a larger draw than just a one person setup.

A less expensive, and I think much more lucrative, approach to speaking is to get yourself on the speaker circuit. There are thousands of associations, users' groups, etc., that host meetings. Sometimes they're even at fun places. Call them up and ask if they need speakers. The Internet is a hot topic, so they should be interested.

To track down organizations that might want you as a speaker, start by checking your yellow pages under the title "associations." Go to the library and ask the librarian for the directory that lists all the associations in the United States. These are listed by location as well as by type. Jot down the ones that interest you.

My advice is to stick with the nontechnical associations. For example, *Inc. Magazine* does a yearly "Growing Your Business" seminar. The Institute of Management Consultants holds a yearly get-together, as does the Direct Marketing Association. These are all nontechnical business groups with a thirst for information about the Internet. And there won't be someone in the audience with lots of knowledge, gunning for you. I've done all these meetings—with great results for my business.

Technical trade shows are listed in the *Computer Industry Almanac*; call (800) 486-8666. While many of the large technical trade show production houses like Blenheim (PC Expo and Unix Expo) have a Web site (*http://www.shownet.com*) where you can download an application form, the general format for getting speaking assignment is:

- Track down the associations that interest you.
- Call them to get the name of the person who handles the conference where you want to speak.
- Write (or fax or e-mail) them a cover letter with an outline covering the topic of your speech; see Appendix A for a sample of what this looks like. Send them your bio as well.

If they're interested, they'll call you. If they're really interested, they might even ask you to be a keynote speaker. Because I've written many books and articles and have been in the field for a while, I get asked to make lots of keynotes. Usually, they pay your expenses and a small honorarium. If it's a large conference with many speakers, and you're not the keynote, you're lucky to get in for free. If it's a large crowd (the Direct Marketing Association had over 1000 people), the money you lay out is well worth it.

In all cases you will discuss with the conference contact such particulars as the length of your speech, the type of audience, the room arrangement, handouts, audiovisual equipment, and whether or not there will be questions and answers at the end.

If you've created a demo CD or disk, you might want to bring a batch of these along as promotional items. In all cases, hang around at the end of your speech and gracefully answer all questions. Stick around for lunches, dinners, and all cocktail parties. Force yourself to mingle. Some folks even wear their business card on their lapels, a great idea! One of the perks of most well-organized conferences is that they make an audio tape of your speech; you'll probably get a free copy. Make sure you get the name and address of the A/V company that made the tape. You will want to make copies to hand out as—you guessed it—a promotional item.

In the end, it's a simple piece of paper that will determine whether you reach your audience successfully. In Chapter 9 we'll continue the paper-based theme as we delve into public relations and advertising.

9

Grow your business using public relations and advertising

Eventually, you'll want to expand your business. You'll want the press and companies beyond your geographic region to know who you are and what you do. There is absolutely no reason why, given the abilities of telecommunications, you can't have customers in all four corners of the globe. The question is, how do you reach them?

> **Tip**
>
> *News Media Yellow Book*, published by Monitor Publishing (212) 627-4140, is a great resource for media contacts for PR purposes. $160

This is where advertising and public relations come in. Like everything else in the marketing arena, it requires some money and a lot of effort. That's what this chapter is about.

Effective advertising

You've probably noticed the rush to advertise on the Web. There might be millions of home pages, but only a few are really worthwhile for advertising. Unfortunately, these chosen few are expensive. For C/Net Online (*http://www.cnet.com*), from the most popular computer-oriented television program, charges are according to two variables: time and CADs (confirmed ads delivered). There are three options for time: 3 months, 6 months, and 12 months. There are five options for CAD level: 200,000, 400,000, 600,000, 800,000, and 1.2 million. Rates begin at $15,000 gross per month for 200,000 CADs, or $12,750 net if you are not working through an agency.

Tip

Want to find out who's linking to the site you want to advertise on? The more links they have the more hits you'll get.

http://www.site.com/

Table 9-1. HotWired Rate Card

Weeks on HotWired:	4 weeks	8 or 12 weeks	16 or 20 weeks	24+ weeks
Pages in Wired:				
0–5 pages/year	$15,000	$14,550	$14,100	$13,650
6–12 pages/year	$15,000	$14,250	$13,800	$13,350
13+ pages/year	$15,000	$13,950	$13,500	$13,050

HotWired's rates are shown in Table 9-1. Other "hot" advertising spots are InfoSeek (*http://www.infoseek.com*), Shareware.com (*http://www.shareware.com*), and Yahoo (*http://www.yahoo.com*). All sites let you request what is known as a rate card, directly from their page.

Because the popularity of Web sites changes daily, it's good to keep track of the "cool" sites as designated by the industry pundits and jump-off places like Netscape, as shown in Fig. 9-1. The appendix of this book lists a load of Internet-related magazines. Read them, or at least leaf through them, on a regular basis.

Of course, there is an alternative to paying money to the likes of Yahoo and HotWired. You can get yourself indexed in as many directories as you can. I've already gone over this at least twice in earlier chapters, and have included lists of directory URLs for you to get started (see Table 6-2). There are a wide variety of pages out there that keep active lists of what they consider to be the most informative sites. For example, the Small Business Administration (*http://www.sba.gov*) keeps track of sites interesting to business.

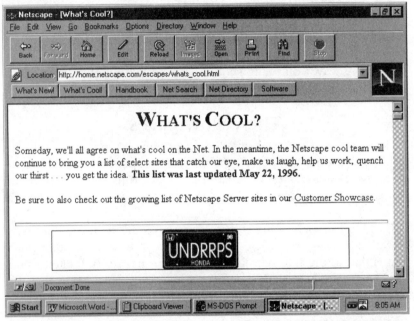

9-1 *There are lots of places to index your site. Netscape is one of them.*

New Art keeps one as well, called HotLinks. I can't tell you how many times I've received e-mail to "please list our site in your HotLinks section." Usually we agree, but request that they link our site to their own home page. Although there's some legal grumbling underway about the copyright infringement possibilities inherent in linking, right now this is still legal and a great way to get folks to come to your page.

Eventually, though, as you grow your business you'll have to start using traditional paper-based methods of advertising. In New York City, Juno (a purveyor of free e-mail on the Internet) is running super-large ads on the sides of buses. Every major manufacturer is printing their URLs right on their glossy color ads. Today the URL is as ubiquitous as the 800 number.

> ### Tip
>
> Need someone to fulfill your orders when you publish your own Internet book? Here are some direct response fulfillment houses:
>
> MATRIXX
> (402) 498-4000
>
> Teletech
> (818) 501-5595
>
> Neodata
> (303) 666-7000

By the way, you really should have an 800 number. They're inexpensive and a great way to get someone to call you.

The yellow pages

Today there are two types of yellow pages; the paper one and the Internet-based one. Although expensive, the paperbound *Business-to-Business Yellow Pages* (a quarter-page ad runs $1100–3000) are probably worth your while. Your ad stays put for a year and people do use it.

The unfortunate thing is that, if you miss the deadline, you have to wait a whole year before you can place your ad. The other problem is that in the Internet business, you are not really limited to doing business only in your own geographic area. This means that you will want to put ads in multiple *Business-to-Business Yellow Pages*.

> ### Tip
>
> Need help with Yellow Page advertising?
>
> O'Halloran is an advertising agency that specializes in this medium.
>
> *http://www.well.com/user/business/ohalloran.htm*
>
> Statistical Research, Inc., provides detailed information on business uses of the Yellow Pages.
> (908) 654-4000

Ad cost depends upon size, the use of color, and even boldfacing. Since you're making a large financial commitment, I recommend spending a little time with the current book to see what other consultants are doing. Are they listing themselves under Internet, Online or Computer—or all three? I would even recommend calling some of them and asking them how the ad in the yellow pages is paying off for them. In fact, I would recommend calling current advertisers in all magazines where you are thinking of advertising, and asking them the same question. A little research can save you a lot of money.

If you can afford it, a big ad is much better than a small ad. People think you're a really big company if your ad is big. The yellow pages are a medium for interested buyers. If they're reading the yellow pages, then they want to buy something, so don't let the yellow pages people write your ad. Let them give you pointers, but write your own or hire someone who's done this before.

You probably know that the yellow and white pages have gone online. The telephone companies have jumped into the fray as quickly as their size allows. I'm an 800-number customer of AT&T. They have a directory online just for me—and you, too, if you have an AT&T 800 number.

Tip

Web Yellow Pages Advertising:
Big Yellow
http://www.bigyellow.com

AT&T Toll Free
http://www.tollfree.att.net/dir800/

American Business Information
http://www.abii.com/

GTE SuperPages
http://www.superpages.com/

Yellow Pages Online
http://www.ypo.com/

Worldwide Yellow Pages
http://www.yellow.com/

The trade ad

If you're going after a particular industry, then you don't want to advertise in *People*. Popular consumer magazines attract a large, fragmented audience. What you don't want is diversity. You want 100 percent of the readership to be interested in what you offer. A recent study by Opinion Research Corporation found that 40 percent of business customers cited trade publications as their chief source of information about their particular product or service.

Let's say you're interested in targeting the computer industry (although this is probably not a good place to find Internet clients, since they can do it for themselves). There are literally dozens of general trade publications from which to choose: *PCWeek, Computer Reseller News,* and *ComputerWorld* are just a few. There are also specialty magazines in the computer industry, such as *LAN Magazine,* which specializes in (you guessed it) networking. The goal is to find the magazines that provide you with the largest audience at the lowest possible cost.

Tip

Places for mailing lists:

Directory of Mailing List Companies
(914) 358-6213

Direct Media
(203) 532-1000

Media Horizons
(203) 857-0770

Although industry directories like the *Computer Industry Almanac* do list the publications in the field, if you want to go after another industry (marketing, for example), you'll need a reference that lists all major publications.

The industry standard, the one that everyone in marketing and public relations uses, is *Standard Rate and Data* (708) 256-6067. This multivolume, fairly expensive reference should be available from your main public library in the business section as a reference book.

SRD lists all magazines and newspapers. Given that there are probably well over 60,000 of them, you can imagine how large this set of books is. Luckily it's organized by industry type (e.g., computers, marketing). Track down your market and then pick through the listings. Information on mission of the magazine as well as size of its readership is listed. Most important, the cost of the advertisement is listed as well.

Tip

Direct mail help: The Advertising Mail Marketing Association represents supporters and users of mail as an advertising and marketing medium.

1333 F St. N.W., #710
Washington, DC 20004-1108
(202) 347-0055

Jot down the phone numbers of magazines that interest you, and when you go back to your office, call the magazines and request a media kit. The media kit tends to be a beautifully designed folder with inserts, and includes a sample of the publication and the rates of all the ads. One nice perquisite is that many publications will automatically put you on their complimentary subscription list when you request a media kit.

Read the magazine carefully. Do your competitors advertise there? If they don't, it might be an indication that this magazine is not an appropriate forum for what you are selling. If there are competing ads, see how long they have been advertising. To get a reduced rate in advertising, usually you have to commit to at least three months' worth of ads. If your competitors have been running their ads for a longer period of time (you can ask the advertising manager of the magazine or check back issues in the library), you can rest assured that the ads probably are drawing some response.

Tip

Al Parinello's *On the Air: How to Get on Radio and TV Talk Shows and What to Do When You Get There* is available from Career Press for about $13. Call (201) 427-0229 or (800) 227-3371.

Business Radio Network provides information on national syndicated radio shows.

888 Garden of God Rd.
Colorado Springs, CO 80907
(719) 528-7040

The ad rate is based on the ad size, use of color, and the number of times the ad is run. Some magazines have different sections. These sections might be priced differently, so check out everything about the publication.

Although trade magazines are less expensive than business or consumer magazines, ads are still expensive. A full-page color ad might run $6000 per month; the same ad in *Forbes* or *Fortune* can cost four times that amount. The unfortunate thing about advertising is that you can't really only do it once. Like direct mail, repetition is what makes it work. You also need repetition to get the lowest rates. Classifieds are much less expensive than display ads. Here you pay by the word and, believe it or not, people do read them. For example, *AdWeek* is a hotbed of classified advertising for Internet consultants. *AdWeek* also has an Interactive Media directory, published once a year, where you can get yourself listed for free.

You can sometimes get yourself a 15 percent discount if you tell them you are your own in-house agency. Advertising agencies usually are the ones who create the ads; so they can make money, the magazines give them a discount. If the ad is $300, for example, the agency pays $300 minus 15 percent, but bills the customer the full $300.

Keep track of your results. If you run more than one display or classified ad, how will you know which one actually works? Put a special extension in the phone number, for example. If they ask for extension 222, then you know it came from magazine A. If they ask for extension 333, you know the lead came from Magazine B. You can do the same with addresses. Attach a different suite number for each magazine.

Here are some more pointers to help you along:

- Make sure your ad has only one message, and that it speaks the language of your audience. If it's a marketing audience, don't speak techie.
- Make sure you have a call to action. No piece of marketing communication should be passive. Make them want to respond to you.
- You can induce them to call you by placing a special offer in the ad, such as a free consultation or a free report.
- Remember that it's not the features but the benefits that sell, so put this in your ad.
- Use great visuals. There's nothing more boring than an ad that's just words.
- Use testimonials if you can.
- Keep the headline short. Write in short sentences.
- Experiment with different ad sizes, shapes, days run, and sections of the periodical.
- Make your small display ads noticeable. Use the word *FREE* in your headline, or put a border around your ad, or use reverse type (i.e., black background and white lettering), or be sure the ad contains a word or two in huge type, or use spot color.

- If you run a full-page color ad, get reprints. You can use them as part of your literature pack or send them as part of a direct mail campaign.

If you run a classified or a black and white display ad, you might be able to get away with sending the magazine camera-ready copy. If you have a good quality laser, then print out your ad and send this in. Your copy will be placed under a camera and the process will proceed from there. The camera sees every flaw, so make sure there are no ink specks and that letters and artwork are all solidly composed. I recommend that you invest in at least a 600 dpi laser printer.

If you are running a color ad, then you might have to use the services of a graphic designer. The magazine probably will want a transparency of composed film; these probably are beyond your capabilities. If you want to play with it yourself, use a good graphics package and the help of a good service bureau. You create the image (sized to the magazine's specifications) using your software. You then send the file to your service bureau, who will compose it to the medium you request. (Make sure the service bureau has compatible software and can read your disk, especially if your computer is a PC and they use the publishing-standard Macintosh.) The final result is sent to the magazine.

How to save money on advertising

You don't want to waste money if you don't have to. Writing the wrong ad leads to wasted money. Some magazines have what is known as a *split run*. This means they run one set of pages in one set of magazines, and another set of pages in a second set of magazines. You can use the split run to test two different ads—all at one price— and see which one works the best.

Nearly all magazines offer impressive merchandising materials, such as easel-back cards for displaying your ad at trade shows and seminars, or reprints and stickers with the name of the magazine (e.g., "As seen in *Newsweek*"). The cost of these tools is low, sometimes free, so check it out with the magazine's sales rep.

If you run small display ads, consider placing classified display ads. You can have your display ad set in the classified section of the magazine. Space rates are usually much lower there, even taking into account the often narrower columns in these sections.

For example, a 1×1.75-inch classified display ad in a major magazine currently costs approximately $330. This compares quite favorably to the regular 1×2.25-inch rate of $860. Your classified display ad will stand out sharply among the regular-format classifieds. Most publications that sell classified advertising by the "word" also sell classified display advertising by the agate line.

There is another valuable benefit to classified display advertising. Many popular publications do not allow regular space advertising of less than ⅙ page. Yet you can run a display ad in the classified section, buying space as small as one column inch. This gives you the opportunity to test display advertising without the need to invest in ⅙ page of space.

Take advantage of frequency discounts where your ad pulls well, or just breaks even at the regular rates. These discounts commonly run from 2 percent to 12 percent. To earn such discounts, you usually have to run a certain number of consecutive inserts, or a certain number of inserts within a 12-month period. You'll find the specifics on each publication's advertising rate card.

When you place the *qualifying insert*, you pay the lower rate and also receive credits for the rate differential on previous inserts. Some publications allow or require you to sign a contract first, committing you legally to the necessary number of inserts for earning the frequency discount. You pay the lower rate immediately. But if you should somehow interrupt the insert schedule, you have to reimburse the publication for the frequency discount rate differential deducted on previous inserts.

Take advantage of ad-size discounts when feasible. Most magazines reduce the per line rate with each increased standard unit of space. These generally are ⅙-page (half-column), ⅓-page (column), ½-page, ⅔-page, and full-page. If your ad is doing very well in ⅙ or ⅓ page of space, it might be worthwhile to test increases in space while incurring significantly lower percentage increases in cost. In one magazine, for example, increasing space from ⅓-page to ⅔-page (100 percent) increases your advertising cost by only 60 percent.

Take advantage of summer or off-season rate discounts offered by many major publications. Such discounts may range from 10 to 25 percent. These are granted by publications as an incentive to stimulate advertising space sales, usually during the slower summer months. You will not find this discount listed on the rate card because a publication's policy in this area can change from year to year, based on space sale projections. If you are on a publication's mailing list as a recent advertiser, you might be notified of the discount by mail a few weeks before the final closing date.

If you are a new advertiser to a publication, ask if it will grant you a one-time test rate to minimize your risk. A test rate can cost you 20–30 percent less than the publication's lowest listed rate. Since decisions are made on an advertiser-by-advertiser basis, publications that do allow test rates usually don't publicize it. Advertisers who are potentially big promotional spenders obviously stand a better chance of being given a test rate. And if you are represented by an advertising agency that gives a publication a large client business, it certainly helps the situation.

Be on the lookout for remnant space opportunities. *Remnant space* consists of one to three pages of unsold advertising space in a publication at press time (national or regional editions). Rather than plugging in non-income-producing editorials, public service announcements, or "house ads," the publication might make last-minute attractive offers to unscheduled advertisers, selling them the open space at large discounts, often 40–60 percent off the regular rates.

To be informed of remnant space when it's available, write to the publications you would be willing to try at lower rates and to those you schedule intermittently. Let them know that you could be interested in purchasing remnant space and ask if they will place you on their contact list. You might also hook up with an advertising agency specializing in such purchases. Quite often, agencies are contacted first when this space becomes available. Establish co-op advertising programs with other mail order advertisers. There are many alternatives here, the two most common are:

- You purchase a large amount of space and take advantage of an ad-size discount. You subcontract smaller portions of that space to other advertisers at a higher line rate than you paid, but at a lower line rate than each advertiser would pay if he purchased that small unit of space directly from the publication.
- You and one or more other advertisers equally share a large amount of space and split the costs accordingly. For example, you reserve a full-page space in a publication at the full-page rate of $2900. You and two other advertisers of related products each run a separately bordered and couponed ⅓-page ad in that space under a common headline. You each pay $966.67 toward the cost of the page. If any of you scheduled your own ⅓-page ad, however, it would have cost $1450. You each save $483.33.

If and when you are able to commit to large amounts of space in any publication in the future, you might be able to "break the rate card." This means negotiating a separate contractual arrangement with the publication, which allows you to purchase fixed amounts of advertising space for long periods of time at rates even below the full-page 12X rate. (This is also referred to as "dealing off the rate card.") Although running large monthly ads in the same publication results in diminishing returns, some advertisers receive such large discounts through such arrangements to make it really worthwhile.

The publicity bandwagon

Publicity is free advertising. It's better, in fact, because it appears unsolicited and gives readers the feeling that you're an expert. Public relations is serious business. It requires a lot of effort. That's why there are public relations firms around. If you can pay a minimum of six grand a month for a retainer, fine. If not, do it yourself. But it must be done.

If you have started an advertising campaign, you've already accomplished the first task of creating a publicity program: figuring out which publications to target. Inside their media kit, along with the rate card, was a sample magazine and an editorial calendar. Keep these as reference.

The object is simple: Get written about. There are two ways to approach this. Either the magazine writes about you, or you write for the magazine. Either way, you get your name in print.

Becoming a writer

I've written a lot of magazine articles in my time and am friends with more than a few editors. I used to write articles as a journalist, with a small byline attached to it at the bottom. When you write as a journalist, you must interview and then quote many sources. The problem is that the readers deem as experts the folks you've quoted, not you. The other problem is that the process of interviewing and writing the article is time-consuming, time better spent in some other endeavor. My advice is to avoid this form of writing. Instead, insist on writing an article as an expert.

Many publications have Talk Back or Readers' Forum columns. These are usually one-page venues. For example, I wrote one for *Byte* about the "productivity paradox." It generated a lot of response and some business. *Byte* even sent a photographer to my office and my photograph was on the Internet for a while.

If you have no writing skill, no style, and/or nothing to say, don't even bother. But if you're itching to get published in a magazine, follow these guidelines:

- Study the magazine to determine its style and audience.
- Determine if they take articles from "experts." Many magazines, particularly those in the computer field, don't like to have expert-written articles. (Go figure.) The business-driven magazines, however, are a great place to get your article placed, particularly if the subject is the Internet.
- Read the editorial calendar to find out what kinds of articles they're publishing. For example, *Pension Management* magazine publishes their software directory in the summer.

Why not find out if they'd be interested in an article about Internet-based retirement planning.

- Make contact with the magazine at least four months prior to the month the issue is to be published. Monthly magazines have long lead times. The weekly magazines have much shorter lead times.
- Send a message to the editor indicating what you'd like to write about. Send your bio, an outline of your proposed article, and a writing sample (if you have one). I personally find e-mail to be a better way to communicate than mail or fax.
- If they don't call you, follow up with a phone call yourself.

Writing for publication is sort of a Catch-22 process. If you haven't written before, they might not want to publish you. Here are some other techniques to get published:

- Join with a colleague and both of you write an article. Sometimes two credentials are better than one.
- Call major publishing houses like McGraw-Hill. Editors often work with authors who are compiling books. My *McGraw-Hill Multimedia Handbook* and the *Ultimate Sourcebook of Multimedia* (the revised version) are compilations. That means I got 70 authors to contribute a chapter to the book. You could have been one of them. The editor can connect you to authors who are working on such projects.
- Offer to write a free column on the Internet for your local paper if they don't want to pay you.
- Refer to your list of associations you've targeted and call the person who publishes the newsletter. Offer to write an article. (Remember that a list of associations is available in the library in the business section.)
- Publish your own newsletter on-line and e-mail editors the URL, along with a proposal to write an article.

Tip

Can't find all the articles you've written or have been written about you? Try a clipping service:

Allen's Press Clippings
(213) 628-4214

Burrelle's
(201) 992-6600

Bacon's
(312) 922-2400

Getting written about

To get written about, you have to lure the publication to you. How is this done?

Magazines are staffed by editors and writers. It's usually the writer, who might indeed be a freelance writer, who does the interviewing and ultimate writing.

Remember those editorial calendars? Go through all of them now and circle the topics that are related to what it is you do. Remember that Internet consultants are conversant with related topics such as telecommunications, intranets, business, and multimedia. Internet consultants also are conversant with seemingly unrelated topics such as unique marketing strategies and doing business globally. The point is to be creative in coming up with a novel slant.

Now update your calendar with the date by which you need to call the publication regarding the article or feature. If the article is to be published in June, then add a note to the March section of your calendar.

Review your calendar frequently. Call the magazine at the appropriate time and ask who's writing the article in which you wish to be mentioned. Call this writer. Convince this person that you have something worthwhile to say. You'll probably have to send along a press kit to pique some interest.

A press kit is almost the same as the literature pack that you send prospective clients. A press kit contains this additional material:

- Your bio, which includes achievements, educational credentials, books and articles written, and anything else you can think of that can make them interested in you.
- A photograph taken with a 35mm camera.
- Press clippings about what your service does.
- Vital statistics. The media love statistics. So if you have been tracking the Internet industry or a particular business segment, fill the reporter in.
- Quote sheet. If others have commented about you or your service, compile your best quotes and insert no more than one to two pages into your media kit.
- Screen prints. There are few publishers would don't use computers today. Take a couple of screen shots of your very best pages and save them as TIFF files. Copy the best one or two to a diskette and insert it in your press kit. Attach a sheet explaining what it is they are looking at.

You'll find that the universe of writers is not that large. If you give good interviews, eventually you'll wind up in the writer's contact database. Soon they'll call you without your having to do anything at all.

> **Tip**
>
> Services that will place your press release:
>
> Radio-TV Interview Report
> (215) 259-1070
>
> Publicity Express
> (800) 541-2897
>
> PR Newswire
> (800) 832-5522
>
> News Broadcast Network
> (212) 889-0888

Giving good public relations

Mastheads of magazines, a box usually found somewhere in the first few pages, list everyone who edits and writes for the publication; some even give e-mail addresses. Create a database to store all this information. Name, address, fax, e-mail, as well as comments on their specialties, should be incorporated. Add freelance writers and industry analysts as well. The names and addresses for the last two categories will require a bit of digging.

Freelancer contact information can be obtained from the magazine. You usually can tell from the byline that this person is a freelancer. Determining who the analysts are and where they hail from will require a bit more research. Publications frequently quote analysts. In the computer industry, for example, magazines love to quote analysts from the Gartner Group and IDC, among others. Read the publication carefully noting, who seems to be quoted frequently. Jot down these names and then look up their addresses. Since journalists have a compulsion for listing location of the firm (e.g., New York-based New Art), a quick call to 555-1212 should get your address. Now that your media database is complete, it's time to use it. Let's send out a press release. But only send out a press release if you have something really worthwhile to report. The reason could be that:

- You're announcing a new service.
- You have a new product release.
- You or your firm won some sort of award.
- You're moving.
- You just released a new book, audio, or video.
- You're sponsoring a contest.
- You're announcing a merger, partnership, or joint venture.
- You're starting a newsletter.
- You completed some market research and are publishing the results.

Tip

Peruse these guides to find the media right for you:

All in One Directory
Gebbie Press
P.O. Box 100
New Paltz, NY 12561-0017
(914) 255-7560

National Radio Publicity Outlets
Morgan-Rand Publishing Company
2200 Sansome St.
Philadelphia, PA 19103
(800) 441-3839

Radio Contacts
BPI Communications Inc.
1515 Broadway, 37th Flr.
New York, NY 10036
(212) 536-5266, (800) 876-8506

Radio/TV Directory
Bacon's Information, Inc.
332 S. Michigan Ave.
Chicago, IL 60604
(312) 922-2400, (800) 621-0561

Talk Shows Selects
Broadcast Interview Source
2233 Wisconsin Ave., Ste. 406
Washington, DC 20007-04104
(202) 333-4904

Television Contacts
BPI Communications Inc.
1515 Broadway, 37th Fl.
New York, NY 10036
(212) 536-5266, (800) 876-8506

TV & Cable Publicity Outlets
Morgan-Rand Publishing Company
2200 Sansome St.
Philadelphia, PA 19103
(800) 441-3839

Here are some tips for creating a press release; a complete sample can be found in Appendix A.

- Keep it short and simple.
- Get right to the point.
- Use the standard press release format, as shown in Appendix A.
- Use professionally printed stationery.
- Include the words PRESS RELEASE on the envelope.
- Use an informative bold headline.
- Keep hyperbole to a minimum.
- Try to get a quote from a customer.
- At a minimum, include a quote from yourself.
- Provide the name, phone number, and e-mail of someone in your organization who can be called for more information.
- Don't defame or slander competitors.
- Use trademark symbols where needed.
- Try to keep it to one page.
- Use fax only if the publication permits it.
- Keep track of which writers and editors like a follow-up phone call and which don't.
- Try to send a press release at least once every 3 months. The more the press sees your name, the more it is they will consider you a player.

If you don't have any of the good reasons listed above to write a press release, then reconsider. They're all good ideas and all worthy of publicity. The publicity stunt is worthy of media attention as well. Publicity stunts are often spectacular feats or events that garner a lot of attention:

- Co-produce an event with a non-profit organization. You'll be doing good works while, at the same time, spreading your name.
- Create a free telephone hot line to answer Internet questions.
- Sponsor a contest: Who has the best computer horror story? Who can surf to the most places in three hours?
- Donate some computers or access time to a local school.
- Start a new association. The business press loves trade associations; the formation of a new one will be most interesting to them. Being president of an association has a lot of other benefits as well, such as vast networking opportunities. There's a lot of work involved in this, however.
- Sponsor a sporting event. How about a 10K Internet run through the park?

All of these ideas merit one or more press releases and some follow-up telephoning.

Actually pitching an editor or writer by phone is entirely different from sending the passive press release. Just as in a telemarketing call, you have to catch their interest within the first 20 seconds. Be personable, warm, and friendly, but do get your message across quickly and factually.

Making TV and radio work for you

This section is not about how to advertise on television or radio. That takes the expertise of a specialist to help you "buy" the right media slots, and then track those slots. This section is about getting interviewed on radio and TV.

Tip

More media guides:

Contacts
(718) 721-0508

Bacon's Media Directories
(800) 621-0561

Power Media Selects
(202) 333-4904

Unless you're really well-known (Bill Gates, for example), producers are not going to be beating down your door. You need to know that right off the bat. If you have an interesting topic or background, however, you might be able to get your foot in.

As usual, research the playing field. Watch TV and listen to the radio. Pick out the programs that might be a good place for you to be interviewed. Jot down the name of the show and host. Add the names you collect to your media database. Send them your press releases.

All of your local television, cable, and radio stations are listed right in the phone book. Call them and ask for the producer of the show. When you get the producer, pitch him or her on your idea. You might be told to mail or fax in your idea. And follow up.

You've probably watched enough TV and listened to enough radio to know what makes for an interesting interview. That the Internet is hot is old news; nobody wants to hear it. Nor do they want to hear that we have a computer revolution, or that businesses will lose out if they're not automated. What producers want is controversy or sizzle. Give it to them. Refute the statistics. Tell them that more women than men are on the Internet. Or tell them that the Internet will make America a third world economy. Come up with an idea that will take their collective breath away. Once you do, then write a simple proposal and attach your bio. This is what you'll send if they ask you, or you'll use as a script if you get to speak to them on the phone.

Tip

Into public speaking? Join the National Speakers Association. A great perk is that they'll list you in their directory, which is given free to meeting planners.

(602) 968-2552

If you wind up speaking on the radio, listen to the host. Try to modulate your speaking voice. Keep your comments brief (don't babble), and don't interrupt the host or callers who ask questions. On TV, make sure you look at the interviewer and not the camera. Smile a lot and don't blush. Wear soft, dark colors (*not* white) with minimal patterns. Avoid clanky jewelry and short skirts. For both media, speak slowly and stay on target with your message, be charismatic, be positive, *and know your material.* Now for the bad news: There are lots of new business shows on cable. If you call them up, you might be in for a surprise or two. Some of them ask you to pay for the privilege of being interviewed.

These shows are professionally produced, and fall into the category of "paid programming." They do not appear in a regular time slot, but viewers get the sense they are real shows. The "producers" of the show line up a bunch of businesses, each of whom chip in several thousand dollars.

The businesses get to be on TV, and get a copy of the videotape that can be duplicated and sent out to prospects. The producers get to keep the difference between what the show costs to produce and what they are paid by the businesses. It's really not such a bad deal. Everyone is a winner. Except, of course, the viewers who think it is a legitimate show.

> **Tip**
>
> Make your own video! Call Medialink:
>
> New York
> (212) 682-8300
>
> Los Angeles
> (213) 465-0111
>
> Chicago
> (312) 222-9850

Hosting your own show

Did you every wonder how the local chiropractor wound up hosting his or her own radio talk show? They paid for it. Some, not all, local radio stations are happy to have you host an hour a week. The catch is you pay somewhere around $3500 per month. But this isn't all bad news:

- You get to host your own show.
- You can take advertising and actually make some money on the deal.
- You can interview all your clients, guaranteeing them publicity.
- You might get to take over for John Tesh if you're good enough.

> **Tip**
>
> Make an infomercial:
>
> American Telecast
> (215) 251-9933
>
> USA Direct
> (612) 945-4391
>
> Gunthy-Renker
> (310) 472-5253
>
> Regal Group
> (212) 682-6000
>
> and read the Infomercial Marketing Report
>
> (310) 472-5253

It's hard to tell you how to track down these stations. Call them all and ask if they need a host for a new program on computers, business, or the Internet. If they're hungry, they're call you back.

If you really want to advertise on TV or radio . . .

If you want to dangle your toe in the shallow end of this particular pool, then try cable television and A.M. talk radio first.

The technique for selecting the right stations is the same as for selecting the right publications. Select only those that your target audience is watching. If you want to attract business, don't advertise on MTV. If you want to attract teenagers, don't advertise on an all-news radio channel.

Call each station and ask to speak to the advertising manager. Ask for the station's rate card. The rates should vary widely. Three o'clock Sunday morning will cost a lot less than weekday drive time (7–10 A.M.) on a radio station.

Radio advertising is the simpler of the two. It requires only a good speaking voice and a tape recorder. Of course, you can get the whole thing done professionally for less than $5000 (in New York City). But where would Carvel be today without the raspy voice of Tom Carvel? Here are some hints for radio advertising:

- Haggle. Radio rate cards are highly negotiable.
- Stay with a 30-second spot. Longer ads might cost proportionally less, but you begin to lose your audience after 30 seconds.
- Add music to your commercial. You can rent it from the station's rights-free music library. They also should have sound effects.
- You have about three seconds to catch a listener's attention. So be interesting during these three seconds.
- You can't run a radio ad just once.
- The best time to run an ad is afternoon drive time. People are in more of a buying mood when they're on their way home.

TV comes in two flavors, cable and broadcast. Cable will be the less expensive of the two. Some cable channels, in fact, go out of their way to help small business advertisers; some even produce a video for you.

I've heard that the price of advertising on TV has come down. Of course, "cheap" here in New York City is "expensive" almost anywhere else. To get the best deal you're really going to have to work with a media buying service. My cousin buys media for a living, and from her conversations I'd say she earns her salary.

Advertising rates depend upon *rating points*. How much a single rating point will cost you in your area depends upon the size and demographics of the area, the competitive situation, the time of day and year, and whether the station is a network affiliate. Points tend to rise around Christmas season and drop during the summer months. Cost ranges between $5 per GRP (gross rating point) in a small town, to about $500 per GRP in a larger city.

Well, we've done it. You're now expert Internet consultants . . . and you know a few things about generating business. But there's one last topic before I let you go. Let's learn how to set fees and get money to grow the business.

10

Let's talk
about money

We all want to make money, but nobody really enjoys keeping track of invoices and bills. Some of us are even squeamish about figuring out what we're netting versus what we're grossing.

> **Tip**
>
> A small but growing number of companies are refurbishing and reselling used computers. One such company is Rumarson Technology Inc., Kenilworth, NJ (908) 298-9300. They pay $100 and up for used computers.

I'm assuming that most of you are already in business, so I'm not going to get into the fine points of the type of business organization you should become, the ins and outs of filing taxes, or the myriad of other subjects that the word *money* usually entails. What I am going to talk about is ways for you to finance yourself—whether from fees you charge your clients, or from folks investing in the future of your company.

What should you charge?

Table 10-1 shows the average fee structure an independent Internet consultant uses when building what I refer to as "Level One" home pages. These are the pages that have forms, frames, backgrounds, minor animation, and graphics.

When you get into database programming, which is what you need if you intend to take orders or respond to inquiries, you're talking about real computer consulting. Here the fee structure is highly variable; the consultant should base his or her fee on what the market will bear. I will tell you that an average computer programmer

Table 10-1. Sample Web page building fees

	Starter	Basic	Plus	Standard	Special	Deluxe
Total Cost	$340	$575	$795	$1,245	$1,875	$2,440
Total Pages	1	2	3	6	12	20
Links	3	6	8	15	30	45
Scanned pictures (in addition to mast and top-of-page graphic)	2	4	5	8	16	24
Words of text (approximate)	200	400	600	1,200	2,400	4,000
Masthead graphic (client-supplied or simple custom graphic incorporation company logo)	yes	yes	yes	yes	yes	yes
Colored lines and bullets	Netscape	Netscape	Netscape	Netscape	Netscape	Netscape
Colored and textured background	Netscape	Netscape	Netscape	Netscape	Netscape	Netscape
Site publicity using Submitlt	yes	yes	yes	yes	yes	yes
Image Map					x	x
E-mail response link to your e-mail address	x	x	x	x	x	x

> ### Tip
> Check out Business Consumer Guide at (800) 938-0088, or on the Internet at:
>
> *http://www.buysmart.com*

prices out at about $300 per day, while a highly experienced one gets over $1000 a day. However lucrative these rates may seem, you have to realize that if you don't work half the year, for whatever reason, your actual yearly gross is fairly low.

In order to determine your own price point, you need to take the following into consideration:

> ### Tip
> To achieve excellence in tax and accounting procedures, consider software. Such packages as CCH Inc.'s *U.S. Master Tax Guide* include information regarding home office deductions, hints on how to choose a tax preparer, etc.
>
> (800) TELL-CCH, $69, Win/Dos, $29.50.

1 What do you need to earn to pay your own personal expenses (mortgage, etc.)?
2 What do you need to pay any staff or temporaries?
3 What do your benefits, such as health care, cost you?
4 What does it cost to run your office (telephone, computers, ISP, etc.)?

More expenses are shown in Table 10-2.

Now multiply 40 hours per week times 52 weeks per year (2080 hours), then deduct for vacations, sick time, and holidays. Deduct un-

Table 10-2. Various business expenses

Office space rental	$_____
Office equipment	$_____
Office supplies	$_____
Insurance	$_____
Utilities (phone, electricity, heat, water)	$_____
Maintenance	$_____
Advertising	$_____
Labor	$_____
Business licenses	$_____

billable professional activities such as appearances, advisory boards, and administration. Now deduct for miscellaneous down time. And definitely don't forget that 20 percent of your time for generating new business. What do have left? Around a thousand billable hours a year?

On the flip side, calculate what you need to earn. Start with your old salary, say $55,000. Now add the cost of items 2 through 4 above. What do you get now? About $100,000? Divide by the 1000 hours of billable time and you find that you have to charge your clients about $100 per hour, or $800 per day. Before you go and print a price sheet, however, check these prices against your competitors so that you don't price yourself out of the market.

Tip

For help in crafting a proposal, contact the Association of Proposal Management Professionals. This group offers conferences, seminars, and brochures.

(714) 240-6246

Many clients will ask you to bid on a particular assignment. They will probably publish an RFP (request for proposal). This is a written document detailing the requirements of the assignment. Read this document carefully. Then proceed to write a proposal (see Appendix A for a sample) that includes the following information:

- Restatement of problem or assignment mission. Convince the reader that you understand the problem.
- Summary of what you intend to do. Tell them what you will do and what you won't.
- Methods or procedures to be used. Detail exactly what you intend to do. If it is an order entry system, for example, talk about the search for an appropriate database, the design of the online order form, etc.
- Materials to be supplied. If you need to buy equipment or software to complete the job, detail it here.
- Personnel required. Provide biographies of all team members who will work on the project. This alone might make or break your deal.
- Time required to perform work. Provide a Gantt chart showing all the milestones of the project, when they start, and when they finish.
- Cost or budget. Detail the total cost of the project, including your fee.

Your fee should include at least a 15 percent administrative charge, which should cover your internal clerical and other costs. Indicate that expenses will be billed separately and provide an upper limit, such as $5000. Make sure you provide receipts for all expenses. Also provide a payment schedule. A typical payment schedule is a third up front, a third in the middle, and the last third at the end.

Tip

Ten expense management techniques:

1 Pay all vendors promptly.
2 Open a corporate credit card and pay whatever you can on it. American Express itemizes all your expenses for you.
3 Make an expense budget and review frequently.
4 Use a travel agent and make preferences clear.
5 Pay your bills twice a month at single sittings.
6 Enter your receivables and expenses into your computer system immediately. Don't wait until they pile up.
7 Automate. Use Quicken, QuickBooks or some other accounting package.
8 Try to buy used equipment.
9 Lease whenever you can.

Whoever said that style doesn't count was wrong. You've all seen that Kinko's commercial where the tiny business person was complimented by the giant company for work well done.

- Print your proposal on good stationery and then bind it between a professional-looking set of covers. You can buy a comb-binding machine for less than $100 at Staples.
- Use your desktop publishing system or word processor to add a slight graphic touch to the proposal. Use an extra-wide left margin and "call out" significant information. Use some color somewhere. Draw a wide, deep box in your header and fill it in with black. Draw a complementary but thinner box in the footer. This will print on every page.
- Include a table of contents.
- Include an appendix with clippings and other information culled from your literature pack.
- Use an overnight service such as FedEx to send it to your prospect, rather than mail it.

Getting an assignment and getting paid for it are two different matters. Get into this mindset: Billing is the most important job you have. Do it before you do any other work:

> **Tip**
>
> Want to assure prompt payment? For $60 and a toll-free call, Dun&Bradstreet's Small Business Services will scrutinize the financial health of any company with whom you are doing business. Tapping its database of 10.5 million companies, D&B will track a company's payment history, etc. For more information call (800) 544-3867.

- Bill each month at the same time.
- Provide detailed information on each invoice.
- Your invoice number should appear on each bill.
- State terms of payment directly on the invoice (i.e., payment due upon receipt).
- Send out a PAST DUE notice as soon as the company is in arrears.
- Don't be shy about using a collection agency. They charge a lot but you'll get satisfaction. We use Dun & Bradstreet collections. Just the name D&B (credit rating?) gets wayward clients to pay.

Financing your business

When you first open your business, you should make an effort to get to know your banker. It's the bank, after all, to whom you will turn when you want to expand. If the bank doesn't know you . . .

> **Tip**
>
> The American Bankers Association offers assistance in understanding the role of banking.
>
> 1120 Connecticut Ave N.W.
> Washington, DC 20036
> (202) 663-5000

What you're going to need is credit. American Express has corporate green and gold cards. Apply for one of them. Not only is there a certain level of credit granted, there are definite benefits to being a cardholder. They itemize all your expenses quarterly, saving you an accountant's fee. Other benefits include discount rates on car rentals, insurance on those car rentals, airline mileage points, and buyer's assurance programs (in which, if you break something, they'll pay to get a new one).

Apply for credit from the company from which you buy your office supplies. We use Quill, (800) 789-1331. They have an enormous variety, great prices, deliver quickly, and bill me at the end of the month.

Tip

Why pay cash if you can barter your services for goods and services? For Information on barter companies, send a self-addressed stamped envelope to International Reciprocal Trade Association, which represents 122 barter companies nationally.

9513 Beach Mill Road,
Great Falls, VA 22066

Eventually you'll need new money to expand. It's more difficult to find financing for service companies than for ones that produce a product, and almost impossible for home-based businesses, try these sources:

- Your local bank
- Friends, neighbors, and relatives
- Venture capital companies
- Lines of credit from vendors (e.g., your ISP or computer retailer)
- Partnerships and stock sales

If you're contemplating using a venture capital company, remember that they wind up owning most of the company and might actually replace you as president. They also want to have lots of input into how you run your company. They're not likely to give funding to a consulting firm, but if you come up with a great idea for a service on the Internet, they might be your best bet.

In deciding how to finance your business, you need to consider certain questions:

- How much control of your new business can you comfortably give up?
- Which facts will debt and equity financiers want to know?
- How do debt and equity requirements differ?
- How highly leveraged do you want your company to be? (The higher the amount borrowed compared to the amount of equity, the higher the leverage.)

> **Tip**
>
> The Small Business Association would like to finance your business. Opportunities include:
>
> 7(a) Loan Guaranty
> Microloan
> 504 Certified Development
> Surety Bond
> Certified and Preferred Lenders
> Small Business Investment Co.
>
> (800) 8-ASK-SBA
>
> *http://www.sba.gov/business_finances/FinancingYourBusiness.html*

In order to answer these questions, it is important that you understand clearly how debt financing and equity financing work, and that you be aware of the advantages and disadvantages of each.

> **Tip**
>
> For banks outside your area, you may want to consult a banking directory such as *Rand McNally's Bankers Directory* or *Polk's World Bank Directory*. Most libraries have copies.

Debt financing

Debt is a direct obligation to pay something (cash) to someone (an investor or lender). In exchange for having lent you the money, an investor will expect to be paid interest. Obviously this means that you will repay more money than you have borrowed. An important feature of debt financing, therefore, is the interest rate you will be charged.

> **Tip**
>
> Get free information about accessing co-op funds by contacting Benard and Company. Call them at (415) 957-5886 and ask for a brochure.

The interest rate usually reflects the level of risk the investor is undertaking by lending you money. Investors will charge you lower interest rates if they feel there is a low risk of the debt not being repaid. Investors will raise interest rates if they are concerned about your ability to repay the debt, or if you have a history of slow payments to lenders, as shown on your personal or business credit reports.

It is important to realize a new business is likely to be charged a higher interest rate than an established business because the lender will feel a new business represents a greater risk. Here's an example of how interest rates can affect your loan repayment amount:

- A 10-year loan for $50,000 at 12 percent interest requires monthly payments of $717.
- A 10-year loan for $50,000 at 15 percent interest requires monthly payments of $807.

A payment difference of $90 each month, over 120 months, makes the second loan almost $11,000 more expensive over the life of the loan.

A debt lender will evaluate your loan request by considering answers to several key questions:

- Can you offer reasonable evidence of repayment ability—either established earnings for an existing business or income projections (profit and loss) for a new business?
- Do you have sufficient management experience to operate the business?
- Do you have enough equity in the business? Equity provides what lenders call a cushion for creditors.
- Do you have a reasonable amount of collateral (assets to be acquired, residential property equity, etc.)?

Tip

Need tax help?

Ernst & Young Tax Corner

http://www.wiley.com/ey/ey.html

IRS - Digital Daily

http://www.irs.ustreas.gov/prod/cover.html

The biggest advantage of debt financing is that it allows you, the business owner, to retain control of your company. You are therefore entitled to all company profits and have ultimate decision-making authority. Since many entrepreneurs start a business for exactly these reasons, a critical advantage of debt financing is that it provides you with some financial freedom: Your debt is limited to the loan repayment period. After you have repaid the borrowed money, the lender has no further claim on your business.

The biggest disadvantage of debt financing is having to make monthly payments on a loan. Cash may be scarce and expenses may be higher than estimated during the early years of a new business.

Even so, the lender must be paid on time. There are severe penalties for late or missed payments, such as additional fees, a poor credit rating, and the possibility that the lender may call the loan due.

Tip

IRS Publication 334, "Tax Guide for Small Business," and Publication 583, "Taxpayers Starting a Business," contain practical explanations of basic bookkeeping requirements. They are available at IRS offices or by calling (800) 829-FORM.

Another disadvantage of borrowing funds is the difficulty in obtaining them. In general, lenders prefer to invest in proven businesses. If your business is new, a lender may charge you a high interest rate or might refuse to make the loan at all. In contrast, if you have been in business for a significant period of time, you may find debt lenders very happy to extend loans.

Equity financing

Equity financing involves no direct obligation to repay any funds. It does, however, involve selling a partial interest in your company. In effect, an equity investor becomes your business partner and will have a degree of control over how your business is run. For example, the sale of stock, one type of equity financing arrangement, typically works as follows:

1 You determine from your analysis that your business will need more funds than you can provide.
2 You consider financing options and decide that you prefer to sell an interest in your company rather than borrow money.
3 You arrange to offer a sale of stock.

Arranging to sell stock can be much more complicated than it sounds, because you must comply with an array of legal and reporting requirements for the life of your business. After shares of your stock are purchased, investors own a portion of your company, which they can keep or sell to others. Equity investors buy part of your company by supplying some of the capital your business requires. Because they will own a share of your business, equity investors are interested in the business's long-term success and future profitability.

Equity investors can resell their interest in your company to other investors. If your business is doing well, they will be able to sell their stake at a higher price than they paid, making a profit. Legally, equity investors are more exposed to risk than are debt investors. If your business fails, equity investors stand to lose more money than debt investors, since creditors are typically paid before owners in the event of business failure. Because equity investors are taking the greater risk, they expect to earn more on their investment than do debt investors.

With equity financing, you do not repay the money invested by others (unless a payoff agreement is made at the time of investment). This can be important when cash is at a premium. Your ideas for making your business successful also might carry more weight with a potential equity investor than with a debt investor. Because it is in an equity investor's best interest for your business to grow and expand, he or she will be more likely to consider sound business ideas than will a debt investor, who is more concerned with the security of the deal proposed.

Tip

Association for Enterprise Opportunity, San Francisco, provides information on alternative funding sources.

(415) 495-2333

The MIT Venture Capital Network links businesses to private wealthy investors for a fee.

(617) 253-7163

Many people who are interested in starting or expanding a business have more ideas than money; this can be an important factor in favor of equity financing. In addition, equity investors, with their genuine interest in your success, can be a good source of advice and contacts for your business. The biggest drawback of equity financing is that you give up some control over your business. You might or might not find this acceptable. Remember, when you accept equity partners, you are selling part of your business. It could be very difficult to regain control in the future.

You also might find your equity investors do not always agree with your plans for the business. However, since they own part of your business, you will have to consider their point of view, even if you do not agree with their choices.

Tip

Check out the MoneyHunter Web site at:
http://www.moneyhunter.com

Finally, equity financing tends to be very complicated and invariably will require the advice of attorneys and accountants. A great deal of paperwork must be prepared and filed. For example, public companies must comply with specific legal regulations that govern their ways of doing business.

More ways of finding money

Insurance companies are a possible source of financing for your business because they make commercial loans as a means of investing unused portions of their income. Generally, insurance companies make term loans and mortgage loans.

If you borrow from an insurance company, you can expect terms and interest rates similar to those available from a commercial bank. Insurance companies can provide your business with a large amount of capital at market interest rates, but you must have assets sufficient to cover the debt, plus 20–30 percent extra. In effect, you mortgage your property to free cash for your business. This allows you to retain title to the property while freeing the cash invested in it. Insurance companies usually have high loan limits; this makes them a good source of funds if you need a large supply of capital. Where can you get more information? Speak with your insurance agent or ask friends to make recommendations. You also might wish to request information packets from insurance companies' loan offices.

A *factor company* can be a useful source of funds if you are already in business and have made sales to customers. Factor companies purchase your accounts receivable at a discount, thereby freeing cash for you sooner than if you had to collect the money yourself. You transfer title of your accounts receivable to the factor company in exchange for a cash payment.

How do they operate? Factor companies provide two types of financing alternatives; recourse factoring and nonrecourse factoring.

Tip

Just starting up? Maybe you need an incubator:

National Business Incubation Association

(614) 593-4331

In *recourse factoring*, you retain part of the risk for ultimately collecting the debts owed to you. The factor company assists you by speeding up the process. For example, the factor company purchases your receivables and advances you cash while the accounts are being collected. If your customers do not pay, however, you will be held responsible for repayment to the factor company.

In *nonrecourse factoring,* you sell all rights and obligations concerning your accounts receivable. The factor company purchases your receivables and collects the debts owed. If a customer does not pay, you will be under no obligation to the factor company. Factor companies can be a useful source of funds for a new or existing business. They are not appropriate as a means of seed capital to start a business, because they require that you have accounts receivable to sell.

Tip

Venture capital on-line:

Accel Partners
http://www.accel.com

Adams Capital Management
http://acm.com/acm

Atlas Venture
http://www.tisco.com/atlas

VistaWEB
http://www.gate.net/vista

Olympic Venture Partners
http://product.com/olympic

Factor companies often advertise in the business sections of newspapers. Usually the advertisement will say "We buy accounts receivable" or something similar. Make sure you work with a reputable company that will not alienate your customers by harassing them for payment.

Venture capital financing is a method used for raising money, but is less popular than borrowing. Venture capital firms, like banks, supply you with the funds necessary to operate your business, but they do it differently. Banks are creditors; they expect you to repay the borrowed money. Venture capital firms are owners; they hold stock in the company, adding their invested capital to its equity base. While banks may concentrate on cash flow, venture capital firms invest for long-term capital gain. Typically these firms look for their investment to appreciate 300–500 percent in 5 to 7 years.

Because venture capital firms are owners, they examine existing or planned products or services and the potential markets for them with extreme care. They invest only in firms they believe can increase sales rapidly and generate substantial profits. Venture capital is risky because of the difficulty of judging the worth of a business in its early stages. Most venture capital firms therefore set rigorous policies for venture proposal size, maturity and management of the seeking company, and "something special" in the plan that is submitted. They also have rigorous evaluation procedures to reduce risks, because their investments are unprotected in the event of failure.

Tip

Interested in exporting?

http://www.exportweb.com

Most venture capital firms are interested in investment projects requiring an investment of $250,000 to $1.5 million. Projects requiring less than $250,000 are of limited interest because of the high cost of investigation and administration. Some venture capital firms will consider smaller proposals, however, if the investment is intriguing enough.

The typical venture capital firm receives over 1000 proposals a year. Probably 90 percent of these will be rejected quickly because they don't fit the established geographical, technical, or market area policies of the firm—or because they have been poorly prepared. The remaining 10 percent are investigated carefully. These investigations are expensive. Firms might hire consultants to evaluate the product, particularly when it is the result of innovation or is technologically complex. The market size and competitive position of the company are analyzed by contacts with present and potential customers, suppliers, and others. Production costs are reviewed. The financial condition of the company is confirmed by an auditor. The legal form and registration of the business are checked. Most important, the character and competence of the management are evaluated by the venture capital firm, normally via a thorough background check.

There are different types of venture firms. *Traditional partnerships* are often established by wealthy families to aggressively manage a portion of their funds by investing in small companies. *Professionally managed pools* are made up of institutional money and operate like the traditional partnerships.

Investment banking firms usually trade in more established securities, but occasionally form investor syndicates for venture proposals. *Insurance companies* often have required a portion of equity as a condition of their loans to smaller companies as protection against inflation.

Finally, *Small Business Investment Corporations* (SBICs) are licensed by the Small Business Administration (SBA) and might provide management assistance as well as venture capital. When dealing with SBIC's, the small business owner/manager should initially determine if the SBIC is primarily interested in an equity position, as venture capital, or merely in long-term lending on a fully secured basis.

In addition to these types of venture capital firms, there are individual private investors and finders. Finders, which can be firms or individuals, often know the capital industry and may be able to help the small company seeking capital to locate it, though they are generally not sources of capital themselves. Care should be exercised so that a small business owner deals with reputable, professional finders whose fees are in line with industry practice. Further, it should be noted that venture capitalists generally prefer working directly with principals in making investments, though finders may provide useful introductions.

Good things to know about venture capital firms

Companies that are just starting or that have serious financial difficulties may interest some venture capitalists, if the potential for significant gain over the long run can be identified and assessed. There are a small number of venture firms that will do start-up financing.

Most venture capital firms concentrate primarily on the competence and character of the management. Venture capital firms usually require that the company under consideration have a complete management group. Each of the important functional areas—product design, marketing, production, finance, and control—must be under the direction of a trained, experienced member of the group.

Venture capital firms seek a distinctive element in the strategy or product/market/process position of the company.

See Appendix A for the format of a venture capital proposal.

Whew! We're through. This book has been brief, but I hope it's been chock full of the stuff you need to know to become a successful Internet consultant. Good luck!

Appendix A

Templates for Internet Entrepreneurs

This appendix differs from the chapters in the main part of the book. It's filled with examples of press releases, sales letters, and proposals to help you speed you on your way. Printed here, it's also available as downloadable files from:

http://www.business-america.com

Sample sales letter

The following is pretty much an all-purpose letter format that can be used to follow up a phone call or, with modification, for a variety of other purposes.

May 24, 1996

Sample Client
Sample Firm
Sample Address
Mendham NJ 07945

Dear George,

It was a pleasure talking to you on Thursday. As promised, I put together a folder of information about my company, as well as samples of our work. I think it pretty much sums up what we do.

Our specialty is Internet Solutions. We have worked with dozens of organizations to implement Web solutions that are not only visually exciting, but also cost-effective. For example, we recently wrote a system for Unisys Corp. that automatically generates over 40,000 Internet files for that company's Web site.

From our conversation, I believe that I understand what you are attempting to do. I also believe that New Art can develop a creative solution for your company. We are experts in the techniques of the Web. This includes graphic design, animation, copywriting, and programming, as well as content advice.

New Art is truly on the Web's cutting edge. You can be assured that if it's available, we not only have used it, we excel in it. So your site will always be, in the vernacular of the Web, a "cool" site.

I will call you next week to set up an appointment. At that time I would like to "surf" the Web with you to show you how others in your industry are using the Web to their competitive advantage.

Sincerely,

Jessica Keyes
President

Sample bio

About Jessica Keyes

Jessica Keyes is president of New Art Inc., a high-technology consultancy. Keyes has given seminars for such prestigious universities as Carnegie-Mellon, Boston University, University of Illinois, James Madison University, and San Francisco State University. She is also the Chief Technology Officer of a new Internet start-up, Worldwide Corporate Network. Keyes is a frequent keynote speaker on the topics of competitive strategy using information technology and marketing on the information superhighway. She is an advisor for DataPro, McGraw-Hill's computer research arm, as well as a member of the Sprint Business Council. Keyes also is a founding Board of Director member of the New York Software Industry Association. She has recently been appointed to a two-year term to the Mayor of New York City's Small Business Advisory Council.

Before to founding New Art, Keyes was Managing Director of R&D for the New York Stock Exchange, and has been an officer with Swiss Bank Co. and Banker's Trust, both in New York City. She holds a Masters from New York University, where she did her research in the area of artificial intelligence.

A noted columnist and correspondent with over 150 articles published, Keyes is the publisher of the *Small Business Journal* and several other computer-related publications. Keyes is also the author of nine books:

The New Intelligence: AI in Financial Services (HarperBusiness, 1990)

The Handbook of Expert Systems in Manufacturing (McGraw-Hill, 1991)

Infotrends: The Competitive Use of Information (McGraw-Hill, 1992)

The Software Engineering Productivity Handbook (McGraw-Hill, 1993)

The Handbook of Multimedia (McGraw-Hill, 1994)

The Productivity Paradox (McGraw-Hill, 1994)

Technology Trendlines (Van Nostrand Reinhold, 1995)

The Ultimate Sourcebook of Multimedia (McGraw-Hill, 1996)

How to Be a Successful Internet Consultant (McGraw-Hill, 1996)

Infotrends was selected as one of the best business books of 1992 by *Library Journal*. *The Software Engineering Productivity Handbook* was the main selection for the Newbridge book club for computer professionals. *The McGraw-Hill Multimedia Handbook* is now in its second reprint, and will be translated into Chinese and Japanese during 1995. Keyes is working on the second edition of the book, which will be retitled *The Ultimate Sourcebook on Multimedia and the Internet.*

Follow-up fax

This fax response is geared to a new, very inexperienced small business client.

It was a pleasure to talk to you today. I will faxing copies of my presentation slides shortly. As I mentioned, creating a Web home page is somewhat like publishing an ad or submitting an article to a magazine. To create one's own page requires mastery of a programming language called HTML and the ability to navigate Unix. In addition, creating one's home page requires one either to create his or her own Web server (with expenses for hardware, software, and the telecom line), or paying for a service provider to host a page for you—both expensive propositions.

The alternative I recommend is to use a company like New Art to publish a home page for you on its own Web site. As I mentioned, we have our own home page (see below). We can create a home page for you on our least expensive server, which is located in San Francisco.

I received the information you provided and, if you provide me with your stationery so that I can scan your logo for your home page, this development task would not be difficult to do in a short period of time.

My estimate (based on what you faxed me is) is: $200 initial document creation charge plus $15 per month storage fee (payable quarterly). If you send me a check for $245 (creation plus 3 months), I can have you up and running within 10 days.

Once your page is up, it can be accessed by 22 million people (if they know where it is). New Art would provide "press releases" to the major Internet directories to let them know you exist. In this way, people who search for all sites on computer components would be able to find you. Of course, you would put your home page address on your stationery, etc., so people know where to find you.

I also recommend that you, since you are an Internet novice, use CompuServe or America Online to get to the Net. Both have what are called Web browsers. I can give you instructions on how to use this facility. In this way you can get to your own home page. (But only to read, not to update. We will have to update it for you. The charge is dependent upon what you want to do.)

Your CompuServe or AOL ID is also your Internet address. If desired, I can add a facility to your home page to direct e-mail directly to your Internet address at CompuServe or AOL. If you wish this facility, please add $50 to the one-time cost of building your home page.

Sample proposal for a speech on the Internet

ACTION FORM for speech at the 15th National Center for Database Marketing: July 26-28, 1995, Sheraton Chicago.

A. MY CONTACT INFORMATION

Full Name:	Jessica Keyes
Prefix:	Ms.
Job Title:	President
Company:	New Art Communications
Address:	200 W 79 Street M/S 8H, NYC, NY 10024
Work Telephone:	212-362-0559
Fax:	212-873-8231
Best time to reach:	Before 10 A.M.

B. TITLE COPY

1 Surviving on the Information Superhighway
2 Cruising the Information Superhighway in a Maserati
3 Don't cruise the Information Superhighway in a Yugo

C. SESSION

The Information Superhighway is indeed the last frontier. It soon may be the only frontier for direct marketing as more and more companies are going digital. But there is danger ahead. Most of the cruisers on the Information Superhighway will stumble along on four flat tires.

This session will provide all the ammunition the attendee will need to survive in this next-generation marketing medium. Through case studies, color slides, and anecdotes, Jessica Keyes will lead attendees through a discussion on building marketing campaigns on what some refer to as the Infobahn.

This session will teach the following: (general outline)

1 What the Information Superhighway is.
2 What the Information Superhighway isn't.
3 What people are doing wrong on the I-way and what they're doing right.
4 Hype vs. reality.
5 What you need to know to get going and keep going.

D. SESSION DESCRIPTION COPY

1 What the Information Superhighway means in terms of marketing potential.
2 Whether the attendee should join the mob scene and cruise Information Superhighway.
3 Who are the 20 million people logged onto the I-way?
4 Ten things you shouldn't do when marketing on the I-way—and ten things you should do.

5 When to not to cruise on the I-way.

6 Where to go for help.

7 How to determine whether your audience is using the I-way.

8 Once you leave this course you'll be able to go back to the office and start your Information Superhighway planning session.

9 A special technique to get yourself some superhighway attention.

10 Why marketing folks are failing on the I-way.

11 Tested non-digital marketing techniques don't work on the I-way.

12 The use of multimedia on the I-way.

13 Techniques sure to get you noticed.

14 Essential rules of etiquette for use on the Superhighway.

15 Proven techniques need not apply.

E. FOCUS OF THE SEMINAR

Market   Both Business-to-Business and Consumer
Track Focus   Can be: Systems/Technology or Interactive Media

F. GUARANTEE COPY

You will:

1 Fully understand the rewards and very real risks in marketing on the Information Superhighway.

2 Have learned how to determine whether or not the I-way is appropriate for your product or service.

3 Be able to separate the hype vs. reality of marketing on the I-way.

4 Have learned what you need to do for successful I-way marketing.

Sample pitch letter

June 12, 1995

Name
Address

Dear Ms. Dwyer,

The Internet is really the place to be. With over 22 million "surfing the net" at any given time, there's a potential for enormous exposure.

Everyone is getting on board. If they don't have a "home page" on the World Wide Web yet, they will have one soon. Internet "home pages" are great for providing information about products, your company, and your industry. Home pages are also great for collecting information about your customers, who can fill out forms, send you e-mail, and even order products and services.

The Internet is also a color medium. Full-color graphics make your home page closely resemble a magazine advertisement. But a home page is really much more. With hyperlinking capabilities you can "jump" to one or more resources either on your own computer— or on a computer 10,000 miles away. For example, the New Art Communications home page (see the insert in our presentation folder) provides dozens of links to business resources, including government, legal and publications—making our home page one of the more popular business places on the Web.

I've sent along our Internet brochure, which explains in depth how we can help your company create a "hot" presence on the Internet. We're experts in technology, graphics, and copywriting. The president of our company, in fact, is editor of the esteemed McGraw-Hill Multimedia and Internet Handbook, now in its second printing with translations due out this year in both Japanese and Chinese. A board member of the New York Software Industry Association, and a charter member of the Sprint Business Advisory Council, Jessica Keyes is truly one of the few people in this business who knows how to "sell on the Internet."

I'll call you in several days to set up a courtesy meeting with Jessica. She'll be happy to assess your requirements. If you have any questions, please feel free to call me at 212.362.0559.

Sincerely Yours,

Debra Nencel
Manager

Sample press release

FOR IMMEDIATE RELEASE   Contact: Rebecca Lakser
                                                    New Art Communications
                                                    200 W 79 Street Suite 8H
                                                    NY NY 10024
                                                    (212) 362-0559

NEW ART RELEASES SURVEY FINDINGS

New York –January 12, 1996 –New Art Communications has re-
leased the 1995 results of its End User Computer Functionality Re-
quirements Survey. Preliminary findings indicate that there
remains a large gap between corporate deployment of end-user com-
puter resources and the productivity derived from it.

In spite of popular press accounts to the contrary, computer
power is neither inexpensive nor always the optimum path to enhanced productivity and efficiency. Rather, if organizations are to
achieve competitive advantage through the use of the computer, they
must assure themselves that computer power is distributed to the
workforce in a way that enhances, rather than detracts from, the
workforce. In addition, organizations also must assure themselves
that, once empowered, the workforce maintains its ability (and desire) to use that power to leverage and enhance individual, work-
group and, ultimately, corporate skill sets.

The **End User Computer Functionality Requirements Sur-**
vey, a proprietary productivity-enhancement tool developed and deployed by New Art Communications, has several steps: Gain a
specific understanding of the needs and requirements of computer
end users; determine the optimal hardware/software mix for end-user
decision support computing; develop a plan for the continued opti-
mization of computing facilities by the end-user community.

In deploying the Survey across 150 organizations during
1995, New Art has determined that there continues to be a
discrepancy between computer power and productivity de-
rived from that computer power. Raw statistics follow: 85 per-
cent of all end users are undertrained in the software

deployed on their computers; end users utilize only 27.5 percent of the functionality of their software; 65 percent of end users are utilizing a non-current version of their software (e.g., earlier versions of Word for Windows); 23 percent of end users utilize their PCs for word processing only; 85 percent of end users indicate that they spend more time than they should on formatting (using word processing, presentation graphics, desktop publishing programs); 90 percent of end users indicate that PC software, particularly Windows-based software, is hard to use, not intuitive, and takes too much time to perform required functionality; 74 percent of end users indicate that PC software "bugs" are prevalent and affect their productivity; 68 percent of end users indicate that they continue to have problems in "getting" their corporate data into the PC for analysis; 90 percent of end users admit that their PC software requests for purchase are a result of advertising blitzes rather than careful consideration of actual requirements on their part.

Founded in 1989, New Art Communications is a management and technology consultancy with a wide range of corporate customers, including many in the technology industry (e.g., Unisys, IBM, Hewlett-Packard). The company specializes in the area of corporate productivity and efficiency, and has developed a number of proprietary practices which serve to increase the competitive edge of deploying organizations. The president of New Art, Jessica Keyes, is the author of nine books and has written over 150 articles on various technology and business topics. She was a founding board member of the New York Software Industry Association, a member of the Sprint Business Advisory Council, as well as a member of New York City's Small Business Advisory Board. Her books, *Infotrends, Solving the Productivity Paradox,* and *The Software Engineering Handbook* are being used by thousands of organizations to increase both end user and systems development productivity.

Sample proposal

Thank you for the additional information. I see no problem in producing a home page as well as subsequent pages for your entire project by July 31, 1997 (see note A). My estimate for the total job is: $4000.

I. Location of home page

There are several alternatives for the location of SAMPLE's home page. One alternative is the installation of a computer, high-speed leased telco line, and Web server software at the SAMPLE location. Since this alternative requires trained personnel and is expensive, the use of a "host" site is the recommended alternative.

There are numerous service providers (i.e., companies who own the necessary hardware, software, and telecommunications and lease it out for a fee) in this country. Prices vary greatly. In addition, not all service providers provide the range of Web services required by SAMPLE.

New Art Inc., which is based in New York City, publishes some of its clients' pages (see attached) using The WELL. The WELL is located in San Francisco and would be a cost-effective alternative for SAMPLE. Their cost is $15 per month with a $2 per hour charge for use. SAMPLE would be required to sign up for an account that New Art would use to upload home and subsequent pages. It is estimated that this would require approximately 2 hours of upload time initially, with subsequent changes to the SAMPLE pages costed according to amount of information changed or added. Note that these charges are payable directly to The WELL and not to New Art Communications.

II. SAMPLE access of home page

Membership at The WELL provides a Unix interface only. Use of Mosaic or Netscape (Web browsers) will require additional software and expenditures, which will be covered in more depth in the final proposal. Note that these charges are minor (software costs approximately $150 and additional WELL charges for PPP access are small).

Since you already have access to the Web through AOL, I suggest that this be the approach SAMPLE continues to use. You will be able to access your home page through AOL. Your URL (address) would be: *http://www.well.com/user/SAMPLE.*

III. Home page

The home page will include an image, as well as hyperlinks to the other SAMPLE topics.

IV. Linked Web pages

This proposal is based upon the categories and page counts you have itemized on the attached table.

Linked Web Pages

Category	Number of pages
Membership	20 pages
Council	estimate: 12 (5 to a page)
Correspondents	1 index page, 20 country pages
History and mission	2 pages
Directory	10 pages
Membership Requirements	1 page
Application template	13 pages + 1 e-mail
Re-registration template	13 pages + 1 e-mail
Standards	3 pages
UBK	20 pages
Newsletter	2 pages
Member news	6 pages
Outreach handbook	10 pages
Public Recognition	estimate: 5 pages + logo
Annual meetings	1 page
Budget	1 page
Bylaws	7 pages
TOTAL	148 pages

V. Links, forms, and e-mail

The first phase of this project will require an analysis of the most appropriate way to design the SAMPLE Web site. It is during this stage that links to SAMPLE topics, as well as external organizations and services, will be determined. In addition, this is the phase where use of forms (e.g., re-registration) will be determined, as well as the use of e-mail. (It is possible for the viewer of the page to automatically submit an e-mail to the owner of the Web site. This technique can be used for registration and re-registration.)

VI. Cost estimates

The final page count is one home page plus 148 adjunct pages. Note that the term "pages" is used to denote screens and not physical Web addresses. However, the page concept is the most appropriate vehicle to use for pricing.

Cost will be figured at $500 plus $100 per hour (billed in 15-minute increments). It is estimated that this project will take 35 hours to complete. New Art is pleased to offer a flat-rate fee of $4000 for the complete job in consideration of your nonprofit status.

Note A: The estimate is based on getting a readable ASCII diskette from SAMPLE.

What goes into a venture proposal

What follows is the basic form of a venture proposal. At minimum, your proposal should address these issues; any other facts, conditions, or situations that would affect the success or profitability of the business also should be included.

Purpose and Objectives Include a summary of the what and why of the project.

Proposed Financing You must state the amount of money you will need from the beginning to the maturity of the project proposed, how the proceeds will be used, how you plan to structure the financing, and why the amount designated is required.

Marketing Describe the market segment you've got or plan to get, the competition, the characteristics of the market, and your plans (with costs) for getting or holding the market segment you're aiming at.

History of the Firm Summarize the significant financial and organizational milestones, describe employees and employee relations, explain banking relationships, and recount major services or products your firm has offered during its existence, and the like.

Description of the Product or Service Include a full description, in detail, of the product (process) or service offered by the firm and the costs associated with it.

Financial Statements Include statements for both the past few years and pro forma projections (balance sheets, income statements, and cash flows) for the next three to five years, showing the effect anticipated if the project is undertaken and if the financing is secured. (This should include an analysis of key variables affecting financial performance, showing what could happen if the projected level of revenue is not attained.)

Capitalization Provide a list of shareholders, how much is invested to date, and in what form (equity or debt).

Biographical Sketches Describe the work histories and qualifications of key owners and employees.

Principal Suppliers and Customers, Problems Anticipated, and Other Pertinent Information Provide a candid discussion of any contingent liabilities, pending litigation, tax or patent difficulties, and any other contingencies that might affect the project you're proposing. List the names, addresses, and the telephone numbers of suppliers and customers; they will be contacted to verify your statement about payments (suppliers) and products (customers).

Provisions of the Investment Proposal What happens when, after the exhaustive investigation and analysis, the venture capital firms decides to invest in a company? Most venture firms prepare an equity financing proposal that details the amount of money to be provided, the percentage of common stock to be surrendered in exchange for these funds, the interim financing method to be used, and the protective covenants to be included.

What goes into a business plan

The following are the basic items to be included in a business plan, together with typical lengths of the sections.

1. *Introduction* Introduce the plan. Explain who wrote it, when, and for what purpose. Give contact details. (1–2 pages)

2. *Summary* Summarize the mission and goals of the plan. Write this last. (1–3 pages)

3. *Mission, Strategies, etc.* What are the central purposes and activities of the planned business? What are its major objectives and key strategies? (1–2 pages)

4. *Present Status of Project* Describe achievements to date, and indicate the parties involved. (1–2 pages)

5. *Product/Service Description* Keep descriptions short and confine them to broad groups. Explain briefly what makes them special. (1–2 pages)

6. *Profile of Target Market(s)* Describe size, segments, trends, competition, and user/customer profiles. (2–3 pages)

7. *Marketing Strategies and Sales Plans* How will the business market products/services and sell to customers? What sales will be achieved in its main markets? How will it deal with competitors? Indicate costs. (2–3 pages)

8. *R&D and Technology* If relevant, explain progress, plans, and resources, and highlight any technological advances. (0–2 pages)

9. *Manufacturing/Operational Plans* Cover distribution and service activities and/or manufacturing. Highlight major elements only. Indicate organization, resources, costings, etc. (2–3 pages)

10. *Management* Introduce the proposed management team, structure, etc. Indicate overhead costs. (1–2 pages)

11. *Financial Position and Projections* Use simple tables to present key financial projections, e.g., summary P&L, cash flows, balance sheets, and key ratios. Place the detailed analyses in appendices. (2–3 pages)

12. *Funding Requirements and Proposals* If applicable, summarize funding requirements, possible sources, likely terms, and, for investors, the projected return on their investment. (2–3 pages)

13. *Conclusion* In a few short paragraphs, explain why the business will succeed and why it should be supported. (1 page)

Appendix B

HTML quick reference

The following elements cover all HTML elements of the level 3.0+ specification. Netscape and Microsoft extensions are listed (and annotated) as well. Remember that this list changes frequently. Get the most recent list at the World Wide Consortium's Web site at *http://www.w3.org*. A good online reference guide can be found at *http://www.woodhill.co.uk/html.*

<!—>	<CENTER>
<A>	<CITE>
<ADDRESS>	<CODE>
<APPLET>	<DD>
<B>	<DIR>
<BASE>	<DL>
<BASEFONT SIZE= >	<DT>
<BGSOUND>	<EM>
<BIG>	<EMBED>
<BLINK>	<FONT COLOR>
<BLOCKQUOTE>	<FONT SIZE= >
<BODY>	<FORM>
 	<FRAMES>
<CAPTION>	<H ALIGN= >

\<H1\>	\<OPTION\>
\<H2\>	\<P ALIGN= \>
\<H3\>	\<P\>
\<H4\>	\<PLAINTEXT\>
\<H5\>	\<PRE\>
\<H6\>	\<SAMP\>
\<HEAD\>	\<SCRIPT\>
\<HP\>	\<SELECT\>
\<HR\>	\<SMALL\>
\<HTML\>	\<STRIKE\>
\<I\>	\<STRONG\>
\<IMG\>	\<SUB\>
\<INPUT\>	\<SUP\>
\<ISINDEX\>	\<TABLE\>
\<KBD\>	\<TD\>
\<LI\>	\<TEXTAREA\>
\<LINK\>	\<TH\>
\<LISTING\>	\<TITLE\>
\<MARQUEE\>	\<TR\>
\<MENU\>	\<TT\>
\<META\>	\<U\>
\<NEXTID\>	\<UL\>
\<NOBR\>	\<VAR\>
\<OL\>	\<WBR\>

\<!--comment--\>

To include comments in an HTML document that will be ignored by
the HTML user agent, surround them with \<!-- and --\>. After the comment delimiter, all text up to the next occurrence of --\> is ignored.
Hence comments cannot be nested. White space is allowed between
the closing -- and \>, but not between the opening \<! and --. Example:

\<!-- Id: The text between these two tags are comments --\>

\<A\> . . . \</A\>

The Anchor element marks text that is the start or destination of a hypertext link. Anchor elements are defined by the \<A\> element. The \<A\>
element accepts several attributes, but either the NAME or HREF attribute
is required. The attributes are listed in the following paragraphs.

HREF

If the HREF attribute is present, the text between the opening and closing anchor elements becomes hypertext. If this hypertext is selected

by readers, they are moved to another document, or to a different location in the current document, whose network address is defined by the value of the HREF attribute. Example:

See <A HREF="http://www.well.com/user/business/">New Art </A>'s information for more details.

In this example, selecting "New Art" takes the reader to a document located at *http://www.well.com/user/business.*

With the HREF attribute, the form HREF="#*identifier*" can refer to another anchor in the same document. Example:

The <A HREF="document.html#glossary">glossary</A> defines terms used in the document.

In this example, selecting "glossary" takes the reader to another anchor (i.e., <A NAME="glossary"><Glossary</A>) in the same document (*document.html*). The NAME attribute is described below. If the anchor is in another document, the HREF attribute may be relative to the document's address or the specified base address.

NAME

If present, the NAME attribute allows the anchor to be the target of a link. The value of the NAME attribute is an identifier for the anchor. Identifiers are arbitrary strings, but must be unique within the HTML document. Example:

<A NAME=coffee>Coffee</A> is an exmple of . . .

An example of this is <A HREF=#coffee>coffee</A>.

Another document can then make a reference explicitly to this anchor by putting the identifier after the address, separated by the hash sign (#):

<A NAME=drinks.html#coffee>

TITLE

The TITLE attribute is informational only. If present, the attribute should provide the title of the document whose address is given by the HREF attribute. The TITLE attribute is useful for at least two reasons. The HTML user agent may display the title of the document before retrieving it, for example, as a margin note, in a small box while the mouse is over the anchor, or while the document is being loaded.

Another reason is that documents that are not marked-up text (such as graphics, plain text, and gopher menus) do not have titles. The TITLE attribute can be used to provide a title to such documents.

When using the TITLE attribute, the title should be valid and unique for the destination document.

REL

The REL attribute gives the relationship(s) described by the hypertext link from the anchor to the target. The value is a comma-separated list of relationship values. Values and their semantics will be registered by the HTML registration authority. The default relationship, if none other is given is VOID. The REL attribute is only used when the HREF attribute is present.

REV

The REV attribute is the same as the REL attribute, but the semantics of the link type are in the reverse direction. A link from A to B with REL="X" expresses the same relationship as a link from B to A with REV="X." An anchor may have both REL and REV attributes.

URN

If present, the URN attribute specifies a uniform resource name (URN) for a target document. The format of URNs is under discussion (1994) by various working groups of the Internet Engineering Task Force.

METHODS

The METHODS attributes of anchors and links provide information about the functions that the user may perform on an object. These are more accurately given by the HTTP protocol when it is used, but it may, for similar reasons as for the TITLE attribute, be useful to include the information in advance in the link. For example, the HTML user agent may choose a different rendering as a function of the methods allowed. For example, something that is searchable may get a different icon. The value of the METHODS attribute is a comma-separated list of HTTP methods supported by the object for public use.

<ADDRESS> . . . </ADDRESS>

The ADDRESS element specifies such information as address, signature, and authorship, often at the top or bottom of a document. Typically, an address is rendered in an italic typeface and may be indented. The ADDRESS element implies a paragraph break before and after. Example:

```
<ADDRESS>
Jessica Keyes<BR>
New Art Inc. New York NY 10024<BR>
Tel (212) 362 0559
</ADDRESS>
```

<APPLET> . . . </APPLET>

Requires start and end tags. This element is supported by all Java-enabled browsers. It allows you to embed a Java applet into HTML documents, e.g., to include an animation. The contents of the element are used as a fallback if the applet can't be loaded. The attributes are: CODE, CODEBASE, NAME, ALT, ALIGN, WIDTH, HEIGHT, HSPACE, and VSPACE. The APPLET element uses associated PARAM elements to pass parameters to the applet.

<B> . . . </B>

The BOLD element specifies that the text should be rendered in boldface, where available. Otherwise, alternative mapping is allowed. For example:

The instructions <B>must be read</B> before continuing

would be rendered as follows:

The instructions **must be read** before continuing.

<BASE>

The BASE element allows the URL of the document itself to be recorded in situations in which the document may be read out of context. URLs within the document may be in a "partial" form relative to this base address. Where the base address is not specified, the HTML user agent uses the URL it used to access the document to resolve any relative URLs. The BASE element has one attribute, HREF, which identifies the URL.

<BASEFONT SIZE= >
Netscape extension

The <BASEFONT SIZE=n> element changes the size of the BASEFONT that all relative changes <FONT SIZE=+n> and <FONT SIZE=–n> are based upon. It defaults to 3, and has a valid range of 1–7. For example, <BASEFONT SIZE=5>.

<BGSOUND>
Microsoft extension

This tag is a Microsoft extension lets you play background sounds or sound tracks while the reader is looking at your page. Attributes follow.

SRC=URL
Specifies source as the Internet address (URL) of the sound file to play.

LOOP=*n* or LOOP=INFINITE

Specifies how many times a sound file will be played. If LOOP=INFINITE or LOOP=–1, the sound file will keep playing indefinitely. Example:

```
<BGSOUND SRC=music.wav LOOP=5>
```

<BLINK>
Netscape extension

Surrounding any text with this element will cause the selected text to blink on the viewing page. This can serve to add extra emphasis to selected text. Example:

```
<BLINK>This text would blink on the page</BLINK>
```

<BLOCKQUOTE> . . . </BLOCKQUOTE>

The Blockquote element is used to contain text quoted from another source. A typical rendering might be a slight extra left and right indent, and/or an italic font. The BLOCKQUOTE element causes a paragraph break, and typically provides space above and below the quote.

Single-font rendition might reflect the quotation style of Internet mail by putting a vertical line of graphic characters, such as the greater than symbol (>), in the left margin. Example:

JFK once might have said

```
<BLOCKQUOTE>
<P>Ask not what your country can do for you  . . . </BLOCKQUOTE>
```

but I am not sure.

<BODY> . . . </BODY>

The Body of a HTML document contains all the text and images that make up the page, together with all the HTML elements that provide the control and formatting of the page. Example:

```
<BODY>
```

The document included here

```
</BODY>
```

The Body element has been enhanced in recent Netscape versions, and there are several attributes.

BACKGROUND

Recent versions of the proposed HTML 3.0 spec. have added a BACK-GROUND attribute to the <BODY> element. The purpose of this attribute is to specify a URL pointing to an image that is to be used as a background for the document. In Netscape, this background image is used to tile the full background of the document-viewing area. Thus, specifying:

```
<BODY BACKGROUND="URL or path/filename.gif">
```

Document here

```
</BODY>
```

would cause whatever text, images, etc., that appeared in that document to be placed on a background consisting of the *filename.gif* graphics file being tiled to cover the viewing area, much like bitmaps are used for Windows wallpaper.

BGCOLOR

This attribute to <BODY> is not currently in the proposed HTML 3.0 specification, but is supported by Netscape 1.1 and above and is being considered for inclusion in the 3.0 spec. Essentially it changes the color of the background without requiring that a separate image be specified that entails another network access to load. The format that Netscape 1.1 understands is:

```
<BODY BGCOLOR="#rrggbb">
```

Document here

```
</BODY>
```

where "#rrggbb" is a hexadecimal red-green-blue triplet used to specify the background color. Clearly, once the background colors/patterns have been changed, it will be necessary to control the foreground to establish the proper contrasts. The following attributes are also recognized as part of the <BODY> element by Netscape 1.1.

TEXT

This attribute is used to control the color of all the normal text in the document. This consists of all text that is not specially colored to indicate a link. The format of TEXT is the same as that of BGCOLOR:

```
<BODY TEXT="#rrggbb">
```

Document here

```
</BODY>
```

LINK, VLINK, ALINK

These attributes let you control the coloring of link text. VLINK stands for visited link, and ALINK stands for active link. The default coloring of these is LINK blue, VLINK purple, and ALINK red. The format for these attributes is the same as that for BGCOLOR and TEXT:

<BODY LINK="#rrggbb" VLINK="#rrggbb" ALINK="#rrggbb">

Document here

</BODY>

Coloring considerations

Since these color controls are all attributes of the <BODY> element, they can be set only once for the entire document. Document color cannot be changed part way through a document.

Setting a background image requires the fetching of an image file from a second HTTP connection, which will slow down the perceived speed of document loading. None of the document can be displayed until the image is loaded and decoded. Needless to say, keep background images small.

If the Auto Load Images option is turned off, background images will not be loaded. If the background image is not loaded for any reason, and a BGCOLOR was not also specified, then any of the foreground controlling attributes (LINK, VLINK, and ALINK) will be ignored. The idea behind this is that if the requested background image is unavailable, or not loaded, setting requested text colors on top of the default gray background may make the document unreadable.

The Line Break element specifies that a new line must be started at the specified point. A new line indents the same as that of line-wrapped text.

The <BR> element has been Netscape-enhanced. With the addition of floating images, it was necessary to expand the <BR> element. Normal <BR> still just inserts a line break. A CLEAR attribute has been added. Specifying CLEAR=LEFT will break the line, and move vertically down until you have a clear left margin (no floating images). CLEAR=RIGHT does the same for the right margin, and CLEAR=ALL moves down until both margins are clear of images.

<CAPTION> . . . </CAPTION>

This represents the Caption for a table. Any <CAPTION> elements should appear inside the <TABLE> but not inside table rows or cells. The caption accepts an alignment attribute that defaults to ALIGN=TOP but can be explicitly set to ALIGN=BOTTOM. Like table cells, any document body HTML can appear in a caption. Captions are always horizontally centered with respect to the table, and they may have their lines broken to fit within the width of the table.

<CENTER> . . . </CENTER>
Netscape extension

All lines of text between the begin and end of the <CENTER> element are centered between the current left and right margins. This new element has been introduced, rather than using the proposed <P ALIGN=CENTER>, because using the <P> element as a container breaks many existing browsers. The <P ALIGN=CENTER> element also is less general and does not support all cases where centering may be desired.

<CITE> . . . </CITE>

The Citation element specifies a citation; typically rendered as italics. For example, this sentence, containing a <cite>citation reference </cite> would look like:

This sentence, containing a *citation reference* would look like:

<CODE> . . . </CODE>

The Code element indicates an example of code; typically rendered as monospaced. Do not confuse with the Preformatted Text element.

<DL> . . . </DL>
<DT> . . . </DT>
<DD> . . . </DD>

A definition list is a list of terms and corresponding definitions. Definition lists are typically formatted with the term flush-left and the definition, formatted paragraph style, indented after the term. Example:

```
<DL>
<DT>Term<DD>This is the definition of the first term.
<DT>Term<DD>This is the definition of the second term.
</DL>
```

If the <DT> term does not fit in the <DT> column (one-third of the display area), it may be extended across the page with the <DD> section moved to the next line, or it may be wrapped onto successive lines of the lefthand column.

   Single occurrences of a <DT> element without a subsequent <DD> element are allowed, and have the same significance as if the <DD> element had been present with no text. The opening list element must be <DL> and must be immediately followed by the first term <DT>.

COMPACT

The definition list type can take the COMPACT attribute, which suggests that a compact rendering be used, because the list items are small and/or the entire list is large. Unless you provide the COMPACT attribute, the HTML user agent may leave white space between successive <DT>–<DD> pairs. The COMPACT attribute also might reduce the width of the lefthand (<DT>) column.

If using the COMPACT attribute, the opening list element must be <DL COMPACT>, which must be followed immediately by the first <DT> element:

```
<DL COMPACT>
<DT>Term<DD>This is the first definition in compact format.
<DT>Term<DD>This is the second definition in compact format.
</DL>
```

<DIR> . . . </DIR>

A Directory List element is used to present a list of items containing up to 20 characters each. Items in a directory list may be arranged in columns, typically 24 characters wide. If the HTML user agent can optimize the column width as function of the widths of individual elements, so much the better. A directory list must begin with the <DIR> element, which is immediately followed by a <LI> (list item) element:

```
<DIR>
<LI>A-H<LI>I-M
<LI>M-R<LI>S-Z
</DIR>
```

<EM> . . . </EM>

The Emphasis element indicates typographic emphasis, typically rendered as italics. For example:

The <EM>Emphasis</EM> element typically renders as Italics.

would render as:

The *Emphasis* element typically renders as Italics.

<EMBED>
Netscape extension

This tag is recognized only by the Windows version of Netscape Navigator, versions 1.1 and above. The <embed> element allows you to put documents directly into an HTML page. The syntax is:

```
<EMBED SRC="images/embed.bmp">
```

The <EMBED> element will allow you to embed documents of any type. Your user needs only to have an application installed on his or her machine that can view the data correctly.

If a width and height are specified, the embedded object is scaled to fit the available space. For example, this is the same bitmap as above, but scaled:

<EMBED SRC="images/embed.bmp"WIDTH=250 HEIGHT=50>

Embedded objects can be activated by double-clicking them in the Netscape window. The application that supports use of the embedded object will be launched, with the object present.

Note: Using the <EMBED> element, you should be sure that the user has a suitable application available that is OLE-compliant. Otherwise the HTML document will not be displayed as expected. This element produces essentially the same results as does embedding objects in Word for Windows: The object is displayed, and can be edited in a suitable application by double-clicking on the object.

<FONT SIZE= >
Netscape extension

Netscape 1.0 and above supports different-sized fonts within HTML documents. This should be distinguished from Headings (the <H*n*> elements). The new element is <FONT SIZE=*value*>. Valid values range from 1–7. The default size is 3. The value given to size optionally can have a + or – character ahead of it to specify that it is relative to the document BASEFONT. The default BASEFONT is 3, and can be changed with the <BASEFONT SIZE= > element.

<FORM> . . . </FORM>

The Form element is used to delimit a data input form. There can be several forms in a single document, but the Form element can't be nested.

ACTION

The ACTION attribute is a URL specifying the location where the contents of the form is submitted to elicit a response. If the ACTION attribute is missing, the URL of the document itself is assumed. The way data is submitted varies with the access protocol of the URL, and with the values of the METHOD and ENCTYPE attributes, described below.

METHOD

This selects variations in the protocol.

ENCTYPE

This attribute specifies the format of the submitted data in case the protocol does not impose a format itself. The Level 2 specification defines and requires support for the HTTP access protocol only.

When the ACTION attribute is set to an HTTP URL, the METHOD attribute must be set to an HTTP method as defined by the HTTP method specification in the IETF draft HTTP standard. The default method is GET, although for many applications, the POST method may be preferred. With the POST method, the ENCTYPE attribute is a MIME type specifying the format of the posted data; by default, it is *application/x-www-form-urlencoded*.

Under any protocol, the submitted contents of the form logically consist of name/value pairs. The names are usually equal to the NAME attributes of the various interactive elements in the form.

Note: The names are not guaranteed to be unique keys, nor are the names of form elements required to be distinct. The values encode the user's input to the corresponding interactive elements. Elements capable of displaying a textual or numerical value will return a name/value pair even when they receive no explicit user input.

Input can take several forms. The following two lines of code would encode radio buttons and checkboxes, respectively:

```
<INPUT TYPE="radio" NAME="heading of button" VALUE="button name">

<INPUT TYPE="checkbox" NAME=
"Signing_from" VALUE="Joes_page">
```

while the coding for pop-up boxes would look like this:

```
<SELECT
NAME="Favorite_Color" SIZE="1">
<OPTION SELECTED>Blue
<OPTION>Red
<OPTION>Yellow
<OPTION>Green
<OPTION>Black
<OPTION>Orange
<OPTION>Purple
</SELECT>
```

<FRAMES>

Frames allow a single Web browser window to be divided into several different areas. Each area can display a different Web page. Frames thus add flexibility to a site. For example, they allow different background colors or images to be used for different parts of the same window, or a table of contents to be available at all times while the user scrolls through the main body of a document. It's not hard to come up with other creative applications for them.

The HTML tags that break a browser window up into several frames are similar to the tags that define lists. Using them is fairly straightforward. First, define a page that gives the frame layout. Second, specify a Web page to put in each frame.

A page that gives a frame layout does not have a BODY; instead, it has a FRAMESET and individual FRAMEs. Every time you use the <FRAMESET> tag, you break the window into columns or rows. Each column or row then may be used as a frame, or broken up into smaller frames by using another FRAMESET tag. Like <BODY>, the <FRAMESET> container must end with the </FRAMESET> tag.

Here's how FRAMESET works. Use it in place of the <BODY> tag in a page. In the tag, specify whether you want to divide the window into rows or columns, and give a list of sizes for the rows or columns. The tag itself looks like this:

<FRAMESET *type* = *"size1, size2, ...">*

Instead of *type*, insert ROWS to divide the window into horizontal frames, or insert COLS to divide the window into vertical frames. In place of each *size*, provide a size for a frame. This can be done in one of three ways:

- Percent of the window size. To specify a frame that's 30 percent of the current window size, enter 30% for the size parameter.
- Absolute size in pixels. To make a frame that's 200 pixels, enter 200 as the size.
- Relative size. A relative-sized frame is defined by using an asterisk * for the size.

After you have set up the layout of the frames, you must tell the browser where to find the Web page that goes into each one. This is done using the <FRAME> tag. The tag works as follows:

<FRAME SRC = "URL">

In place of the URL place holder above, give the actual URL of a page, image, newsgroup, telnet session, or whatever you want.

Example 1: Two frames

The following HTML creates two equal, vertical frames side-by-side:

```
<HTML>
<HEAD>
<TITLE>Example 1</TITLE>
</HEAD>

<FRAMESET COLS = "50%, 50%">
<FRAME SRC = "wpage1.html">
<FRAME SRC = "wpage2.html">
</FRAMESET>
</HTML>
```

Example 2: Nested frames

Frames also can be nested. Once you have divided the window into frames, you then may divide each frame into smaller frames. This is again accomplished by using the <FRAMESET> tag, and is illustrated in the code below:

```
<HTML>
<HEAD>
<TITLE>Example 2</TITLE>
</HEAD>

<FRAMESET COLS = "50%, 50%">
<FRAME SRC = "wlogo.gif"> - This is the first frame

<FRAMESET ROWS = "50%, 50%"> - The second frame is itself a set
of two more frames
<FRAME SRC = "wpage1.html">
<FRAME SRC = "wpage2.html">
</FRAMESET>

</FRAMESET>

</HTML>
```

Example 3: HTML for non-frame browsers

Not all browsers support frames. You should make provisions for those people. The FRAMESET tag has a complementary NOFRAMES tag. A browser that does support frames will skip over everything between <NOFRAMES> and </NOFRAMES>. Browsers in general ignore tags that they do not recognize, so for other viewers you can put the HTML definition of a standard Web page between the two tags. Frames-incapable browsers can "see" it and will display it, as illustrated in this HTML:

```
<HTML>
<HEAD>
<TITLE>Example 3</TITLE>
</HEAD>
<FRAMESET COLS = "50%, 50%">

<NOFRAMES>
<BODY>
If you can see this, your browser does not support frames.<P>

<A HREF = "net3.html#ex3">Go back to Example 3</A>
</BODY>
</NOFRAMES>

<FRAME SRC = "wpage1.html">
<FRAME SRC = "wpage2.html">
</FRAMESET>

</HTML>
```

The individual frames may be modified in several ways. First, scroll bars may be added or removed. Normally this is done automatically; if a Web page doesn't fit into its frame, Netscape adds scroll bars. When the frames are defined, the author may choose to force scroll bars to be present at all times, or prevent them from ever appearing. This is done by using the SCROLLING modifier to the FRAME tag, as follows:

```
<FRAME SCROLLING = "YES" SRC = "wpage1.html">
```

If this tag were used in one of the preceding examples, the frame containing the Web page *wpage1.html* would always have scroll bars. Replacing the "YES" with "NO" would prevent scroll bars from ever appearing in the frame, regardless of how small the user resized the window.

Viewers also can be prevented from resizing the frames within the window (but not the window itself) by adding the NORESIZE modifier to the FRAME tag. Note that this fixes all edges of the frame, so it also will prevent some parts of the adjacent frames from being manually resized. To use this modifier, just add NORESIZE to the FRAME tag in the following manner:

```
<FRAME NORESIZE SRC = "wpage1.html">
```

The frames also can be named, by using the NAME modifier to the FRAME tag. The syntax is very simple; to create a frame named "frame1," use the following tag:

```
<FRAME NAME = "frame1" SRC = "wpage1.html">
```

Targets are the complement to links. A *link* tells the browser what file to display. A *target* tells the browser where to display it. You can use targets to specify a frame in a current window, for example, or call up a new window when a link is selected.

Example 4: Default and specific targets
There are two primary ways to specify the target of a link. First, a target can be given for an individual link. Second, a default target can be specified. Let's look at each of these in turn.

To create targets for individual links, The TARGET modifier is added to the <A HREF> tag in the following manner:

```
<A HREF = "url" TARGET = "targetname">Hit me</A>
```

Here *url* is the URL of the new Web page or file, and *targetname* is the name of the target. If it matches the name of an existing frame (see the NAME modifier to frames, above), whatever is stored at the URL will be displayed in that frame. If *targetname* does not match any frame names, a new window will be created.

To establish a default target for all links, the BASE tag is used at the beginning of a document to specify a target for all links that do not have a target already given in the manner shown above. The syntax is very simple, but note that this tag belongs in the *header* section of your HTML document:

```
<HEAD>
<BASE TARGET = "maintarget">
</HEAD>
```

If no TARGET is given in a particular link, the link will behave as if TARGET = "*maintarget*" had been added to it.

Here is the complete code for Example 4, showing both default and explicitly specified targets:

```
<HTML>
<HEAD>
<TITLE>Example 4</TITLE>
```

```
<BASE TARGET = "frame3">
</HEAD>

<FRAMESET COLS = "50%, 50%">
<FRAME SRC = "frame4a.html">

<FRAMESET ROWS = "50%, 50%">
<FRAME NAME = "frame2" SRC = "blank.html">
<FRAME NAME = "frame3" SRC = "blank.html">
</FRAMESET>
</FRAMESET>

</HTML>
```

The name of targets must begin with a number or letter. There are four special target names that always can be used. They all begin with the underscore character. The syntax is the same:

TARGET = *"specialname"*

where *specialname* is one of the following four special target names:

- **_blank** causes the link to be loaded into a new blank window.
- **_self** causes the link to be loaded into the same window or frame in which it was clicked upon by the user. This comes in handy when a default target was specified using the BASE tag.
- **_parent** causes the link to load in the parent document. This is useful if more than one window has been created.
- **_top** causes the link to load in the full window. This is useful for wiping out a frameset without creating a new window.

<H ALIGN= >
HTML 3.0

Included in the proposed HTML 3.0 specification is the ability to align Headings. Basically, LEFT, CENTER, and RIGHT attributes have been added to the <H1> to <H6> elements. For example:

<H1 ALIGN=center>Hello, this is a heading</H1>

would align a type 1 heading in the center of the page.

<H*n*> . . . </H*n*>

HTML defines six levels of heading. A Heading element implies all the font changes, paragraph breaks before and after, and white space necessary to render the heading.

<H1> . . . </H1>

The highest level of heading is <H1>. It is bold, in a very large font, centered, with one or two blank lines above and below.

<H2> . . . </H2>

Bold, large font, flush left, with one or two blank lines above and below.

<H3> . . . </H3>

Italic, large font, slightly indented from the left margin, with one or two blank lines above and below.

<H4> . . . </H4>

Bold, normal font, indented more than <H3>, with one blank line above and below.

<H5> . . . </H5>

Italic, normal font, indented as <H4>, with one blank line above.

<H6> . . . </H6>

Bold, indented the same as normal text, more than <H5>, with one blank line above only.

<HEAD> . . . </HEAD>

The head of an HTML document is an unordered collection of information about the document. It requires the Title element between <HEAD> and </HEAD> elements, thus:

```
<HEAD>
<TITLE> Introduction to HTML </TITLE>
</HEAD>
```

The <HEAD> and </HEAD> elements do not directly affect the look of the document when rendered. The following elements are related to the head element. While not directly affecting the look of the rendered document, they do provide (if used) important information to the HTML user agent.

<BASE>	Specifies base address of HTML document.
<ISINDEX>	Allows keyword searching of document.
<LINK>	Specifies relationships between documents.
<NEXTID>	Creates unique document identifiers.
<TITLE>	Specifies title of document.
<META>	Specifies document information usable by server/clients.

<HR>

A Horizontal Rule element is a divider between sections of text, such as a full-width horizontal rule or equivalent graphic.

Note: The <HR> element has been Netscape-enhanced. The <HR> element specifies that a horizontal rule of some sort (the default being a shaded engraved line) be drawn across the page. To this element, Netscape has added four new attributes that allow the author of the document to describe how the horizontal rule should look.

SIZE

The SIZE=n attribute lets the author give an indication of how thick he or she wishes the horizontal rule to be.

WIDTH

The default horizontal rule is always as wide as the page. With the WIDTH=n and WIDTH=n% attributes, the author can specify an exact width in pixels, or a relative width measured in percent of document width.

ALIGN

Now that horizontal rules no longer have to be the width of the page, the author must be able to specify whether they should be pushed up against the left margin, the right margin, or centered in the page. Values for the ALIGN attribute are LEFT, RIGHT, or CENTER.

NOSHADE

Finally, for those times when a solid bar is required, the NOSHADE attribute lets the author specify that the horizontal rule should not be shaded at all. There are no values for this attribute.

<HTML> . . . </HTML>

This element identifies the document as containing HTML elements. It should immediately follow the prologue document identifier and surrounds all of the remaining text, including all other elements. The document should be constructed thus:

<HTML>

Here is all the rest of the document, including any elements.

</HTML>

The HTML element is not rendered visibly by the HTML user agent, and can contain only the <HEAD> and <BODY> elements.

<I> . . . </I>

The Italic element specifies that the text should be rendered in italic font, where available. Otherwise, alternative mapping is allowed. For example:

Anything between the <I>I elements</I> should be italics.

would render as :

Anything between the <PROGRAMLISTING-ITALC>*I elements* should be italics.

<IMG. . .>

The Image element is used to incorporate inline graphics (typically icons or small graphics) into an HTML document. This element cannot be used for embedding other HTML text.

HTML user agents that cannot render inline images ignore the Image element unless it contains the ALT attribute. Note that some HTML user agents can render linked graphics but not inline graphics. If a graphic is essential, you may want to create a link to it rather than put it inline. If the graphic is not essential, then the Image element is appropriate.

The Image element, which is empty (no closing element), has several attributes, described in the following paragraphs.

ALIGN

The ALIGN attribute accepts the values TOP or MIDDLE or BOTTOM, which specify whether the following line of text is aligned with the top, middle, or bottom of the graphic.

ALT

Optional text as an alternative to the graphic for rendering in non-graphical environments. Alternate text should be provided whenever the graphic is not rendered. Alternate text is mandatory for Level 0 documents. Example:

<IMG SRC="triangle.gif" ALT="Warning:"> Be sure to read these instructions.

ISMAP

The ISMAP ("is map") attribute identifies an image as an imagemap. Imagemaps are graphics in which certain regions are mapped to URLs. By clicking on different regions, different resources can be accessed from the same graphic. Example:

```
<A HREF="http://machine/htbin/imagemap/sample">
<IMG SRC="sample.gif" ISMAP>
</A>
```

Note: To be able to employ imagemaps in HTML documents, the HTTP server that will be controlling document access must have the correct CGI software installed to control imagemap behavior.

SRC

The value of the SRC attribute is the URL of the document to be embedded; only images can be embedded, not HTML text. Its syntax is the same as that of the HREF attribute of the <A> element. SRC is mandatory. Image elements are allowed within anchors. Example:

```
<IMG SRC ="triangle.gif">Be sure to read these instructions.
```

Note: The <IMG> element has received possibly the largest Netscape enhancement. The <IMG> attribute is probably the most extended element in HTML. The attributes follow.

ALIGN

The ALIGN attribute accepts the values LEFT, RIGHT, TOP, TEXTTOP, MIDDLE, ABSMIDDLE, BASELINE, BOTTOM, and ABSBOTTOM. The additions to your ALIGN options need a lot of explanation. Images with the LEFT and RIGHT alignments are an entirely new floating image type.

Using LEFT will float the image down and over to the left margin (into the next available space there), and subsequent text will wrap around the righthand side of that image. With RIGHT, the image aligns with the right margin, and the text wraps around the left.

The TOP value causes the image to align itself with the top of the tallest item in the line. With TEXTTOP, it aligns itself with the top of the tallest text in the line; this usually, but not always, is the same as using ALIGN=TOP.

The MIDDLE value aligns the baseline of the current line with the middle of the image, while ABSMIDDLE aligns the middle of the current line with the middle of the image.

BASELINE aligns the bottom of the image with the baseline of the current line; BOTTOM aligns the bottom of the image with the baseline of the current line; and ABSBOTTOM aligns the bottom of the image with the bottom of the current line.

WIDTH, HEIGHT

The WIDTH and HEIGHT attributes were added to <IMG> mainly to speed up display of the document. If the author specifies these, the viewer of the document will not have to wait for the image to be loaded over the network and have its size calculated.

BORDER

This attribute lets the document author control the thickness of the border around an image displayed. Be careful, though, when setting BORDER=0 on images that also are part of anchors. It may confuse your users, as they are used to a colored border indicating an image is an anchor.

VSPACE, HSPACE

It is likely that the document author does not want floating images pressing up against the text wrapped around the image. The VSPACE attribute controls the vertical space above and below the image, while HSPACE controls the horizontal space to the left and right of the image.

LOWSRC

By using the LOWSRC attribute, it is possible to use two images in the same space. Example:

```
<IMG SRC="highres.gif"LOWSRC="lowres.jpg">
```

Browsers that do not recognize the LOWSRC attribute cleanly ignore it and simply load the image called *highres.gif.* Netscape Navigator, on the other hand, will load the image called *lowres.jpg* on its first layout pass through the document. Then, when the document and all of its images are fully loaded, Navigator will do a second pass through and load the image called *highres.gif* in place. This means that you can have a very low-resolution version of an image loaded initially; if the user stays on the page after the initial layout phase, a higher-resolution (and presumably bigger) version of the same image can "fade in" and replace it.

Both GIF (normal and interlaced) and JPEG images can be freely interchanged using this method. You also can specify width and/or height values in the IMG element, and both the high-res and low-res versions of the image will be appropriately scaled to match.

If the images are of different sizes and a fixed height and width are not specified in the IMG element, the second image (the image specified by the SRC attribute) will be scaled to the dimensions of the first (LOWSRC) image. This happens because, by the time Netscape knows the dimensions of the second image, the first image already has been displayed in the document at its normal dimensions.

<INPUT>

The Input element represents a field, the contents of which may be edited by the user. Attributes of the Input element are described below.

ALIGN

Specifies vertical alignment of the image. For use only with TYPE= IMAGE in HTML Level 2, the possible values are exactly the same as those for the ALIGN attribute of the Image element.

CHECKED

Indicates that a checkbox or radio button is selected. Unselected checkboxes and radio buttons do not return name/value pairs when the form is submitted.

MAXLENGTH

Indicates the maximum number of characters that can be entered into a text field. This can be greater than specified by the SIZE attribute, in which case the field will scroll appropriately. The default number of characters is unlimited.

NAME

Symbolic name used when transferring the form's contents. The NAME attribute is required for most input types and normally is used to provide a unique identifier for a field, or for a logically related group of fields.

SIZE

Specifies the size or precision of the field according to its type. For example, to specify a field with a visible width of 24 characters, you'd do the following:

INPUT TYPE=text SIZE="24"

SRC

A URL specifying an image, for use only with TYPE=IMAGE in HTML Level 2.

TYPE

Defines the type of data the field accepts, defaulting to free text. Several types of fields can be defined with the type attribute.

The value CHECKBOX is used for simple boolean attributes, or for attributes that can take multiple values at the same time. The latter is represented by a number of checkbox fields, each of which has the same name. Each selected checkbox generates a separate name/value pair in the submitted data, even if this results in duplicate names. The default value for checkboxes is *on*.

With HIDDEN, no field is presented to the user, but the content of the field is sent with the submitted form. This value may be used to transmit state information about client/server interaction.

The IMAGE value creates an image field upon which you can click with a pointing device, causing the form to be submitted immediately. The coordinates of the selected point are measured in pixel units from the upper left corner of the image, and are returned (along with the other contents of the form) in two name/value pairs. The x coordinate is submitted under the name of the field with ".x" appended, and the y coordinate is submitted under the name of the field with ".y" appended.

Any VALUE attribute is ignored. The image itself is specified by the SRC attribute, exactly as for the Image element.

Note: In a future version of the HTML specification, the IMAGE functionality might be folded into an enhanced SUBMIT field.

PASSWORD

This is the same as the TEXT attribute, except that text is not displayed as it is entered.

RADIO

This is used for attributes that accept a single value from a set of alternatives. Each radio button field in the group should be given the same name. Only the selected radio button in the group generates a name/value pair in the submitted data. Radio buttons require an explicit VALUE attribute.

RESET

This is a button which, when pressed, resets the form's fields to their specified initial values. The label to be displayed on the button may be specified just as for the SUBMIT button.

SUBMIT

As might be surmised, this is a button which, when pressed, submits the form. You can use the VALUE attribute to provide a non-editable label to be displayed on the button. The default label is application-specific. If a SUBMIT button is pressed in order to submit the form, and that button has a NAME attribute specified, then that button contributes a name/value pair to the submitted data. Otherwise, a SUBMIT button makes no contribution to the submitted data.

TEXT

This attribute is used for a single-line text entry field, and is used in conjunction with the SIZE and MAXLENGTH attributes. Use the Textarea element for text fields that can accept multiple lines.

VALUE

The VALUE attribute determines the initial displayed value of the field if it displays a textual or numerical value, or the value to be returned when the field is selected if it displays a boolean value. This attribute is required for radio buttons.

<ISINDEX>

The Isindex element tells the HTML user agent that the document is an index document, meaning the reader can either read it or use a keyword search. The document can be queried with a keyword search by adding a question mark to the end of the document address, followed by a list of keywords separated by plus signs.

Note: The Isindex element is usually generated automatically by a server. If added manually to a HTML document, the HTML user agent assumes that the server can handle a search on the document. To use the Isindex element, the server must have a search engine that supports this element.

Note also that the <ISINDEX> element has been Netscape-enhanced. To the <ISINDEX> element Netscape authors have added the PROMPT attribute. The <ISINDEX> tag indicates that a document is a searchable index. PROMPT has been added so that text, chosen by the author, can be placed before the text input field of the index.

<KBD> . . . </KBD>

The Keyboard element indicates text typed by a user, typically rendered as monospaced. It's the sort of thing that might be used in an instruction manual.

<LI>

The List Item element is a sort of general-purpose tag used with the <dir>, <menu>, <ol>, and <ul> list container elements. It serves to delimit each entry within a list, and requires no closing tag. For example:

```
<UL>
<LI>First list item
<LI>Second list item
<LI>Third list item
</UL>
```

<LINK>

The Link element indicates a relationship between the document and some other object. A document may have any number of Link elements.

The Link element is empty (it does not have a closing element), but takes the same attributes as the Anchor element. It typically is used to indicate authorship, related indexes and glossaries, older or more recent versions, etc. Links can indicate a static tree structure in which the document was created, for example by pointing to a parent, next, and previous document.

Servers also may allow links to be added by those who do not have the right to alter the body of a document.

MARQUEE
Microsoft extension

The Marquee element lets you create a scrolling text area. This is a useful space for advertising or other information. There are a number of attributes that let you control the use of Marquees.

ALIGN
Specifies the location of text around the marquee; values can be either TOP, MIDDLE, or BOTTOM.

BEHAVIOR
Determines how the text will move within the marquee. Use the value SCROLL and the text will move in from one side, and disappear off the other. If you use SLIDE, the text will move in from one side, then stop when it touches the other. The value ALTERNATE will make the text bounce back and forth within the marquee.

BGCOLOR
Specifies the background color for the marquee. Instead of using the hexadecimal RGB triplet (e.g., #FFFFFF), you can use a Color Name.

DIRECTION
The direction in which the text should scroll. It can be either LEFT or RIGHT.

HEIGHT
The height of the marquee as an absolute pixel value, or as a percentage of screen height.

HSPACE
The distance between the left and right margins of the marquee, and the surrounding text (in pixels).

LOOP
Specifies how many times text will scroll across the marquee. Setting LOOP=n makes it scroll n times; if LOOP=INFINITE or LOOP=-1, the text will repeat indefinitely.

SCROLLAMOUNT
Specifies the number of pixels between each successive draw of the marquee text.

SCROLLDELAY
Specifies the number of milliseconds between each successive draw of the marquee text.

VSPACE
The distance between the top and bottom margins of the marquee, and the surrounding text (in pixels).

\<MENU\> . . . \</MENU\>

A Menu is a list of items, typically with one item per line. The Menu list style is more compact than that of an unordered list. A Menu list must begin with a \<MENU\> element, which is immediately followed by an \<LI\> (list item) element. Example:

```
<MENU>
<LI>First item in the list.
<LI>Second item in the list.
<LI>Third item in the list.
</MENU>
```

<META>

The Meta element is used within the Head element to embed document meta-information not defined by other HTML elements. Such information can be extracted by servers and clients for use in identifying, indexing, and cataloging specialized document meta-information.

Although it is generally preferable to use named elements that have well-defined semantics for each type of meta-information (such as title), this element is provided for situations where strict SGML parsing is necessary and the local DTD is not extensible.

In addition, HTTP servers can read the content of the document head to generate response headers corresponding to any elements defining a value for the attribute HTTP-EQUIV. This provides document authors a mechanism (not necessarily the preferred one) for identifying information that should be included in the response headers for an HTTP request. Attributes follow.

HTTP-EQUIV

This attribute binds the element to an HTTP response header. If the semantics of the HTTP response header named by this attribute are known, then the contents can be processed based on a well-defined syntactic mapping, whether or not the DTD includes anything about it. HTTP header names are not case sensitive. If not present, the NAME attribute should be used to identify this meta-information, and it should not be used within an HTTP response header.

NAME

This is the meta-information name. If the name attribute is not present, then the value can be assumed to be equal to the value HTTP-EQUIV.

CONTENT

The meta-information content to be associated with the given name and/or HTTP response header.

<NEXTID>

The Nextid element is a parameter read by and generated by text editing software to create unique identifiers. This element takes a single attribute, which is the next document-wide alphanumeric identifier to be allocated, in the form Z*nnn*. For example:

```
<NEXTID N=Z127>
```

When modifying a document, existing anchor identifiers should not be reused, as these identifiers may be referenced by other documents. Human writers of HTML usually use mnemonic alphabetic identifiers. HTML user agents may ignore the Nextid element. Support for the Nextid element does not impact HTML user agents in any way.

<NOBR>
Netscape extension

The <NOBR> element stands for "no break." This means all the text between the start and end of the <NOBR> elements cannot have line breaks inserted. While <NOBR> is essential for those character sequences that don't want to be broken, please be careful. Long text strings inside of <NOBR> containers can look rather odd, especially if, during viewing, the user adjusts the page size by altering the window size.

<OL> . . . </OL>

The Ordered List element is used to present a numbered list of items, sorted by sequence or order of importance. An ordered list must begin with the <OL> element, which is immediately followed by an <LI> (list item) element. For example:

```
<OL>
<LI>Click the Web button to Open the URL window.
<LI>Enter the URL number in the text field of the Open URL
window. The Web document you specified is displayed.
<LI>Click highlighted text to move from one link to another.
</OL>
```

The Ordered List element can take the COMPACT attribute, which suggests that a compact rendering be used.

Note that the <OL> element has been Netscape-enhanced. The average ordered list counts 1, 2, 3,. . ., etc. Netscape authors have added the TYPE attribute to this element to allow authors to specify how the list items should be enumerated.

TYPE=A	capital letters A, B, C,. . .
TYPE=a	small letters a, b, c,. . .
TYPE=I	large roman numerals I, II, III,. . .
TYPE=i	small roman numerals i, ii, iii,. . .
TYPE=1	arabic numerals (default) 1, 2, 3,. . .

For lists to start at values other than 1, the new attribute START is available. START is always specified in the default numbers, and will be converted based on TYPE before display. Thus START=5 would display either an E, e, V, v, or 5, based on the TYPE attribute.

<OPTION>

The Option element can only occur within a Select element. It represents one choice. There are two attributes available, SELECTED and VALUE.

SELECTED

This attribute indicates that the option to which it is applied is the one initially selected. In the following example, Blue is the color initially selected:

```
<SELECT
NAME="Favorite_Color" SIZE="1">
<OPTION SELECTED>Blue
<OPTION>Red
<OPTION>Yellow
<OPTION>Green
<OPTION>Black
<OPTION>Orange
<OPTION>Purple
</SELECT>
```

VALUE

When present, this attribute indicates the value to be returned if the option to which it is applied is chosen. The default returned value (if no other is specified) is the contents of the Option element itself.

<P ALIGN>
HTML 3.0

Included in the proposed HTML Level 3.0 specification is the ability to align paragraphs. In essence, the left, center, and right attributes have been added to the <P> element. Example:

```
<P ALIGN=LEFT>. . .</P>
```

All text within the paragraph will be aligned to the left side of the page layout. This setting is equal to the default <P> element.

```
<P ALIGN=CENTER>. . .</P>
```

All text within the paragraph will be aligned to the center of the page.

```
<P ALIGN=RIGHT>. . .</P>
```

All text will be aligned to the right side of the page.

Note: To account for the commonly used yet nonstandard <CEN-TER> element, Mosaic (2.0b4) will change the default ALIGN=LEFT attribute of all paragraph and header elements to ALIGN=CENTER until a </CENTER> element is read. Mosaic also will allow internally defined alignment attributes to take precedence over a wrapping <CENTER> element. Mosaic authors would like to encourage all HTML authors to conform to the HTML 3.0 way of centering HTML, and no longer use the nonstandard <CENTER> element.

<P> . . . </P>

The Paragraph element indicates a paragraph. The exact indentation, leading, and other characteristics of a paragraph are not defined and may be a function of other elements, style sheets, etc. The closing tag is not mandatory.

Typically, paragraphs are set off by a vertical space of one line or half a line. This is usually not the case within the Address element, and is never the case within the Preformatted Text element. With some HTML user agents, the first line in a paragraph is indented. Example:

```
<H1>This Heading Precedes the Paragraph</H1>
<P>This is the text of the first paragraph.
<P>This is the text of the second paragraph. Although you do not need
to start paragraphs on new lines, maintaining this convention facilitates
document maintenance and source code readability.
<P>This is the text of a third paragraph.
```

<PRE> . . . </PRE>

The Preformatted Text element presents blocks of text in fixed-width font, and is suitable for text that has been formatted on screen.

The <PRE> element may be used with the optional WIDTH attribute, which is a Level 1 feature. The WIDTH attribute specifies the maximum number of characters for a line and allows the HTML user agent to select a suitable font and indentation. If the WIDTH attribute is not present, a width of 80 characters is assumed. Where the WIDTH attribute is supported, widths of 40, 80, and 132 characters should be presented optimally, with other widths being rounded up. The rules of use are:

1 Line breaks within the text are rendered as a move to the beginning of the next line.

2 The <P> element should not be used. If found, it should be rendered as a move to the beginning of the next line.

3 Anchor elements and character highlighting elements may be used.
4 Elements that define paragraph formatting (headings, address, etc.) must not be used.
5 The horizontal tab character (encoded in US-ASCII and ISO-8859-1 as decimal 9) must be interpreted as the smallest positive nonzero number of spaces that will leave the number of characters up to that point on the line as a multiple of 8. Its use is not recommended, however.

<SAMP> . . . </SAMP>

The Sample element indicates a sequence of literal characters, typically rendered as monospaced.

<SCRIPT> ... </SCRIPT>

This pair of tags marks the beginning and end of a Netscape/Sun Javascript script, such as the following:

```
<script><!— Beginning of JavaScript ——————————>

function scrollit_r2l(seed)
{
        var msg = "VISIT the SoftStore........ Best prices on the Web.....
Coming soon!"
        var out = " ";
        var c  = 1;
</SCRIPT>
```

<SELECT> . . . </SELECT>

The Select element allows the user to choose one of a set of alternatives described by textual labels. Every alternative is represented by the Option element. The attributes follow.

MULTIPLE
The MULTIPLE attribute is needed when users are allowed to make several selections, for example <SELECT MULTIPLE>.

NAME
Specifies the name that will be submitted as a name/value pair.

SIZE

Specifies the number of visible items. If this is greater than one, then the resulting form control will be a list.

The <SELECT> element is typically rendered as a pull-down or pop-up list. For example:

```
<SELECT NAME="flavor">
<OPTION>Vanilla
<OPTION>Strawberry
<OPTION>Rum and Raisin
<OPTION>Peach and Orange
</SELECT>
```

If no option is initially marked as selected, then the first item listed is selected.

<SMALL> ... </SMALL>

Text within this container is rendered in a small font.

<STRIKE> ... </STRIKE>

Text between these two tags appears in strike-through mode, usually a horizontal line through each of the characters.

<STRONG> . . . </STRONG>

The Strong element indicates strong typographic emphasis, typically rendered in boldface.

_{...}

SUB places text in subscript style.

^{...}

SUP places text in superscript style.

<TABLE> . . . </TABLE>

This is the main wrapper for all the other Table elements; all other table elements will be ignored if they aren't enclosed by a <TABLE> . . .<TABLE> structure. By default, tables have no borders; borders will be added if the BORDER attribute is specified.

At the time is written, the <TABLE> element has an implied line break both before and after it. This is expected to change, allowing as much control over placement of tables as is currently available for the placement of images: aligning them to various positions in a line of text, as well as shifting them to the left or right margins and wrapping text around them.

```
<TABLE BORDER=3 CELLSPACING=2 CELLPADDING=
2 WIDTH="80%">
<CAPTION ALIGN=bottom> ... table caption ... </CAPTION>
<TR><TD> first cell <TD> second cell
<TR> ...
...
</TABLE>
```

All the attributes on TABLE are optional. By default, the table is rendered without a surrounding border. The table is generally sized automatically to fit the contents, but you can also set the table width using the WIDTH attribute. BORDER, CELLSPACING, and CELLPADDING provide further control over the table's appearence. The ALIGN attribute can be used to position the table to the LEFT, CENTER, or RIGHT. The CAPTION element is used for captions; these are rendered at the top or bottom of the table depending on the optional ALIGN attribute.

Each table row is contained in a TR element, although the end tag can always be omitted. Table cells are defined by TD elements for data and TH elements for headers. Like TR, these are containers and can be given without trailing end tags. TH and TD support several attributes: ALIGN and VALIGN for aligning cell content; and ROWSPAN and COLSPAN for cells which span more than one row or column. A cell can contain a wide variety of other block- and text-level elements, including form fields and other tables.

BORDER

This attribute appears in the <TABLE> element. If present, borders are drawn around all table cells. If absent, there are no borders, but by default, space is left for borders, so the same table with and without the BORDER attribute will be of equal width.

By allowing the BORDER attribute to take a value, document authors gain two things. First, they gain the ability to emphasize some tables with respect to others; a table with a border of four containing a sub-table with a border of one looks much nicer than if both share the same default border width. Second, by explicitly setting border to zero, they regain that space originally reserved for borders between cells, allowing particularly compact tables.

CELLSPACING

This is a new attribute for the <TABLE> element. By default, Netscape uses a cell spacing of two. For those fussy about the look of their tables, this gives them a little more control. Just as it seems, cell spacing is the amount of space inserted between individual cells in a table.

CELLPADDING

This is a new attribute for the <TABLE> element. By default, Netscape uses a cell padding of one. Cell padding is the amount of space between the border of the cell and the contents of the cell. On a table with borders, setting a cell padding of zero might look bad because the edges of the text could touch the cell borders. CELLSPACING=0 and CELLPADDING gives the most compact table possible.

WIDTH

When this attribute appears in the <TABLE> element, it is used to describe the desired width of this table, either as an absolute width in pixels, or a percentage of document width. Complex heuristics are applied to tables and their cells to attempt to present a pleasing display. Setting the WIDTH attribute overrides those heuristics; instead effort is put into fitting the table into the desired width specified. In some cases it might be impossible to fit all the table cells at the specified width, in which case Netscape will try to come as close as possible.

When this attribute appears on either the <TH> or <TD> element, it is used to describe the desired width of the cell, either as an absolute width in pixels, or a percentage of table width. The same considerations for WIDTH in a <TABLE> element also apply here.

<TD> . . . </TD>

This stands for Table Data, and specifies a standard table data cell. Table data cells must appear only within table rows. Each row need not have the same number of cells specified; short rows will be padded with blank cells on the right. A cell can contain any of the HTML elements normally present in the body of an HTML document.

The default alignment of table data is ALIGN=LEFT and VALIGN=MIDDLE. These alignments are overridden by any alignments specified in the containing <TR> element; those alignments in turn are overridden by any ALIGN or VALIGN attributes explicitly specified on this cell. By default, lines inside of table cells can be broken up to fit within the overall cell width. Specifying the NOWRAP attribute for a <TD> prevents line breaks for that cell. The <TD> structure also can contain the COLSPAN and ROWSPAN attributes.

<TEXTAREA> . . . </TEXTAREA>

The Textarea element lets users enter more than one line of text. For example:

```
<TEXTAREA NAME="address" ROWS=64 COLS=6>
New Art Inc.
200 West 79 Street
NY NY 10024
</TEXTAREA>
```

The text up to the end element </TEXTAREA> is used to initialize the field's value. This end element is always required, even if the field is initially blank. When submitting a form, lines in a Textarea should be terminated using CR/LF.

In a typical rendering, the ROWS and COLS attributes determine the visible dimension of the field in characters. The field is rendered in a fixed-width font. HTML user agents should allow text to extend beyond these limits by scrolling as needed.

Note: In the initial design for forms, multiline text fields were supported by the Input element with TYPE=TEXT. Unfortunately, this causes problems for fields with long text values. SGML's default (Reference Quantity Set) limits the length of attribute literals to only 240 characters. The HTML 2.0 SGML declaration increases the limit to 1024 characters.

<TH> . . . </TH>

This stands for Table Header. Header cells are identical to data cells in all respects, with the exception that header cells are in a bold font, and have a default ALIGN=CENTER. The <TH>. . .</TH> structure also can contain VALIGN, NOWRAP, COLSPAN, and ROWSPAN attributes.

<TITLE> . . . </TITLE>

Every HTML document must have a Title element. The title should identify the contents of the document in a global context, and may be used in history lists and as a label for the windows displaying the document. Unlike headings, titles are typically not rendered in the text of a document itself. The Title element must occur within the head of the document, and may not contain anchors, paragraph elements, or highlighting. Only one title is allowed in a document.

The length of a title is not limited; long titles may be truncated in some applications, however. To minimize the possibility, titles should contain fewer than 64 characters. Also keep in mind that a short title, such as "Introduction" might be meaningless out of context. An example of a meaningful title might be "Introduction to HTML Elements."

This is the only element that is required within the Head element. The other elements described are optional and can be implemented when appropriate. For example:

```
<HEAD>
<TITLE> Introduction to HTML </TITLE>
</HEAD>
```

`<TR> . . . </TR>`

This stands for Table Row. The number of rows in a table is exactly specified by how many `<TR>` elements are contained within it, regardless of cells that might attempt to use the ROWSPAN attribute to span into nonspecified rows. The `<TR>` element can have both the ALIGN and VALIGN attributes, which, if specified, become the default alignments for all cells in this row.

`<TT> . . . </TT>`

The Teletype element specifies that the text should be rendered in fixed-width typewriter font.

`<UL> . . . </UL>`

The Unordered List element is used to present a list of items, which typically are separated by white space and/or marked by bullets. An unordered list must begin with the `<UL>` element, which is immediately followed by an `<LI>` (list item) element:

```
<UL>
<LI>First list item
<LI>Second list item
<LI>Third list item
</UL>
```

The Unordered List element can take the COMPACT attribute, which suggests that a compact rendering be used.

Note: The `<UL>` element has been Netscape-enhanced. The basic bulleted list has a default progression of bullet types that changes as you move through indented levels, from a solid disc to a circle to a square. Netscape authors have added a TYPE= attribute to the `<UL>` element, so that no matter what the indent level, the bullet type can be specified by the values DISC, CIRCLE, or SQUARE.

<VAR> . . . </VAR>

The Variable element indicates a variable name, typically rendered as italic. For example:

When coding, <VAR>LeftIndent( )</VAR> must be a variable

would render as:

When coding, *LeftIndent( )* must be a variable.

<WBR>
Netscape extension

The <WBR> element stands for Word Break. This is for the very rare case when a <NOBR> section requires an exact break. The <WBR> element does not force a line break; it simply lets Netscape Navigator know where a line break is allowed to be inserted if needed.

Appendix C

The Keyes annotated Internet products and services guide

There's a plethora of Internet-related products out there. There's also a plethora of guides that list each of these products in painful detail. What I've done here, at the risk of incurring the wrath of literally hundreds of Internet vendors, is list the ones that were most interesting to me. Since I have the same background as most of you, I think you'll find these products to be interesting as well. But buyer beware: The field is ever-changing. What's in business today might not be in business tomorrow, and what's popular today might not be popular tomorrow.

3D tools

Crystal Kaleidoscope
This 3D animation dream suite answers all your dreams and desires, multimedially speaking. It features Crystal TOPAS Professional 5.1, an extremely user-friendly 3D animation software tool.
CrystalGraphics
3110 Patrick Henry Drive
Santa Clara, CA 95054
(800) TOPAS-3D

Viewpoint Data Labs
The world's largest 3D library is available at one low price per title: no royalties and one low flat fee.
Viewpoint Data Labs
625 South State St.
Orem, UT 84058
(800) 328-2738

Animation

Photorealism
That's what Strata calls their series of packages for the Mac, and there's a bunch of them. Stratavision 3D is a 3D animation program; Stratatextures are collections of realistic-looking materials that can be applied to objects.
Strata
2 W. Saint George Blvd.
Suite 2100
St. George, UT 84770
(801) 628-5218

DPS Personal Animation Recorder
Version 2.5
Personal Animation Recorder, an IBM-PC compatible recorder, complements all 3D applications, including 3D Studio and TOPAS Professional. Record your animations onto a dedicated hard drive and play them back in real time, for 3D animations without the expense of single-frame tape decks.

ElectriImage Animation System features speed and quality. The color jumps and shouts; the images can make you forget you're watching Macintosh-generated computer graphics. This package is the only per-frame renderer anywhere.

Electric Image Inc.
(818) 577-1627 ext. 224
sales@electricimg.com

Real3D

A full-featured 3D animation, modeling, and rendering program for the Amiga, which enables objects to "rock and roll" and react to their environment with "intelligence."
RealSoft
544 Queen St.
Chatham, Ontario N7M 2J6
Canada
(407) 539-0752

Animator Pro

This one has won a bunch of awards. It's a high-resolution, 2D paint and animation software program for the PC, and provides a repertoire of special effects like tweening and color cycling.
Autodesk, Inc.
2320 Marinship Way
Sausalito, CA 94965
(415) 332-2344

3D Studio

This is the superb animation product that made Autodesk a household name. It comes with over 500MB of 3D objects, textures, and animation. It's not cheap, though.
Autodesk, Inc.
2320 Marinship Way
Sausalito, CA 94965
(415) 332-2344

Cyberspace Developer Kit

One of Autodesk's superb animation products, it's a complete tool set for 3D visualization and simulation. In other words, it lets you create virtual reality applications.
Autodesk, Inc.
2320 Marinship Way
Sausalito, CA 94965
(415) 332-2344

Animation Works Interactive

This is a sophisticated animation system with interactivity support, multimedia extensions support, and MCI support.

Gold Disk Inc.
5155 Spectrum Way, Unit 5
Mississaauga, Ontario L4W 5A1
Canada
(310) 320-5080

Creative Toonz 2D CEL
This is animation software for Silicon Graphics workstations that enables animators to experiment with up to 32 different fill colors, add 3D animations, build a picture base of images, and use a scanner for input.
Softimage Inc.
660 Newton-Yardley Rd., Suite 202
Newton, PA 18940
(215) 860-5525

Liberty
This is a Unix-based, high-end graphics package coupled with animation tools.
Softimage Inc.
660 Newton-Yardley Rd., Suite 202
Newton, PA 18940
(215) 860-5525

3D Choreographer
3D Choreographer is a model-based 3D animation program for Windows. Users create animated sequences with predrawn people, 3D shapes, etc. Each character is customizable and has an extensive library of predefined actions.
AniCom Inc.
PO Box 428
Columbia, MD 21045
(800) 949-4559

Animation Gallery
Animation Gallery contains more than a hundred 3D animations for use with any presentation manager that handles Audodesk 3D Studio (FLI) files.
Wizardware Multimedia Ltd.
918 Delaware Ave.
Bethlehem, PA 18015
(800) 548-5969

Animation How-To CD

This intermediate-level book/disc offers hands-on explanations that show users how to create dynamic moving objects. Each animation idea is explained, and then the steps required to produce it are presented.

Waite Group Press
200 Tamai Plaza
Corte Madera, CA 94925
(800) 368-9369

Animation Paint Box

Animation Paint Box for Windows offers exceptional productivity tools for 8-bit animators. Features include resizeable frame ranges, extensive file conversion, partial loads of large animations, etc.

Azeena Technologies Inc.
PO Box 29169
Long Beach, CA 90806
(310) 981-2771

Animation Master

Animation Master, the three-dimensional motion picture studio, is a powerful and affordable, spline-based modeling and animation program, specifically designed for classic character animation. Features include inverse kinematics, time-based materials, image mapping, etc.

Hash Inc.
2800 E. Evergreen Blvd.
Vancouver, WA 98661
(206) 750-0042

Caligari trueSpace

Caligari trueSpace for Windows enables users to create advanced 3D graphics easily. In real-world 3D perspective, users can twist and bend simple cylinders and spheres into sophisticated, organic shapes with free-form deformation and point editing.

Caligari Corp.
1955 Landings Dr.
Mountain View, CA 94043
(800) 351-7620

Frame By Frame Graphic Animation System

Frame By Frame Graphic Animation Systems enable producers to capture Video for Windows or QuickTime movies and computer

graphics directly to Panasonic videodisc recorders, for instant playback or full-screen, full-resolution video and animation.
Image Management Systems
239 W. 15th St.
New York, NY 10011
(212) 741-8765

MicroScribe-3D
Compatible with most currently available 3D graphics packages
(including AutoCAD, 3D Studio, Wavefront, SoftImage, Alias and
Form-Z), this tool enhances 3D animations without heavy out-of-
pocket expenses. It's customizable and has an extensive library of
predefined actions.
Immersion Corporation
2158 Paragon Dr.
San Jose, CA 95131
(800) 893-1160
immersion@starconn.com

Authoring

Java WorkShell
Joe (client/server extension to Java)
Need I say more? About $295.
Sun Microsystems
http://www.sun.com

Power Media
Able to run on all major computing platforms (Windows, Macintosh,
Unix), this object-oriented, drag-and-drop authoring kit gives you all
the power you need without complex flowcharts and graphs. Its total
Internet connectivity provides all the global access you might require.
RAD Technologies
745 Emerson St.
Palo Alto, CA 94301
(415) 617-9430

Internet Publishing Kit
For Windows or Macintosh, it's a complete publishing toolkit featuring HotMetal Pro and Netscape Navigator, plus text, sound and
graphics editing tools, Web-age templates, and much more.
Ventanna Communications
(800) 743-5369
http://www.vmedia.com

Sapphire/Web
One of the more popular packages, it's a visual, open development tool that lets you generate C and C++.
> Bluestone
> (609) 727-4600
> *http://www.bluestone.com*

AnchorPage
This tool fully automates concept extraction and hypertext anchoring in HTML documents, and offers end users four different methods of referencing document content.
> ICONOVEX Corporation
> 7900 Xerxes Ave. South, Suite 550
> Bloomington, MN 55431
> 1-800-943-0292
> *http://www.iconovex.com*

HTML.edit
For the Macintosh, it does an excellent job of putting a friendlier face on top of HTML. Nearly every feature of HTML is accessible from easy-to-use dialog boxes and pop-up menus.
> Murray Altheim
> *http://www.metrics.nttc.edu/tools/htmledit/HTMLEdit.html*

Site Writer Pro
For the Macintosh, this tool splits the edit window into three panes for the header, body, and footer of a document. It supports even the most recent extension to the HTML tag set.
> Rik Jones
> *http://www.ric.dccd.edu/Human/SWPro.htm*

Web Weaver
For Macs only, it's one of the category of "paste attribute" editors that help isolate the user from the need to know HTML tags.
> Robert Best
> *http://www.potsdam.edu/Web.Weaver/About.htm*

Simple HTML Editor
For Macs only, it's a very basic text editor with only the barest of HTML editing tools.
> Eric Morgan
> *http://www.lib.ncsu.edu/staff/morgan/simple.html*

HTML Editor

A Mac-based utility, it provides a good basic environment in which to work. It offers most commonly used HTML structures through pop-up menus and buttons.

Rick Giles
http://dragon.acadiau.ca/~giles/HTML/Editor/Documentation.html

HTML tools for desktop publishing

BBEdit and HTML Tools
Lindsay Davies
http://www.york.ac.uk/~idn/BBEditTools.html

HTML Extensions
Carles Bellver
http://www.uji.es/bbedit-html-extensions.html

Beyond Press (for QuarkXPress users)
Astrobyte
(303) 534-6344
support@astrobyte.com
http://www.astrobye.com

XPress to HTML Converter (maps Quark styles to HTML)
Jeremy Hylton
http://the-tech.mit.edu/~jeremy

HTML Xport (maps Quark styles to HTML)
Eric Knudsstrup
ftp://mars.aliens.com/pub/Macintosh/HTML Xport.sit

WebSucker (for PageMaker)
Mitch Cohen
http://www.iii.net/users/mcohen/websucker.html

Web-It (for Claris)
University of Michigan
http://www.umich.edu/~demonner/Primer_main/primer_main.html

HTML+
Leonard Rosenthol
leonard@netcom.com

XL2HTML.XLS (for Microsoft Excel)

This Visual Basic macro for Excel helps turn Excel 5.0 data into HTML tables, maintaining simple text formatting.

Jordan Evans
http://www710.gsfc.nasa.gov/704/dgd/xlzhtml.html

1-Way

Create hyperlinked information on a PC, Mac, or Unix workstation without dealing with HTML syntax. Make information readily available for Net surfers without file conversion and transport.

ForeFront Group Inc.
1360 Post Oak Road
Suite 1660
Houston, TX 77056
(800) 867-1101
info@ffg.com

InContext Spider
This is an HTML editor and Web browser, a package that helps you create imaginative pages without muss and fuss. It speaks directly to the Web, thus allowing dynamic home page creation and Web cruising. There's no limit to what you can produce.
InContext Corporation
2 St. Clair Avenue West
16th Floor
Toronto, Ontario M4V 1L5
Canada
(800) 263-1027
http://incontext.ca

HTML.edit
For the Mac, it does an excellent job of putting a friendly face on top of HTML. Nearly every feature of HTML is accessible from easy-to-use dialog boxes and pop-up menus.
Murray Altheim
http://www.metrics.nttc.edu/tools/htmledit.html

Arachnid
Arachnid is a Mac tool that features on-screen support for most HTML tags. It shines in the creation of forms.
Robert McBurney
http://sec-look.uowa.edu/about/projects/arachmin-page.html

HotMetal Pro
For use with either Windows, MacOS, or Unix, it provides such useful features such as spell checker, search/replace, and thesaurus.
SoftQuad Corp.
http://www.wq.com/hmpro.html

HTML Pro
A great environment for both novices and expert Mac users. Two editable windows allow novice users to begin in the preview window and watch the HTML representation being built as they work.
Niklas Frykholm
http://www.ts.umu.se:80/~rad/shareware/htmlpro_help.html

HTML Assistant Pro
This is shareware gone public, and has all the bells and whistles.
Brooklyn North Software Works
(800) 349-1422
http://fox.nstn.ca/~harawitz/index.html

Webtor (Web Editor)
A great tool for beginners, it does a good job of isolating the page author from the complexities of HTML. It displays text, URLs, and in-line graphics onscreen.
Jochen Schales
http://www.igd.fhg.de/~neuss/webtor/webtor.html

Clip art

Artmaker's MegaRom
For Mac and PCs, over 1000 top-quality clip art and graphics on CD-ROM.
The Artmaker Company
1420 N. Claremont Blvd., #205-D
Claremont, CA 91711
(909) 626-8065 (credit card orders)

Encyclopedia of Stock Photography CD-ROM Vol. 6
This CD contains over 21,000 professional stock photographs from more than 40 diverse subject categories.
Comstock Inc.
The Comstock Building
30 Irving Place
New York, NY 10003
(800) 225-2727

Signature Series
Transcend the boundaries of traditional stock photography with this collection of stunning photos from world-renowned photographers. Each disc features a single photographer, with 100 thematic images. All photos are drum scanned for incredible resolution.
PhotoDisc Inc.
2013 4th Avenue
Seattle, WA 98121
(800) 528-3472

Ad Art: Logos & Trademarks CD-ROM 3.0
A collection of the most popular corporate symbols and service marks used to advertise and display products and services, this CD-ROM

contains more than 1200 Encapsulated PostScript images, representing organizations, manufacturers, and corporations. All trademarks represented in this collection are registered by their respective owners and are designed for editorial and advertising use.

Innovation Advertising & Design
41 Mansfield Ave.
Essex Junction, VT 05452
(800) 255-0562

Corel Stock Photo Library

More than 20,000 photographs, all royalty-free, high-resolution images for use in everything from newsletters to t-shirts. The Kodak Photo CDs are PC- and Mac-compatible, and also include such utilities as Corel Photo CD Lab, Corel Mosaic Visual File Manager, and Corel Artview Screen Saver.

Corel Corporation
(613) 728-0826 ext. 3080

Archive Films/Archive Photos

Historical image library of more than 14,000 hours of historical stock footage drawn from newsreels, TV news, Hollywood feature films, silent films, historical documentaries, etc. All footage is listed on a computer database for quick retrieval.

Archive Films/Archive Photos
530 W. 25th St.
New York, NY 10001
(800) 876-5115

Backgrounds for Multimedia

These are high-quality, full-screen, 8- and 24-bit images specifically designed with video, slide, animation, and texture mapping applications in mind. Extras include tips, onscreen examples, and instructions for use in many software applications.

Airbeats
PO Box 709
Myrtle Creek, OR 97457
(800) 444-9392

CD Link Volume 1

A CD-ROM designed to be used with multimedia authoring tools such as IBM's LinkWay, Storyboard Live, and Windows, it includes 300 sound effects and music clips that can be used by educators and students to add pizzazz to their presentations. License rights to use the clip sounds also are included.

Educational Renaissance Inc.
2474 Woodchuck Way
Sandy, UT 84093
(801) 943-0841

Corel Gallery 2
Able to work with all Windows-based application, this CD-ROM clip
art library provides 15,000 clipart images, 500 fonts, 500 photos, 75
sound clips, and 10 video clips, as well as a powerful multimedia file
manager.
Corel Corporation
(613) 728-0826

CD-ROM drives and accessories

CD 4000
This expansion cabinet can hold up to eight CD-ROM drives and/or
hard drives. It's a cost-effective path for providing additional drives to
a CD-ROM network.
Logicraft
22 Cotton Rd.
Nashua, NH 03063
(800) 880-5644

CD-R Cube
A desktop processing system for CD replication, it creates CD-ROM
discs from files and scanned images for archiving, imaging, multimedia, etc.
Todd Enterprises Inc.
224-49 67th Ave.
Bayside, NY 11364
(800) 445-8633

CD/Maxtet
Designed for sharing CD-ROM-based information over a network,
this tower can hold up to seven discs, allowing a file server to share
them out over a network.
Optical Access International Inc.
500 W Cummings Park Drive
Woburn, MA 01801
(800) 433-5133

Philips CDD522

This CD recorder supports all CD formats and includes such in-demand features as write-once CD format, data addition to recorded discs, double- or single-speed recording and playback, and a motorized tray for ease of loading.

Philips Laser Magnetic Storage
4425 ArrowsWest Dr.
Colorado Springs, CO 80907
(800) 777-5674

PxCDS, PiCDS

Two multisession Photo CD, MPC, and XA-compatible drives. Both have an average access time of 490ms, and feature tray loading, 3-way eject, and stereo headphone jack with volume control. Internal and external version accepts 12 cm or 8 cm diameter CDs, and plays CD audio.

Procom Technology
2181 Dupont Drive
Irvine, CA 92715
(800) 800-8600

CDR100

A Yamaha drive that reads and records faster than ever—4 times as fast! It's a space-efficient design that fits easily into a 5.25-inch disk drive bay.

Yamaha
100 Century Center Court
San Jose, CA 95112
(800) 543-7457

JVC CD Recording System

Provides totally integrated CD recording solutions. This leading technology firm both manufactures CD-Recording drives and designs software to work effortlessly with the most technologically developed drives.

JVC Information Products Company of America
17811 Mitchell Ave.
Irvine, CA 92714
(714) 261-1292

Master CD

This desktop recorder/player allows the user to create his or her own CDs, and can save up to 650MB of data (including audio and video). It works with either a Macintosh or PC.

MicroNet Technology Inc.
80 Technology
Irvine, CA 92718
(800) 650-DISK

MultiSpin

NEC offers a series of high-quality CD-ROM drives. What makes them unique is their "MultiSpin" technology, which makes them exceptionally fast—about 280ms average access time, compared to 800ms for typical, low-cost, catalog-quality CD-ROM drive.

NEC Technologies, Inc.
1255 Michael Drive
Wood Dale, IL 60191
(800) NEC-INFO

Chinon 435

This is an MPC- and QuickTime-compatible drive with 150K/sec sustained transfer rate and 64K data buffer. It has built-in RCA jacks for stereo audio output, plus headphone jack with volume control.

Up to seven drives can be daisy-chained. Bundled software includes Multimedia Encyclopedia, The Animal MPC, World/US Atlas MPC, Sherlock Holmes MPC, Chess Master 3000 MPC, Mavis Beacon Typing MPC, and Chinon Selectware.

Chinon America
615 Hawaii Avenue
Torrance, CA 90503
(800) 441-0222

MacCD Station

This SCSI drive is QuickTime-compatible, featuring 380ms seek time, 150K/sec sustained transfer rate, and stereo audio output. Both amplified speakers and lightweight headphones are included. Mozart Dissonant CD Companion, Sherlock Holmes, Procom's Musical Sampler, Illustrated Encyclopedia, World Atlas, shareware, and Nautilus sampler are bundled.

Procom Technology, Inc.
2181 Dupont Drive
Irvine, CA 92715
(800) 800-8600

CD Porta-Drive

This is a SCSI CD-ROM drive for laptop, portable, and desktop computers, and uses the Toshiba XM-3401 mechanism. It features 200ms

average access time and 330K/sec transfer rate, and weighs in at 3.0 pounds. Audio output is through dual RCA phono/headphone jack.
CD Technology, Inc.
766 San Aleso Avenue
Sunnyvale, CA 94086
(408) 752-8500

LapDrive
LapDrive is a portable lightweight CD-ROM drive with a rechargeable battery, providing up to 4 hours of use.
TACSystems
P.O. Box 650
Meridianville, Alabama 35759
(205) 828-6920

Personal ROMMaker CD-Recording System
Get the most from your Macromedia programs with a JVC Personal RomMaker CD recording system. It provides Red Book audio recording mixed mode, CD-I, CD-ROM XA, and unique hybrid dual-platform disc formatting.
JVC
17811 Mitchell Avenue
Irvine, CA 92714
(714) 261-1292

Rimage CD-R Printer
Need a label? This is the world's first silkscreen-quality CD-R printer that offers versatility on demand. It features 300 dpi resolution, fast print speed (4 CD's per minute), and uses standard CD-R media.
Rimage
7725 Washington Avenue South
Minneapolis, MN 55439
(612) 944-8144

CD Recording System
Copy files to a mounted recordable CD, mount and use discs in standard CD-ROM drives, and add additional data at any time with this remarkable CD recording system. This system is ideal for storing, archiving, and distributing data.
Optima Technology
(714) 476-0515 ext. 244

CDD 521CW Desktop CD Recorder

This is Philips Consumer Electronics's entry into the make-your-own CD arena, and comes bundled with CD-WRITE publishing software. It also will create audio discs.

Philips Consumer Electronics Company
One Philips Drive
P.O. Box 14810
Knoxville, TN 37914
(615) 521-4316

CD Studio

For the IBM RS/6000, CD Studio is a combination of hardware and software that enables organizations to master their own CD-ROMs. It consists of Makedisc, which is premastering software; CD Studio Controller, which is proprietary hardware, software, and dedicated hard drive; and the Philips CDD 521 CD-WO drive.

Young Minds
P.O. Box 7399
Redlands, CA 92375
(714) 335-1350

Personal RomMaker, Mixed Mode RomMaker

The first unit is JVC's personal solution for in-house CD-ROM mastering. The Mixed Mode model enables you to record data (Yellow Book) and audio (Red Book) on the same disc.

JVC
19900 Beach Blvd.
Suite 1
Huntington Beach, CA 92648
(714) 965-2610

RCD-202

This is an affordable (less than $4000), recordable CD-ROM drive for Mac and PC computers, which allows you to create your own HFS, ISO 9660, or audio CDs within minutes.

Pinnacle Micro
19 Technology
Irvine, CA 92718
(714) 727-1913

Personal Scribe

This probably is the cheapest and easiest way of making your own ISO 9660-compatible CD-ROMs. All you have to do is pick the directories and files you want and hit the Enter key. Another advantage is

that you don't need excessive hard disk space. Prices start at less than $3000.
Meridian Data Inc.
5615 Scotts Valley Drive
Scotts Valley, CA 95066
(408) 438-3100

TOPiX
This is basically a desktop mastering system that is affordable and easy to use, and supports all CD-ROM standards.
Optical Media International
180 Knowles Drive
Los Gatos, CA 95030
(408) 376-3511

PCD LAN Writer 200
This is a package that bundles Kodak's writable CD products with Netscribe Access Client Software from Meridian Data. The net result is a turnkey system that lets any DOS or Windows user on a Novell network produce CD-ROM discs.
Eastman Kodak
343 State Street
Rochester, NY 14650
(800) 242-2424 ext. 52

CD-ROM mastering services
Here are just a few of the many mastering labs available to you. Full-service providers will master your CDs, pack, ship, and distribute them.
Technicolor Optical Media Services
3301 E. Mission Oaks Blvd .
Camarillo, CA 93012
(800) 656-8667

Northern Digital Recording, Inc.
2 Hidden Meadow Lane
Southborough, MA 01772
(508) 481-9322

MultiMedia PC Enterprises Inc.
3 Hanover Square
Suite 19A
New York, NY 10004
(212) 509-9636

Electronic Publishers International Corporation
P.O. Box 17006
Winston-Salem, NC 27116
(800) 258-4423

International Teleproduction Society
350 Fifth Ave.
Suite 2400
New York, NY 10118
(212) 629-3265

Technidisc
2250 Meijer Drive
Troy, MI 48084
(313) 435-7430

Prerecorded Optical Media
3M Center Blvd.
223-5N-01
St. Paul, MN 55144
(612) 733-2142

Firewalls

SmartWall
A smart card provides one of the most secure rides through the Internet. Electronic commerce, digital signature, encryption for files/sessions are all available now.
Virtual Open Network Environment
12300 Twinbrook Pkwy.
Rockville, MD 20852
(800) 881-7090
http://www.v-one.com

BorderWare Firewall Server
Easy to install, easy to use, this secure internet gateway is unique among firewalls in that it integrates packet filters and circuit-level gateways with application servers into a single highly secure, self-contained system.
Border Network Technologies Inc.
20 Toronto St.
Toronto, Ontario M5C 2B8
Canada
http://www.border.com
info@border.com

The Black Hole

A highly-effective firewall, invisible within the Internet, this private network protects your data from cyber-criminals.
Milkyway Networks Corporation
255-2650 Queensview Dr .
Ottawa, Ontario K2B, 8H6
Canada
(613) 596-5549

Sidewinder

Featuring a patented type enforcement mechanism, this internetwork (including the Internet) security technology prevents unauthorized access to your data. It actually traps intruders, going beyond the capabibilities of traditional passive firewalls.
Secure Computing Corporation
2675 Long Lake Rd .
Roseville, MN 55113
(800) 692-LOCK

Graphics

addDepth for Windows

A graphics application tool that adds 3D impact to type and line art. Users enter text or choose their artwork; depth and perspective are added automatically.
Ray Dream Inc.
1804 N. Shoreline Blvd.
Mountain View, CA 94043
(800) 846-0111

Color Tools

Color Tools is a complete graphics solution for multimedia presentation. It provides a comprehensive set of line drawing tools, paint and effect brushes, and enhancement capabilities for all types of presentation screens, information displays, training applications and more.
Time Arts Inc.
1425 Corporate Center Pkwy.
Santa Rosa, CA 95407
(707) 576-7722

Creative License

Users can create and edit images, textures, and backgrounds with this affordable graphics package. It contains a broad range of pressure-sensitive drawing and painting tools.

Time Arts Inc.
1425 Corporate Center Pkwy.
Santa Rosa, CA 95407

Designer 4.0

Featuring a 32-bit graphics engine, this tool allows users unequaled precision, power, and performance for illustration on a PC. Features include streamlined interface, precision symbol creation, and editing with 29 drawing tools.

Microgrfx Inc.
1303 E. Arapaho
Richardson, TX 75081
(800) 326-3576

Lumena

Lumena is a powerful raster paint, vector draw, animation, and video-graphics software package for DOS-based systems.

Time Arts Inc.
1425 Corporate Center Pkwy.
Santa Rosa, CA 95407
(707) 576-7722

Professional Ddraw

Professional Ddraw is a precision illustration program with built-in desktop publishing and high-end color control. A snap-top modifier palette allows precise size and placement of objects on the fly.

Gold Disk Inc.
3350 Scott Blvd., Bldg. 14
Santa Clara, CA 95054
(800) 465-3375

Altamira Composer 1.01

A revolutionary image composition application for Windows that allows image elements to be automatically masked and anti-aliased through "dynamic alpha" technology, and float as independent objects in an infinite stack.

Altamira Software Corp.
150 Shoreline Hwy.
Suite B-27
Mill Valley, CQ 94941
(800) 425-8264

Chroma Tools
This is a file conversion utility for TARGA users. It converts TGA, PCX, GIF, TIF, BMP, Mac TIF, and VST images to TGA, PCX, GIF, TIF, VST, BMP, Mac TIF, and color or black and white PostScript. It supports all screen modes and includes multiple color reduction algorithms.
    Videotex Systems Inc.
    11880 Greenville Ave., #100
    Dallas, TX 72524
    (214) 231-9200

Image-in
A Windows-based editing tool that provides utilities for drawing, painting, and editing or manipulating color, black and white or grayscale images.
    CPI Inc.
    1820 Gateway Dr., Bldg. 3, Suite 370
    San Francisco, CA 94404
    (800) 345-3540

"Pixel Perfect" Graphics
A CD-ROM that contains more than 2000 images in 11 formats, in 300 dpi resolution. Categories include animals, business, computers, food, high tech, holidays, states, countries, etc.
    Wizardware Multimedia Ltd.
    918 Delaware Ave.
    Bethlehem, PA 18015
    (610) 866-9613

Digital Morph
With an easy-to-use image manipulation tool, users now can add exciting visual impact to presentations with this sophisticated morphing tool. Users can morph from one still image to another, or between moving images.
    HSC Software
    6303 Carpinteria Ave.
    Carpinteria, CA 93013
    (805) 566-6200

Image Partner
A full-featured image processing and analysis program that offers high resolution, with up to 1024×768×256-grayscale imaging displayable on Super/Extended VGA systems. Unique capabilities in-

clude video camera characterization, permitting users to understand
and quantify the systematic errors in imaging systems.

Image Automation
7 Henry Clay Dr.
Merimack, NH 03054
(603) 598-3400

JAG for Windows
Concerned with the quality of digital images, JAG can be used to
smooth out the stairstepped edges in color and grayscale graphics. It
works with the popular paint, graphics, and image editing packages.

Ray Dream Inc.
1804 N. Shoreline Blvd.
Mountain View, CA 94043
(800) 846-0111

Picture Publisher 5.0
Picture Publisher is a professional image editing program that provides a combination of speed, functionality, and ease of use. Features
include object layers, intuitive interface, an image browser, etc.

Micrografx Inc.
1303 E. Arapaho
Richardson, TX 75081
(800) 326-3576

3-D Modeling Lab
Crystal-clear, hands-on examples helps users learn 3D modeling, rendering, and animation for the PC. They can design 3D images and animation for products, presentations, etc.

Waite Group Press
200 Tamal Plaza
Corte Madera, CA 94925
(800) 368-9369

Cheetah 3D
Render and animate complex 3D images with this powerful multimedia tool. Standard rendering features include up to 10 parallel light
sources with specular and ambient light controls. High-end features
include multiple-area rendering, bitmap textures, etc.

Looking Glass Software
11222 La Cienga Blvd., Suite 305
Inglewood, CA 90304
(310) 348-8240

Envision

With unparalleled realism and rendering quality, this tool allows users to see their finished designs in photorealistic detail and 24-bit color. It renders any image and applies surface details, textures, or finishes on any background image.

ModaCAD
1954 Cotner Ave.
Los Angeles, CA 90025
(310) 312-6632

Fractals for Windows

With zoom box, menus, and a mouse, users can create new fractals and control more than 85 different fractal types. Bundled with Win-Fract, this package speedily computes mind-bending fractals.

Waite Group Press
200 Tamal Plaza
Corte Madera, CA 94925
(800) 368-9369

Imagine

A 3D image processing program that lets users create any kind of character, with numberless effects applied to that character. Once users have snared the look that they have imagined, they can make those characters live through the extensive use of Imagine's animation capabilities.

Impulse Inc.
8416 Xerxes Ave. North
Brooklyn Park, MN 56544
(800) 328-0184

MacroModel

This package enables users to twist or bend 3D objects. Since there is a version for the Mac as well as for the IBM PC platform, images created on one can be transferred easily to the other.

Macromedia, Inc.
600 Townsend St.
San Francisco, CA 94103
(800) 288-8229

223 – The Stereo Paint System

A paint system that provides the ability to create true 3D, stereoscopic images. Also permits conversion of pre-existing 2D images into 3D images.

Latent Image Development Corporation
Digital Media Group
111 Fourth Ave.
New York, NY 10003
(212) 388-0122

Adobe Illustrator
A powerful professional design tool, it enables designers to draw
from scratch or work with existing images. Illustrator supports 16.7
million colors, handles text, generates separations, allows custom
views and page sizes, and does object manipulation such as dividing,
slicing, and combining.
  Adobe Systems Inc.
  1585 Charleston Road
  P.O. Box 7900
  Mountain View, CA 94039
  (800) 833-6687

Painterly Effects
This is a Unix-based set of filters that lets you turn boring images into
classical art.
  Softimage Inc.
  660 Newton-Yardley Rd.
  Suite 202
  Newton, PA 18940
  (215) 860-5525

Digital cameras and video

Canon Still Video Camera RC-360, RC-570
Records color images on small floppy disks instead of using film. Us-
ing a separately purchased video card, you can input these images di-
rectly into your computer.
  Canon USA
  One Canon Plaza
  Lake Success, NY 11042
  (615) 488-6700

FlexCam
FlexCam is a small, flexible camera with built-in stereo microphones.
Having the same quality as a Sony camcorder, the FlexCam looks
somewhat like a desktop high-intensity lamp. It can be hooked up di-

rectly to the PC through any video board. By pointing down at a desk, the FlexCam also can be used as a scanner.

VideoLabs
Minneapolis, MN
(612) 897-1995

DS-100 Memory Card Camera

Cardinal Technologies and Fuji Photo Film have combined forces to create this PC-ready digital camera. Twenty-one photos can be stored on a reusable memory card. Capabilities include auto flash/focus/exposure, and 3X zoom.

Cardinal Technologies, Inc.
1827 Freedom Road
Lancaster, PA 17601
(800) 722-0094

FotoMan Plus

This is a 10-ounce, pocket-size portable camera that lets you take grayscale digital photos. Costing about $800 retail, FotoMan is a one-button camera that holds up to 32 images and downloads those images through a serial interface. Bundled software completes the package.

Logitech Inc.
6505 Kaiser Dr.
Fremont, CA 94555
(510) 795-8500

Kodak DC40/DC20

This is a low-cost digital camera that plugs right into your PC or Mac.

Eastman Kodak
343 State Street
Rochester, NY 14650
(800) 242-2424 X 52
http://www.kodak.com/daiHome/DCS/DCSGateway.shtml

Casio QV Digital Cameras

They make the QV series that I happen to use. It's a real joy to grab hold of images I take, directly into my PC.

Casio
(800) 962-2746

Connectix Color QuickCam

Their videocamera is cheap and does stills, too. It's a basic component of Internet videoconferencing.

Connectix Corporation
2655 Campus Drive
San Mateo, CA 94403
(800) 950-5880, (415) 571-5100
http://www.connectix.com

Digital video

Adobe Premier
It's the hot ticket for Macs and even was profiled on the Discovery
Channel.
Adobe Systems Inc.
1585 Charleston Road
P.O. Box 7900
Mountain View, CA 94039
(800) 833-6687

CameraMan
CameraMan is a "screen movie" capture utility for Windows computers. Unlike screen capture utilities, which can capture only static pictures of the screen, CameraMan records in real time everything that
takes place on the screen into a standard movie file.
Motion Works USA
524 Second St.
San Francisco, CA 94107
(800) 800-8476

D/Vision
This product enables you to produce edited videotapes and multimedia video. Using Intel's *i*750/Indeo digital video board, it enables instant revision and playback of edit decisions. Both models offer good
price for the power.
   D/Vision uses SupeRTV, an enhancement of Intel's RTV (Real
Time Video). It lets you "print" high-quality, full-screen video directly
to videotape. There are two versions of this software. The basic system (under $500 retail) is touted as the lowest-cost nonlinear editing
software on the market. The Pro version (slightly under $4000) turns
your PC into a professional video production studio, and it even
stores over 70 hours of accessible, online digital video.
TouchVision Systems Inc.
1800 Winnemanc Ave.
Chicago, IL 60640
(312) 989-2160

VGA Producer Pro
This VGA-to-NTSC genlockable encoder enables you to transfer your multimedia work of art to broadcast-ready videotape. (That's what the genlock means.) It promises to be flicker-free.
Magni Systems Inc.
9500 SW Gemini Drive
Beaverton, OR 97005
(503) 626-8400

DVA-4000
This is a family of full-motion digital video adapters for PC/AT, PS/2, or Mac computers.
VideoLogic, Inc.
245 First Street
Cambridge, MA 02142
(617) 494-0530

Mediator
High-quality computer graphics can be converted to video for Mac and VGA displays.
VideoLogic, Inc.
245 First Street
Cambridge, MA 02142
(617) 494-0530

Pro Movie Spectrum
This is a playback, capture, and editing add-in board with bundled software. It enables user to bring synchronized, full-motion video sequences to the PC.
Media Vision
3185 Laurelview Court
Fremont, CA 94538
(800) 845-5870

Bandit
Bandit simplifies the process of transferring images between your computer and VCR or video camera. Bandit is a peripheral device that works in the Mac and PC environments by connecting to either a SCSI or serial port.
Fast Forward Video
18200-C West McDurmott
Irvine, CA 92714
(714) 852-8404

Bravado
Bravado combines full-featured, onboard VGA with live NTSC or PAL video-in-a-window and controllable pass-through audio in one board. Apparently it's a single-board multimedia presentation engine.

Truevision
7240 Shadeland Station
Indianapolis, Indiana 46256
(317) 841-0332

Super Still-Frame Compression
This product reduces storage requirements for captured video through JPEG (8:1 to 75:1) compression.

New Media Graphics
780 Boston Road
Billerica, MA 01821
(800) 288-2207

VideoSpigot for Windows
VideoSpigot captures digital video from cameras, VCRs, laser discs, etc. It includes Microsoft Video for Windows, which enables editing motion video sequences for embedding in any OLE-compliant application. CinePak software compression lets you stores AVI files at a fraction of their original size.

Creative Labs
1901 McCarthy Blvd.
Milpitas, CA 95035
(800) 428-6600

Videovue
This product grants the ability to extract images from motion or still-frame video. Incoming video can be PAL, NTSC, composite, or S-Video.

Video Associates Labs
4926 Spicewood Springs Road
Austin, Texas 78759
(800) 331-0547

Intel Smart Video Recorder
One-step recording and Indeo compression allows a 50MB, 60-second clip to be stored in a relatively small 9MB file.

Intel Corp.
2200 Mission College Blvd.
Santa Clara, CA 95052
(800) 538-3373

DigiTV
Built-in 122-channel, cable-ready TV tuner with onboard 4-watt stereo audio amplifier lets you watch TV through your PC.
Videomail, Inc.
568-4 Weddell Dr.
Sunnyvale, CA 94089
(408) 747-0223

Video Machine
This product enables broadcast-quality video editing, right on the desktop.
Fast Electronics
5 Commonwealth Road
Natick, MA 01760
(508) 655-FAST

TelevEyes
An inexpensive tool for converting computer VGA to recordable composite video, TelevEyes allows displaying computer screens on any standard composite video monitor or recording VGA screens to videotape.
Digital Vision Inc.
270 Bridge Street
Dedham, MA 02026
(617) 329-5400

WatchIT
This is an add-in board that allows you to watch TV on your PC. It runs under DOS or Windows using a pop-up remote control for TV adjustment.
New Media Graphics
780 Boston Road
Billerica, MA 01821
(509) 663-0666

PC Tele-VISION PLUS
This is a board that allows a PC-compatible computer to display NTSC or composite video in a window of variable size on a VGA or SVGA monitor.
50/50 Micro Electronics
1249 Innsbruck Dr.
Sunnyvale, CA 94089
(408) 720-5050

TapeIT

TapeIT is an inexpensive video encoding board that converts VGA signals to NTSC (North America) or PAL (Europe) formats.

New Media Graphics
780 Boston Road
Billerica, MA 01821
(800) 288-2207

The Indy Workstation

I haven't listed any multimedia PCs here because all vendors seem to be offering them. This one, however, is unique. Silicon Graphics is now offering a workstation with a built-in color video camera for under $4995.

Given the price of a multimedia-enabled PC nowadays, this workstation is worth a look-see. (Remember, Silicon Graphics are the guys who brought you the special effects for *Jurassic Park*.)

Silicon Graphics
2011 N. Shoreline Rd.
P.O. Box 7311
Mountain View, California
(800) 800-7441

928Movie

This is a single-slot ISA or VL bus Windows and multimedia accelerator that delivers up to six times the performance of ordinary VGAs, and visibly improves the quality of CD multimedia titles by scaling up video clips to full-color, full-screen movies.

VideoLogic Inc.
2245 First St.
Cambridge, MA 02142
(617) 494-0530

Rapier 24

A two-page graphics processor that brings workstation-class, 24-bit true color performance to Windows Autodesk and TIGA applications. It provides resolutions from 640×480 to 1152×882, and allows the user to select from a wide range of third-party multisync VGA and Apple monitors.

VideoLogic Inc.
245 First St.
Cambridge, MA 02142
(617) 494-0530

SynchroMaster 300AV
A synchronizer, switcher, fader, and dissolve unit for data display projectors. It provides instantaneous clean cuts between two computer sources of up to 1280×1024 resolution, as well as fades and dissolves.
RGB Spectrum
950 Marina Village Pkwy.
Alameda, CA 94501
(510) 814-7000

Vivid 3D
A sound enhancement system for video games and multimedia, it creates dynamic 3D sound from only two speakers.
NuReality
2907 Damier St.
Santa Ana, CA 92705
(714) 442-1080

DigiTracker
This uncomplicated digital tracker combines a multiple-sensor motion tracker (up to 30 sensors) with a 3D digitizer that allows for easy creation of 3D models. Mesh files can be created simply by positioning the stylus on any point on a model and pressing a button to enter the coordinate.
Visual Circuits
3309 83rd Ave. North
Brooklyn Park, MN 55443
(612) 560-6205

LiveWindows
A collection of routines to provide real-time display and scaling of live video within a window or multiple windows on the VGA screen. The card plugs into a 16-bit slot and connects to a VGA card via the card's "feature connector."
Software Interphase
82 Cucumber Hill Rd., Suite 258
Foster, RI 02825
(800) 542-2742

Super Video Windows - ISA
A professional quality frame grabber and video windowing board that accepts up to three composites or S-VHS inputs from camera, VCR, or videodisc, and displays full-motion video in a scalable window.

New Media Graphics Corp.
780 Boston Rd.
Billerica, MA 01821
(800) 288-2207

Video-It!

A high-performance video capture card, featuring real-time capture and compression. Available in ISA, PCI, and VESA local bus versions, it can display live video-in-a-window at any graphics resolution.
ATI Technologies Inc.
33 Commerce Valley Dr. East
Thornhill, Ontario L3T 7N6
Canada
(905) 882-2600

VideoSurge

A full-motion, 24-bit color video display and capture board that can do chromakey and lumakey effects, and forms the basis of any video processing studio. Features include three independent audio and video sources, audio pass-through, and optimal support for 24-bit VGA color.
AITech International
47971 Fremont Blvd.
Fremont, CA 94538
(800) 882-8184

Encoder/decoders and scan converters

Audio/Video Key-PC Presentation Kit

This add-on comprises two external interfaces that connect a DOS computer to a wide range of audio/visual hardware. With the included presentation software, HSC Interactive, Audio/Video Key is a portable multimedia presentation system.
Comedge Inc.
2211 S. Hacienda Blvd. #100
Hacienda Heights, CA 91745
(818) 336-7522

Chroma Gold

This is a 32,768-color VGA display adapter with NTSC composite output. It supports all VGA and SVGA modes with standard VGA outputs.

Ventura Technologies
4820 Adhor Lane, Suite M
Camarillo, CA 93012
(805) 445-4411

CVC

The CVC converts interfaced 15 Hz RGB analog video to studio-quality component video in selectable Betacam or Mll formats.
Visual Circuits
3309 83rd Ave. N
Brooklyn Park, MN 55443
(612) 560-6205

Delta VC

An integrated PC solution for creating interactive and linear-play video programs. It combines real-time MPEG video and audio compression technology with powerful interactive design and mastering tools.
Optimage
7185 Vista Dr. West
Des Moines, IA 50266
(800) 234-5484

Genie Scan Converter

Genie is an external portable box that converts PC graphics to TV video. Genie is a true, 100-percent hardware scan converter; it requires no software and is truly plug and play.
Jovian Logic Corp.
47929 Fremont Blvd.
Fremont, CA 94538
(510) 651-4823

TV Link

TV Link delivers precision computer images to any standard TV system. It handles VGA resolution up to 640×480 with as many as 16 million colors.
KDI/Precision Products Inc.
60 S. Jefferson Rd.
Whippany, NJ 07981
(201) 887-5700

Captivator ProTV

Coupled to VESA Media Channel (VMC) graphics systems, Captivator ProTV for VMC displays crystal-clear TV pictures on a PC screen. The user has total control of the picture attributes (brightness, contrast, etc.) through an easy-to-use control panel. The live-video window can be set to stay on top of the display, enabling the user to monitor the TV while working with another application. It's simple to install and use, making it ideal for home use.

VideoLogic
245 First Street
Suite 1403
Cambridge, MA 02142
(617) 494-0530
usa@videologic.com

MPEG Player for VMC

Using VideoLogic's PowerStream video processor and associated proprietary SmoothScale algorithms to deliver sensational quality video, this peripheral equips today's PCs to take advantage of MPEG, the dominant standard for exceptionally high-quality digital video and audio. It features the highest quality video playback, full support for application developers, outstanding CD audio, and easy installation.

VideoLogic
245 First Street
Suite 1403
Cambridge, MA 02142
(617) 494-0530
usa@videologic.com

MovieLine

Full-featured, low-cost MovieLine enables users to create dynamic presentations with digital effects and animation. MovieLine includes Movie Machine Pro with Motion-JPEG option, Adobe Premiere, Animator Pro, and XingCD MPEG encoding.

Fast Electronic
393 Vintage Dr.
Foster City, CA 94404
(800) 864-MOVIE

Alladin Media Printer

Alladin integrates a seven-input digital switcher with a fully programmable 3D DVE, and bundles a graphics software package for paint, character generation, 3D modeling, and animation. The open architecture enables users to customize the product to meet specific needs.

Pinnacle Systems Inc.
870 W. Maude Ave
Sunnyvale, CA.
408-720-9669

Asii Switcher
This is a plug-in, broadcast-quality switcher that utilizes the latest technology to provide various digital effects. PC control allows users to set up multiple events, allowing the editor to preselect and store a series of digital effects.
Hotronic Inc.
1875 S. Winchester Blvd.
Campbell, CA
(408) 378-3883

AmiLink CIP Desktop Video Editing Systems
This editing tool allows true A/B roll editing with consumer- or industrial-level video equipment, and lets users upgrade to professional editing and still use their CIP equipment. It comes with extensive edit list tools.
RGB Computer & Video Inc.
4152 Blue Heron Blvd. West
Suite 118
Riviera Beach, FL 33404
(808) 563-7876

Edit-San
This is a low-cost A/B roll system that provides the professional features requested by most editors. It lets users create tape logs right from the editing software, and then build edit decision lists directly from the tape logs.
TAO Inc.
PO Box 1254
Roll, MO 65401
(800) 264-1121

The Executive Librarian
This system features multiuser access for fast, full text searches of thousands of records. Pull lists are generated from query results and may be further edited, saved, or e-mailed.
Imagine Products Inc.
581 S. Rangeline Rd. Suite B3
Carmel, IN 46032
(317) 843-0706

Matrox Studio
The Matrox Studio PC-based video editing suite combines the productivity of nonlinear editing with the quality and versatility of linear, tape-based online production.

Matrox Graphics Inc.
1025 St. Regis Blvd.
Dorval, Quebec H9P 2T4
Canada
(800) 362-9343
http://www.matrox.com

Media Merge
Video editing software designed to edit video in Windows. It enables
users to choose source material from popular video, paint, spreadsheet, animation, presentation, word processing, or desktop publishing packages and combine it into a new video presentation.
ATI Technologies
33 Commerce Valley Dr. East
Thornhill, Ontario L3T 7N6
Canada
(905) 882-2600

Scene Stealer
Scene Stealer is a PC/AT circuit board and software for automatic
scene detection and video logging, saving hours of logging drudgery.
The on-board frame grabber examines incoming video to determine
when a cut takes place.
Dubner International Inc.
13 Westervelt PL
Westwood, NJ 07675
(201) 664-6434

Strassner SES-2000 Thru 3000
Fulfills an editor's wish list of artistic tools. These features provide the
ultimate in offline and online editing applications, and every Strassner system has, built in, the capacity for upgrading and adding new
features.
Strassner Editing Systems
104-19 McCormick St.
North Hollywood, CA 91601
(800) 836-3348

Studio Magic
This product enables users to display VGA output on any TV screen.
It can capture full-size, full-color video images and store them on disk
for later use. The heart is an online video production studio.

Studio Magic Corp.
1690 Dell Ave.
Campbell, CA 95008
(408) 378-3638

U-Edit
A very affordable news and video magazine edit controller.
Based on the PC platform, U-Edit converts a user-supplied 286 or bet-
ter computer into a frame-accurate, 99-event editor.
Editing Technologies Corp.
11992 Challenger Ct.
Moorpark, CA 93021
(805) 529-7074

ScreenPlay 2.2
An audio/video editing package that offers 24-bit, true-color playback
and is able to run on Windows-based applications, as well as Apple's
QuickTime. It's fully licensed to allow people the right to distribute
the ScreenPlay 2.2 Viewer and ScreenPlay-formatted movies over the
Internet.
RAD Technologies
745 Emerson St.
Palo Alto, CA 94301
(415) 617-9430

MediaSpace
A cost-effective means to add video wherever needed, this digital
video board allows you to record, edit, and play back in real time. It
includes Adobe Premiere and works with more than a hundred Video
for Windows compatible applications.
VideoLogic Inc.
245 First St.
Suite 1403
Cambridge, MA 02142
(617) 494-0530

Captivator
Captivator is a low-cost video capture card that brings desktop video
to office and home PCs. Easily installed, this card enables high-quality video to be displayed in any size and in 8-, 16-, or 24-bit color.
VideoLogic Inc.
245 First St.
Suite 1403
Cambridge, MA 02142
(617) 494-0530

Magazines and journals

InterActivity
Multimedia and the Web are covered all in one place.
411 Borel Avenue
Suite 100
San Mateo, CA 94402
(415) 358-9500

Advanced Imaging
It covers all facets of imaging, including video. It's monthly and free.
PTN Publishing
445 Broad Hollow Rd.
Melville, NY 11747
(516) 845-2700

The Net
It's the directory for interesting things on the Web.
Imagine Publishing
150 North Hill Drive
Brisbane, CA 94005
http://www.thenet-usa.com

Boardwatch Magazine
Actually directed to online users of bulletin boards, it's still a good source of information on cyber-issues.
5970 South Vivian Street
Littleton, CO 80127
(800) 933-6038

Business Publishing
Specifically for those interested in corporate publishing, it provides information on desktop publishing and electronic delivery. Published monthly, it's $24 per year.
Hitchcock Publishing Co.
191 S. Gary Ave.
Carol Stream, IL 60188
(800) 234-0733, (708) 665-1000

Computer Pictures
A wonderful bimonthly graphics publication, $40 per year.

Montage Publishing Inc.
(Knowledge Industries Publications Inc.)
701 Westchester Ave.
White Plains, NY 10604
(914) 328-9157

Desktop Video World
Similar to *Digital Video* magazine, it's bimonthly and $19.97 per year.
Desktop Video World
PO Box 594
Mt. Morris, IL 61054

Digital Media
A monthly Seybold publication providing the usual high level of Seybold insight, $395 per year.
Seybold Publications
428 E. Baltimore Pike, PO Box 644
Media, PA 19063
(215) 565-2480

Interactive Age
A magazine that deals with doing business via the Internet.
Interactive Age
PO Box 1194
Skokie, IL 60076
(708) 647-6834

Inside the Internet
A monthly magazine that offers tips on how to retrieve information on the Internet, as well as covering a wide range of Internet tools. Subscription price is $49 per year.
Cobb Group Inc.
9420 Bunsen Parkway, Suite 300
Louisville, KY 40220
(800) 223-8720, (502) 493-3200

Internet Business Advantage
A monthly newsletter, costing $69 per year, that shows business professionals how to use the Internet to their company's advantage.
Internet Business Advantage
9420 Bunsen Parkway, Suite 300
Louisville, KY 40220
(800) 223-8720, (502) 493-3200

Internet Week
It's a newsletter, costing $495 per year.
Phillips Business Information
1201 Seven Locks Rd.
Potomac, MD 20854.
(301) 424-3338

Internet World
Published monthly at $29 per year, it focuses on developments within
the World Wide Web, the Internet, electronic networking, etc.
Mecklermedia Corp.
20 Ketchum St.
Westport, CT 06880
(203) 226-6967

NetGuide
This magazine reviews Internet sites, online services, and related
hardware and software. It's published monthly, at $22.97 per year.
CMP Publications
600 Community Dr.
Manhasset, NY 11030
(516) 562-5000

New Media
A slick, enjoyable magazine, with great ads. A bargain.
Hypermedia Communications Inc.
901 Mariner's Island Blvd., Suite 365
San Mateo, CA 94404
(415) 573-5170

Virtual Reality Report Magazine
A must-have if you're into VR, and another of the fine Meckler publications.
Meckler Corporation
11 Ferry Lane West
Westport, CT 06880
(203) 226-6967

Webweek
I read it each and every week. Good stuff!
Mecklermedia Corporation
20 Ketchum Street
Westport, CT 06880

InterAd Monthly

Every month the publication provides competitive monitoring, trends and statistics, and relevant news—everything one needs to know in terms of online corporate marketing and communications.

Webtrack
9 E. 38th St., 8th Floor
New York, NY 10016-0003
(212) 725-5328
info@webtrack.com

WEB Developer

Another of the excellent Mecklermedia publications. A technical resource for Internet developers.

Mecklermedia Corporation
20 Ketchum Street
Westport, CT 06880
subs@mecklermedia.com

WebServer

This is a bimonthly magazine for those who need to run a server.

Computer Publishing Group
320 Washington Street
Brookline, MA 02146
(617) 739-7001

WEBTechniques

Everything you need to know about developing on the Web.

Miller Freeman
600 Harrison Street
San Francisco, California 94107
(303) 661-1885 (fax)

Internet Business Report

A newsletter centered on doing business on the Internet.

Jupiter Communications
627 Broadway
New York, NY 10012
(212) 780-6060
http://www.jup.com

Internet World

PO Box 713
Mt. Morris, IL 61054
iwsubs@kable.com

Media clips

Wallace Music & Sound

Wallace Music & Sound, Inc., provides original music and sound effects for software developers and publishers.

Wallace Music & Sound, Inc.
6210 West Pershing Ave.
Glendale, AZ 95304
(602) 979-6201

Soundtrack Express

Compatible with all authoring and presentation tools, it's an unlimited source of professional-quality music for multimedia.

BlueRibbon Soundtracks Ltd.
PO Box 8689
Atlanta, GA 30306
(800) 226-0212

Multimedia Music Library

Multimedia Music Library is a collection of more than 100 pop and orchestral musical sequences, royalty-free.

Midisoft Corporation
P.O. Box 1000
Bellevue, WA 98009
(206) 881-7176

Killer Tracks

Killer Tracks is a series of music selections.

Killer Tracks
6534 Sunset Blvd.
Hollywood, CA 90028
(800) 877-0078

HyperClips

HyperClips for Windows is a CD-ROM volume containing hundreds of high-quality animation and sound clips designed to accent business, sales, and technical presentations.

The HyperMedia Group
5900 Hollis Street
Suite O
Emeryville, CA 94608
(510) 601-0900

DigiSound Audio Library

The DigiSound Audio Library brings exciting, full-fidelity sound to multimedia with professionally produced MIDI music, sound effects, and DigiVoice clips.

Presentation Graphics Group
270 N. Canon Dr.
Suite 103
Beverly Hills, CA 90210
(310) 277-3050

MediaClips

Aris Entertainment offers several sets of CD-ROMs for Windows, MacOS, and DOS platforms that contain a combination of sound effects, full-color photographs, and/or video clips. Under the trade name MediaClips, the following sets illustrate the Aris offerings: Worldview (space images and sounds), Wild Places (North American photos and audio clips), Majestic Places (nature photos and audio clips), and Business Background (photos, audio clips, and sound effects).

Aris Entertainment, Inc.
4444 Via Marina, Suite 811
Marina del Rey, CA 90292
(310) 821-0234
(800) 228-2747

Digital Zone

Digital Zone hires professional photographers to take stunning photos. The photos are then stored on Kodak's Photo CD and are free for use by purchasers of one of the collections.

Digital Zone Inc.
P.O. Box 5562
Bellevue, WA 98006
(800) 538-3113

Archive

Archive Films/Archive Photos contain thousands of hours of historical and entertainment footage and stills, produced from 1894 to the present. Includes Albert Einstein, John Jacob Astor, Hollywood, presidents, kings, the Depression.

Archive New Media
530 West 25th Street
New York, NY 10001
(212) 620-3980

CBS News Archives
Exactly that.
CBS
524 West 57 Street
New York, NY 10019
(212) 975-2875

Buyout Music Library
Hours of royalty-free original music on CD.
Musi-Q
P.O. Box 451147
Sunrise, Florida
(305) 572-9276

Station Break
Station Break contains collections of license-free music. Pick selections by theme, such as crime, haunted house, etc.
Station Break Music
40 Glen Street
Suite 1
Glen Cove, NY 11542
(800) ON-AIR-99

VTL
Video Tape Library offers news clips such as L.A. riots, gang shootings, and sports.
VTL
1509 N. Crescent Heights Blvd.
Suite 2
Los Angeles, CA 90046
(213) 656-4330

PhotoDisc
PhotoDisc contains, on each CD, 336 multipurpose images from award-winning photographers of landscapes, rain forests, deserts, animals, etc. Shots are arranged in a user-friendly slide show.
PhotoDisc
2013 4th Ave.
Seattle, WA 98121
(206) 441-9355

Clipper
Clipper is a monthly clip art subscription service. You have the choice of medium: paper, floppy, or CD-ROM. Each month, subscribers get

a variety of themed images designed especially for Clipper by leading artists.

Dynamic Graphics Inc.
6000 N. Forest Park Drive
P.O. Box 1901
Peoria, IL 61656
(800) 255-8800

Masterclips

A collection of 6000 images in 60 different categories.

Masterclips, Inc.
5201 Ravenswood Rd.
Suite 111
Ft. Lauderdale, FL 33312
(800) 292-2547

Morphing

If you've seen *Terminator 2*, then you know what morphing is. You select a starting image and an ending image, and then let the computer make the gradual transition between the two. You've also seen this done in one too many music videos.

Morph

A general-purpose tool for morphing one image to another.

Gryphon Software Corporation
7720 Trade Street
Suite 120
San Diego, CA 02121
(619) 536-8815

HSC Digital Morph

With an easy-to-use image manipulation tool, users now can add exciting visual impact to presentations with this sophisticated morphing tool. Users can morph from one still image to another, or between moving images.

HSC Software
1661 Lincoln Blvd.
Suite 101
Santa Monica, CA 90404
(310) 392-8441

Packaging

Ames Specialty Packaging

Here are some folks to check out:

Ames Specialty Packaging
21 Properzi Way
P.O. Box 120
Somerville, MA 02143
(617) 776-3360

Photo CD

Kodak Photo CD

Instead of having your trip to the beach printed from negative to photo paper, you get it on a CD. Although targeted primarily at consumers, Photo CD offers opportunities to businesses as well.

Eastman Kodak Company
343 State Street
Rochester, NY 14650
(716) 724-6404

Scanners

Kodak Professional RFS 2035 Plus Film Scanner

The Kodak Professional RFS 2035 Plus Film Scanner is an ultrafast, 200 dpi, 12-bit per color area array scanner for 35mm slides and negatives. The scanner provides adjustable scanning resolutions, auto exposure, auto color balance, and other features.

Eastman Kodak Co., Professional Imaging
343 State St.
Rochester, NY 14650
(800) 242-2424

Polaroid CS-500i Digital Photo Scanner

A high-speed, high-resolution digital scanner which, along with the accompanying software, scans and manipulates reflective images up to 4x6 inches. Scanned images can be stored in industry-standard file formats.

Polaroid Corp.
575 Technology Sq.
Cambridge, MA 02139
(800) 225-1618

ScanMan Color
A 24-bit color, hand-held scanner that captures up to 16.7 million colors, as well as true 256 grayscale data. It is bundled with FotoTouch Color Image Editing Software.
　Logitech Inc.
　6505 Kaiser Dr.
　Fremont, CA 94556
　(800) 231-7717

Sound

20-20 Sound Editor
A Windows program designed to deal with the audio part of multimedia presentation, its features include fast, nondestructive waveform editing, powerful 8-track audio file mixer, and a versatile multimedia browser.
　MKS Compu-Group Inc.
　1730 Cunard St.
　Laval, Quebec H7S 2B2
　Canada
　(514) 332-4110

Ballade for Windows
Record, play back, and print out sheet music with this production package. Pick and choose from a variety of musical sounds and sound effects contained in the computer sound card.
　Dynaware
　950 Tower Ln. Suite 1150
　Foster City, CA 94404
　(415) 349-5700

Cakewalk Home Studio
Your PC can be turned into a multitrack recording studio with this innovative software package. Features include a virtual piano to record music with the keyboard or mouse.
　Twelve Tone Systems
　PO Box 760
　Watertown, MA 02272
　(800) 234-1171

The Editor Plus

Record one stereo sound file while listening to another with this software helpmate. It plays the file in the bottom waveform display window and records the new sound in the top window.

Digital Audio Labs
114505 21st Ave., Suite 202
Plymouth, MN 55447
(612) 473-7626

Knowledge Media Audio Plus

Audio contains public domain, freeware, and shareware applications and data files, covering hundreds of sounds, sound effects, and MOD files.

Knowledge Media Inc.
436 Nunneley, Suite B
Paradise, CA 95969
(800) 782-3766

MIDI Programmer's ToolKit for Windows

The MIDI Programmer's TookKit provides tools and documentation to assist Windows programmers in developing MIDI applications. All ToolKit features are found in a dynamic link library (DLL), which provides functions to access Standard MIDI files easily.

Music Quest Inc.
1700 Alma Dr., Suite 330
Plano, TX
(214) 881-7408

Power Tracks Pro

A full-featured, integrated 48-track MIDI sequencer and music notation program for Windows 3.1, Power Tracks Pro can record, play back, and edit MIDI data.

P.G. Music Inc.
266 Elmwood Ave., Suite 111
Buffalo, NY 14222
(800) 268-6272

MusicPrinter Plus

A notation-based sequencer program that's chock full of such features as page view, automatic measure numbering, extended print to print, PCX files, accurate performance of artistic notation and rubato markings, and more.

Temporal Acuity Products
300 120th Ave. NE, Bldg. 1, Suite 200
Bellevue, WA 98005
(800) 426-2673

Sound Impression

Manage MIDI data, waveform audio data (.WAV files) and CD audio with this full-featured program. Among its attributes are the ability to create scores for multimedia presentations, an interface that appears and operates like a stereo component rack, and extensive OLE support.
Midisoft Corp.
15379 NE 90th St.
Redmond, WA 98052
(800) 776-6434

AudioMan

A portable, hand-held device with a built-in microphone, speaker, and 8-bit sound digitizer, AudioMan was built to let you add verbal notes to your work, rather than handwritten ones.
Logitech Inc.
6505 Kaiser Dr.
Fremont, CA 94555
(510) 795-8500

PortAble Sound

A portable, parallel-port sound device with bundled DOS and Windows software.
Digispeech, Inc.
550 Main Street
Suite J
Placerville, CA 95667
(916) 621-1787

SoundXchange

A business-level audio solution using a telephone instead of a microphone.
Interactive
204 N. Main
Humboldt, SD 57035
(800) 292-2112

Sound Blaster Deluxe
Sound Blaster Pro Deluxe
Sound Blaster 16 ASP

A variety of cards of every need. Creative Labs creates sound cards for those interested in gaming (Sound Blaster Deluxe), as well as those interested in 16-bit, CD-quality sound (Sound Blaster 16 ASP).

    Creative Labs
    1901 McCarthy Blvd.
    Milpitas, CA 95035
    (800) 428-6600

Wave Blaster

A MIDI add-on daughter board to the Sound Blaster 16 card. Wave Blaster provides realistic, wave table instrument sounds instead of FM synthesized sound.

    Creative Labs
    1901 McCarthy Blvd.
    Milpitas, CA 95035
    (800) 428-6600

Audioport
Microkey

Two products that let you take sound on the road. With Audioport you can both record and play sound; with Microkey you can only play. Both devices are tiny and fit into the parallel port of your laptop computer. It uses 12-bit sampling and a 3:1 compression ratio for storage.

    Video Associates Labs
    4926 Spicewood Springs Road
    Austin, TX 78759
    (800) 331-0547

Audioport

Antex's Audioport (not to be confused with the Creative Labs product of the same name) is an external device that offers broadcast-quality digital audio. It interfaces with PCs via the parallel port and records or plays digital audio direct-to-disk.

    Antex Electronics Corporation
    16100 South Figueroa Street
    Gardena, CA 90248
    (310) 532-3092

AdLib Gold

This board is one of the standards in multimedia sound, roughly equivalent to Creative Labs Sound Blaster. Both of these boards are popular on the gaming side of the industry. Quality may not be what you're looking for in the professional arena.

AdLib Multimedia
(800) 463-2686

Port Blaster

A portable solution for "on-the-road" business or multimedia presentations. Works with a parallel port.

Creative Labs
1901 McCarthy Blvd.
Milpitas, CA 95035
(800) 428-6600

UltraSound

Can perform mixing of CD audio, digital audio, synthesizers, a microphone, and line-level input.

Advanced Graphics Computer Technology
Vancouver, British Columbia
Canada
(604) 431-5020

Microsoft Sound System

Built primarily to add verbal notes to Windows applications such as your spreadsheet or word processing document, it also has a facility (ProofReader) that provides an audible proofing of numbers, and another (Voice Pilot) that enables users to execute commands by voice.

Microsoft Corporation
One Microsoft Way
Redmond, WA 98052
(206) 882-8080

Roland SCC-1 Sound Card

This card seems to be quite popular with those interested in recording high-fidelity music.

Roland Corporation
7200 Dominion Circle
Los Angeles, CA 90040
(213) 685-5141

Audio Solution Board

Basically available through OEMs, IBM's Audio Solution Board supports Windows, OS/2, and DOS. Available either in ISA or Micro Channel bus versions (the latter for IBM's own PS/2 series), this board enables 16-bit audio.

IBM
White Plains, NY
(800) 426-3333

Sound Galaxy
Offers 8- or 16-bit sounds cards, as well as multimedia upgrade kits.
Aztech Labs, Inc.
46707 Fremont Blvd.
Fremont, CA 94538
(510) 623-8988

Midisoft Studio for Windows
MIDI recording/editing software that delivers the power of a professional music studio to your multimedia PC.
Midisoft Corporation
15513 NE 52nd St.
Redmond, WA 98052
(206) 881-7176

Trax
Easy-to-use software for the MIDI beginner.
Passport Designs, Inc.
100 Stone Pine Rd.
Half Moon Bay, CA 94019
(415) 726-0280

Wave for Windows
Professional audio software for Windows.
Turtle Beach Systems
P.O. Box 5074
York, PA 17405
(717) 843-6916

Monologue
A software product for Windows that adds speech to your applications.
First Byte
19840 Pioneer Ave.
Torrance, CA 90503
(800) 545-7677

IBM Speech Recognition Family
Brings the power of speech to AIX and OS/2 workstations. It has an active vocabulary of over 20,000 words and a sophisticated language model.

IBM
Multimedia Information Center
P.O. Box 2150
Atlanta, GA 30301
(800) 772-2227

Read My Lips
Not a George Bush record, but software for the Macintosh that lets users record voice or sounds and attach digitized audio clips to documents.
Praxitel
Box 452
Pleasanton, CA 94566
(510) 846-9380

MCS Stereo
The complete interface to your computer's audio capability, it controls CD-ROMs, plays/records/edits WAV files, and has an integrated database for all your audio sources.
Animotion Development
3720 4th Ave. South #205
Birmingham, AL 35222
(205) 591-5715

FluentLinks
This is a NetWare Loadable Module that enables multiple users to retrieve and play motion video and audio segments over industry-standard networks.
Fluent, Inc.
One Apple Hill
594 Worcester Rd.
Natick, MA 01760
(508) 651-0911

ACS300.1 Computer Speaker System
Lets users hear digital audio sound with their computers. Users can plug this computer speaker system into any audio or video card to enhance any business presentation, etc., with the same level of recording quality as a music CD.
Altec Lansing Multimedia
PO Box 277
Milford, PA 18337-0277
(800) 648-6663

AudioPrisma

A professional Digital Audio Workstation, integrated onto a single system board. It contains everything needed for complete audio editing and production for multimedia applications.

Spectral Synthesis
19501 144th Ave. NE Suite 100A
Woodville, WA 98072
(206) 487-2931

The CardD Plus

Specifically created for professional recording applications, this product delivers sonic performance equal to none. It comes complete with a Windows 3.1 driver and can be used with any Windows-compatible sound editing software.

Digital Audio Labs
14502 21st Ave., Suite 202
Plymouth, MN 55447
(612) 473-7626

SoundMan Wave

SoundMan Wave is a wave table synthesis board coupled with up-to-the-minute, 16-bit stereo. Audio will no longer sound computer-generated.

Logitech Inc.
65505 Kaiser Dr.
Fremont, CA 94555
(800) 231-7717

Virtual reality

Since this is a category unto itself, I've decided to lump hardware and software together.

Mandala

It's almost impossible to explain. Using a video camera, this software puts you in your own virtual world. Mandala currently is used by the Nickelodeon cable channel.

The Vivid Group
317 Adelaide Street W
Suite 302
Toronto, Ontario M5V 1P9
Canada
(416) 340-9290

Head-mounted displays
Optics for head-mounted displays, cyberface head-mounted displays, and other stereo optical equipment (cameras, etc.).
Leep Systems
241 Crescent Street
Waltham, MA 02154
(617) 647-1395

WorldToolKit
WorldToolKit is a virtual reality applications development toolkit that runs on a variety of robust hardware platforms. It's basically a rendering, or visualization, software package that makes the impossible possible.
SENSE8 Corporation
4000 Bridgeway, Suite 101
Sausalito, CA 94965
(415) 331-6318
C:\WINDOWS\DESKTOP\MYBRIE~1

ADL-1 Tracker
A sophisticated and inexpensive 6D tracking system that converts position and orientation information into computer-readable form. The ADL-1 calculates head/object position with six degrees of freedom via a lightweight, multiple-jointed arm. Sensors mounted on the arm measure the angles of the joints. The microprocessor-based control unit uses these angles to compute position-orientation information in a user-selectable coordinate system, which is then transmitted to the host computer.
Shooting Star Technology
1921 Holdon Avenue
Burnaby, British Columbia V4B 3W4
Canada
(604) 298-8574

Spaceball 2003
The Spaceball 2003 is a 3D control device. With six simultaneous degrees of freedom, users are able to manipulate 3D screen models or conduct virtual scene walk-throughs or fly-throughs, as easily and intuitively as if they performed these tasks in the real world. The Spaceball consists of a tennis ball-sized sphere fixed on a stand.
A user places a wrist on the stand and grasps the ball with the fingertips. By gently pushing, pulling, or twisting the ball, the 3D screen object can be moved, in corresponding directions and speeds, in real

time. Screen object or screen movement is smooth and dynamic. The Spaceball is supported on major workstation and person computer platforms and in a host of applications from mechanical CAD to Virtual Reality.

Spaceball Technologies, Inc.
600 Suffolk St.
Lowell, MA 01854
(508) 970-0330

Flight Helmet

A head-mounted display for VR.

Virtual Research
Sunnyvale, CA 94089
(408) 748-8712

Grip Master

A force-sensing input device.

EXOS, Inc.
8 Blanchard Road
Burlington, MA 01803
(617) 229-2075

Cyberspace Developer Kit

One of Autodesk's superb animation products, it's a complete tool set for 3D visualization and simulation. In other words, it lets you create virtual reality applications.

Autodesk, Inc.
2320 Marinship Way
Sausalito, CA 94965
(415) 332-2344

Distant Suns
VistaPro

Use your PC to simulate the night sky (Distant Suns) or create electronic landscapes. I heard that Arthur C. Clarke (author of *2001: A Space Odyssey*) is using this software to get "images" for his next book.

Virtual Reality Laboratories
2341 Ganador Court
San Luis Obispo, CA 93401
(805) 545-8515

EYEGEN 3

This is a head-mounted display that uses monochrome CRTs and color wheels to improve resolution and decrease weight. EYEGEN 3 has a screen resolution of 369,750 color elements. Adjustments/features include interpupilary distance (IPD), focus, display release, and a double-ratchet headband.

Virtual Research
3193 Belick St. Suite #2
Santa Clara, CA 95054
(408) 748-8712

Smart 3D

This is a 3D rendering system that lets both Mac and Windows users manipulate objects in real time. The nice thing about this package is that the images wind up taking up little space, about 200–500K, compared to 100MB in other packages.

Macromedia Inc.
600 Townsend St.
San Francisco, CA 94103
(800) 288-8229

Telephony

Internet Phone

Internet Phone is a software package that allows the user to talk for free via the Internet. Free demo copy can be downloaded from *http://www.vocaltec.com/it.html*

VocalTec Inc.
157 Veterans Dr.
Northvale, NJ 07647
(201) 768-9400
info@vocaltec.com

Digiphone

This software package allows natural, two-way conversations, and offers such services as conference calling, caller ID, call screening, and voice mail. It includes an interface for connecting to the Internet and other online services.

Third Planet Publishing
Camelot Place
17770 Preston Rd.
Dallas, TX 75652
(214) 713-2607

Web servers

Website

A new server software kit for Windows NT 3.5 and Windows 95 users to publish, at very low cost, via the Internet. Easy training is provided by a complete tutorial and online help.

O'Reilly & Associates Inc.
103A Morris Street
Sebastopol, CA 95472
(800) 998-9938
catalog@online.ora.com

Explore OnNet

A package that enables Internet access in as little as 5 minutes. Windows-based, it features an enhanced NCSA Mosaic Internet browser, Gopher+ information retriever, e-mail, etc.

FTP Software
100 Brickstone Sq.
Andover, MA 01810
(800) 282-4FTP, ext. 455
http://www.ftp.com
Info@ftp.com

Purveyor

Point-and-click graphical interface allows easy access to the Web. It also features sample home pages, hot links to registration and support, sample forms, report generators, and excellent security and password protection.

Process Software Corporation
959 Concord St.
Framingham, MA 01701
1-800-722-7770
info@process.com
http://www.process.com

Sun Netra Internet Server

Just plug it in and, quick as can be, your PC LANs can be on the Internet. All the system software, application software, and administration tools have already been installed.

Sun Micosystems Inc.
2550 Garcia Ave.
Mountain View, CA 94043
(800) 786-0785 ext 110

Apple Internet Server

Installed with a simple click of a mouse, this server makes creating a Web site a sail of calm seas. It comes bundled with Adobe Acrobat Pro.

Apple
(800) 538-9696, ext 830
http://abs.apple.com

BSDI Internet Server

An affordable Internet package, easy to set up and administer. Even novices can get running and set up a home page in record time.

Berkeley Software Design Inc.
7759 Delmonico Dr.
Colorado Springs, CO 80919
1-800-800-4273
info@bsdi.com
http://ww.bsdi.com

Alibaba

This is a server running on a Windows 95 or Windows NT platform. Access is granted through group, host, IP, user. It uses the Secure Sockets Layer (SSL) security type. Price and secure price are $24 and $599, respectively.

Aspect Software
(808) 539-3782
http://alibab.austria.eu.net

SiteBuilder

A server running under Novell NetWare, no security type specified. Access is granted through directory, group, host, IP, NDS and bindery (NetWare), user. The price is $1495.

American Internet
800) 425-1112
http://www.american.com

Apache

Server running on Unix platforms, available free. Security type is SSL and access is granted through IP, user.

Apache
http://www.apache.org

CERN W3C HTTPd

Versions available to run under MacOS, OS/2, Unix, VMS, and Windows NT, available free. No security type. Access granted through group, IP.

CERN W3C
http://www.w3.org

SPRY Web Server, SafetyWeb Server

Runs under Windows NT 3.51 Workstation or Server. Cost is $245 standard or $895 for SafetyWeb. Security type SSL, with access granted through directory, file, group, host, IP, user.

CompuServe Internet
(800) 557-9614
http://www.spry.com

InterWare

Web server running under Windows NT, costing $1495. No security type specified. Access is granted through group, IP, user.

Consensys
(800) 328-1896
http://www.consensys.com

WebWare

Runs under NetWare, cost $999. No security type specified; access is granted through IP.

Electronic Dimensions
http://www.edime.com.au

HTTP Server

Runs under Windows NT. No security type specified. Available free.

EMWAC
http://emwac.ed.ac.uk

SuperWeb Server

Runs under Windows NT, costs $795. No security type specified; access granted through directory, file, group, IP, user.

Frontier Technologies
(800) 929-3054
http://www.frontiertech.com

Worldgroup Internet Server

Runs under DOS, costs $1995. No security type specified; access granted through IP, user.

Galacticomm
(800) 328-1128
http://ww.gcom.com

GLACI-HTTPD
Runs under NetWare, costs $475. SSL security tupe; access granted through directory, document group, host, IP, time, user.
Great Lakes Area Commercial Internet
http://www.glaci.com

Internet Connection Server
Runs under AIX (Unix) or OS/2. Costs range between $1199–$2699. Security type S-HTTP and SSL. Access granted through directory, document group, host, IP, user.
IBM
(800) 426-4968
http://ww.ibm.com/internet

FolkWeb
Runs under Windows 95 or Windows NT, and costs $120. No security type specified; access granted through IP.
ILAR Consulting
http://www.ilar.com

InterServer Publisher
Runs under MacOS, costs $495. No security type specified; access granted through directory, IP, realms.
Intercon
(800) 468-7266
http://www.intercon.com

Commerce BuilderPro
Runs under Windows 95, Windows NT. Costs $495–$995. Security type is SSL. Access granted through directory, group, host, IP, realm, time, user.
Internet Factory
(800) 229-6020
http://www.aristosoft.com

Internet Information Server
Runs under Windows NT, and is available free. Security type is SSL, with access granted through host, IP, user.

Microsoft
(800) 426-9400
http://www.microsoft.com

GNNserver
Runs under Unix and Windows NT, and is available free. Security type SSL, with access granted through directory, document group, host, IP, time, user.
Navisoft/AOL
(800) 529-9166
http://www.navisoft.com

HTTPd 1.4
Runs under Unix, and is available free. No security type specified; access granted through directory, group, IP, user.
NCSA
http://hoohoo.ncsa.uiuc.edu

Chameleon
Runs under Windows 3.1, Windows 95, and Windows NT. Cost is $400. No security type specified, and no access permission required.
NetManage
(408) 973-7171
http://www.netmanage.com

FastTrack Server
Enterprise Server
Both products run under Unix and Windows NT. FastTrack costs $299, Enterprise is $995. Both are security type SSL. Access for both is granted through directory, document, group, host, IP, user.
Netscape
(415) 254-1900
http://www.netscape.com

NetWare Web Server
Runs under Novell NetWare and costs $995. No security type specified; access granted through directory, file, group, host, IP, user.
Novell
(801) 429-7000
http://www.novell.com

WebServer
Runs under Unix and Windows NT, and costs $1495–$1995. Security types are both S-HTTP and SSL. Access is granted through browser type, directory, document, host, group, IP, time, user.
Open Market
245 First Street
Cambridge, MA 02142
(617) 621-9500
http://www.openmarket.com

Webserver 2.0
Runs under Unix, and costs $2495. No security type specified; access granted through directory, document, group, host, IP, time, user.
Oracle
(800) 423-0166
http://www.oracle.com

WebSite
Runs under Windows 95 and Windows NT. Cost is $379. No security type specified; access granted through directory, group, host, IP, user.
O'Reilly & Associates
(707) 829-0515
http://website.ora.com

Purveyor
Runs under NetWare, OpenVMS, Windows 95, and Windows NT. No security type specified. Costs between $295–$1195. Access is granted through directory, document, group, host, iP, realm, time, user.
Process Software
http://www.process.com
(800) 722-7770

WebServer
Runs under Windows and costs $170. No security type specified; access granted through document, group, host, user.
Quarterdeck
(310) 309-3700
http://www.qdeck.com

WebStar
WebStar 95/NT
WebStar runs under MacOS, WebStar 95/NT runs under Windows 95 and NT. The Mac version costs between $499–$599 and uses SSL se-

curity. The Windows 95 version is $99, with no security type. Access
for the Mac product is granted through directory, document, group,
host, IP, user. Win 95 access is through activity, group, host, user.

Quarterdeck (StarNine)
(800) 525-2580
http://www.qdeck.com

Webquest

Runs under Windows 95, Windows NT. Win 95 version is $295; Win-
dows NT is $495. No security type; access granted through group,
user.

Questar Microsystems
http://www.questar.com
(800) 925-2140

Glossary

account An area partitioned for a user of a particular host computer. To assure validity, account holders cannot gain access without using assigned login and password information.

address An individualized name (or number) identifying a computer user or computer, used in network communications for the transmission of messages for a particular person or machine.

Air Mosaic A Web browser that supports hypermedia.

anonymous FTP A means of allowing users to retrieve documents, files, programs, and other archived data from anywhere in the Internet, without having to establish a user-id and password on the system where the material resides. By using the special user-id "anonymous," the network user will circumvent local security checks and have access to publicly accessible files on the remote system. Most systems that permit anonymous login require the user's e-mail address as the password.

application Software that executes a particular task, such as word processing or spreadsheet analysis.

Archie A method of automatically gathering, indexing, and serving information on the Internet. Archie's initial implementation offered an indexed directory of filenames from all anonymous FTP archives on the Internet. Later versions provided additional collections of information. See also: *archive site, Gopher, Wide Area Information Servers.*

archive site A mechanism that renders access to a collection of files across the Internet; also, a computer on which such a collection is stored. For example, an "anonymous FTP archive site" allows users to access this material via the FTP protocol.

ARPAnet The experimental network, established in the 1970s but no longer in existence, where the theories and software on which the Internet is based were tested.

ASCII The acronym for American Standard Code for Information Interchange, the standard method for encoding characters as 8-bit sequences of binary numbers, allowing a maximum of 256 characters. Text files are customarily called "ASCII files." ASCII has codes representing upper- and lowercase letters, the numerals, and punctuation.

authentication The process of identifying users before they are allowed access to computer systems or networks, typically by userids and passwords.

backbone A high-speed connection within a network that links shorter (usually slower) branch circuits. An example is the NSFNet, generally considered to be the backbone network of the Internet in the United States.

bandwidth Strictly speaking, the difference in Hertz (Hz) between the highest and lowest frequencies a transmission channel is capable of passing. In common usage, however, it refers to the amount of data that can be transmitted through a given communications circuit.

baud rate In data transmission, the number of times per second the transmission medium's state can change. For example, a "2400-baud" modem changes the signal it transmits on the phone line 2400 times per second. Modern modem technology can encode more than one bit per state change, however, making bits per second (bps), kilobits per second (kbps), or megabits per second (mbps) the more meaningful measures of line speed.

binary file Any file that is not a text file. Any arrangement of bits that is meaningful to a computer, without regard to any correspondence to a human-readable character set.

BITNET An acronym for Because It's Time Network, a cooperative education and research network. BITNET primarily provides e-mail services.

bits per second (bps) The rate at which bits are transmitted over a communications medium.

BTW An abbreviation for "by the way," commonly used in mail and news.

Bulletin Board Systems (BBSs) Computers accessed by remote users via modems for discussion, file downloads, and other BBS services. BBSs typically are stand-alone systems not on the Internet, though many have gateways.

CERT Computer Emergency Response, a clearing house of information about network security, etc., providing security protection for the Internet.

C shell A user interface for those whose Internet providers offer only character-based, command-line access to a Unix system (hence the term "shell account").

CIX Commercial Internet Exchange, a pact between network providers that allows them to do accounting for commercial traffic.

client A computer application that requests support from another program, often called a *server*, which usually runs on a remote computer.

CoSN Consortium for School Networks, a nonprofit group whose members include K-12 teachers, hardware and software vendors, and Internet providers.

cracker Someone who attempts to thwart computer security systems.

datagram A formatted set of electronic data used in communication between computer systems. Datagrams consist of two parts, the data proper (which may be part of a longer message) and the header (which indicates the source, the destination, and the type of data).

DDN Defense Data Network, a segment of the Internet that links to U.S. military bases and contractors, used for unsecured communications.

DECnet A set of proprietary networking protocols utilized (instead of TCP/IP) by Digital Equipment Corporation's operating systems. These protocols are not compatible with the Internet.

dial-up As opposed to *dedicated*, a type of computer linkage using regular telephone lines, generally referring to the kind of connection one makes when using a terminal emulator and a regular modem.

directory An organizational unit for file storage on a computer system; also, a listing of the files residing within such a unit. Files on many computer systems are organized in this way. Directories for users' private files and directories for public files can be found on most systems. Files common to a topic are often grouped into separate subdirectories.

directory service A service on a network that relays information about sites, computers, resources, or users in the area.

DOD Department of Defense, the branch of government whose Advanced Research Projects Agency began the creation of the Internet.

domain A unique name (a classification category) by which a computer is known to the larger network.

Domain Name System (DNS) A general-purpose, replicated, distributed data query service for looking up host IP addresses based on host names. The DNS is hierarchical, consisting of domains, subdomains, sites, and hosts. Unique names are formed from smallest unit to largest, and are of the form *user@host.site.subdomain.domain*, where *host* and *site* are often optional. Some well-known and often referred-to domains are: *.com* (commercial), *.edu* (educational), *.net* (network operations), *.gov* (U.S. government), and *.mil* (U.S. military). Most countries also have a domain name, e.g., *.us* (United States), *.uk* (United Kingdom), and *.au* (Australia).

download/downloading The process of transferring files to your local machine using communications software and a modem, often the final, vital step necessary to have your "own" copy of a file.

EFF Electronic Frontier Foundation, a nonprofit organization concerned with Internet-related privacy and access issues.

encryption The process of scrambling a message so that a key, held only by authorized recipients, is needed to unscramble and read.

e-mail Electronic mail; online communications between computer users.

e-text The full text of a document available in electronic format, typically via FTP.

EARN European Academic and Research Network, the European equivalent to BITNET. EARN uses BITNET-type protocols.

edu The domain name used to identify educational institutions.

Ethernet Computers on the Internet use the TCP/IP protocols are frequently connected to the Net over an Ethernet link. Ethernet supports communication at 10 mbps over several different types of wiring.

FAQ Frequently Asked Questions, a document that attempts to respond to the most asked questions about a particular subject. FAQs exist for most topics relating to the Internet.

finger A program that attempts to retrieve information about a particular user, or all users, logged on the local system or on a remote system. Fingering typically shows full name, last login time, idle time, terminal line, and terminal location (where applicable). It may also display plan and project files posted by the user.

flame A frank, inflammatory statement in a newsgroup posting or electronic mail message, which often evokes equally "hot" criticism or strong opinions in return. It is courtesy to precede a flame with an indication of pending fire (e.g., FLAME ON!). *Flame wars* result when online communicants start flaming one another for the act of flaming, the topic that provoked the original flame often being forgotten.

followup A reply to a Usenet posting.

Free-Net An open-access, community-sponsored and maintained computer network, affiliated with the National Public Telecomputing Network.

freeware Non-copyrighted software, for which no compensation is asked.

FTP File Transfer Protocol, a basic Internet application that allows for the transfer of files from one computer to another. The term is often lowercased as *ftp*, and used as either noun or verb.

For Your Information (FYI) A subseries of RFCs that are not technical standards or descriptions of protocols. FYIs convey general information about subjects related to TCP/IP or the Internet. See also: *Request For Comments*.

gateway A computer that links two networks, routing IP datagrams and often converting protocols or messages from one network to the other. The term also can refer to a system capability that provides direct access to other remote networks or services.

gopher A distributed information service that uses a simple protocol to make available hierarchical collections of information across the Internet. Allowing a single gopher client the ability to access information from any accessible gopher server, it provides the user with a single "gopherspace" of information. Public domain versions of the client and server are available. (The name comes from the mascot of the University of Minnesota, where the service was developed.)

host A computer system that is the source of network services; also, the site where you can hold an interactive session.

HTML HyperText Markup Language, a document tagging specification used for World Wide Web documents.

HTTP HyperText Transfer Protocol, the client-server protocol upon which the World Wide Web is based.

hypermedia A blending of hypertext and multimedia.

hypertext The links within one document that allows it to connect to and display another document. Selecting a hypertext link automatically displays the second document.

HYTELNET A program that provides an easily adaptable and fluid connection to a multitude of networked information resources, including library catalogs.

IAB Internet Architecture Board, the "regulatory body" that makes decisions about standards and other vital issues.

IETF Internet Engineering Task Force, a voluntary group that investigates and resolves technical problems, as well as making recommendations to the IAB.

IMHO An acronym commonly used in e-mail and news, meaning "in my humble opinion."

Internet The worldwide network of networks based on the TCP/IP protocol. Also, when not capitalized, any interconnected set of networks.

Internet Relay Chat (IRC) A mechanism that allows for a number of Internet users to connect to the same network node and chat in real time.

InterNIC Internet Network Information Centre for the United States, which is made up of three separate commercial organizations, and provides government-contracted services.

IP Internet Protocol, number 1 among the protocols on which the Internet is based. IP allows a packet to travel through multiple networks on the way to its ultimate destination.

IP address A unique number assigned to every computer directly connected to the Internet, for example, 192.35.222.222. See also: *DNS*.

ISDN Integrated Services Digital Network, a digital phone service which allows the phone lines to carry digital rather than analog signals.

ISO International Organization for Standardization, an association that has defined a different set of network protocols, known as the ISO/OSI protocols, that are in line to replace those currently in use on the Internet.

ISOC The Internet Society (ISOC), a group made up of members who support a worldwide information network. It is also the governing body to which the IAB reports.

JANET Joint Academic Network, the academic and research network in the United Kingdom.

Jughead A program, used in conjunction with gopher, that provides the means to search all of the menu selections within a particular gopher server.

Knowbot A registered trademark of the Corporation for National Research Initiatives. Knowbots are robots designed to seek out files on the Internet.

leased line A dedicated (as opposed to dial-up) telephone line typically used to link a moderate-sized local network to an Internet Service Provider.

Listserv A program that allows users to mass-distribute messages that form conferences, as well as archiving files and messages that can be searched for and retrieved.

LAN Local Area Network, a network of computers covering a relatively small geographical area, such as an office, building, or campus. Some LANs are attached to the Internet.

login, logon The initial identification procedure to gain access to a system as a legitimate user. The usual requirements are a valid user name and password.

logout, logoff The concluding steps for formally ending a session with a system. Physically disconnecting or powering down a terminal does not necessarily result in a logout.

lurking A subscriber who doesn't actively participate in mailing list or Usenet newsgroup discussions. One who lurks is just listening to the discussion. Lurking is advised for beginners who need to get up to speed on the history, mores, and etiquette of the group.

Lynx A character-based client program for the World Wide Web.

mail reflector A specialized address from which email is automatically forwarded to a set of other addresses, commonly used to implement a mail discussion group.

MILNET A part of the DDN network that makes up the Internet, centered on nonclassified military communications.

MIME Multipurpose Internet Mail Extensions, extensions to the Simple Mail Transfer Protocol (SMTP), that allow the transmittal of non-text information (graphics, etc.) via e-mail.

mirror A duplicate of an FTP site.

modem Modulator-demodulator, hardware that connects a computer to a data transmission line.

Mosaic The World Wide Web client program developed by the National Center for Supercomputing Applications.

MUD Multi-User Dungeon. Modeled on the original Dungeons and Dragons, it is a group of role-playing games that have been used as conferencing tools and educational aids.

multimedia Documents that combine different kinds of data, e.g., plain text, video, graphics, and audio.

name A lexical string that is mapped to an IP address, e.g., *cutl.city.unisa.edu.au.*

name server A networked computer responsible for the guardianship of DNS name and address mapping tables, and for providing that information upon request from other computers.

netiquette The rules of etiquette in cyberspace.

NIC Network Information Center, an electronic site where users can hunt down information about specific capabilities of a network. NICs are customarily maintained by regional networks and by institutions. The U.S. national NIC is backed financially by the National Science Foundation, and is called the InterNIC. Depending on context, the abbreviation NIC can also mean *network interface card*, the hardware that connects an individual computer to a network.

NFS Network File System, a set of protocols that offers users access to other files on other networked computers as if they were local.

NNTP Network News Transfer Protocol, the protocol used to transfer Usenet pieces on the Internet.

NOC Network Operations Center, a site or group that is responsible for the daily care and maintenance of a network.

node One computer within a network.

NREN National Research and Education Network, a U.S. attempt to link networks operated by different federal agencies into a single, high-speed network.

NSFNet National Science Foundation Network, currently the Internet backbone network of the United States.

NTP Network Time Protocol, a protocol used to synchronize time between computers on the Internet.

octet Alternate term for a set of eight bits, i.e., a byte.

OSI Open Systems Interconnect, a conceptual model and set of protocols for networks, promulgated by the ISO.

packet A unit of data of standardized size, into which information is divided for transmission over a network. Each of the packets that comprise a message travels the internetwork independently; the message is reassembled from its component packets at the destination.

PEM Privacy Enhanced Mail, an encryption standard generally used to secure Internet mail.

ping A diagnostic utility that determines whether a remote computer is active and where it can be contacted.

POP Post Office Protocol, which makes available client-server e-mail messaging. Also, *Point of Presence* in the context of telecommunications companies and ISPs.

PPP Point-to-Point Protocol, a protocol for transmitting TCP/IP packet-type data over serial (modem-type) communications lines, an eventual replacement for SLIP.

port A point of I/O access to a computer or system. Also, to convert a program from one platform to run on another, e.g., from Unix to MS-DOS or MacOS.

protocol The "must follow" regulations that govern the transmission and receipt of information across a data communications link. In sets or *suites*, protocols rule communication between entities, including the type, size, and format of data units.

RFC Request for Comments, the documents that contain the standards and other information for the TCP/IP protocols and the Internet in general. They can be found at several sites through anonymous FTP.

relevance feedback Documents retrieved in a search that are used to further refine the search.

routing The process of locating the most efficient or effective pathway through a network to a destination computer. Routing is commonly handled by the network or communication software.

RTFM "Read the [*deleted*] manual," a common response to trivial or obvious questions in e-mail and newsgroups.

server The application (or more commonly, the computer) that provides services such as files or database access to the (usually remote) client.

Service Provider A business that provides connections to a part of the Internet.

signature A 3- or 4-line message, used to identify the sender of an e-mail note or Usenet article, that appears at the end of either communication. Signatures longer than 5 lines are generally frowned upon, and should be avoided.

SLIP Serial Line Internet Protocol, a predecessor of PPP, which allows TCP/IP packeted data to travel over serial connections, typically modem access through dial-up telephone lines. SLIP and PPP create an option for directly connecting a computer to the Internet without a dedicated connection.

SMTP Simple Mail Transfer Protocol, the standard protocol on the Internet for transferring electronic mail messages.

SRI A research institute, based in California, that runs the Network Information Systems Center.

switched access A network connection that can be created and eliminated as necessary.

T-1, T-3 High-speed digital lines that provide data communication speeds of 1.544 megabits (T-1) and 45 megabits (T-3) per second.

TCP/IP Transmission Control Protocol/Internet Protocol, the common designation for the suite of protocols that govern the operation of internets and the Internet.

Telnet The Internet formalities that allow remote logins to distant computers. Also, the name of the program implementing the protocol.

timeout What occurs when one computer fails to respond to another within a predetermined interval during a conversation.

tn3270 A version of Telnet software that allows connection to IBM mainframes by emulating the widely used IBM 3270 family of terminals.

token ring One of several combinations of electrical, packet-format, and procedural specifications used for transmitting information over a medium.

The trademark Token-Ring refers to IBM's implementation of this scheme. See also: *Ethernet.*

UDP User Datagram Protocol, another of the protocols on which the Internet is based.

Unix A computer operating system, originally developed at AT&T Bell Laboratories, that is compatible with a wide range of computer systems. Ultrix, Solaris, AIX, HP/UX, BSD, Linux, and System V are among its numerous descendants.

URL Uniform Resource Locator, a draft standard for specifying the location of a file on the Internet.

Usenet A worldwide network that supports e-mail transmissions to distributed servers and features BBS-like "newsgroups."

username, user-id An address that designates a personal account on a large computer, for example, *ptadc@ntx.city.unisa. edu.au.*

UUCP Unix-to-Unix Copy, originally a program that ran under the Unix operating system and allowed one Unix system to send files to another via dial-up phone lines. At present, the term generally is applied to the large international network that uses the UUCP protocol to pass news and electronic mail.

Veronica A gopher service that provides keyword pursuit of gopher menu items.

VMS The native operating system of Digital Equipment Corporation's VAX computers.

VT100 The DEC terminal (actually the terminal's operating parameters and command set) generally used to define the notion of "standard computer terminal." Countless other terminals, as well as PC telecommunications programs, can emulate the VT100.

Wide Area Information Servers (WAIS) A distributed information service that offers simple, natural-language input, with indexed searching for fast retrieval, and a "relevance feedback" mechanism that allows the results of initial searches to influence future searches.

World Wide Web, WWW A user-friendly, client-server software system that easily interfaces with text, graphics, moving images, sounds, and other types of information transmitted among computers directly linked to the Internet.

Z39.50 A U.S.-based protocol (with international OSI counterparts) that allows stress-free information exchange (i.e., full-text or catalog records) between dissimilar computer systems.

Tip

For a more inclusive glossary of Internet and World Wide Web terms, see the Unisys *Information Superhighway Driver's Manual*:

http://www.unisys.com/OfInterest/Highway/highway.html

Or check out the comprehensive glossaries from Interactive Insights:

http://www.cbs.com/dweebs/cyberguide.html

Or Internet Literacy Consultants:

http://www.matisse.net/files/glossary.html

Index

Illustrations are in **boldface**.

ABOUT THE AUTHOR

Jessica Keyes is president of Techinsider/New Art, Inc., a technology consulting and research firm specializing in productivity and high-technology applications. Formerly managing director of technology for the New York Stock Exchange and an officer with Swiss Bank Co. and Banker's Trust, she publishes Techinsider Reports and Computer Market Letter. Keyes is a frequent contributor to such well-known publications as *Software Magazine* and *Computerworld*, and is the author of several best-selling books, including *Infotrends, Software Engineering Productivity*, and *Solving the Productivity Paradox*.